The St. Martin's
Workbook
Sixth Edition

Lex Runciman
LINFIELD COLLEGE

BEDFORD/ST. MARTIN'S
BOSTON ♦ NEW YORK

For Bedford/St. Martin's

Developmental Editor: Nathan Odell
Senior Production Supervisor: Dennis J. Conroy
Marketing Manager: John Swanson
Project Management: Books By Design, Inc.
Cover Design: Donna L. Dennison
Composition: Achorn International
Printing and Binding: R. R. Donnelley & Sons Company, Inc.

President: Joan E. Feinberg
Editorial Director: Denise B. Wydra
Editor in Chief: Karen S. Henry
Director of Development: Erica T. Appel
Director of Marketing: Karen Melton Soeltz
Director of Editing, Design, and Production: Marcia Cohen
Manager, Publishing Services: Emily Berleth

Library of Congress Control Number: 2007925937

Manufactured in the United States of America.

For information, write: Bedford/St. Martin's, 75 Arlington Street,
Boston, MA 02116   (617-399-4000)

ISBN-10: 0-312-43119-8
ISBN-13: 978-0-312-43119-8

Acknowledgments

Definition of "compose." Adapted and reproduced by permission from *The American Heritage Dictionary of the English Language, Fourth Edition*. Copyright © 1996 by Houghton Mifflin Company.

Rachel Carson. "The Birth of an Island." Excerpt from *The Sea Around Us* by Rachel Carson. Copyright © 1950 by Rachel Carson. Published by Oxford University Press. Reproduced by permission of Pollinger Ltd. and the proprietor. Used by permission of Frances Collin, Trustee.

Clifford Odets. "Joe and Edna," Scene I from *Waiting for Lefty* by Clifford Odets. Copyright © 1935 by Clifford Odets; renewed 1962 by Clifford Odets. Used by permission of Grove/Atlantic, Inc.

Dylan Thomas. 13 lines from "Fern Hill." From *The Poems of Dylan Thomas*. Copyright © 1945 by the Trustees for the Copyrights of Dylan Thomas. Reprinted by permission of New Directions Publishing Company and David Higham Associates.

Preface

The St. Martin's Workbook is a multifaceted resource for both teachers and student writers. Everything in this book proceeds from two assumptions: one is that every college student can become a skilled and successful writer; the other is that successful writing proceeds from knowledge of how English works and knowledge of what writers do.

This workbook is devoted to discussion and exercises dealing with the formal complexities and conventions of written English as it is typically used in college writing. A working knowledge of these conventions encourages writers to believe that English is indeed their language and can be used to serve their own purposes—in a college essay, a research paper or technical report, a job application, a short story, or a poem.

Overall, this book attempts to give student writers a realistic image of the good writer. Students tend to think that good writers write effortlessly, quickly, and perfectly. That is simply not so. All writers struggle with questions of content, purpose, and audience. All writers must sometimes look up fine points of grammar and punctuation. And when at last we see that our words communicate almost precisely what we wish them to, when we have worked through and conquered the confusions, looked up misspellings, and nailed down every comma, the elation we feel is real and well earned. *The St. Martin's Workbook* aims to make such success more practically and more frequently attainable.

The St. Martin's Workbook shares its organization with Parts 1, 2, and 5–11 of *The St. Martin's Handbook,* covering the art and craft of writing, critical thinking and argument, the effective use of language, grammar, clarity, style, punctuation, mechanics, and special help for multilingual writers. The books' chapter and part numbers and titles parallel each other, and the numbers that follow major text heads in the *Workbook* (1a, 1b) correspond to numbered *Handbook* sections in which the same material is covered. The two texts can easily be used together, with the *Workbook* providing many additional exercises. Like the *Handbook*, the *Workbook* highlights the twenty errors most commonly found in college essays, providing explanations and exercises to enable student writers to identify such errors and to correct them. The *Workbook* may also be used alone, as either a primary or a supplemental text.

The sixth edition of the *Workbook* has been revised to be a better companion for *The St. Martin's Handbook*. Opening each chapter of the *Workbook* are "Everyday Use" exercises that link material in the Workbook with students' lives beyond the classroom. Chapters on expectations for college writing and on visual thinking have been added to correspond to new coverage in the *Handbook*.

To accompany *The St. Martin's Workbook*, an Instructor's Manual is available, containing suggested answers and strategies for using the *Workbook*'s exercises. Instructors who wish to may use exercises in this book as the basis for classroom discussion and as the basis for work in small groups; the Instructor's Manual identifies exercises that particularly lend themselves to this approach. Such collaboration is widespread in business and professional writing and is encouraged in many rhetoric texts; it is time for such strategies to find their way into workbooks.

Books of the type and size of the *Workbook* depend on the collaboration and cooperation of many individuals, and I want to thank at least a few of them here. First, thanks must go to all the good people at Bedford/St. Martin's. Special thanks to Carolyn Lengel, Kristin Bowen, and Nathan Odell, who shepherded this edition through the revision process. Continued thanks also go to *The St. Martin's Handbook* author Andrea Lunsford.

Writers, like everyone else, need human encouragement, and it helps immensely to work among folks with similar interests. So thanks to my colleagues at Linfield College for your encouragement and friendship. Finally, thanks to my family—to Debbie, Beth, and Jane. You are wonderful, fascinating people; what can I say—we have a good time.

Lex Runciman

A Note to Students

Think about the word *writing*, and you will realize that it has two basic meanings. Writing is what you're reading now, but writing is also the process writers go through as they write. It's a process that involves considerable thinking: thinking about what you want to say, thinking about whom you're saying it to, thinking about how the material can be organized, and so on. Writing teachers often distinguish these various activities by calling them planning, drafting, and revising. Put that way, it sounds as though writing—the process—moves forward in a straight line: you plan first, then you draft, and then you revise. That's a neat model for what writers do, but it makes the process look orderly and predictable, when in fact most writers will quickly acknowledge that writing often means planning, drafting, revising, drafting some more, researching answers to unanticipated questions, drafting again, revising some more, and so on. Notice how often the word *revising* gets mentioned. If you depend on one draft, you can be smart only once. If you revise, you can be smart many times.

If you are a student opening *The St. Martin's Workbook* for the first time, you will find that it focuses most of its attention (and therefore most of yours) on making revision easier and less troublesome and more correct. The majority of the explanations and writing activities you find here will help you understand and practice the ways that sentences and paragraphs can be put together accurately and concisely. And the hope is that completing exercises in this book will give you the understanding and the confidence to use these same strategies and techniques when you write and revise your own sentences.

Good writing needs to be substantially correct; it needs basic clarity, or its readers will be lost. But good writing is the result of much more than a concern for sentence-by-sentence correctness. Good writing begins with a decision to think and a decision to engage yourself in a process of discovery and learning, a process that will make clear to you what you want to say and how it ought to be said. Large questions of strategy and approach are discussed in Part 1, but these chapters are not meant to be complete by themselves. See them as introductions, useful as such.

The very term *college writing* can provoke a certain amount of worry. Sometimes people aren't sure they can measure up. Sometimes people fear that they just weren't born with the right equipment. We as instructors know that college writers are made, not born; and we know that the key factors are study and practice; to become a better college writer, you must write. If you don't now consider yourself a "college writer," you can become one, and this book will help. If you already know you can excel as a college writer, this book will help you add to your set of tools for using that astonishingly versatile and powerful set of conventions called the English language.

Contents

THE ART AND CRAFT OF WRITING

"Writers (our memories and experiences) and the world around us are sources, and it's likely that most anything we write will involve some form of reading and research: for inspiration, for details, for enriching memories, for learning."
— MELISSA GOLDTHWAITE

PREVIEW QUESTIONS

These questions are designed to help you decide what you need to study. Read each statement, and indicate whether it is true or false. (Answers to preview questions are at the back of the book.)

1. Skillful writers do not need to revise. ___F___

2. Writing is always done alone. ___F___

3. Most writers pursue a writing process that is neatly linear. ___T___

4. Writers should never consider the nature of their readers when writing. ___F___

5. The thesis of an essay may change as a writer completes a draft. ___T___

6. An essay should be drafted as quickly as possible and usually in one sitting. ___F___

7. Revision helps writers understand what they want to say and how readers are likely to interpret their words. ___T___

8. In the early stages of revising a piece of writing, it isn't necessary to pay attention to small errors of punctuation and spelling. ___F___

9. An outline is useful because it allows writers to see the organization of an entire paper and spot inconsistencies. ___T___

10. All the sentences in an essay should be roughly the same length. ___F___

11. Details can help a paragraph hold a reader's interest. ___T___

12. Writing an introduction should always be the first step in composing your rough draft. ___F___

13. Any visuals must be clearly integrated with the text of an essay. ___F___

14. Writers often use common patterns such as problem-solution or comparison/contrast to organize their work. ___T___

15. A paragraph is a group of sentences focusing on one main point. ___T___

16. Transitional words and phrases help both the writer and the reader make connections and achieve clarity in a paragraph. ___T___

Expectations for College Writing

1

First-year college students often feel that their instructors expect certain things from them without stating those expectations directly. To understand such expectations, you need to realize that most instructors see themselves as doing much more than simply preparing students for a particular job after graduation. Rather, in addition to imparting knowledge of their specific field, they hope to help students develop the kinds of skills that will benefit them in many areas of life, whether on the job or not — skills such as critical thinking and reasoning, active problem solving, thorough research abilities, and effective communication. Obviously, you will often demonstrate these skills through writing, so it is important that you understand what is expected of you as a writer.

EXPECTATIONS FOR WRITING IN EVERYDAY USE

Think about the expectations that *you* bring to the various texts that you read. What are your expectations when you pick up a newspaper? when you look through a popular magazine? when you begin a new novel? when you open an email, enter an online chat room, or access a Web site? when you open a textbook for the first time? Obviously, you bring different expectations to each of these kinds of reading. Think about how you have come to have such expectations. How might you apply this sort of learning to your learning about what will be expected of you as a college writer?

Expectations about college writers (1b)

Above all, writers in U.S. academic situations are expected to *demonstrate authority* and to *be direct*. You may not feel like an authority as you write a paper for an instructor (who presumably knows quite a bit about the subject), but this feeling should not stop you from displaying your own knowledge and critical thinking. You have, after all, done some form of research and considered your topic — you have your own ideas and do not need to simply repeat what someone else has said. To demonstrate authority, you should do the following:

- Have opinions (but make sure that you are informed about the subject — uninformed opinions are not likely to impress an instructor). Your audience will expect you to discuss the opinions you have formed.
- Draw conclusions about material you read, and include these conclusions in your writing.
- Demonstrate that you are becoming an authority — prove in your writing that you have done the required homework or reading for the assignment.
- Consider the ideas of others as long as you give a reasonable explanation for your critique and avoid negative or destructive criticism.

In U.S. academic writing, directness is prized. Your instructors will expect your writing to make its point sooner rather than later and to contain nothing that is unrelated to that point.

Here are some tips for making your writing more direct:

- Don't overqualify statements with phrases such as *I think* or with words such as *possibly*. Instead of saying "I think that the statistics show" or "The statistics may show," say "The statistics show."
- Don't use too many prepositional phrases in a row, which can be a sign of indirection. "The need for additional nurses in many hospitals in the United States is desperate" is less direct and gripping than "Many U.S. hospitals desperately need additional nurses."
- Don't digress. When you include a story, example, or anecdote, ask yourself whether it relates directly to your main point. If it does not, omit it.
- Do show your confidence as a writer. This task will be much easier if you have done the necessary preparation to make you *feel* confident.

Expectations about college readers (1c)

Most people have established reading habits by the time they get to college, but if your reading habits do not meet the expectations of your instructors, you should consider trying to change your habits. In U.S. academic situations, instructors will ask you to read actively by being assertive, talking back to the text, and offering informed opinions on what the text says. Instructors do not view this kind of critique as negative or belligerent; instead, such dialogue shows the reader's engagement with and respect for the text. Here are some guidelines for meeting most instructors' expectations as you read:

- Understand the *context* of the assignment, and be able to provide a brief summary of the context.
- Think *critically*, and analyze what you read. Think about the connections between sentences and paragraphs, and relate what you notice to the selection overall. Also look for recurring images and themes, structural patterns, choices

of diction, and organizational patterns; then think about why the author made those choices. Lastly, consider the author's attitude about the subject and any assumptions that he or she seems to make; then think about how the author's attitude and assumptions affect his or her position.

Expectations about college texts (1d)

Expectations for your writing will vary depending on the class, instructor, and assignment, but here are some general guidelines that you should follow whenever you write at the college level in the United States:

- Consider your purpose and audience carefully, making sure that your topic is appropriate to both. In a college context, this usually means selecting a formal topic, or addressing a casual topic in a formal way. For instance, you might propose steps to prevent the spread of AIDS in Africa (a formal topic) or you might think about the economics of collecting baseball cards (a formal approach to a casual topic).

- Remember to state your main point clearly and to support it explicitly. If your main point requires background information, keep the information as brief as possible and show how it relates directly to your main point. Be sure that your clearly stated main point is supported by examples, statistics, anecdotes, or conventionally accepted authorities (see Chapters 8–10).

- If an assignment asks you to answer a question before providing your own interpretation or argument, be sure to answer the question completely. Consider this example: "What did Lincoln accomplish by signing the Emancipation Proclamation? Analyze the effectiveness of the document and of Lincoln's Civil War strategy for the North." Before proceeding with your analysis, remember the question.

- If your work requires outside research, be sure to document your sources correctly. In particular, be careful not to cut and paste material from the Internet into your own papers without using quotation marks and correct documentation.

- Make clear transitions from paragraph to paragraph and from point to point. Think of these transitions as a handshake: the first sentence of the second paragraph reaches back to the last sentence of the first paragraph, like two hands meeting in a greeting.

- Use conventional grammar, spelling, punctuation, and mechanics (as discussed throughout this book).

- Use conventional margins, double spacing, and an easy-to-read font size, color, and typeface for your papers, whether they be lab reports, documented essays, literature reviews, proposals, or what have you. If your instructor does not explicitly tell you how to format your paper, you may want to consult the style guides in a handbook, such as *The St. Martin's Handbook*, to see what is standard practice in your discipline.

EXERCISE 1.1   ESTABLISHING AUTHORITY

NAME _____ **DATE** _____

Choose a recent piece of writing you have done for a class assignment. Answer the following questions as completely as you can.

1. Where in the piece of writing do you present your own opinions? Do you think you said enough in this piece about what you thought? Why, or why not?

2. What conclusions have you drawn in the piece? Have you made any comments on the opinions of others? Why, or why not? If you have not, what conclusions might you have included in this piece of writing?

EXERCISE 1.2   BEING DIRECT

NAME _____ **DATE** _____

Write *D* if a statement is appropriately direct and *I* if a statement is too indirect.

EXAMPLE   ___I___   It seems to me that the author might be criticizing the system of inheritance.

1. _____ Many people who emigrate here from other countries find Americans' easy access to firearms surprising.

2. _____ In my opinion, it might be more difficult to live in a large city than in a small town.

3. _____ The political climate in Washington in current days seems to be marked by polarization and a sense of discord between the major parties.

4. _____ The film has a strong cast and an evocative setting; however, its script lacks focus, and its direction comes off as overly self-conscious in too many scenes.

5. _____ The fossil record shows that North America was once home to many species of very large animals, but archaeologists and paleontologists disagree about what caused these giant creatures' extinction.

6. _____ Facing my brother's addiction to alcohol was, I guess, probably one of the most difficult things I ever had to do.

7. _____ Compact fluorescent lightbulbs cost three or four times as much as an ordinary lightbulb, but they save much more than three or four times as much electricity. My electric bills showed the difference after I made the switch to compact fluorescents.

8. _____ Emergency agencies estimate that every year two hundred Americans die and more than seven hundred are injured because of being struck by lightning. This fact doesn't surprise me because my cousin was once almost struck by lightning.

9. _____ I think that the administration's new policies regarding offensive speech on campus may be somewhat difficult to enforce.

10. _____ The increase in the number of patients with atrial fibrillation in the United States is a matter of concern for many physicians and medical researchers.

EXERCISE 1.3   UNDERSTANDING EXPECTATIONS FOR READERS

NAME _____ **DATE** _____

Choose a reading assignment that an instructor has given you, either for this class or for a different one. Then answer the following questions about this assignment.

A.

1. How did you respond to the assignment when you first received it? Write a paragraph explaining as completely as you can how you prepared to read the assignment, what you did as you read it, and how well you think you met the instructor's expectations.

2. Now, read the assignment again, making an effort to read actively. What did you do differently this time? Write a paragraph explaining the differences between the two readings and the effect active reading has on your understanding of the assignment.

B.

1. Write a brief summary of the assignment, reading it again if you need to.

2. What do you notice about the author's attitudes and assumptions in this assignment? Write a brief paragraph explaining what you have discovered in your reading and how the author's views are apparent.

Reading, Writing, and Research

2

Consider the many things you read and write every day. You may read magazines, billboards, course assignments, school newspapers, emails, Web site banner ads, sports scores and weather warnings crawling across the bottom of a television screen, cereal boxes, recipes, novels, horoscopes, poems, junk mail, and credit-card bills. You may write instant messages, notes for your roommate, grocery lists, fan fiction, essays for class, diary entries, love letters, comments in your friends' yearbooks, limericks, screenplays, protest letters, and song lyrics. Some of the things you read and write may look pretty much the same today as they looked twenty-five years ago; many others, however, look very different or did not exist a quarter century ago. Writing and related activities, such as reading, talking, and listening, have changed tremendously because of new technologies and increasing amounts of contact between people all over the world.

READING, WRITING, AND RESEARCH IN EVERYDAY USE

Do you associate reading, writing, and research exclusively with school? It is important to realize that people engage in reading, writing, and research all day long and in endless ways. Consider a popular movie that's out right now. Studying the poster for the movie, watching a preview, reading a review, discussing the movie with a friend, and scanning the newspaper or the Internet for showtimes are all examples of reading and research. Emailing your brother or sister about your favorite scene and participating in an online chat about one of the movie's stars are both examples of writing. Think for a moment about the reading, writing, and research you have done recently. Have you registered for classes? bought a car? paid a bill? hired a babysitter? Select one such experience, and then make a short list detailing how this experience involved reading, writing, and research.

Writing now carries all kinds of meanings—some old, some new. As the meaning of writing has expanded, the act has evolved as well. Today, writing offers both new opportunities and added responsibilities. As a writer, you can take advantage of innovative media, improve communication by using not only words but also images and graphics, and benefit from the talents of classmates and co-workers through collaboration (a frequent activity in modern writing). More than ever before, however, writers must be careful and thoughtful in order to be effective. As you write, you are quite likely to reach a diverse audience (your college instructors and peers or a wider group); writers today may truly be writing for the world. Remember that some members of your audience may not share your culture or values. Considering diversity allows you to ensure that the message of your writing is not misunderstood.

Writing processes (2b)

A strong, finished piece of writing is usually the result of a collection of activities known as the *writing process*, a term that you may be familiar with from other courses or textbooks. This process may have been described as a step-by-step march from plan to outline to draft to final copy. Most writers, however, do not proceed in such a neat, linear way; indeed, parts of the process often overlap and occur simultaneously. Writers also engage in various steps "out of order" or more than once, perhaps outlining, drafting, and revising, then planning, outlining, and drafting some more. Parts of the writing process flow into and influence each other. Such nonlinear activity is called *recursion*, and thus writing is often called a *recursive activity*.

Of course, each stage of the writing process is important. But it is the process as a whole that produces strong, inspired writing, and the process may unfold in endless ways. Here are the stages in the writing process:

- *Exploring.* During this stage, you consider the rhetorical situation. What is your purpose? Who is your audience? You also engage in a preliminary investigation of your topic, brainstorming, reading, browsing online resources, or discussing your ideas with friends or classmates.

- *Narrowing a topic and researching.* At this stage, you think about what you already know about your topic, narrow your topic to a manageable size, devise a working thesis, and gather information through research.

- *Organizing and designing.* At this stage, you shape your thesis and put your ideas in order. Think about the best way to organize your argument and how you might use charts, photos, or other design elements to support your thesis.

- *Drafting.* Drafting includes writing ideas down, as well as coming up with new ideas as you write. No matter how thoroughly you have explored your topic, you will almost certainly discover more about it while drafting. Therefore, don't worry about making your writing come out perfectly the first time. Drafting is not about producing a finished copy but rather about getting your ideas onto the page or screen, continuing to explore, and perhaps realizing that you need to change your organization or your thesis, gather more information, or approach your subject from a different angle.

- *Reviewing.* During this stage, you look at your draft critically and objectively to see what's missing, what needs explaining, where the organization is flawed, what examples could be improved, whether sentence structures are varied and word choices are correct, and whether your attitude toward your topic and audience is what you intended. At this stage, you also should try to get responses from other people.

- *Revising.* Revising means reworking the draft after you and others have reviewed it. You may polish the language, add sentences or paragraphs, change the organization, rewrite the introduction, or make any number of other alterations — including throwing the draft out and starting again.

- *Editing, formatting, and proofreading.* During this stage, you turn your draft into a finished product. Editing involves correcting errors in grammar, usage, mechanics, and other conventions. Formatting involves deciding on fonts, page layout, and color (if any). Proofreading, your final step, means checking for misspellings and typographical errors.

Reading processes and research (2c, 2d)

Reading is a wonderful way to teach yourself to be a strong and effective writer. Think about the reading you enjoy most, and notice the writing. What makes that writing good? As you read, paying attention to what you like—and what you don't like—will help you strengthen your own writing skills. Try to develop the habit of slowing down enough to really examine the print, electronic, and visual texts you are reading.

When reading for research or an assignment, take the time to preview, annotate, and summarize the material. These skills can help you to understand, remember, and master what you read. Analyzing material critically and rereading also help you to understand the text and to know how you feel about it.

Writers today do a great deal of online reading in school, on the job, and at home. Online reading is different from print reading in several ways. When reading online text, you may encounter hyperlinks, video, and sound. Hyperlinks can change the organization of a piece of writing, allowing you to experience text in your own way, finding your own beginning and ending points. In addition, studies show that online readers skim more than print readers and—unexpectedly—are more likely than print readers to read words before looking at pictures.

Observe your own online reading habits. Being aware of what you read or look at first can sharpen your critical-thinking skills by helping you identify what the Web designer thinks is most important and is trying to draw your attention to most quickly. If you are not interested in visuals, use the Web site's print-friendly or text-only option if one exists; this will give you faster access to the site's information and make it easier for you to print or save the material.

Talking and listening (2e)

Speaking and listening are often treated separately from reading, writing, and researching, but it is both impractical and unwise to draw strict boundaries between the various communicative arts. Writers are often readers of their own texts; they may hear their texts read aloud or read their texts aloud themselves; and they will often discuss their texts with other people. Indeed, talking and listening can be extremely helpful to the writing process. Discussions allow writers to explore material and test ideas, consider new perspectives, receive and offer feedback, and ask and answer questions. The flip side of talking is listening, of course. Indeed, becoming an attentive, purposeful listener may yield rewards in every area of your life.

Taking notes (2f)

Good note-taking is a survival skill in college, one that can form the basis for your success as a critical reader, writer, and listener. Before taking notes, consider your purpose. Are you collecting ideas to use in a piece of writing? Are you studying for a test? Are you recording personal responses to an assignment? Knowing your purpose will help you decide what to write down. Also consider your own style. Do you take the best notes writing by hand or typing on a laptop? Do you prefer to jot things down while someone is speaking or after the lecture has concluded? Whatever your style when taking notes, always look for the main points and their relationship to one another. And remember to label and organize your notes in a way that allows you to make good use of them later.

EXERCISE 2.1 YOUR WRITING PROCESS

NAME _____ **DATE** _____

Assume that you have been asked to write a paper describing the most interesting piece of writing you have ever done. Answer these questions as specifically and truthfully as possible.

1. Would you have difficulty coming up with material for this paper? Why, or why not?

2. Describe the step-by-step process you might use to complete this assignment. Be detailed. What would you do first? second? after that? Include all significant steps, including any expected procrastination.

3. How happy are you with the process you just described? Would this process allow you to write your best paper? Explain.

4. Is the writing process that you just described typical of the way you work? Have you always worked in this way? Do you feel you are the "victim" of your writing habits or that you are in control of them?

EXERCISE 2.2 YOUR READING PROCESS

Choose a sample of someone else's writing that you enjoyed reading. Answer these questions as specifically and completely as you can.

1. Why did you enjoy this material? How would you persuade someone else that it is worth reading?

2. What one sentence impressed you most? Why?

3. What is the *least* effective part of this piece of writing? Why? Did you skim or skip any parts? Explain.

EXERCISE 2.3   YOUR READING AND WRITING HISTORY

NAME _____ **DATE** _____

Answer these questions with detailed, truthful sentences. There are no right or wrong answers here, only incomplete ones.

1. What kinds of writing do you read most frequently—novels? newspapers? online chats? class assignments? other material? Give examples.

2. What are your strengths and weaknesses as a reader? How could you make the most of your strengths? How could you minimize the impact of your weaknesses? Give examples.

3. What are your strengths and weaknesses as a writer? How could you make the most of your strengths? How could you minimize the impact of your weaknesses? Give examples.

4. What kinds of writing do you do most often—homework assignments? email? memos for your job? essay tests? Give examples.

EXERCISE 2.4   TAKING NOTES

Choose a reading assignment. Preview the assignment before you read, and make notes of your observations. Then read the assignment once carefully, annotating as you read. Finally, write a brief summary of the assignment.

EXERCISE 2.5   TALKING AND LISTENING

After you complete exercise 2.4, find a partner in the class. Take turns reading your summaries of the assignment aloud and explaining where you would each begin if you were asked to write a short essay in response to the reading. Discuss your ideas, listening to and questioning each other carefully. Then write a paragraph explaining what you learned about the assignment from talking with and listening to your partner.

Rhetorical Situations

3

Analyzing assignments (3d)

As you know if you have worked through Chapter 2, writing is more than something others read. It is also something writers *do*. Experienced writers know what kinds of activities and writing strategies work for them, and they have learned the importance of beginning early. They begin thinking about writing as soon as the task is assigned. And they often begin that thinking by considering the **audience** they're writing to (the person or group they most want to reach) and the **purpose** they have in writing (the goals established by the writing task, the person assigning the task, and the writer).

RHETORICAL SITUATIONS IN EVERYDAY USE

You can probably remember a time when something you wrote failed to achieve your purpose or, worse yet, backfired on you. That's why even a fairly routine piece of writing calls for careful thinking about its audience and its purpose. For example, a thank-you note or email sent to a grandparent in response to a birthday present will differ considerably from a note or email thanking a prospective employer for an interview or a message expressing gratitude to co-workers for their help on a group project. Make a list of some thank-you messages you have either sent or received. Then briefly explain how these messages differed according to their purposes and audiences.

You will have occasion to write for many purposes and to address many audiences — to amuse your friends, to reassure your parents that you are still alive and well, to inform a credit-card company about an error in your bill, to explain a sales campaign to employees, to persuade your local government to lower its assessment of the value of your house, and so on. Here are five questions you can use to help you understand any new writing assignment in terms of its audience and its purpose.

1. Who will read what you write?
2. What do your readers already know or believe?
3. What is it that only you can tell your readers?
4. What judgments or actions do you want your readers to make?

5. What information will effectively convince your readers to make these judgments or take these actions?

Suppose that your instructor's first assignment asks you to introduce yourself by telling a story about yourself. You can choose to write a story about some big event, or you can choose to write about something that happens almost every day but reveals something significant about you. Your instructor plans to ask you to read over your rough draft with others in the class, so you're supposed to think of your readers as being your instructor and your classmates. Here is how you might use the five questions to decide whether you've chosen a good story.

1. Who will read what you write?

My instructor and classmates will read this.

2. What do your readers already know or believe?

My readers here really don't know anything about me except what I give them to read. They sure don't know anything about the car wreck — where it happened, how it happened, and who was in the car.

3. What is it that only you can tell your readers?

I'm the one who knows this story. Because they don't know any of it, I have to think about how much background to give. I could start by talking about how the afternoon was so much fun. I need to make sure they know who Treavor and Lea are — how long we've known each other. I have to make sure that I answer readers' questions.

4. What judgments or actions do you want your readers to make?

First of all, I want my readers to understand how the events went — what happened first, second, and so on. And I want them to understand how I felt that evening, how it seemed that I should have been hurt and not the others (since I was driving). I want them to know how humiliating it was to fail the breath test and how scared I was about Treavor. So I want my readers to understand, and then I guess I want them to see how this should never have happened.

5. What information will effectively convince your readers to make these judgments or take these actions?

If I leave out the details, I'm in trouble. Then they'll have to stop reading and try to figure out the part I didn't include. And that means they're not reading the story, not staying inside it. The accident itself and what happened just after it — this is crucial. The woman with her shopping bag, the police officer, how at first I couldn't move, seeing the blood, how quiet it was after the skidding. . . .

As you can see, those five questions can be tremendously useful. As you answer them, you make real progress toward understanding how your audience and your purpose affect what you write.

Purposes and rhetorical stance (3e, 3g)

Although your audience and its needs are important any time you write, it is also important for you to consider your own opinions, your own understandings, and your own purposes—in short, your **rhetorical stance**. You may start with no stance at all, especially if the assigned topic is new to you. In other situations, you might begin with a well-developed stance, especially if you can bring to the topic some personal experience or earlier study.

Suppose that because of tight budgets your school was considering dropping certain sports programs—soccer, swimming, and volleyball. Suppose further that your composition instructor asked you to write a paper arguing either to save such sports programs or to cut them. What's your stance? If you have played on a volleyball team, then your experience—if it was positive—might immediately give you a stance: save the volleyball program. Examining your stance even further here will help you understand what you have to say.

However, suppose that you begin the assignment with little or no prior knowledge, little or no opinion. Your task then is to develop a stance. In fact, that becomes one of your central purposes in writing.

Here are five questions to help you analyze your own rhetorical stance:

1. What knowledge or experience do you already have on this subject?
2. What are your feelings about this topic: strong opinion? curiosity? dislike?
3. What interests you most about this topic? Why?
4. What interests you least about this topic? Why?
5. What do you expect to conclude about this topic?

Here's how a volleyball player in the situation mentioned earlier might use the questions to more fully develop a stance.

1. What knowledge or experience do you already have on this subject?

Since I've been on volleyball teams for over three years, I bring considerable knowledge to this subject. I know the kind of support system that a team sport can provide. My first year here, I was homesick and unsure about college. It was the volleyball team and the help they gave me that made me feel that I could make it. And I know about the kind of personal dedication that sports can inspire. Volleyball has taught me a lot about my own potential; I know that hard work can pay off.

2.   What are your feelings about this topic: strong opinion? curiosity? dislike?

Strong opinion. I really feel that I'm right about this topic.

3.   What interests you most about this topic? Why?

Now that I think about it, I guess I'm interested in how much volleyball has given me — things that a fan in the stands would never be able to see. It's so much more than just winning or losing. And I'm also curious about the reasons other people have for dropping these sports. Is their argument only about money? Should it be only about money? This topic is a good one for me because I bring so much of my own interest to it.

4.   What interests you least about this topic? Why?

I guess the budget questions interest me the least: How much do these sports cost? How much do they cost compared to big spectator sports like basketball or football? Are there ways to trim the budgets and still keep the programs? I know that budget questions are probably important, but my own interest comes from having actually played on one of these teams. I want people to see how important that experience has been (and still is) to me.

5.   What do you expect to conclude about this topic?

I expect to conclude that these sports should be kept, not cut. I'll want to say whatever I can to support that.

Clearly, these answers show a writer with a strong stance. Answering the questions helps clarify it, and answering the questions helps this writer develop a personal interest and motivation. What might have started out as just another writing assignment becomes an activity with some personal interest and passion.

Now suppose you start with little or no prior knowledge. Suppose you're asked to write a paper outlining the controversy over the death penalty. We've all had some exposure to this question in the media, but maybe you haven't really studied it, nor do you have any direct experience with it. The assignment seems boring. Again, answering the five questions should help you begin to develop a personal stance and the personal interest that goes with it. If you're starting with practically no knowledge or initial interest, question 3 becomes crucially important in helping you analyze your stance. Your answer to this question must be something useful, rather than a one-sentence indication that nothing about this topic is interesting. The key here is to take advantage of the chance to explore and learn.

1.   What knowledge or experience do you already have on this subject?

I have no direct experience with this topic, no knowledge beyond what I've heard on television or seen in the papers.

2. What are your feelings about this topic: strong opinion? curiosity? dislike?

My own feelings at this point are somewhere between dislike and curiosity.

3. What interests you most about this topic? Why?

I guess I have always thought it was weird that the law could call murder a horrible crime yet make killing a justified, legal punishment. There's something inconsistent here, isn't there? I remember seeing the daughter of someone who'd been shot. She was interviewed after a jury had sentenced her mother's killer to death, and she was glad! She said it made her mother's death worth more. I'm not sure what she meant. So, what interests me most about this topic? Part of it is the emotion of it all. How can anyone not be emotional about killing someone? And I'm interested in finding out what *I* think. I'm a citizen of this state, and if the state uses the death penalty (notice we don't say *if the state kills someone*), then in some ways do I share responsibility for this?

4. What interests you least about this topic? Why?

The extremists are least interesting to me. They're sure. And I think they often make complicated issues too simple. Besides, I don't know where I stand on this issue. I want to focus on the reason and the values here, and I have a feeling they're pretty complicated.

5. What do you expect to conclude about this topic?

I may not conclude anything, and I'm glad now that this assignment is supposed to be an overview. I won't have to argue a position in the paper. Still, I hope the reading and thinking I do will help me decide what I privately think.

Audience (3h)

Almost all the writing you do is read and used by other people. Instructors read what you write and use it to assess your course performance. Prospective employers will read your job application letters. Once on the job, you may be asked to write a variety of requests, memos, evaluations, and so on. Thinking about your audience will often make your writing task clearer. Remembering your readers' point of view will also help you determine an appropriate tone and even in some cases an effective organization for what you write.

Think about how closely audience and purpose are linked. Suppose that in an Introduction to Physics course you are asked to write out an explanation of what happens when a baseball is hit for a home run. In this case, you can probably assume your audience has seen a baseball game and knows what a home run is. But can you assume your audience understands specific concepts of physics — things such as accelerations and velocity — or should you take the time to explain these terms? If you're writing to explain the physics of home runs to your roommate, a history major, you'd better explain the terms.

Considering your audience becomes especially important whenever you're trying to argue or convince. The first test of a written argument is whether readers actually read it. If an argument loses readers after the first paragraph, then it's a failure despite the shining logic on page 3. Keeping your audience in mind should help you make useful decisions about your writing.

Here are five questions you can use to analyze audience members and make decisions that will help you reach them effectively:

1.   Who will read and use your writing? If you can see more than one group of readers, what group should you consider your first (or primary) audience?
2.   As audience members finish reading your writing, what do you want them to see or feel or understand or agree to?
3.   What is your relationship to your audience? Can you approach your readers as friend to friend? expert to novice? expert to expert? novice to novice?
4.   What assumptions do you make about your audience's beliefs and about what your readers think and value?
5.   What assumptions will your audience make about your topic or about you as a writer on this topic? Are these assumptions useful to you? If so, how can you take advantage of them? If they will cause you problems, how can you neutralize them?

As you consider these questions, see if you can arrive at a tentative decision about your writing. Suppose that as a student in a community college you want to convince voters in your community college district to support a new tax so that your college can stay open. You know the budget allows for maintaining current quality, not for any expansion. Here's how the five questions just listed might help you write a persuasive letter to the local paper.

1.   Who will read and use your writing? If you can see more than one group of readers, what group should you consider your first (or primary) audience?

   Although my instructor will read this and grade it, I should think of local newspaper readers as my primary audience here.

   Decision: Write to local newspaper readers.

2.   As audience members finish reading your writing, what do you want them to see or feel or understand or agree to?

   I want readers to decide to vote yes on the new tax.

3.   What is your relationship to your audience? Can you approach your readers as friend to friend? expert to novice? expert to expert? novice to novice?

I live in the same community, so I can approach readers as a neighbor. But I also go to the community college, so I have some inside information. And I'm a taxpayer, too, so I can talk to readers as one taxpayer to another.

Decision: The taxpayer-to-taxpayer relationship is the one to make use of here. That relationship stresses the connection I have with readers. I can bring in the student-taxpayer relationship after I establish the taxpayer-taxpayer relationship .

4. What assumptions do you make about your audience's beliefs and about what your readers think and value?

I assume people don't want to pay more taxes. I also assume that they believe education is important. I assume that my readers don't want me to just tell them how wrong they are.

Decision: Maybe begin by agreeing that taxes are high, that it would be easy to vote no without really looking at what the tax money supports.

5. What assumptions will your audience make about your topic or about you as a writer on this topic? Are these assumptions useful to you? If so, how can you take advantage of them? If they will cause you problems, how can you neutralize them?

Since I want to increase the votes for the new tax, I want to focus on those readers who might vote the other way. I suppose some of them are tired of hearing about any new tax. Once they find out I'm a student at the community college, they might dismiss what I say. They might also think the community college is doing too much already and that some parts of the curriculum could be cut.

Decision: Maybe begin with something that diverts attention away from the tax issue itself. Whatever opening I use shouldn't sound dull; it should hook people into reading. And the letter needs to talk about why the college offers such a range of programs.

EXERCISE 3.1   ANALYZING AN ASSIGNMENT

NAME _____ **DATE** _____

Suppose your composition instructor gives you the assignment below. Read the assignment carefully, and then use the five questions to help you analyze it.

Think of a person who has had a strong effect on your life. Identify the person, and tell your readers why he or she is important to you. For this assignment, assume that you are writing to the other members of the class.

1. Who will read what you write?

_____

2. What do your readers already know or believe?

_____

_____

_____

3. What is it that only you can tell your readers?

_____

_____

_____

4. What judgments or actions do you want your readers to make?

_____

_____

_____

5. What information will effectively convince your readers to make these judgments or take these actions?

_____

_____

_____

EXERCISE 3.2   DETERMINING YOUR STANCE

NAME _____ **DATE** _____

Use the five questions to help you analyze your stance for writing assignments 1 and 2.

ASSIGNMENT 1

Identify some out-of-school activity that you enjoy—a hobby or sport or other activity. Talk about this activity, and show your readers why you find this activity enjoyable or rewarding. Ultimately, your paper should encourage readers to give your activity a try. Your audience is other college students who are unfamiliar with your topic.

1. What knowledge or experience do you already have on this subject?

_____

_____

_____

2. What are your feelings about this topic: strong opinion? curiosity? dislike?

_____

_____

_____

3. What interests you most about this topic? Why?

_____

_____

4. What interests you least about this topic? Why?

_____

_____

5. What do you expect to conclude about this topic?

_____

_____

This time consider a larger topic: the concept of patriotism. In your essay, explain what you think it means to be patriotic and the extent to which your ideas about patriotism are shared by your fellow citizens. How many different ways are there to be patriotic? For this essay, assume a wide audience, such as the people reading your local newspaper.

1. What knowledge or experience do you already have on this subject?

_____

_____

_____

2. What are your feelings about this topic: strong opinion? curiosity? dislike?

_____

_____

_____

3. What interests you most about this topic? Why?

_____

_____

4. What interests you least about this topic? Why?

_____

_____

5. What do you expect to conclude about this topic?

_____

_____

EXERCISE 3.3   FOCUSING ON YOUR AUDIENCE

NAME _____ **DATE** _____

Use the following questions to help you analyze your audience for the writing assignment. Note that you should make some decisions based on questions 1, 3, 4, and 5.

ASSIGNMENT

An organization you belong to wishes to raise $5,000 to aid victims of a recent natural disaster, but everyone seems to have a different opinion about the kinds of fund-raising activities that could achieve this goal most effectively and quickly. Your assignment is to write a three-page paper discussing the best ways for your organization to raise the $5,000 in the shortest amount of time.

1. Who will read and use your writing? If you can see more than one group of readers, what group should you consider your first (or primary) audience?

_____

_____

Decision: _____

_____

2. As audience members finish reading your writing, what do you want them to see or feel or understand or agree to?

_____

_____

_____

3. What is your relationship to your audience? Can you approach your readers as friend to friend? expert to novice? expert to expert? novice to novice?

_____

_____

_____

Decision: _____

_____

_____

_____

4. What assumptions do you make about your audience's beliefs and about what your readers think and value?

_____

_____

_____

Decision: _____

_____

_____

5. What assumptions will your audience make about your topic or about you as a writer on this topic? Are these assumptions useful to you? If so, how can you take advantage of them? If they will cause you problems, how can you neutralize them?

_____

_____

_____

_____

Decision: _____

_____

_____

_____

Visual Thinking

4

The average writer at the beginning of the twenty-first century has the ability to incorporate visuals into his or her work in ways that were unheard of even thirty years ago. Photographs and other images can easily be inserted into documents, software exists to create sophisticated charts and graphs, and text can be highlighted using color and a range of font styles. This almost overwhelming number of options means that writers face some difficult choices in crafting the messages they wish to send. Visuals need to meet readers' needs and support the purpose for writing. They should be clearly integrated with the document's words. They should not detract from the impact of the document as a whole. In other words, visual thinking is critical to your strategic thinking as a writer.

CONSIDERING VISUAL THINKING IN EVERYDAY USE

In your community and on your college campus — on bulletin boards, light and telephone poles, billboards, and virtually anywhere announcements and advertising can be posted — you will likely encounter numerous documents, all competing for your attention. Take the time to study a collection of these. Why do some draw your eye more immediately or compellingly than others? Is it the use of different typefaces or color? Is it the use of graphics? Is it something about the overall visual design? What kinds of visual thinking do the most effective of these documents exhibit? What do they suggest to you about strategic visual thinking in terms of document design?

Document design conventions (4a)

Business letters, résumés, academic essays and lab reports in various disciplines — each follows specific conventions in terms of overall design that make it immediately recognizable to informed readers. In composing such documents, you need to familiarize yourself with and follow these conventions. Many books and online resources are available to provide you with models. In specific courses, your instructors may well have their own preferred guidelines for you to follow. In general, proper document design shows that a writer respects his or her reader's expectations.

Visuals and their associations (4b)

Visuals create particular mental associations for readers. Obvious examples of this can be found in advertising, which often includes images of attractive models and cute children and pets that are intended to create positive associations with the product being advertised. When you see a popular company logo, for instance, you often make an immediate connection with the company and its product or service. Notice how quickly you can associate each logo shown in this flag with the company it represents.

Reprinted with permission of Adbusters.

The same image may even create different associations among different readers. For instance, to some this flag may be saying that the strength of the United States stems from its strong economy, which has flourished thanks to the American tradition of entrepreneurship. To others, this flag may represent the excessive political sway that corporate lobbyists have over the U.S. government. In deciding what visuals to include in a document, keep your audience in mind. What associations of their own are your readers likely to bring to a particular image? Remember that some readers may find a meaning in your message different from the one you intend to send.

Tone (4c)

The attitude you convey toward your subject and audience — whether serious or humorous, formal or casual, neutral or passionate — is reflected in the tone of your writing. Your choice of language contributes to creating your tone, of course, and so do the types of visual images you include in your document. In considering visuals, be sure that they accurately reflect the tone established by your language.

Cartoons, for example, might be appropriate if you are approaching your subject and audience from a humorous or lighthearted perspective, but they would not be appropriate for a more serious academic topic, when you would probably rely on photographs and charts. An impassioned argument against eating meat might include graphic images of animal slaughter, but such images would not be appropriate in a more neutral essay on the health benefits of vegetarianism.

A visual that varies in tone from the text of a document may confuse or put off readers and interfere with their reception of your message. (For more on tone, see Chapters 6 and 21.)

Pairing words and visuals (4d)

When including visuals in your writing, you need to clearly integrate text and images. In most types of academic writing, it is a good idea to refer to a visual explicitly. Readers may not recognize the purpose of visuals that simply "hang" in the text. You may also wish to explain to readers the significance of the visual or even to point out specific elements of the visual you want readers to take note of.

One common means of doing this is to give each visual a number (Figure 1, Figure 2, and so forth) and to mention the figure number at an appropriate point in the text, using language such as "As Figure 1 suggests . . . ," for example, or including a parenthetical citation: "(see Fig. 1)." It is also a good idea to provide each figure with a brief title that describes it or suggests its significance (though such titles need not be repeated in the text).

The point is that your text and visuals need to work together to have the maximum effect on your intended audience. You need to think carefully about what kinds of information can best be conveyed graphically; but you need to realize as well that readers must understand your purpose for including each visual image, a purpose that the image by itself often will not make clear. You also need to make certain that each image you include actually conveys the point you wish to make. If possible, during the revision process ask several readers to evaluate your visuals as well as the text of your work. If they are at all unclear as to the meaning of an image, then you probably need to revise, replace, or delete it.

EXERCISE 4.1   DOCUMENT DESIGN CONVENTIONS

NAME _____ **DATE** _____

Identify the kind of document represented by each of the following pages. Then write a sentence or two to explain the design elements of the document that help you identify it.

1.

2.

3.

1. Type of document _____

Explanation _____

_____

2. Type of document _____

Explanation _____

_____

3. Type of document _____

Explanation _____

_____

EXERCISE 4.2   VISUAL ASSOCIATIONS

NAME _____ **DATE** _____

A. Think of the logo for a popular or well-known company, such as McDonald's golden arches, Jack of Jack in the Box, the NBC peacock, the Microsoft Network butterfly, the Nike "swoosh," or another that comes to mind. Then on the lines below write about what associations your mind makes when you encounter that logo. Finally, share what you have written with several other students, and discuss how their mental associations differ from yours. How might these differences be accounted for?

_____

_____

_____

_____

_____

_____

B. Visit a bookstore or magazine stand and consider the covers of the various popular publications displayed there. Then, using your own paper, write about the ones that you are most drawn to as well as about the ones that you view more negatively. What positive and negative associations do you have with the images displayed on these particular covers?

EXERCISE 4.3   CONSIDERING THE TONE OF VISUALS

NAME _____ **DATE** _____

Look through a chapter or two in a textbook assigned to you for another course, and think particularly about the tone conveyed by the textbook's visual images. Then examine the images you find in a popular magazine you enjoy reading. Finally, answer the following questions.

1. How do the textbook's visuals differ from the magazine's visuals?

2. What tone is suggested by the visuals in each case?

3. To what extent do you find the visuals particularly appropriate (or inappropriate) for each type of publication? What makes you think as you do?

EXERCISE 4.4   ANALYZING HOW WORDS AND VISUALS ARE PAIRED

NAME _____ **DATE** _____

As in exercise 4.3, look through a chapter or two in a textbook assigned to you for another course, as well as through a popular magazine you enjoy reading. Then answer the following questions.

1. How clearly does each publication integrate visuals with text?

2. What methods does each publication use to do so?

3. What have you learned about integrating visuals with text from examining the two publications?

Exploring, Planning, and Drafting

5

Analyzing your assignment, determining your rhetorical stance, and focusing on your audience are crucial steps toward a rough draft. After these analyses, what should you do next? Should you go directly to a rough draft? Should you go to the library to look up every single bit of information on your topic? Should you try to talk to your instructor or a classmate to find out what others are doing? Or should you just hope you'll get some ideas by the time your paper is due?

Many experienced writers have a strategy for exploring a new, perhaps strange, topic systematically. Four modes of exploration are discussed here: brainstorming, freewriting, looping, and questioning. Each of these methods can help you explore a topic and determine your interest in and level of knowledge about the topic.

EXPLORING, PLANNING, AND DRAFTING IN EVERYDAY USE

If you have ever written a love letter, you probably know all about exploring a topic and working hard on a draft. You might have spent days, even weeks, exploring the ideas you wanted to convey and considering the effects your language might have. And you may have drafted, torn up the draft, and then drafted some more, searching for the right words to express something deeply felt but difficult to put down on paper.

Thank goodness few writing tasks are as demanding as a love letter, but most of the writing you do will call on you to give some serious thought to what you want to say and how you want to say it. Make a list of some other occasions outside of school when you thought long and hard about something you needed to write — a letter to a friend asking for a special favor, a personal statement to accompany a job application, and so on. Then, for one of these occasions, briefly explain how you went about exploring your topic and planning what to say.

Brainstorming

To **brainstorm**, simply make a list of words or phrases that seem connected to your topic. The idea is to push yourself to focus on the topic without judging your results.

Work fast, and do not censor yourself. At the top of a notebook page, jot down your topic; then note under it anything that comes to mind. Figure 5.1 shows what a brief brainstorming session might produce after some reading or class discussion of the Industrial Revolution.

Brainstorming works best when writers already have some knowledge of their topic. It is even more effective in a group. Even two people brainstorming together will normally produce much more material than an individual. And talking with others, tossing out ideas, is a way to hear what you already know and what you need to find out more about.

> *Industrial Revolution*
> *new machines to speed up production*
> *all kinds of products → like what? textiles – weaving*
> *   mass productions – clothes, household goods*
> *"Sweatshops"   working conditions – long hours*
> *safety – child labor*
>
> *Shift from country to city*
> *less reliance on agriculture / weather / forces of nature / God*
> *more dependence on mill owners, market forces*
> *– lives out of control?*
> *standardized products, not unique handmade ones*
>
> *Pollution   rich get richer / poor get poorer*
> *   less self-sufficiency*
> *transportation vastly improved*

Figure 5.1 Brainstorming

Freewriting and looping

Like brainstorming, **freewriting** asks writers to suspend judgment, banish hesitation, and simply think on paper. Instead of making notes, freewriting involves writing sentences or something approximating sentences. What do you write? You write whatever comes into your head after you have thought for a minute. The key to freewriting is to keep right on going even if all you are writing is "I don't know what to say now." If you write "I don't know what to say now" two or three times and you really seem stuck, go back to the last substantive sentence and recopy it. But keep writing. How long should you keep going? Plan on no more than ten minutes. Set a timer if you like. Write nonstop for ten minutes, and if there is more to say, keep on saying it.

Here is a freewrite on "one aspect of the Industrial Revolution":

> I'm supposed to write on one aspect of the Industrial Revolution. That's a big one. There's what happened to technology — all those machines doing things that people used to do. Lots more efficient in comparison with the old ways. I need some examples

here. But what's the price? the consequences of all this? Were people better off? happier? Some probably were, some not. So which ones were happier and which ones were not? Fine, all I'm coming up with are questions. And now I'm running out of things to say about the Industrial Revolution. Except that word revolution revolution revolution revolution—something→connected to other revolutions. These are big changes we're talking about here—generation gaps. TVs with 2-inch screens, and my grandparents didn't know tv at all as kids. Not to mention space travel.

Not everything this student has written would go directly into her European History paper; the instructor is probably not interested in reading about space travel. But that's fine—nobody grades your freewriting. It's intended to help you get started. When this student looked back over what she had written, she found herself most interested in a question she had posed, then dropped, in the middle of freewriting: Who was better off, and who suffered, as a consequence of the Industrial Revolution? She had found a way into her topic and a starting point for exploration.

Freewriting can be effective as you begin a writing task, and it can be equally effective later on as you explore a subtopic. Freewriting is so easy that you can try it on several possible topics as a way of helping to settle on one.

Writers can also see repeated freewriting in a method that the writer and educator Peter Elbow calls **looping**. Suppose your freewrite looks something like the one shown in Figure 5.1. Choose a sentence in it that for some reason appeals to you—for instance, "So which ones were happier and which ones were not?" These words become the starting point for your second freewrite, and your goal is to explore further the ideas contained in that sentence.

Questioning

One of the oldest ways to explore a topic is to ask questions about it systematically. You can pose and answer questions entirely on your own, or you can use any of the sets of questions in this section as a basis for group discussion.

The ancient Greek philosopher Aristotle first proposed four questions as a way to generate information.

1. What is it? (definition or description)
2. What caused it? (cause and effect)
3. What is it like or unlike? (comparison/contrast)
4. What do others say about it? (testimony)

The journalistic questions *who, what, when, where, why,* and *how* are also widely used and are particularly helpful if your overall purpose is to explain.

Finally, the modern philosopher Stephen Toulmin designed a way to help writers analyze their thinking when their aim is to persuade. Toulmin's analytic model is shown here in modified form as a series of brief questions.

1. What is the *claim* I am making?
2. What are the *grounds* or *good reasons* that support my claim?

3. What *underlying assumptions* support the grounds of my claim?
4. What *backup evidence* do I have or can I find to add further support?
5. What *refutations* can be made against my claim?
6. In what ways is or should my claim be *qualified*?

Note that these question sets may require that you perform research to answer them thoroughly. Such research may be useful and necessary, but there is no point in conducting research until you have some idea of how you will use the information you gather. At an early stage in the writing process, you may not need to answer any of these questions completely. Their value lies in their ability to focus your thinking so that you can begin to determine what you know and what you need to find out.

Drafting a working thesis (5c)

As writers explore a topic, their major goal is to develop a working thesis to guide them as they begin to draft. A **thesis** is a one-sentence statement that presents an essay's main point and suggests the writer's purpose for that essay. A **working thesis** is tentative and subject to change or refinement. Your working thesis evolves as you explore your topic; it eventually becomes your final thesis. Although a working thesis is likely to change, establishing one early makes the drafting proceed smoothly.

A good working thesis has two parts: a topic portion and a comment portion. The **topic** portion states the subject, and the **comment** portion makes an important point about that subject.

TOPIC	**COMMENT**

Genetic engineering can lead to astonishing cures, and it will also lead to ethical and moral questions we have yet to answer.

COMMENT	**TOPIC**

We have not yet fully understood the effects of economic globalization.

Note that both of these examples are not yet well focused. What are the astonishing cures? What are the ethical questions? How many of each will be discussed? And what exactly are the possible effects of economic globalization? Is this paper going to talk about the outsourcing of jobs from the United States to other parts of the world? Will it discuss the exploitation of foreign workers or the rise in wages in previously undeveloped countries? In short, a working thesis gives you a place to start.

After writing a working thesis, you can begin looking at what it promises that your paper will do. As you think about your thesis, you almost certainly will change it somewhat. Remember, the point of a working thesis is to get you working.

FIRST VERSION

TOPIC	**COMMENT**

My friend Rosa is an important friend I have known for years.

- *Interest.* Certainly this must be interesting to the writer, someone who has known Rosa for a long time and presumably shared many experiences with her.

Readers might not yet find this interesting. Readers (strangers, after all) do not know Rosa and may not know the writer. So this working thesis seems to leave readers out of the picture.

- *Specificity and clarity.* The topic focus on Rosa is clear. The comment section, however, is very vague. Why is Rosa important? Is it simply that the writer has known her for years? The writer needs to answer this question and then rephrase the working thesis to make it more specific.

- *Manageability.* Right now it is difficult to judge the manageability of this working thesis. If the writer plans to discuss the entire friendship with Rosa, the topic is probably too large.

- *Assessment.* This working thesis needs revising, particularly so that the comment part is more specific. That specificity should help make the working thesis more interesting to readers and also should limit the topic so that it can be reasonably handled by the writer.

	TOPIC	COMMENT

REVISED WORKING THESIS   I learned what friendship is from Rosa, particularly in the two weeks I roomed with her after my apartment was burglarized.

Notice that in the revised working thesis the topic has shifted to "what friendship is," a topic with much broader interest. Notice, too, that the comment part has been focused much more specifically. The writer of this working thesis has moved to a much clearer and more carefully defined plan. This revised working thesis tells the writer what to write about: the burglary, those two weeks with Rosa, and what those two weeks taught the writer about friendship.

Gathering information (5d)

After you carefully consider your audience, explore your topic, and establish a working thesis, ask yourself whether you already have enough information to begin writing a draft. Your working thesis can be a guide. If it is tightly focused and specific, you may already have enough information to feel comfortable drafting. But if your own sense of your topic is still vague or somewhat confused, then you probably need to gather additional information.

Begin gathering information by listing the questions that you need to answer. Let's say you've been assigned to write a report on a job or career that interests you (your audience is other college students) and you've decided to write on photography. You have a topic; you may have a vague, still-unfocused working thesis such as "photography can be an interesting and profitable career." Here are some questions you might still need to answer:

- What exactly do I mean by "interesting"?
- What career options are open to photographers? Do I want to talk about all of those options?

- How much do photographers make?
- What kind of hours do they keep?
- What do they think is the best part of their job?

Listing questions like these helps you decide what information you're looking for, and it should help you figure out where to look.

One option is to consult written sources. In many academic writing situations, the textbooks you already have will provide the information you need in order to begin drafting. If you need additional information, consult your college library. (Don't forget, you *must* document your research by citing your sources. Ask your instructor for information on documenting sources.)

Information can also be obtained through interviews, field observation, and surveys. If, for example, you want to know what photographers think of their job, one obvious thing to do is to interview some local photographers.

Don't forget the important role that your audience plays in deciding what information you need. If your audience is other college students, they won't understand (or have the patience for) a chemically precise description of how color prints are made. As someone interested in photography, you may find this topic fascinating, but you will probably have to stay away from that sort of highly technical discussion with this audience.

Organizing verbal and visual information (5e)

When writers actually start drafting depends on their own inclinations. Some writers don't begin drafting until they have written an outline; they use the outlining process to help them decide on their organization. Other writers begin drafting right away; they use the drafting and revising process itself to help them understand and organize what they are writing about.

Whatever your inclinations, you should be aware of some common organizational patterns. Recognizing these patterns in the information you gather will often help you organize your essay. The simplest organizational pattern is based on time: first this, then this, then this. Whenever you have to tell a story, you're using this organizational pattern. Sometimes this **chronological** pattern can be used for an entire piece of writing—an account of your auto accident for your insurance company, for instance. Sometimes chronological organization will be part of a larger structure.

Several common essay forms are based on logical relationships. The **cause-effect** pattern can work in either of two ways: by trying to explain why something happened (thus working from effect back to cause) or by trying to forecast something that is likely to happen (thus working from current causes to possible effects). A newspaper article that tries to explain a politician's defeat may begin by acknowledging an effect (the defeat) and then discuss its probable causes. A business report analyzing a proposed price change would discuss the price change (the cause) and its probable effect on sales.

The **problem-solution** pattern identifies and describes a problem, explores possible solutions, and typically ends by recommending one solution. Such a pattern would be appropriate, for example, in a paper urging commuters to solve their parking problems by taking the bus.

An essay employing **illustration** provides concrete examples to support the essay's main idea. If your essay's purpose is to describe the promising future awaiting liberal arts graduates, you might begin by proposing that thesis and then using examples to illustrate it.

Closely related to the illustration essay is the **definition** essay, which describes what something is and, often, what it is not. For example, an essay that sets out to define the character of people raised in the Midwest would essentially be a definition essay. This same topic could also be organized as a **comparison/contrast** essay. By its nature, a comparison/contrast essay focuses on two main topics or subjects, examining their similarities and their differences. Thus a writer might contrast midwestern cultural values with southern cultural values.

Writers can organize comparison/contrast essays in two ways. Using **block comparison**, an essay would speak about one topic (the first block), then discuss the second topic in light of the first (the second block). Here is an organizational sketch for a paper comparing and contrasting American factory working conditions in 2000 and 1900:

A. Introduction
B. Block 1: Working conditions in 2000 (hours, pay, safety)
C. Transition
D. Block 2: Working conditions in 1900 (hours, pay, safety)
E. Conclusion

The other possibility is to organize comparison/contrast essays by major points, comparing each point separately and then moving on to the next. This is called **alternating comparison**:

A. Introduction
B. Working hours in 2000 vs. working hours in 1900
C. Brief transition
D. Pay scales in 2000 vs. pay scales in 1900
E. Brief transition
F. Workers' safety in 2000 vs. workers' safety in 1900
G. Conclusion

Two other logical relationships can also form the basis for essay organization: **division** and **classification**. An essay based on division begins by examining an idea in its entirety and then proceeds to identify and discuss parts of it. Suppose you are asked to write an essay that describes "the good teacher." You might identify and discuss the components that you believe go into a good teacher—knowledge of subject, enthusiasm, respect for students, and so on. You might then follow this discussion with your explanation of how these various traits are related to one another.

To classify means to group according to categories. You might choose to describe your particular college courses this term by classifying them as science/math or liberal arts.

Writers often use some combination of these organizational strategies. Considering this question of organization before beginning a rough draft should give you a sense of direction, control, and confidence as you begin drafting.

Drafting (5g)

At some point, your thinking, information gathering, and planning must lead you to writing sentences and paragraphs that will eventually add up to a rough draft of your essay. Where should you begin? You could begin with the introduction if you know what it should say. But if beginning with the introduction seems difficult (as is often the case), start drafting some middle part of the paper—some part you know well. But do begin. (For more on writing introductions, see Chapter 6.)

What, in general, can be said about the drafting process?

- *Drafting demands flexibility.* As you write, you are thinking—concentrating with more intensity and interest than earlier. As a result, you will probably find it necessary to revise your plan as you go along. This should not surprise or dismay you; in fact, you should expect that as you draft you will probably not follow your own plan to the letter.

- *Drafting demands paying attention to your content and to your process.* What should you do if you realize as you draft that you lack certain information or that you are not making use of information that you spent hours gathering? All writers encounter such situations at one time or another. They are normal and must be accepted. Sometimes that means continuing to draft but writing a note to remind yourself that you skipped over a key point and need to come back to it later; or it might mean that you will simply omit some information to provide a tighter, more manageable focus for your paper. Such adjustments should not be cause for panic or frustration.

- *Drafting demands time.* No matter how much planning you have done or how much information you have gathered, chances are that your drafting will proceed fitfully and will require more than one sitting. If your drafting goes forward without a hitch, consider yourself lucky. The advice here is to anticipate that your drafting will take longer than you want it to, so be sure to avoid last-minute, hurried drafting if you wish to rise above mediocrity. Also realize that juggling other concerns and responsibilities is part of the writer's lot. Even full-time writers cannot entirely escape the sometimes chaotic reality of their daily lives.

Perhaps the most important advice about drafting is this: generate a train of thought, and stay with it. Do not stop to look up words in the dictionary (circle them and come back to them later). Do not stop to ponder paragraph breaks or rules about quotation marks. Write in bursts of at least ten minutes—longer, if the words are coming easily. If you have access to a computer, consider drafting at the keyboard.

If you cannot finish a draft in one sitting, stop at a point where you know what you will say next. Suggest that information with a couple of phrases jotted on the page. You will be grateful for those notes to yourself when you next look at the draft.

What if you get absolutely stumped and can see no way to proceed? Do not panic. Reread what you have written, looking for wrong turns or imprecise expressions in the last page or so of your writing. If you are still stumped, set the draft aside and do something entirely different, something that will allow you to forget the writing task altogether. Jog. Do laundry. If your deadline allows you to stay away from the writing overnight, do so. A brief time away will often give you a new perspective and enable you to resume drafting. One more possibility is to skip the section that is giving you trouble. This may be possible if you know what you want to say further on. By the time you have written the rest of the paper, you will probably have figured out how to address the problem portion of the draft.

↵ You can try all of these tactics by yourself, but perhaps the best remedies involve other people. Talk to someone about your writing. If your campus has a writing center, talk to one of the writing assistants. Talk to your instructor. Talking about a draft helps you see that draft more objectively, and that new outlook may be all you need to continue drafting.

EXERCISE 5.1   EXPLORING A TOPIC

NAME _____ **DATE** _____

Read the assignment below, and then use the specified strategies to help you explore the assigned topic.

ASSIGNMENT

Write a personal essay about lies and lying. In your essay, you should answer this question: "How have I been personally affected by lies and lying, either as the one telling the lie or as the one being lied to?" Since this is such a wide-open topic, begin by finishing the following sentence and then freewriting for at least five minutes.

When I think of experiencing lies and lying, the first thing that comes to mind is

_____

_____

_____

_____

_____

_____

_____

_____

_____

_____

_____

_____

_____

_____

Use these journalistic questions to help you continue exploring the question "How have I been personally affected by lies and lying, either as the one telling the lie or as the one being lied to?"

1. Who was involved?

   _____

   _____

2. What happened?

   _____

   _____

   _____

3. When did it happen?

   _____

   _____

   _____

4. Where did it happen?

   _____

   _____

   _____

5. Why did it happen?

   _____

   _____

   _____

6. How did it happen?

   _____

   _____

   _____

Based on your initial freewrite and your answers to the journalistic questions, explain to a partner (or small group) what you think you will write about in your personal essay about lies and lying. Listen to your partner's (or your group's) questions, and make notes about whatever you think you need to add or make clearer. Then switch roles and be the listener. Listen to what your classmate might write about, and try to help that classmate make his or her story clearer and more complete. Once this discussion process is finished, write a paragraph explaining how it was useful to you to freewrite, to use journalistic questions, and to discuss your topic with others.

_____

EXERCISE 5.2 ESTABLISHING A WORKING THESIS

NAME _____ **DATE** _____

A. Underline the topic part of each working thesis, and circle the comment part. Remember, the topic portion answers the question "What is this about?" and the comment portion makes a claim or description or another important point about the topic.

>   **EXAMPLE**   For a report to appear in a general-interest magazine: <u>Drift-net fishing</u> is
>
>   an efficient method but an environmentally disastrous international problem.

1. For a paper aimed at other new students: The first week of college is filled with unexpected challenges.

2. For a college newspaper: The career counseling center offers many opportunities for students who are uncertain about what course of study they might pursue.

3. For a paper in your U.S. history class: Prohibition was not as complete a failure as many modern Americans believe, for U.S. consumption of alcohol remained dramatically down from pre-1919 levels one year after Prohibition was repealed.

4. For a brochure issued by an environmental organization: The importation of certain foreign plant species has had an adverse effect on the fragile ecosystems of wetlands.

5. For an opinion piece in a film class: Although the screenplay is brilliant, it is Orson Welles's revolutionary filmmaking techniques that truly dazzle in *Citizen Kane*.

B. Write out a possible working thesis for each topic area. Underline the topic part, and circle the comment part.

EXAMPLE TOPIC AREA	Pollution in your area (for a feature article in the local newspaper).
EXAMPLE WORKING THESIS	<u>Cleaning up after the bankrupt United Chrome Company</u> (continues to be a time-consuming and expensive process.)

1. Topic area: The need for a particular government policy change (to be written for your local or campus newspaper).

   Working thesis: _____

   _____

2. Topic area: Ways to choose a major (to be written for students entering college).

   Working thesis: _____

   _____

3. Topic area: The importance of learning good time-management skills (to be written for high school students going on to college).

   Working thesis: _____

   _____

4. Topic area: Types of teachers (to be written for other college students).

   Working thesis: _____

   _____

5. Topic area: A popular television or radio program (to be written for critics of the program).

   Working thesis: _____

   _____

C. Use the questions below to test your working thesis for any one of the topic areas in part B. Then revise your working thesis accordingly.

1. *Interest.* Why are you interested in this topic? Does your thesis statement make this interest clear to readers?

   _____

   _____

   _____

   _____

2. *Specificity and clarity.* Is the topic focus clear and specific, or is it so vague that readers will have to guess at it? Is the comment section clear, or will it leave readers guessing?

   _____

   _____

   _____

   _____

3. *Manageability.* Can this topic and comment be handled in five pages, or will they require a more lengthy report? If the topic and comment seem to require more than five pages, how can the topic and comment be made more manageable?

   _____

   _____

   _____

   _____

   Your revised working thesis:

   _____

   _____

   _____

EXERCISE 5.3   ORGANIZING AND PLANNING A DRAFT

NAME _____ **DATE** _____

Respond to the questions below to help you see your own methods for planning and drafting.

1. This chapter identifies four methods for exploring a topic: brainstorming, freewriting, looping, and questioning. Of these four, which one seems most useful to you? Why?

   _____

   _____

   _____

2. For a class on organizational psychology, you have been asked to choose a well-known figure, alive or dead, and to write a paper explaining what qualities make him or her an effective leader. What two techniques from this chapter would you use in drafting your thesis? Be specific.

   First technique: _____

   _____

   _____

   Second technique: _____

   _____

   _____

3. You were asked to bring to class the working thesis for the organizational psychology assignment described in question 2. The instructor has each student examine a classmate's working thesis and comment on it. The thesis you are asked to discuss reads: "Chief Crazy Horse had many traits that contributed to his ability to lead." Would you encourage the writer of this working thesis to begin drafting, or would you urge this writer to refine the working thesis? Explain your recommendation in a helpful way.

   _____

   _____

   _____

Reviewing, Revising, and Editing

6

Revision strategies (6a, 6b, 6c, 6d, 6e)

We revise and edit all the time—even in our conversations. Directions to a child on how to measure the ingredients for cupcakes may have to be revised on the spot if the child isn't understanding. A story told to friends may be revised in the telling to get the sequence of events right. Like speakers, writers are likely to find that their first efforts are often sketchy or wandering or incomplete, which is hardly a surprise since they are first efforts. Good writers don't confuse first drafts with final copy; they know those first drafts will need reworking. For experienced writers, **revising** may include rethinking the thesis, assessing the draft's logic and organization, adding or changing material, gathering more information to develop or support a point, or reshaping sentences. Typically, writers revise for two main reasons. Revision helps them understand what they really think, what they really want to say. And revision helps writers make their prose communicate clearly to readers.

Revising often goes hand in hand with drafting. In fact, every time you reread what you've written (which you probably do often as you draft), you are using one of the most important revision strategies.

REVISING AND EDITING IN EVERYDAY USE

You may well remember a time when you consciously edited what you were saying in order to be tactful or considerate of someone's feelings. For example, a woman seeing a new baby for the first time was stuck for what to say, for the baby struck her as anything but cute. Revising and editing rapidly in her head, she stumbled on what she hoped was a tactful as well as an honest response. "What a baby!" she exclaimed. "What a baby!"

For a portion of a day, listen carefully for revising and editing in conversations you hear or take part in. Then analyze what kinds of revisions you heard and what seemed most interesting about them. Summarize your analysis of each conversation in a sentence or two.

Revision strategy 1: Rereading to see what you've said

As you reread, pay attention to your thoughts, and don't worry about small errors in punctuation or spelling (be sure to fix them later in the process). As you reread, do so with a reason in mind. Do you have the nagging sense that your draft has veered off somewhere? Reread to see whether you can find the wrong turn. Or do you have a sense that even though your teacher asked for five pages, your two-page draft says everything it should? In that case, reread to look at your examples or illustrations to decide whether they really tell readers all that they need to know.

Remember, rereading should lead you toward revising—adding or changing—what you already have. Here are some questions to keep in mind as you reread.

1. What does the opening paragraph promise that the rest of the paper will discuss? Is this promise clear and focused? How can this opening be sharpened or clarified?

2. Can you tell what the assignment is just by reading the draft? Can you identify the intended audience for this assignment? If not, what should be added or rephrased?

3. As the draft moves from point to point, can you understand its logic? If the paper seems to jump around, where are the jumps? Where do you get lost? What needs to be added or rearranged?

4. What conclusion is the draft working toward? What makes this conclusion clear to you? What doesn't?

5. How will your readers react to this draft? Will they find enough explanation? Will they draw the conclusions you want them to draw?

6. What is the best, clearest, most compelling part of the draft now?

Revision strategy 2: Asking objective readers to mirror, question, and discuss your content

Whenever you write, your first reader is yourself. But nearly all your college and work-related writing will be read and acted on by others. Thus asking for an objective response to a draft is a tremendously powerful revision strategy. Outside readers will have only what is on the page to read and understand. They are often able to spot incomplete explanations or missing transitions.

Before you ask for a response, identify some questions to help guide your reader. Saying "Will you read this and tell me what you think?" will probably give you a response such as "This is good" or "I like most of it." Hearing those things might make you feel good, but those responses don't help much when it comes to revising. As you work on your own draft, you will naturally feel confident about some parts, uneasy about others. Ask readers to help you with the problem areas. For example, you could say something such as "This part on the top of page 2 has been giving me trouble. What does it say to you?" You may have a number of such questions, and the questions that you considered as part of revision strategy 1 will work here to help outside readers give you specific feedback.

Above all, get your outside readers to talk about your draft. Ask them to explain the paper's purpose. Ask them to identify its major points. Ask them what has been left out. Their answers will help you see your own draft and hear its strengths and weaknesses in someone else's words.

Revision strategy 3: Making a revision plan

Sometimes it is easy to feel lost in the writing process, especially if you are writing about new material or writing with a new purpose (say, your first scholarship application). When this sense of being lost hits, stop and review what you've done. Take out a sheet of scratch paper, and begin by briefly writing out your assignment: What are you writing? Why are you writing it? Who will read it? Underneath that, list the things you've already done to make progress. What parts have you drafted so far? What questions have you researched, and what sources have you consulted? As you read your draft, what questions are you yourself sure of? Which ones are you still unsure about? What answers do you need to find? You might, for instance, realize that you need to reread something or that you need to locate some new answers.

Once you've begun to take stock in this way, identify what specifically you will do next. Will you reread something before you try to do more drafting? Will you skip to another section and work on it for now? Will you head to the library to look for some specific answers? Will you ask an objective reader for some input and response? What can you do next to make progress?

Revision strategy 4: Charting the organization of your draft

Sometimes with short writing assignments, and especially with longer ones, writers have trouble keeping track of their logic and organization. The simple solution here is to use some method to make that logic clear to yourself. Outlining is one way to accomplish this, for by outlining your draft you will see how it is put together. Alternatively, you might try numbering each paragraph of your draft and then writing a sentence or phrase summarizing each one. Write the summaries consecutively on a piece of scratch paper. Once they are written, you should be able to see whether you need to rearrange some sections, cut some sections, or add new ones.

Revision strategy 5: Giving yourself time

If you have worked hard drafting, you will eventually get tired and lose your concentration. At this point, your best revision strategy is to take a break. If you have the luxury of stepping back for several hours or a whole day, you might find that when you return, the draft—which seemed jumbled and hopeless before—now announces its flaws so that you can see how to deal with them. This strategy can be helpful even if you have only a few minutes or an hour for a break. Take a walk, do some laundry, jog—anything that's not too demanding but that will take you away from the desk for a little while. When you come back, you should come back fresh and ready to apply one of the other strategies.

Editing strategies (6f, 6g, 6i)

Once you have a mostly complete draft that you feel says pretty much what it should say, it is time to begin considering editing strategies. **Editing** turns to the smaller elements of a draft: the paragraphs, the separate sentences, and even the individual words — especially as they create the essay's tone. Careful editing means checking each of these elements for effectiveness, variation, and correctness.

Editing strategy 1: Reconsidering your title and introduction

The title and opening paragraph should introduce the essay's topic. They also should convey the writer's reasons for writing.

What makes a good title?

- A good title is specific; it would be appropriate only with the paper that follows it.
- A good title is interesting, intriguing; it asks questions or raises expectations that readers will want to satisfy.

It is useful to ask yourself to come up with one or two alternative titles. By forcing yourself to come up with alternatives, you give yourself choices; revision involves making such choices.

An introduction can take any of these forms:

- a general-to-specific paragraph that states a generality and then modifies and limits it, thus indicating the essay's limited topic (for more on the general-to-specific paragraph, see Chapter 7)
- a quotation that the essay will either agree with or contradict
- a brief story that dramatizes the essay's topic
- a question or series of questions that the essay will address
- a strong assertion of opinion

To draft an effective introduction, you need to review your purpose and your topic. Then consider which form best suits the purpose and topic. Ask yourself questions like these: Should I begin with a thesis statement or with an example? What if I tried it the other way? I know that stories make statistics come alive. If I am beginning now with statistics, could I begin instead with a story, even a fictional story identified as such? If I'm beginning now with a story, would beginning with statistics be a better way to start?

Editing strategy 2: Reconsidering paragraphing, sentence structure, word choice, and tone

Once you feel reasonably happy about an essay's content and organization, and your draft has assumed the overall shape it will probably keep, reread with an eye toward technical choices. As you reread, consider the following questions about paragraphs, sentences, word choice, and tone.

■ *Paragraphs*

- Do the paragraphs group sentences effectively?
- Are the paragraphs consistently too long? Do I pack too much information into one paragraph?
- Are the paragraphs consistently too short? Do they lack examples and explanations?
- Are the transitions from one paragraph to the next smooth and clear?

If you charted the organization of your draft as suggested earlier in this chapter, you have an easy way to check your transitions between paragraphs. Your chart will tell you where your major shifts in thought occur. Chapter 7 discusses the use of transitions *within* paragraphs, and those same devices can be used between paragraphs.

■ *Sentences*

- Are all of the sentences the same length?
- Do all of the sentences employ the same structure?

A paragraph of short sentences sounds like a grade-school text: "I went to the store. Jack went with me. At the store, bread filled at least four shelves. I could not decide which kind to buy. Finally, I recognized our usual brand." A series of unnecessarily long sentences, however, often exasperates the reader and makes meaning hard to grasp. Varying sentence length helps to hold readers' attention.

Readers also welcome variation in sentence structure. The most common (and most direct) English sentence structure is the simple one-clause declarative sentence: subject → verb → object. This structure is excellent. But if every sentence sounds and looks the same, the ideas in those sentences will seem the same, too. Varying sentence structure will help you accentuate some ideas and downplay others. Thus variation allows you to be more expressive as a writer. (For more on varying sentence structure, see Chapter 29.)

■ *Word Choice*

- Does the essay use specific words rather than general ones—*spaghetti* rather than *dinner*, *sneakers* rather than *shoes*, *sprinted* rather than *ran*?
- Does the essay use active verbs whenever reasonable, and does it stay away from excessive use of the verb *be* (*is*, *was*, *were*)?

Words such as *fun*, *large*, *messy*, *great*, and *slow* are all defined by context, as are generic nouns such as *food*, *movie*, and *building*. If the writing does not provide a detailed context, these words often leave readers in the dark. How big is *large*? How messy is *messy*? Which *movie* did you see? What kind of *building* was it? When you revise to use more specific words, you give your readers far more information. (For more on word choice, see Chapter 14.)

Remember, too, that essay writing improves when writers use the active voice. In addition to simply conveying more action, the active voice demands subjects as the agents of the verbs' actions. (For more on active and passive voice, see Chapter 30.)

> The original house on the property was destroyed in 2001. [*What destroyed it?*]

> A hurricane destroyed the original house on the property in 2001. [*Now we can picture it, and we have more information.*]

Writers often employ the passive voice in a variety of useful ways, but if you find that you lapse repeatedly into the passive, try rewriting in the active.

■ *Tone*

- Do the word choices create a tone appropriate to the topic and intended audience?
- Is the language too formal? too informal?
- Does the essay employ words your readers will find out of place or offensive?

If you and your audience possess similar values and backgrounds, your instinctive word choices will probably not offend your readers. However, if your readers possess values or attitudes quite different from your own, you will probably need to pay close attention to your use of language. Contrast the vocabulary you would use in writing to a friend with the vocabulary you would use in writing to a prospective employer. (For more on tone and appropriate word choice, see Chapters 12, 13, and 14.)

Editing strategy 3: Checking for correctness

In most cases, experienced writers check for correctness only after completing their large-scale revisions; there is little point in correcting sentences that will be changed or possibly cut later. Since editing often comes nearly last in the writing process, it is a step that inexperienced writers sometimes skip. The result may be a clearly organized piece of writing that contains numerous errors.

What do writers look for as they check their own work? They look for errors—especially errors that have given them trouble before. Reading for correctness involves training yourself to pay *little* attention to your content and *close* attention to individual sentences and words. Reading aloud often helps writers focus in this way. Many writers also read backward, sentence by sentence. Such backward reading makes the content difficult to follow and frees the mind to concentrate on spelling and punctuation. Whatever your method of rereading, simply mark each error (or possible error), and keep reading. Then return to reexamine and remedy the errors.

If you write infrequently, you will probably find it hard to recall the rules and hard to check your own work. In some cases, a sentence may sound wrong or look wrong, but you cannot say why. If you suspect an error, note the sentence, finish your reading, and then ask someone to help you with the problem sentences — your course instructor, a knowledgeable student, or a writing assistant in your writing center. Do not let any of these resource people simply correct your work. Besides being unethical, such correcting by others robs you of the opportunity to learn. Ask instead for an explanation of the error. Once you understand, you can make the correction.

If none of these resource people are available, you will need to do what many experienced writers do: consult a source book. This workbook is one such book. The table of contents and the index should help you locate answers to specific questions of punctuation and grammar. If you need to review the meanings of various grammatical terms, Chapter 16 should prove useful.

In addition, maintain your own personal editing checklist — a record of the sorts of errors caught during editing. Include the errors you catch and those your instructor notes. Most writers make the same errors over and over. By identifying these trouble spots, you should be able to recognize and correct them next time. Reviewing your checklist before editing a new paper should help you catch the kinds of errors made on previous papers. Here is an example of a checklist:

MARKED ERROR	IN CONTEXT	LOOK FOR
wrong preposition	*to* for *on*	use of *to*
spelling	*seperate* for *separate*	*seperate*
sentence fragment	starts with *-ing* word	use of *-ing* words at start of sentence
apostrophe	*it's* for *its*	use of *it's*
comparison of unlike things	"a winter as cold as Buffalo" should be "a winter as cold as Buffalo's"	"as . . . as"

If you find that many or most of your checklist entries refer to spelling errors, consider keeping a separate spelling checklist (see Chapter 15).

➔ **CHECKING YOUR WRITING FOR THE TOP TWENTY ERRORS FOUND IN STUDENT WRITING**

The authors of *The St. Martin's Handbook* have conducted extensive research into the error patterns of college writers. This research has resulted in a list of the twenty errors most often made by college students in their writing. Throughout this workbook you will find coverage of the rules and guidelines you need to correct each of these problems. Each of the specific errors requires more explanation than can be provided here, but the list that follows identifies each error and the chapter that will help you with it.

1. Wrong word (see Chapter 15)
2. Missing comma after an introductory element (see Chapter 31)
3. Incomplete or missing documentation
4. Vague pronoun reference (see Chapter 19)
5. Spelling (including homonyms) (see Chapter 15)
6. Mechanical error with a quotation (see Chapter 35)
7. Unnecessary comma (see Chapter 31)
8. Unnecessary capitalization (see Chapter 37)
9. Missing word
10. Faulty sentence structure (see Chapter 16)
11. Missing comma with a nonrestrictive element (see Chapter 31)
12. Unnecessary shift in verb tense (see Chapter 21)
13. Missing comma in a compound sentence (see Chapter 31)
14. Unnecessary or missing apostrophe (including *its/it's*) (see Chapter 34)
15. Fused (run-on) sentence (see Chapter 23)
16. Comma splice (see Chapter 23)
17. Lack of pronoun-antecedent agreement (see Chapter 19)
18. Poorly integrated quotation
19. Unnecessary or missing hyphen (see Chapter 40)
20. Sentence fragment (see Chapter 24)

Since so many student errors fall into these twenty error patterns, chances are that several of them may end up on your personal editing checklist. You could *begin* your checklist by looking through your writing for some of the twenty errors just listed. After all, one of the hardest things about correcting your own writing is knowing what mistakes to look for. This list can give you some ideas, but bear in mind that learning what mistakes you routinely make will take time. You will probably keep adding items to your checklist long after you finish using this book. As you do, you will be actively making yourself a stronger, more accomplished writer.

Document design (6h)

Once editing has been completed and you are ready to retype or print out your final version, take some time to consider the way you want your writing to look on the page. For example, if your paper is longer than two or three pages, you might consider whether to use subheadings to guide your readers, showing them where your writing shifts to a new topic. Thus a paper reporting on the history of the Sierra Club might begin with a subheading called "Origins," followed by "The Sierra Club to 1970," followed by "From 1970 to the Present."

In addition, this is your last chance to consider whether you want to add any charts or illustrations. If you are working with a word processor or if you have a graphics program, you can consider using different fonts or other visual cues to change the appearance of your draft and help guide the reader.

Proofreading the final draft (6j)

As a writer, you need to **proofread** to make your final draft as correct as you can make it. That means one final rereading even after you think you have caught every single error. Read aloud slowly. Check for punctuation marks, letters left out or transposed, and any other typographical errors. If you have been doing your drafting and revising on a computer, you should be able to produce an absolutely clean and error-free copy. However, if you catch any last-minute errors to correct after your final draft has been printed out, don't be shy about doing so right on the paper you're about to turn in. Your instructor would rather see you correcting your own errors than receive a totally uncluttered typescript full of uncorrected errors.

EXERCISE 6.1 ACTING AS A READER

Here is the first draft (written in class) of what is supposed to become a two-page essay that discusses the writer's first week in school. Read the draft, and then, using your own paper, write out your responses to the writer's questions.

I don't know what to say about this first week. It's been a struggle. Registration wasn't too hard — I'd expected some foul-ups. Buying my books just took a long time, standing in line to get into the bookstore and standing in line again to check out. Not much different from going to the grocery store the day before Thanksgiving. The big problem is that after all this time away from school I'm worried that I won't be able to handle it. I'm used to being busy, between working and taking care of Aaron and the kids, but I haven't had to do much deep thinking. At least I'm still used to reading — even if it's just been email at work and novels or magazines at night.

Humanities looks OK, but the reading list is long. The books cost a lot, too, and two aren't in yet. The class starts with the Greeks, so I'll soon see if I can remember anything about mythology. My computer class sounds tough, but I'm used to debugging and solving software problems. The big difference is that I'm not used to writing much about it — just talking to my supervisor. And my writing class — well, I haven't written anything long in a long time — just grocery lists, letters, and memos. It all seems overwhelming, but I'm determined. This is something I've wanted to do for two years now. And getting through this first week means I've started. I'm nervous about it, but at least I've made a start.

WRITER'S QUESTIONS

1. This seems wandering and too informal to me, but I don't know what else to do. Can you suggest some ways to organize what I want to say?

2. I know I'm not including all that you need to know about me and about my first week back. What have I left out?

3. Is there anything good about this draft?

EXERCISE 6.2   DRAFTING AND REVISING

Think about this chapter and about your own drafting and revising habits as you answer these questions on your own paper.

1. What kind of writing have you done most frequently in the past?

2. How would you describe the drafting and revising process for this writing? Was this kind of writing always a straight-line, clear process? What made it easy? What made it difficult?

3. Of the five revision strategies discussed in this chapter, which one is most effective for you? When you use this strategy, what is the key to making it work?

4. Of the five revision strategies discussed in this chapter, which one seems most promising to you, even though you have not used it much before? Why does it seem promising?

5. When it comes to drafting and revising, what two pieces of advice would you give to less experienced writers? Why would it be important for them to follow this advice?

EXERCISE 6.3   CONSIDERING TITLES AND INTRODUCTIONS

TITLES

Five pairs of titles are given. For each pair, indicate the title that would be more likely to move you to read whatever would follow it. Then explain briefly the reason for your choice. Use your own paper for this exercise.

EXAMPLE

Looking at College Life after Two Years Away *or* Returning to College: Back in the Saddle Again

The second version, "Returning to College: Back in the Saddle Again," would be my choice. Besides giving a fairly clear indication of the essay's topic, this version suggests a somewhat humorous tone, which suits the topic. The first version does a good job of identifying the topic but does not have the human interest of the second version.

1. Why Instructors Should Give More Tests *or* More Testing Means More Learning

2. Building Homes, Building Lives *or* The Goals of Habitat for Humanity

3. Exercise for Health *or* Fitness: A Way of Life

4. Making Communities Safe for Bicycles *or* Give Bike Riders a Break

5. Perils in the Beauty Industry *or* Cosmetic Surgery: It's Not Always Safe

INTRODUCTIONS

You want to write a persuasive paper aimed at convincing high school students that they ought to attend a driver safety seminar your campus is offering. The seminar lasts two hours and is free for local students. You have statistics on the number of accidents involving teenage drivers. You have talked with a person who was badly injured in an automobile accident she caused when she was seventeen. You have interviewed several students who are reluctant to attend the seminar, so you know why they are reluctant. You have interviewed the person conducting the seminar, who has explained that the seminar is geared to teenage drivers and that follow-up surveys found 90 percent of attendees thought the seminar was informative.

1. Specifically identify two ways that this persuasive paper could be introduced.

2. Explain how you would begin this paper. What factors will influence your decision?

EXERCISE 6.4   REVISING PARAGRAPHING, SENTENCE STRUCTURE, AND WORD CHOICE

Read this passage, and answer the questions that follow it. Use your own paper for this exercise. (The sentences are numbered for easy reference.)

(1) In Kansas, where I grew up, there was often the threat of a tornado on summer afternoons. (2) The familiar "bing-bong" tone would interrupt radio and television programs. (3) Everyone would gather around to watch the words crawl across the bottom of the television screen and to wonder. (4) It might be a tornado warning or just a tornado watch. (5) What counties were affected? (6) The answers to these questions determined the rest of the afternoon. (7) We might stay close to the house and listen to a transistor radio. (8) We might go on about our usual business. (9) For fourteen years, I was seeing tornado watches for our area come and go without incident. (10) Someone had once told me about an ancient prediction that no tornado would strike where two rivers crossed. (11) This supposedly meant that my town was safe. (12) The person assured me that my town sat at the intersection of two underground rivers. (13) How convenient! (14) Anyhow, this prediction made me feel safe, and I stopped worrying about tornadoes. (15) One day, however, this all changed. (16) The "bing-bong" tone interrupted the soap opera I was watching on the sly while my parents were out. (17) I was supposed to be doing something else. (18) The crawling words mentioned a tornado weather watch in our county. (19) I rolled my eyes, but then I saw the greenish-black sky and a little twinge of worry was felt. (20) "Tornado weather" could mean a violent thunderstorm as well as high winds. (21) My parents rushed in just ahead of the rain. (22) I heard another "bing-bong," and we headed to the basement. (23) The sound of an oncoming train was in the air. (24) Fortunately, our neighborhood was passed by. (25) It damaged some crops on the edge of town, but no one was hurt. (26) So much for the ancient prophecy, I thought.

1. Does this text really need to be just one paragraph, as it is now? Would you recommend reparagraphing? If so, how? If not, why not? Explain your reasoning.

2. Would you recommend any changes in sentence length or sentence structure? Identify your changes, if any. Explain your reasoning.

3. Would you recommend any changes in word choice? If so, what words would you change?

4. What else would you say to help this writer improve the passage? Discuss both strengths and weaknesses.

EXERCISE 6.5   CONSTRUCTING AN EDITING CHECKLIST

NAME _____ **DATE** _____

Assume that you have been employed for some time as a retail salesperson at a small store in your local mall. You must regularly close the shop at the end of your shift, so you know the procedures well. The manager has asked you to write down those procedures for new employees who will be hired over the holiday season.

You have written a draft that you feel is complete and worded as you want it. Your next step is to edit. Read the following passage, first to acquaint yourself with its content and then a second time to edit it. Underline any errors you find. Then enter those errors in the editing checklist begun below. (The first error has been underlined, and a checklist entry has been made.)

Instuctions for Locking the Store

1. At ten minutes before closing, turn off half of the store lights. Marked in red on the electir-ical panel, which you'll find on the north wall in the overstock room.
2. After turning out half the lights. Ring up any last minute purcheses', and then let any remaining customers no that the store will be closing at 7 pm. Be freindly!
3. At 7, walk from the back of the store up the front. Keeping any remaining customers in front of you. Usher them out the door (tell them "thanks for shopping at Smith's") lock the door behind them. Put the closed sine in the window.
4. Check and clean the fitting rooms. Look for any stray pins have been removed from the carpets!
5. Check the bathroom. Turn the light.
6. Close cash register, tally receipts (see the separate list instructions for this task).
7. Connecting the off-hours answering machine.
8. Check the front door once more turn out remaning lights. Exit out the employee's door. Locking it behind you.

MARKED ERROR	IN CONTEXT	LOOK FOR
spelling	*instuctions* for *instructions*	letter left out

Developing Paragraphs

7

A **paragraph** usually is a group of sentences that are set off as a unit (sometimes a paragraph consists of a single sentence). A long piece of writing is built from paragraphs, each one focusing on a main point or idea. Of all the paragraphs in a piece of writing, none is more important than the first. In fact, outside of the classroom — in job applications, newspaper articles, and fund-raising appeals, for example — the quality of the opening paragraph often determines whether readers bother to read further. After you have caught their attention with your first paragraph, you indicate to your readers that you are moving from one idea to the next by ending that paragraph and beginning a new one.

Fitting your writing into paragraphs sends useful signals to your readers, who can tell from your paragraph breaks where you want them to shift gears from one train of thought to another. As you develop paragraphs, you will progress in your ongoing effort to think and communicate clearly.

Some writers working at the drafting stage ignore paragraphs altogether; their drafts look like one big paragraph. Other writers actually draft their essays using paragraph breaks right from the beginning. But whatever their habits at the drafting stage, nearly all writers recognize that paying attention to paragraphing is a vital part of the revision process.

PARAGRAPHS IN EVERYDAY USE

One high school student, Ted Frantz, found himself concentrating hard on his opening paragraph as he worked on an essay describing his "major academic interest" to accompany his college application. Here is the paragraph he came up with to get his readers' attention and introduce his subject.

> Picture a five-year-old boy with a stack of cards in his hands, not baseball cards but presidential flashcards. He would run around asking anybody to question him about presidents; this kid knew incredible facts and could name every president in the correct order from George Washington to Bill Clinton. I was this little boy, and ever since I was five, I have had a passion for studying history.

Look at some opening paragraphs in the reading you normally do: newspapers or magazines, textbooks, charitable appeals, and junk mail. (Your instructor may ask you to bring the paragraphs you find to class for discussion.) Then briefly analyze how such paragraphs grab and hold your attention.

Constructing unified, coherent, and fully developed paragraphs (7a, 7b, 7c, 7d, 7e)

Developing your ability to construct effective paragraphs puts you well on the way to completing successful full-length essays. Let's take a look at three qualities that all well-written paragraphs share: **unity, coherence**, and **development**. A paragraph is unified if it focuses on one main idea; it is coherent if the reader can easily see how all of its parts fit together; and it is developed if its main idea is supported with specifics.

Making paragraphs unified: Focusing on a main idea

One good way to bring unity to a paragraph is to include one sentence in which you state the main idea or topic clearly. The other sentences then relate in one way or another to the topic sentence, often supporting it by adding examples and details.

Must the topic sentence come first in the paragraph? Can it come later in the paragraph? Those are good writing questions — ones that a writer must answer on the basis of both material and purpose for writing. As you continue reading this chapter, you will find topic sentences in many positions. The position of the topic sentence is less important than paragraph unity — the end to which the topic sentence is only a means.

Consider this paragraph (the topic sentence is underlined):

My Monday mornings are often difficult. Part of the problem lies with my own internal body clock. It's set to keep me awake and alert until late in the evening. When the clock radio comes on at 6:06, my internal clock says it's way too early to climb out of bed. Since I'm groggy and not exactly eager to wake up, I tend to be grouchy. Even after I've had my shower and begun to feel conscious, I can get irrationally angry when there isn't a full bowl's worth of Grape Nuts left; never mind that there's an unopened box of Raisin Bran in the pantry. If it's raining when I go out to get the paper, I'll probably curse the weather and the paper.

As you can see, the topic sentence is the first sentence in the paragraph. Every sentence that follows it adds some new example or detail to support the statement made in the topic sentence.

In a unified paragraph, all the information contributes to the paragraph's main point; nothing irrelevant is included. In paragraphs that deal with ideas, unity sometimes presents problems. Consider this paragraph:

Sarah Vowell's *The Partly Cloudy Patriot* identifies what makes the United States a great country while showing the author's discomfort with some expressions of patriotism. It's interesting that this book appeared so soon after the controversial ruling on the Pledge of Allegiance, a ruling that inspired some political maneuvers that probably disturbed Vowell. I read somewhere that the phrase "under God" was added to the Pledge of Allegiance in the 1950s, and most Americans seem pretty well used to saying it that way. Vowell doesn't discuss the Pledge controversy; instead, she focuses on the unique people and places that make her proud to be an American.

What is this paragraph about? It starts by discussing a book, Sarah Vowell's *The Partly Cloudy Patriot*. From the opening sentence, you could reasonably expect that the entire paragraph would focus on the book and especially on Vowell's view of the greatness of America. But that's not where the paragraph goes. Instead, it wanders to a discussion of the Pledge of Allegiance. This kind of wandering is often what our minds do, and this kind of paragraph is common in first drafts. The only cure for such a disunified paragraph is revision. The writer needs to make some decisions about the paragraph's main point. The writer could decide to keep the focus on the book. In that case, the paragraph needs more discussion of Vowell's ideas. Or the writer could decide to focus the paragraph on how Vowell's book connects with the writer's own feelings about patriotism. In that case, the paragraph needs a new opening that accurately establishes this focus. But the paragraph cannot be effectively revised until the writer decides what's really important.

To analyze a paragraph for unity, first identify its topic sentence. Then ask yourself whether each of the other sentences illustrates, explains, or adds to your knowledge of the main point set forth in the topic sentence. If you cannot identify the paragraph's topic sentence, the paragraph probably needs substantial revision.

Making paragraphs coherent: Fitting details together

In a coherent paragraph, the sentences are related to one another not only by their content but also by their sentence structures and word choices. As a writer, you should be aware of four important techniques for creating coherence: repetition, pronoun usage, parallelism, and transitions.

Repetition is the multiple use of key phrases or words. The following paragraph uses repetition to achieve coherence:

> Why do some college students succeed while others struggle? Some succeed because their educational backgrounds have prepared them for college-level work. Others succeed because they are effective time managers: they have set aside time for study and time for play. Others succeed because they are motivated. If a class seems too difficult, they recognize the difficulty and seek help. Successful students are also determined students. And, finally, successful students do not ask themselves to be superhuman; they are aware of their strengths and not discouraged by their weaknesses.

As you can see, several words and phrases are repeated from sentence to sentence, including the word *succeed* and the phrase *successful students*. This paragraph uses just about the maximum amount of repetition that any paragraph can stand without sounding affected, forced, or tedious.

In this sample paragraph, one important noun phrase is *college students*. Three pronouns—*some*, *others*, and *they*—consistently refer to the college students named in the topic sentence. This **pronoun usage** reminds readers that the paragraph is still addressing the subject it began with. It is another way writers can link ideas and increase the coherence of their paragraphs.

The next paragraph uses the third technique to add coherence. In this example, the sentences are related by **parallelism**, the use of grammatically similar structures. Notice how many of the subjects and verbs (underlined) are positioned right next to each other without any clauses or phrases between them. Besides adding coherence, this parallel sentence structure emphasizes the variety of actions the paragraph discusses.

> For two days, streets that normally know the rumbling of buses and the honking of angry drivers were filled with food booths, arts and crafts booths, and all the hubbub that is this city's ArtQuake celebration. Street <u>musicians played</u> jazz for change. <u>Tie-dyers sold</u> sweatshirts and head scarves. <u>Children sat</u> patiently while artists dressed as clowns painted their faces with stripes or flowers or turtles or hummingbirds. Their <u>parents eyed</u> landscape photographs of sand dunes or a series of doorways photographed on the island of Paros. Other <u>browsers tested</u> the weight of hand-thrown mugs and bowls glazed in shiny browns and reds. A <u>fortune-teller tempted</u> passersby with tarot cards. Here and there a <u>dog roved</u> at the edges of the action, looking for a discarded hamburger or dropped ice-cream cone. The <u>sun shone</u>, a steady <u>breeze moved</u> the awnings, and <u>people chatted</u>, stopped to look, and then moved on. <u>No one hurried</u>, and by the festival's end <u>merchants reported</u> brisk sales.

Another way of bringing coherence to a paragraph — of helping readers to see clearly how ideas are related — is to use transitions from sentence to sentence. **Transitional words and phrases** such as the ones listed here are writers' tools for making connections; they signal how one sentence relates to the next, showing the connections among ideas and the progression within the paragraph.

as a result	in short	of course	other
but when	nevertheless	often	when

If you have not consciously been using transitional words and phrases, doing so will probably make a big difference in the way readers react to your writing. In addition, consciously using transitional words forces writers to make sure that their paragraphs are indeed carefully organized. If you have difficulty making a transition, then either one or more sentences have been left out of the paragraph or the paragraph has jumped to a new topic. Paying careful attention to transitions is an important part of the revision process.

Developing paragraphs fully: Providing details

Often the difference between a well-written paragraph and a poorly written one is the inclusion of details. Without them, a writer's message is a mystery. With them, the message is clear and unmistakable.

Consider this short paragraph:

> Even though the movie featured some big-name stars, I thought it flopped. The story itself was poorly developed, and at several points it seemed truly confused. The chases were meant to be exciting, but without any real sense of suspense, they seemed more like distractions. There were some good points, but mostly it was a dud.

This paragraph is not an example of good writing because it raises more questions than it answers. We don't know which actors starred in this movie, we haven't been given any real discussion of the story, and (worst of all) the movie itself hasn't even been named. All of these things are details — crucial ones. Without them, this writing works to exclude us as readers. We have a vague sense that the writer wants to tell us something, but mostly we know that the writing isn't telling us very much.

All good paragraphs present details. They may be **sensory details** — how something looks, tastes, smells, feels, or sounds. They may be **intellectual details** — the specific nuances of ideas. They may be **emotional details** — how something made someone feel. But how do you present these details? How do you decide what order they should follow?

If you are having difficulty drafting a paragraph, there are various patterns you can consider to help you decide what to include. These patterns also are useful during revision. When you have a paragraph that seems disorganized or meandering, you can try rewriting it using any one of the following patterns to make your point more plainly.

■ *Illustration and Examples*

You might develop your paragraph by **illustration**, using specific examples and good reasons to support your point. Notice how this paragraph illustrates a main idea by means of several examples:

> An amazing variety of wildlife has managed to survive and even thrive in urban areas. Squirrels and mice are almost as common in cities as in rural areas, and songbirds sometimes share the airspace with more ordinary pigeons and sparrows. Raccoons and skunks will probably turn up anywhere food is available, which means anywhere — country, suburb, or city — garbage cans are found. Coyotes, also scavengers, have been spotted in big-city parks and yards from coast to coast. Peregrine falcons nest on highrises and bridges, apparently having decided that one cliff dwelling is as good as another. Cougars on the jogging path, bears on the golf course — more and more wildlife keeps turning up in surprisingly urban places.

You also could use illustration by presenting a single extended, fully detailed example.

■ *General-to-Specific Pattern*

A **general-to-specific** paragraph begins with its most general sentence, the topic sentence, which introduces the main idea. The second sentence limits and focuses the writer's message, and the rest of the paragraph illustrates or supports this narrower focus.

> Pets have been a part of human society at least since the days of the pharaohs. Recently, however, doctors and other health care workers have begun to use pets as an integral part of their recommended treatments, particularly with children and the elderly. In some children's hospitals, cancer wards use dogs and cats, even gerbils, as means of

providing patients with unrestricted acceptance. Kids whose hair has fallen out or who find themselves in casts or bandages sometimes wish to withdraw from contact with their family or friends because they do not wish to be seen "that way." But pets don't care. Their love is unconditional. The elderly respond to pets in much the same way as children do. To these people, often in pain and sometimes without nearby family or friends, pets provide instant companionship and instant distraction. As a result, some older folks take a greater interest in their own well-being and in the life around them.

■ Specific-to-General Pattern

As you no doubt have guessed, a **specific-to-general** paragraph is organized so that the sentences providing explanations or examples come first. Positioned at the end of the paragraph, the topic sentence serves to unite the explanations and examples. This method of organization creates a quite different reading experience. A successful specific-to-general paragraph draws readers in with its specifics and then unites those specifics with a topic sentence that provides a neat summary.

> Originally they filled whole rooms, and occasionally bugs would crawl in and interfere with the circuits. Their earliest uses were mostly government sponsored, either for military purposes by such organizations as the CIA or for space exploration efforts by NASA. Over the years, they shrank in size and price, even as their usefulness and variety of applications dramatically increased. By 2000, the machine that once filled a room now filled a shoebox, and data input had shifted from the clumsiness of punched cards to the ease of keyboards and graphic user interfaces. In this way, computers evolved from behemoths only governments or large corporations could afford to personal computers affordable to many families and individuals. What was once an obscure, unknown, and even scary piece of equipment has become a routine tool at home, in business, and in school.

■ Problem-Solution and Question-and-Answer Patterns

A **problem-solution** paragraph states a problem first and then provides one or more solutions. Similarly, a **question-and-answer** paragraph opens by raising a question and then providing one or more answers.

■ Process Analysis Paragraphs

A **process analysis** paragraph is chronologically organized. It specifies a particular action or set of actions and then proceeds to tell readers how they regularly occur. Here is a nontechnical process analysis describing how a car is started:

> The process of starting a car begins when the driver inserts the car key into the ignition. Turning the key (typically to the right) completes a circuit and sends electricity from the car's battery to the starter motor and to the spark plugs. The starter motor sets the pistons in action. The spark plugs begin to fire, and the pistons begin to rise and fall on their own. At this point, the driver disengages the starter motor, and the fuel injection system gives the cold engine the fuel it needs.

■ *Cause-Effect Paragraphs*

A **cause-effect** paragraph examines why something happened (emphasis on causes), tries to predict what will happen (emphasis on effects), or does both (cause and effect given equal billing). The typical television weather forecast is often a cause-effect analysis with an emphasis on effects.

■ *Comparison/Contrast Paragraphs*

Another quite useful organizational pattern is **comparison/contrast** (you *compare* similar things; you *contrast* dissimilar things). This pattern is discussed in Chapter 5 as an essay organizational format.

■ *Narrative Paragraphs*

A **narrative** paragraph tells a small story in order to support some main point. The story usually moves from beginning to end in chronological order, and the ending usually forms the story's climax, making the point of the story clear to readers. For example, a writer who wants to urge readers to seek help for substance abuse problems might choose to include the story of a friend or family member who has successfully sought help. A narrative paragraph (or a series of paragraphs) presenting this story might start with the recognition of the problem, move to the decision to seek treatment, then present the treatment period itself, and end with the individual's continuing recovery. Once the story has been told, the writer then uses additional sentences to underscore the point that the story makes and to link that story to the larger issue.

Narrative paragraphs have the advantage of making large issues personal and immediate. Readers identify with the people in a story. However, if your aim is to persuade readers to some new understanding or new action, narrative paragraphs might not be enough by themselves. Especially with controversial issues, readers need to be convinced that a personal story—however dramatic—is typical and applies to more than just one person. Thus narrative paragraphs are often linked with statistics in order to bring the statistics and the larger issues to life.

Composing special-purpose paragraphs (7f)

Occasionally essays, especially narrative essays, use **quoted dialogue** to present the actual words of several speakers. The conventions of paragraphing dialogue are simple: every time you present a new speaker, start a new paragraph. Recognizing that convention, you know how to write and how to read this exchange:

> "Want to jump rope?"
> "Nah. I'm tired."
> "Want to play gin rummy?"
> "Nah."
> "Want to watch TV?"

"We've already watched an hour's worth, and you know what Mom said."

"Well, then—"

"What about if we kick the soccer ball in the backyard?"

"I thought the ball was flat."

"It was until Mom pumped it up again."

"OK, let's go."

Short stories and novels follow the same convention for quoted dialogue: every time there is a new speaker, there is a new paragraph.

The introduction and conclusion of an essay, as discussed in Chapter 6, require special types of paragraphs that relate to the entire essay. Transitions from paragraph to paragraph also need special attention; consult the part of Chapter 6 that deals with the use of transitions between paragraphs.

EXERCISE 7.1   FINDING PARAGRAPH BREAKS

NAME _____ **DATE** _____

This is an excerpt from Rachel Carson's *The Sea around Us*. Here Carson discusses the way volcanic action creates islands in the sea. Read the passage, and determine where you think the paragraph breaks should be. Mark each paragraph break with a slash (/). Underline the topic sentence of each paragraph you identify. (The sentences are numbered for easy reference.)

(1) Millions of years ago, a volcano built a mountain on the floor of the Atlantic. (2) In eruption after eruption, it pushed up a great pile of volcanic rock, until it had accumulated a mass a hundred miles across at its base, reaching upward toward the surface of the sea. (3) Finally its cone emerged as an island with an area of about 200 square miles. (4) Thousands of years passed, and thousands of thousands. (5) Eventually the waves of the Atlantic cut down the cone and reduced it to a shoal—all of it, that is, but a small fragment which remained above water. (6) This fragment we know as Bermuda. (7) With variations, the life story of Bermuda has been repeated by almost every one of the islands that interrupt the watery expanses of the oceans far from land. (8) For these isolated islands in the sea are fundamentally different from the continents. (9) The major land masses and the ocean basins are today much as they have been throughout the greater part of geologic time. (10) But islands are ephemeral, created today, destroyed tomorrow. (11) With few exceptions, they are the result of the violent, explosive, earth-shaking eruptions of submarine volcanoes, working perhaps for millions of years to achieve their end. (12) It is one of the paradoxes in the ways of earth and sea that a process seemingly so destructive, so catastrophic in nature, can result in an act of creation. (13) Islands have always fascinated the human mind. (14) Perhaps it is the instinctive response of man, the land animal, welcoming a brief intrusion of earth in the vast, overwhelming expanse of sea. (15) Here in a great ocean basin, a thousand miles from the nearest continent, with miles of water under our vessel, we come upon an island. (16) Our imaginations can follow its slopes down through darkening waters to where it rests on the sea floor. (17) We wonder why and how it arose here in the midst of the ocean. (18) The birth of a volcanic island is an event marked by prolonged and violent travail: the forces of the earth striving to create, and all the forces of the sea opposing. (19) The sea floor, where an island begins, is probably nowhere more than about fifty miles thick—a thin covering over the vast bulk of the earth. (20) In it are deep cracks and fissures, the results of unequal cooling and shrinkage in past ages. (21) Along such lines of weakness the molten lava from the earth's interior presses up and finally bursts forth into the sea.

EXERCISE 7.2   UNDERSTANDING TOPIC SENTENCES AND PARAGRAPH UNITY

NAME _____ **DATE** _____

As you read each paragraph below, identify its topic sentence, and indicate any sentences that undermine paragraph unity because they do not illustrate or relate to the topic sentence. Then briefly explain your reasoning. (The sentences are numbered for easy reference.)

EXAMPLE

(1) My typical Monday morning starts sometime after 6:06. (2) That's when the clock radio comes on to bring me the early traffic report and the weather forecast. (3) However, we don't set the alarm on weekends. (4) After twenty minutes of dozing and groaning about how hard it is to climb out of bed, I get up and stumble into the kitchen to make coffee. (5) Half consciously my hands know what to do: measure the water and pour it into the coffee maker, and so on. (6) But I don't really wake up until the shower water hits my face. (7) I know other people who seem bright and awake the minute the alarm sounds. (8) After showering, it's breakfast time—more coffee, vitamins, a bowl of cereal. (9) On Sunday, I usually linger and read the paper.

Topic sentence ____1____

Unnecessary sentences ___3, 7, 9___

Explanation The topic sentence identifies Monday morning as the paragraph's focus. Sentence 3 talks about weekends, not Mondays. Sentence 7 talks about people different from the writer, and again this is off the subject. Sentence 9 talks about Sunday rather than Monday.

1. (1) Identifying an Internet hoax usually requires only a few simple steps. (2) The first step is recognizing that unsolicited emails can be a source of misinformation and that not every plea to find a missing child, warning about the dangers of deodorant, or notice of a new computer virus is legitimate. (3) People who are new to the Internet often forward such messages—my sister-in-law sent them out almost daily when she first got an email account. (4) If a message ends with the phrase, "Forward this to everyone in your address book," be extremely skeptical of the contents of the message. (5) Other giveaways are the use of inflammatory language, claims that "the media" are conspiring to keep the news secret, the frequent use of capital letters for emphasis, and far too many exclamation marks. (6) A hoax message may try to appear legitimate by including the name of a professional person or respectable agency, but the message probably won't include a link to the agency's Web site or any contact information for the person. (7) If a message makes you suspicious, the next step is to look at one of the many Internet sites devoted to publicizing widespread hoaxes and Internet chain letters. (8) Some people simply forward hoaxes, concluding that there's no real harm in them and that the information might help someone. (9) The harm, according to government agencies, is that forwarding bogus messages indiscriminately to dozens of people slows down flow of legitimate information on the Internet, costing users money. (10) If a message you have received is identified as a hoax on a

debunking Web site, you can be sure the information isn't genuine—so don't forward the email. (11) Finally, never act on medical tips that come in unsolicited messages; check with a doctor first.

Topic sentence _____

Unnecessary sentences _____

Explanation _____

_____

_____

2.   (1) Lorraine Hansberry's landmark play, *A Raisin in the Sun*, focuses on the dreams of the Youngers, an African American family living on Chicago's South Side in the late 1950s. (2) There is also a musical version of the play called *Raisin*. (3) The matriarch of the family, Mama, has received a $10,000 check from her husband's life insurance policy and wants to use the money to move her family from their cramped inner-city apartment to a house in the white suburbs. (4) Her son, Walter Lee, who is a cab driver, wants to use the money to buy a liquor store, which he believes will ensure the family's financial security. (5) Daughter Beneatha dreams of earning a medical degree and hopes to use some of the money toward this goal. (6) She is different from the rest of the family because she celebrates her African roots. (7) Walter Lee's wife, Ruth, agrees with Mama, hoping for greater opportunities and a better life for their son, Travis. (8) Learning that Ruth is pregnant, Mama makes a down payment on a house in a suburban development, and although a representative of the development comes to offer the family money not to move in, the family eventually decides not to take the money but rather to pursue the dream of a new life. (9) The man is disappointed with the family's decision but leaves when he realizes their minds are made up. (10) Mama also gives Walter Lee what is left over from the down payment for a liquor store, but his partner runs off with the money. (11) The play ends as the family is moving out of their apartment and looking forward to their future. (12) Despite the uncertainty of what is in store for them in the unwelcoming suburbs, we feel a sense of optimism that unlike the title of the Langston Hughes poem, "A Dream Deferred," a line from which provides the title of the play, the Youngers' dream will be fulfilled.

Topic sentence _____

Unnecessary sentences _____

Explanation _____

_____

_____

NAME _____   DATE _____

The paragraph below uses repetition, parallel sentences, and pronouns to achieve coherence. Read the paragraph, and take note of these devices. Then answer the questions that follow. (The sentences are numbered for easy reference.)

(1) Like many mothers, my mother does not approve of the green-haired boys who play rebellious punk songs on MTV. (2) Like many mothers, she rolled her eyes when I used to buy records by these bands. (3) But unlike most mothers, mine has nothing against the piercings, tattoos, and gravity-defying rainbow-colored tresses of the performers in so-called alternative rock bands. (4) No, she has a different reason for objecting to their acts. (5) My mother sneers, "They stole all their ideas from the Sex Pistols"—or the Ramones, or some other punk rockers from the late 1970s. (6) Unlike most mothers, mine sang in a punk band when she was nineteen years old. (7) Unlike most mothers, mine was a rebel who really did wear army boots. (8) Her hair was green before anyone in my generation was even born, as she doesn't hesitate to remind me. (9) Like my mother, I have my rebellious moments. (10) Like her, I use music to express my rebellion. (11) But the music I used to listen to annoyed my mother for all the wrong reasons, so I've moved on to something else. (12) Now, when I really want to drive my mother crazy, I have a better solution: I play Merle Haggard.

1. Identify at least four important words (not pronouns) that are repeated and that help give this paragraph coherence.

   _____

2. Identify three pairs of sentences using parallel structures to add coherence.

   _____

3. What pronouns are repeated, and how does that repetition add coherence?

   _____

   _____

   _____

EXERCISE 7.4   CHOOSING A PATTERN OF DEVELOPMENT

NAME _____ **DATE** _____

In each case below, you are given a writing task and a question to help you analyze the task. After analyzing the task, choose a pattern of development: problem-solution/question-and-answer, process analysis, cause-effect, or comparison/contrast.

EXAMPLE   *Writing task*: Use a paragraph to explain how to hit a golf ball out of a sand trap.
Question: What pattern will make it easiest for you to explain how to hit this golf shot?

Your choice: <u>Write a process analysis paragraph.</u>

1. *Writing task*: As the assistant manager of a small clothing store, you have been asked by your manager to write out instructions to new employees explaining the procedures to follow in closing up the store at the end of the business day.
Question: How can you organize these instructions so that new employees can easily understand what to do?

   Your choice: _____

2. *Writing task*: In your environmental studies class, you are asked to write about the human-related factors that have led to an increase in global warming.
Question: Given these conditions, what pattern would you use to best organize your answer?

   Your choice: _____

3. *Writing task*: Your political science instructor wants you to explain the similarities and differences between a democratic system of government and a parliamentary one.
Question: What pattern will help you address this assignment?

   Your choice: _____

4. *Writing task*: Writing task: For an essay contest sponsored by a campus alumni group, you have elected to respond to the question "What constitutes a good education?"
Question: What pattern will help you organize your answer?

   Your choice: _____

5. *Writing task*: For a club you belong to, you are asked to research and write a brief paper exploring whether the treasury can best be increased through higher dues or through a candy sale.
Question: What pattern will best help you organize your paper?

   Your choice: _____

6. *Writing task*: You wish to write a letter to your local newspaper describing a particularly dangerous traffic intersection in your neighborhood and explaining what you think the city should do to make it less dangerous.
   Question: What pattern will best allow you to present your ideas?

   Your choice: _____

7. *Writing task*: In your health class, you are asked to write about the benefits of regular exercise.
   Question: What pattern will let you explore these benefits most clearly?

   Your choice: _____

8. *Writing task*: Writing task: For a linguistics class, you are asked to explain the stages children go through in acquiring language.
   Question: What pattern will best help you address this assignment?

   Your choice: _____

9. *Writing task*: Your writing instructor asks you to write a paragraph discussing the ways your approach to writing has changed over the semester.
   Question: How can you present your information in order to highlight the differences between the beginning of the semester and the present?

   Your choice: _____

10. *Writing task*: In the group project for your environmental studies class, you plan to predict what would happen to the economics of recycling if consumers increased their purchases of recycled goods by 5 percent.
    Question: What pattern will allow you to make this prediction?

    Your choice: _____

EXERCISE 7.5   USING PATTERNS OF DEVELOPMENT

NAME _____ **DATE** _____

Each writing task below specifies a pattern of development and a set of possible topics. Choose one of the topics, and write a topic sentence introducing your choice. Then list at least four details of supporting information.

1. Process Analysis
    Topics: how to make tacos (or some other dish) / how to buy a used car (or some other item) / how to find a job / how to ruin a roommate relationship / how to do research on the Internet / how to clean a bathroom (or some other place or object)

    Topic sentence: _____

    _____

    Details and support:

    a. _____

    b. _____

    c. _____

    d. _____

2. Problem-Solution/Question-and-Answer
    Topics: why taking time off between high school and college is (or is not) a good decision / what the best movie of the year is / how you would define success, art, stress, or another abstract term / when confrontation is (or is not) the right choice / what should be done to solve a particular problem (which you identify) at school or in your community

    Topic sentence: _____

    _____

    Details and support:

    a. _____

    b. _____

    c. _____

    d. _____

3. Comparison/Contrast
   Topics: doing a task (which you specify) with or without a particular tool / shopping online versus shopping at stores / the advantages of one class you are taking versus those of another / living alone versus living with a roommate (or living with a family) / the similarities and differences between two movies, books, video games (or another topic of your choice)

   Topic sentence: _____

   _____

   Details and support:

   a. _____

   b. _____

   c. _____

   d. _____

4. Cause-Effect
   Topics: why your favorite local team did (or did not) win the championship this year / what makes horror movies frightening (or boring) / why you decided to go to college / how a person (whom you identify) influenced your life for the better (or the worse) / why you did well (or poorly) in response to a recent challenge

   Topic sentence: _____

   _____

   Details and support:

   a. _____

   b. _____

   c. _____

   d. _____

EXERCISE 7.6 USING TRANSITIONS

NAME _____ **DATE** _____

Transition words and phrases have been left out of the following paragraph. Select from the list of words and phrases below the paragraph the most appropriate transition word or phrase for each blank. Write the number of the blank next to the appropriate word or phrase. (You will not use every word or phrase in the list.)

Traffic in most parts of the country keeps getting worse, ____(1)____ most experts believe that not much can be done to help the situation. ____(2)____, the number of registered vehicles is growing at alarming rates. Since 1970, the number of vehicles has doubled, ____(3)____ it is hardly surprising that the roads seem more crowded; ____(4)____, they are. ____(5)____, building more roads is not likely to solve the problem. New roads often have the effect of adding more drivers; ____(6)____, people who commuted by public transportation decide to drive if a new road makes driving easier. ____(7)____, even if new roads would decrease traffic congestion, it is almost impossible to get permission to build them if they would displace homes and businesses—which they would do in any place where traffic congestion is bad. ____(8)____, most people have some kind of public transportation option, ____(9)____ the trick is convincing them to use it when cars are so much more convenient. How bad do traffic jams have to get before people willingly ride buses and commuter trains? ____(10)____ the answer seems to be "a lot worse"—a situation that may yet become reality.

_____ and   _____ eventually   _____ in addition   _____ of course

_____ as a result   _____ for one thing   _____ in fact   _____ so

_____ but   _____ frequently   _____ nevertheless   _____ unfortunately

EXERCISE 7.7 SUMMARY EXERCISE: WRITING PARAGRAPHS

For this exercise, you will draft and revise a paragraph. To begin, read the following writing tasks, and choose one that interests you. Circle your choice.

Your assignment for Foods and Nutrition class asks you to list the contents of your refrigerator and then arrive at a conclusion about your diet.

In your educational psychology class, you're studying learning styles. You're asked to tell the story of one instance in which you learned something very easily (or with great difficulty). Your paragraph should pay special attention to your reactions to this learning situation.

In a freshman composition class, you are asked to write a paragraph answering this question: "What is your general attitude toward writing?"

For a communications class, you are asked to write a paragraph discussing the differences between the way a television news show and a newspaper depict a current event.

Draft a topic sentence, and indicate at least four pieces of evidence that will explain and support your topic sentence.

Topic sentence: _____

_____

Evidence/support:

a. _____

b. _____

c. _____

d. _____

Using your own paper, write a first draft of your paragraph. Make sure that your evidence is clear and that there is enough of it to answer readers' questions. Once you have your draft, use these questions to help you revise:

- **Do all your sentences refer to and explain or support your topic sentence?**
- **Have you effectively used transition words and phrases?**
- **Have you made your paragraph coherent by using devices such as repetition, parallel sentences, and pronouns?**

After you finish your paragraph, number your sentences and answer these questions.

1. Which sentence is your topic sentence? _____
2. What transition words or phrases have you used to make your paragraph more readable?

_____

_____

3. What words or phrases have you repeated to make your paragraph more coherent?

_____

4. What sentences are parallel or use pronouns to increase coherence?

_____

Turn in this page and all the work you have done on this paragraph.

CRITICAL THINKING
AND ARGUMENT

"So much of what we receive from others — from family and friends to thirty-second blurbs on TV — is intended to persuade. Recognizing how this is done gives greater power to choose."
— VICTOR VILLANUEVA JR.

PART 2

PREVIEW QUESTIONS

Decide whether each statement below is true or false. If it is true, write *T* in the space after the sentence; if it is false, write *F*.

1. Nearly every use of language involves an element of persuasion. _____

2. Arguments found on a Web site are almost always authoritative. _____

3. An argument must make a debatable claim. _____

4. "Event A happened before event B, and therefore event A caused event B" is not a good logical argument. _____

5. An image alone cannot make an argument. _____

6. A strong argument should never appeal to the emotions of its intended audience. _____

7. Many good arguments present viewpoints that are opposed to what is being argued. _____

8. An effective argument can be based entirely on personal narratives. _____

9. "Two people were killed and more than fifty injured in the fire that broke out at the nightclub" is a good thesis statement for an argument. _____

10. Rather than attempting to convince readers, an argument may share information and perspectives so that readers can make an informed choice. _____

Analyzing Arguments

8

More so today than ever before, we are surrounded by language that is meant to persuade us. Advertisements, news stories, textbooks, political speeches, comedy routines, Web sites, and email petitions, for example, all compete for our attention and argue for our agreement. We need to be able to recognize and question language that vies for our support, our values, our money, and our souls. We also need to be able to construct and put forth effective arguments of our own.

ANALYZING ARGUMENTS IN EVERYDAY USE

Every day, you encounter arguments carefully crafted to persuade you to do, buy, or believe something. Collect a few examples of advertisements, music or movie reviews, newspaper editorials, or other arguments that you encounter. What exactly does each argument want you to do? How can you tell? What method does each one use in attempting to persuade you to take the desired action? Do you find the method convincing? Why or why not?

Recognizing argument (9a)

Any text, image, or speech that attempts to persuade an audience can be considered an argument—and almost every use of language does try, in some sense, to persuade. When a Web site includes a link to another site, the creators of the original site are arguing that the link is important in some way. When a teenager tapes a poster to her bedroom wall, she is making an argument in support of the subject of the poster. And when your friend complains about how difficult his geology test was, even he has a persuasive purpose: to receive sympathy, encouragement, or commiseration about a hard-hearted professor. Although persuasion may not always be the most important purpose of a verbal or visual text, it is nevertheless almost always present. To see for yourself, try to figure out the argument made in the lyrics of your favorite song or in the visuals of your favorite movie.

Critical thinking (9b)

Critical thinking is the process by which we make sense of information. The goal of critical thinking is to construct your own ideas and reach your own conclusions, which eventually you must assess as well. The first step in thinking critically about arguments is to recognize that arguments surround you. The next step is to make sense of all the information these arguments present. One way to do this with a particular argument is to play the *believing game* and the *doubting game*. These games require you to put aside your own views for a few moments in order to gain different perspectives.

First, play the believing game. Consider the argument as if you were the person who created it. Try to put yourself in that person's place, adopt that person's outlook, and generally do all you can to understand how and why that person arrived at those conclusions. When you feel that you have given the argument a sympathetic reading, play the doubting game. Consider the argument again, but this time skeptically. Question every claim and piece of evidence to see how well—or whether—the evidence supports the claim. Assume that the argument is flimsy, and search thoroughly for anything that will back up this assumption. Eventually, this process of first believing and then doubting will become a habit, helping you to consider both the merits and the pitfalls of any argument.

When you analyze arguments, it is essential to *ask the right questions*. Here are some good ones:

- What is the agenda—the unstated purpose—behind this argument?
- Why does the argument's creator hold these ideas or beliefs? What larger social, cultural, economic, political, or other conditions may have influenced him or her?
- What does the argument's creator want readers to do? Why?
- What reasons are offered in support of the argument? How good are these reasons?
- What sources does the argument rely on? How current and reliable are they? What agendas do these sources have? Are any perspectives left out?
- What objections might be made to this argument?
- What assumptions are behind this argument? Are they acceptable? Why, or why not?
- If the argument is found on the Web, ask yourself what individual or group is responsible for the site and the argument it makes. What can you learn about this sponsor? Does the information come from accurate sources? Can you confirm the accuracy of the information presented?
- If the argument contains visual or audio aspects, ask yourself how these appeal to the reader or listener. What do they contribute to the argument? Why are they used?

After asking those questions, you may discover that *additional information* is necessary in order to decide whether the argument is persuasive. Finding more about a subject will often help you *learn about other perspectives* that you might not have considered, perspectives that will contribute to your ability to analyze an argument.

You also will need to *interpret and assess the information* presented in an argument. Remember: no information presented in language is completely neutral; information always has a perspective, or spin. For example, politicians spin the information they present so that people see it only from the politicians' angles of vision. You yourself have probably spun information to explain a late paper or a missed appointment or to soften bad news. But when you are the person receiving information, you need to be aware of what the presenter wants you to see—as well as what he or she would rather you didn't notice. You must be able to evaluate the information, its sources, and the context in which it appears. In this way, you will be able to reach your own conclusions about an argument.

Emotional, ethical, and logical appeals (9d)

The ancient Greek philosopher Aristotle identified three basic kinds of appeals that arguments can make: emotional, ethical, and logical. Aristotle's types of appeals can help you break down an argument and thus begin to analyze it.

- *Emotional appeals* try to convince you by stirring up your feelings and reminding you of your deeply held values. A visual or verbal text that attempts to evoke laughter, sadness, anger, or fear makes an emotional appeal. Most arguments include emotional appeals because such appeals make people care about the argument. However, be aware of the difference between appeals that engage your emotions legitimately and appeals that aim to manipulate your feelings.

- *Ethical appeals* try to convince you by pointing out the credibility, moral character, and goodwill of the creator. In an ethical appeal, the argument's creator tries to prove that he or she knows the subject well, has a trustworthy character, and has the best interests of readers—including you—at heart. When you recognize that an argument is making an ethical appeal, ask yourself whether the creator successfully demonstrates that he or she actually has the knowledge, trustworthiness, and empathy for the reader that he or she claims to have.

- *Logical appeals* try to convince you by supplying fact-based evidence such as experimental data, observation, testimony, statistics, and personal experience. Western culture tends to value "facts," so logical appeals are often viewed as particularly trustworthy. But remember: facts can be easily manipulated, authorities can be cited out of context, statistics can be misinterpreted, and sources can be unreliable. Thus even an argument based on apparent facts requires critical investigation.

The elements of an argument (9e)

According to Stephen Toulmin, a modern philosopher, most arguments contain common elements: a *claim* or *claims, reasons, warrants, evidence,* and *qualifiers.* Identifying these elements in an argument provides an excellent framework for an analysis of the argument's strengths, weaknesses, and overall effectiveness.

- *Claims* are statements of fact, opinion, or belief that form the backbone of an argument. A claim must be debatable and is only as good as the reasons attached to it.

- *Reasons* provide support for claims. They may be drawn from facts, authorities, personal experience, or examples. Test each reason by asking how directly it supports the claim and what counter-reasons you could offer.

- *Warrants* are assumptions that connect the claim to its reasons. Warrants are often unstated and can be difficult to detect. They often reflect the cultural biases or beliefs of the argument's creator—biases and beliefs that you may or may not agree with. If an argument is based on an assumption that contradicts your own views or experience, then the warrant of the argument is a weak link. It is crucial to identify the warrants in any argument you analyze.

- *Evidence,* or backing, includes facts, authoritative opinion, personal experience, statistics, and examples that are meant to support the truth of the claim, reasons, or warrant of an argument. Don't take the validity of evidence for granted. Instead, evaluate each piece of evidence, asking whether it is relevant, appropriate, timely, and reliable.

- *Qualifiers* are words such as *few, many, often, in these circumstances, rarely,* and *typically,* which narrow a claim in order to make it as precise as possible. A claim that does not use any qualifiers may be too general and therefore easy to refute. Look for qualifiers in the arguments you analyze, because qualifiers affect the strength of an argument's claim.

Here's an example of how to use the Toulmin system to label the parts of an argument. Consider the assertion "The death penalty should be abolished in most cases because innocent people have occasionally been convicted and sentenced to die." The *claim* is "The death penalty should be abolished"—a debatable statement. The *reason* is that "innocent people have occasionally been convicted and sentenced to die." The unstated *warrant* is that innocent people should never be sentenced to death. The *qualifier* is "in most cases," which makes the argument easier to prove than an argument that asserted that the death penalty should never be used. A complete argument would also include *evidence* that people are occasionally convicted and sentenced to death for crimes they did not commit.

Fallacies (9f)

You may have heard fallacies described as serious flaws that weaken an argument. Because arguments occur in a particular place and time, however, the part of an argument that seems to be a fallacy to one audience in one context might seem perfectly acceptable to other audiences elsewhere. Instead of thinking of fallacies as flaws that discredit an argument, it may be more fruitful to view them as barriers to common ground and worthwhile debate. Recognizing common fallacies is important. It is helpful to identify fallacies by associating them with the major appeals of argument — ethical, emotional, and logical.

Ethical fallacies unjustly attack an opponent's character rather than attacking the issue.

- *Ad hominem* (Latin for "to the man") charges directly attack someone's character or appearance and suggest that because a person is somehow untrustworthy or unlikable, his or her opinions are also invalid. "Governor Baldwin is a raving lunatic who supports sex education in our high schools," for example, calls the governor names and does not address the issue of whether sex education is a good idea.

- *Guilt by association* attacks someone's credibility by linking that person with an activity or person the audience will see as bad, suspicious, or untrustworthy. The statement "The mayor's ancestors owned slaves in Alabama before the Civil War" impugns the mayor for an unsavory connection that he could not control.

- *Appeals to false authority* use a person, group, or institution to back up an argument even though the person, group, or institution has no expertise in the area of argument. Someone who says "My history professor drives a Honda Civic, so I know that it is a reliable car" makes the unreasonable assumption that a history expert must also be an automobile expert.

Emotional fallacies attempt to overcome readers' good judgment with overblown or unfair emotional appeals.

- *Bandwagon appeals* suggest that the reader would be a fool or a traitor not to be swept up in a movement that is under way. "Everyone is switching to Bubble-Fizz soda!" urges readers not to be left behind.

- *Flattery* tries to persuade readers to act by suggesting that they are especially thoughtful, intelligent, fashionable, or perceptive (which they may be — but the arguer has no way of knowing this). "You're too smart not to shop at the Big Q" tries to win readers over by complimenting them.

- *In-crowd appeal*, a special kind of flattery, invites readers to identify with an elite group. An advertiser who says "People with good taste know that the food at Jack's Burger Palace tastes great" hopes that readers will flock to Jack's to prove that they are part of the elite group with good taste.

- *Veiled threats* try to frighten readers by suggesting that they will suffer adverse consequences if they do not take specific action. "John Hudson, a young pilot, received this letter, but he decided not to pass it on and was severely injured a week later when his plane crashed during a routine takeoff" is a typical chain-letter argument attempting to intimidate readers into continuing the chain.

- *False analogies* make comparisons between two situations that are not essentially alike. "Right now, investing in high-tech stocks is as bad an idea as pitching a fastball to Barry Bonds" compares two subjects—putting money into certain investments and pitching to a famous home-run hitter—that seem connected only by the arguer's statement that both are bad ideas.

Logical fallacies are usually defined as errors in formal reasoning. They often sound plausible, however, and can be used to convince unwary readers.

- *Begging the question* treats an unanswered question as if it has already been answered, creating a circular argument. "That TV news provides accurate and reliable information was demonstrated conclusively on last week's *60 Minutes*" says in effect that television news is accurate and reliable because TV news says so.

- The *post hoc fallacy* (from Latin for "after this") assumes that because event B occurred after event A, it was caused by event A. Such events, however, are often completely unrelated. "I took a new medicine, and two days later my cold was gone" implies that the medicine caused the end of the cold, when in fact the cold may have simply run its course.

- A *non sequitur* (Latin for "it does not follow") tries to tie together logically unrelated items as if they were related. "An owl hooted outside my window last night, and when I woke up, my goldfish was dead" is an example of such reasoning.

- An *either-or fallacy* oversimplifies a complicated situation by implying that only two possibilities exist and that one is clearly better than the other. In fact, many other possibilities may have been overlooked—or purposefully omitted in order to emphasize the arguer's preferred outcome. A teenager's argument "I need to get a car for my sixteenth birthday, or I'll have to hitchhike to school and maybe get killed" fails to consider other options, such as taking the bus, getting a ride from parents or friends, or riding a bicycle.

- A *hasty generalization* draws a conclusion based on too little evidence or on evidence that is bad or misinterpreted. "I couldn't understand the lecture today, so I'm sure this course will be impossible" is an example of such a conclusion.

- *Oversimplification* misunderstands the relationship between a cause and an effect. "If everyone were permitted to carry a concealed weapon, no one would ever commit a crime" oversimplifies the relationship between gun ownership and crime. It is likely, for example, that crimes of passion would still occur.

EXERCISE 8.1   CRITICAL THINKING

Using your own paper, answer each of the following questions as completely as you can.

1. Choose a Web site, a newspaper or magazine article, a television program, or some other source (including one assigned by your teacher) that takes a clear and debatable stand on an issue that interests you, and play the believing game with the argument being made. Briefly describe the issue. What is a believer's point of view on this issue? How does a believer arrive at this view?

2. Using the argument you chose for question 1, play the doubting game. What parts of the argument make you most skeptical? Why?

3. Using the same argument, write down the most important questions that you would ask about this piece if you were writing an analysis of the argument. Can you answer them without further research? If so, how would you answer them? If not, what else do you need to know?

EXERCISE 8.2   IDENTIFYING EMOTIONAL, ETHICAL, AND LOGICAL APPEALS

Using a source that you found for exercise 8.1 or another example of an argument that interests you, answer the following questions as completely as you can. Use your own paper for this exercise.

1. What is the main type of appeal to the audience — emotional, ethical, or logical — used in this argument? Explain your answer.

2. Does the argument use another type of appeal as well? If so, which type or types?

3. Does the use of the main type of appeal seem legitimate in this argument? Why, or why not?

EXERCISE 8.3   IDENTIFYING THE ELEMENTS OF AN ARGUMENT

A. Using either a source that you found for one of the previous exercises or another example of an argument that interests you, answer the following questions as completely as you can. Use your own paper for this exercise.

1. What claim is made by this argument?

2. What are the reasons?

3. What warrants can you identify?

4. What evidence is supplied?

5. What qualifiers can you identify?

B. After identifying the elements in part A, answer the following questions on your own paper.

1. Is the claim debatable? Why, or why not?

2. Do the reasons support the claim? Why, or why not?

3. Are the warrants stated or unstated? Do you think that every reader is likely to agree with these assumptions? Why, or why not?

4. Is the evidence sufficient to support the reasons? Is other evidence needed? If so, what kind? Do you see any problems with the evidence?

5. What problems do you see with the qualifiers, if any? Explain.

NAME _____ **DATE** _____

The following sentences contain ethical, emotional, or logical fallacies. After reading each sentence, indicate whether you see an ethical fallacy, an emotional fallacy, or a logical fallacy. Write out a sentence or two to explain your reasoning.

EXAMPLE   When I think of you—the good, responsible residents of this city—I know you will vote yes on the urban renewal plan.

Fallacy: _emotional_

Explanation: _Flattering voters is a way of distracting them from looking at any of_ _the benefits or problems associated with the proposed urban renewal plan._

1. The candidate presents an attractive appearance on television, so she would clearly make a good mayor.

   Fallacy: _____

   Explanation: _____

   _____

2. Federal income tax rates should be lowered because people pay too much in taxes.

   Fallacy: _____

   Explanation: _____

   _____

3. In the two months since his taking office, the governor and his administration have reduced the unemployment rate by 5 percent.

   Fallacy: _____

   Explanation: _____

   _____

4. Because of budget cuts, the school must drop the men's soccer program or raise student fees.

   Fallacy: _____

   Explanation: _____

   _____

5. Anyone who is well read on the issue knows that global warming is not caused by the burning of fossil fuels.

Fallacy: _____

Explanation: _____

_____

6. My boss at the car dealership supports the current administration, so its policies must be sound.

Fallacy: _____

Explanation: _____

_____

7. Students who are major sports fans do not appreciate the fine arts.

Fallacy: _____

Explanation: _____

_____

8. An increase in the minimum wage will drive small companies out of business.

Fallacy: _____

Explanation: _____

_____

9. Professor Parvi admits that he smoked marijuana in the 1970s, so his views on drug testing should not be taken seriously.

Fallacy: _____

Explanation: _____

_____

10. As a reader of this magazine, you obviously have the good taste to appreciate the quality of our products.

Fallacy: _____

Explanation: _____

_____

Visual Arguments

9

Arguments can be made visually as well as verbally. You've seen television commercials in which the camera lingers lovingly on melted cheese, on the sleek lines of a new sports car, or on the acne-free face of an attractive teenager; and you know exactly what such images mean and what the advertisers want from you. But advertising photos are not the only images that persuade us or lead us into debates. Most Americans associate another image—the picture of a huge fireball erupting from the World Trade Center—with discussions about a wide range of topics, including the nature of heroism, personal and national security, civil liberties, terrorism, and America's place in the world. Images can influence us powerfully. It is therefore essential to be able to recognize and analyze the arguments they make.

VISUAL ARGUMENTS IN EVERYDAY USE

Since September 11, 2001, American flags have become ubiquitous—they flutter from car antennas, hang from student backpacks, and fly from flagpoles in front of private homes all over the country. Flags also make guest appearances as backdrops for public service announcements, campaign advertisements, and commercials of all kinds. Make a list of some of the places you see the American flag. In which of these locations did you regularly see the flag before the September 11 attacks? Do any of these locations for the flag surprise you? Which of these displays are making an argument? What are these visual arguments claiming?

Visual literacy (10a)

Although the idea of "reading" a visual argument may initially seem strange, you are probably more accustomed to reading images than you think. Whenever you watch television, see billboards, look at magazine covers or product labels, read cartoons or comic books, glance at Web sites, go to movies, or participate in any number of everyday activities, you are absorbing and processing visual information. How do you begin to analyze a visual argument? The process is pretty much the same as analyzing any other argument: you begin by looking at the content—claims, reasons, warrants, and so on—and deciding what kind of appeal the argument is making. You then consider whether any cultural influences are evident in the argument. Finally, you analyze how the design, color, sound (if any), and arrangement of visual elements influence the argument's impact and effectiveness.

Design as a persuasive element (10b)

Creators of visual arguments understand that nearly every aspect of design — including placement of elements, choice of color, and the inclusion of sound and video — can be used to persuade. Therefore, in analyzing a visual argument, you need to analyze the argument's design. Ask yourself these questions (and any others that come to mind) when you are examining a visual argument:

- What attracts your eye first? Why is your attention drawn to this part of the image? What is the effect of this attention-getting device?
- What is in the foreground (front) and what is in the background of the image? Pay attention to the placement of various elements, noticing what is high, low, large, and small. What effects does this placement of elements have?
- Are any words or images downplayed, hidden, or tucked away in a corner? If so, why do you think the designer made the decision to do this? How does it affect the argument?
- Are sound and video used? If so, are they effective in enhancing the argument?
- If words are included, how effectively are they combined with the images? What is the relationship between the two?
- Do you notice any repetition of words or images? If so, why do you think the repetition is used?
- If you are looking at a Web page, what overall impression does it give? Is your impression after a close examination the same as your first impression? Is the page easy to navigate, and does it guide you? How do these considerations affect your view of the page's argument?

Analyzing visual arguments (10c)

The Toulmin system (see Chapter 8) offers a simple and effective way of identifying and analyzing parts of an argument. You can use the Toulmin system to break down and think critically about visual arguments as well as verbal ones. According to the Toulmin system, the main elements of an argument include

- the *claim* being made
- the *reasons* attached to the claim
- the *warrants*, or assumptions, connecting the claim to the reasons
- the *evidence* that supports the reasons

Look at the political cartoon by Mike Luckovich that uses characters from Charles M. Schultz's comic strip *Peanuts*.

By permission of Mike Luckovich and Creators Syndicate, Inc.

The cartoon contains very few words, yet it makes a series of subtle arguments. What do you think Luckovich intended to suggest with this picture? As you begin to analyze this visual argument, ask what claims the photograph makes. The following claims (and others) might come to mind:

POSSIBLE CLAIM	The threat of bioterrorism affects people in different ways.
POSSIBLE CLAIM	A symbolic security blanket no longer offers protection.

What reasons might support the second claim? You might word your reason like this: *Because biological or chemical attacks on American soil now seem like a serious threat, the kind of innocence associated with Charlie Brown's America is no longer possible.* You could offer evidence that Charlie Brown's America was a more innocent place where clutching a blanket was enough for Linus to feel secure. You might also note the different meaning *security* has taken on since the fall of 2001 and the widespread view in the United States that further terrorist attacks are a possibility. Armed with this material, you would have made a strong start in analyzing this visual argument.

When you analyze a visual image, you will also want to look at the appeals it makes (see Chapter 8) and the cultural values it seems to support or criticize. Consider the following appeals and questions:

- *Emotional appeals* attempt to provoke particular emotions — such as pride, horror, anger, desire, or happiness — in a viewer. What feelings does the visual argument elicit? How does it do this? What specific elements in the visual argument create these emotions in the viewer?

- *Ethical appeals* attempt to prove the character or credibility of the image. If an image makes an ethical appeal, how is credibility or character demonstrated?

What kinds of authorities or symbols are used in the image to support the ethical appeal?

- *Logical appeals* attempt to persuade viewers with evidence. Are images in a visual argument arranged logically? Do important elements command more space than less important elements, for example? Do words and images work together to show a cause-and-effect relationship? Are examples used?

- *Cultural values* appeal to a particular audience. Do the images in a visual argument reflect any specific values? Does the visual argument seem to approve of these values, or does it poke fun at them?

EXERCISE 9.1 ANALYZING VISUAL ARGUMENTS

A. Choose an image—such as an advertisement, a cartoon or comic strip, a news photograph, or an image assigned by your teacher—that appears to make an argument. Using your own paper, answer the following questions about the image as completely as you can.

1. What *first* makes you aware that this image makes an argument? What response do you think the creators of the image expect?

2. What claim does the visual argument seem to make?

3. What reasons does the visual argument supply for the claim?

4. What warrant or warrants does the argument assume?

5. Does the image supply evidence to support the reasons? If so, what? If not, do you think the viewer is expected to supply evidence? What kind of evidence do your knowledge and experience supply?

B. Using the visual argument you discussed in part A, answer the following questions.

1. What kind of appeal does this image rely on *most*? Explain how the appeal is supposed to affect viewers. Does it have this effect on you? Why, or why not?

2. What cultural values are evident in this visual argument? Do they influence your view of the image? Why, or why not?

C. Write a brief paragraph explaining why the visual argument is or is not convincing to you.

EXERCISE 9.2 ANALYZING THE DESIGN OF VISUAL ARGUMENTS

A. Using either the image you chose for exercise 9.1 or another image that makes an argument, answer the following questions as completely as you can. Use your own paper for this exercise.

1. How does the visual argument attract your attention? Why do you think it was designed to attract your attention in this way?

2. Describe the placement of visual elements. What is in the foreground and background? What parts of the image are large and what parts small, what parts high and what parts low? How does this placement affect the way you look at this argument?

3. Does the visual argument include words? If so, how important are they? What is their effect on the image, and what is the effect of the image on the words? Would the argument be possible without the words? Why, or why not?

4. Do you notice any repetition in the visual argument? If so, what effect does the repetition create?

B. Based on your analysis of the visual argument in part A, how convincing and effective do you consider the design of this argument to be?

Constructing Arguments

10

The ability to think critically about the many arguments you encounter each day is an essential skill for many reasons. One of the most important is that understanding what makes other people's arguments succeed or fail enables you to make effective arguments of your own. This chapter will guide you in putting your critical-thinking skills to work in crafting powerful, persuasive arguments with purposes that range from winning debates with other people to inspiring change within yourself.

CONSTRUCTING ARGUMENTS IN EVERYDAY USE

You have probably been crafting convincing arguments since you were old enough to talk. If you ever convinced a schoolmate to play hopscotch instead of tag, got a parent's permission to stay out late or attend a concert, persuaded a group at school or work to try your approach to a project, or simply talked friends into coming over to watch your favorite video again, you made a convincing argument. Over the next couple of days, pay attention to the arguments you make and the arguments you hear, and make note of several interesting ones. Can you identify the purpose in each of these arguments? Do the successful arguments have anything in common? How about the unsuccessful ones?

The purposes of argument (11a)

All language is in some sense argumentative, and everything you say or write has a purpose. An argument can have many different purposes.

- One purpose of argument is *to win*. When people argue in formal debates, in courtroom trials, or in business, for example, they argue to win — to control the audience and triumph over opposing views.

- Another, more frequent goal of argument is *to convince* other people to change their minds or to take a specific action. This kind of argument requires the arguer to make such a compelling case that the audience must agree.

- Argument can also be used *to reach a decision or explore an issue*. This type of argument often takes the form of a conversation; the arguer seeks not to triumph, or even convince, but rather to share information and perspectives with other people so that they can make an informed choice.

- You may also argue *to change yourself*. This kind of argument may resemble an intense meditation on a theme or idea as you seek to transform some part of yourself or to find peace of mind.

Determining whether a statement can be argued (11b)

Straightforward, factual statements do not provide a good basis for argument. "This bus goes downtown" or "Guy Ritchie directed that movie" are *not* seriously debatable; a look at the bus map or the credits of the film will conclusively answer any questions about whether these statements are true. However, sentences such as "The bus is the best way to get downtown" or "Guy Ritchie should never direct Madonna in another film" *are* debatable because reasonable people might have other opinions.

In general, an arguable statement has the following characteristics:

1. It attempts to convince readers of something, or it urges them to do something.
2. It addresses a problem that has no easily acceptable solution, or it asks a question that has no absolute answer.
3. It presents a position on which readers might realistically have different perspectives.

The statement "The Indian Point nuclear power plant is located less than fifty miles north of New York City" is not arguable because it is easy to verify or refute. In contrast, "In the aftermath of September 11, nuclear power plants should be closed" meets the criteria for an arguable statement: it tries to convince readers, it addresses a problem that has no easy solution, and it presents a position about which people can — and do — disagree.

Formulating a working thesis (11c)

After determining that a statement is arguable, you need to develop a working thesis (see Chapter 5). One way to do this is to use Stephen Toulmin's system (see Chapter 8). Begin with your arguable statement, or *claim*; identify one or more *reasons* for your claim; and then identify your *warrants*, or assumptions that link the claim and reasons together. Once you have articulated these three elements, you can formulate a working thesis. Let's apply this approach.

First, state the claim.

CLAIM   In the aftermath of September 11, nuclear power plants should be closed.

Then, attach a good reason.

REASON   Nuclear power plants offer a tempting target for terrorists.

Then combine the claim and the reason into a working thesis.

WORKING THESIS   In the aftermath of September 11, nuclear power plants should be closed because they offer a tempting target for terrorists.

After you have your working thesis, it is a good idea to examine your warrants. Doing so can help you test your reasoning and strengthen your argument. You may identify numerous warrants that support your working thesis.

WARRANT 1   Terrorists want to cause mass destruction to America.

WARRANT 2   Nuclear power plants would emit dangerous radiation if attacked by terrorists.

WARRANT 3   Nuclear power plants and everyone who lives near them are now vulnerable to terrorist attacks.

In addition, Toulmin suggests that once you have an argumentative thesis, you may want to use qualifiers to make it more precise and thus easier to support.

WORKING THESIS WITH QUALIFIERS   In the aftermath of September 11, nuclear power plants near major metropolitan areas should be closed because they offer a tempting target for terrorists.

Limiting your argument so that it refers only to nuclear power plants near big cities will make it easier to prove and more difficult to refute.

Ethical appeals (11e)

To make your argument convincing, you must establish your credibility with your readers—in other words, you must make an ethical appeal. Ethical appeals aim to persuade the audience to respect and trust your argument. There are three main ways to create an effective ethical appeal: by demonstrating knowledge, by establishing common ground, and by demonstrating fairness.

Demonstrating knowledge

You can establish credibility by demonstrating knowledge about the topic at hand. To begin, think about your basis for deciding that you know enough about your subject to create an argument in the first place. Perhaps you have personal experience that is relevant, or perhaps you have done research or simply thought carefully about the topic. Next, consider the information you have gathered about the subject: What sources can you include? How reliable are they? Do they contradict one another in any way? If they do, what can you do to resolve the contradiction? Will personal experience help support your claim? Thinking about these questions will help you figure out what additional research you may need to do in order to successfully demonstrate knowledge.

Establishing common ground

Common ground is the starting point of agreement—something all sides of an argument can support—and establishing common ground is often an essential element of persuasion. Common ground almost always exists, yet lack of common ground dooms many arguments to failure. In attempting to find common ground with potentially opposing members of your audience, consider the following questions: What are the differing perspectives on the issue at hand? How can you discover opinions different from your own? What aspects of the issue do all sides agree on? How can you express such agreement clearly to all sides? How can you use language (formal or informal, occupational or regional, slang or ethnic varieties of language, for example) to establish common ground with those you address?

Demonstrating fairness by considering counterarguments

Considering opposing viewpoints (also called counterarguments) is an important way to demonstrate fairness. You can establish evenhandedness and credibility by discussing counterarguments reasonably, rather than ignoring opposing viewpoints. Indeed, an effective argument anticipates and addresses any significant counterarguments. Ask yourself how you can demonstrate that you have considered all evidence carefully and that you understand and sympathize with other points of view. Such demonstrations of fairness make highly effective ethical appeals.

Logical appeals (11f)

An effective ethical appeal can be an important element in an argument, but an ethical appeal alone is not usually enough to convince an audience. Indeed, many people view the logic of an argument—the reasoning behind it—as even more important than the character of the arguer. Effective types of logical appeals include providing examples, precedents, and narratives; citing authority and testimony; establishing causes and effects; and using inductive and deductive reasoning.

Examples, precedents, and narratives

Examples, precedents, and narratives will enliven your argument and support your claims, helping to make them seem logical or even obvious.

Examples bring generalizations or abstractions to life. The case history of a child who witnessed violence against his mother and then grew up to abuse his own spouse would illustrate a generalization such as "Domestic violence can have serious and long-lasting effects on children who witness it." To check your use of example, ask yourself whether your examples are representative of your argument, whether they are strong enough or numerous enough to support a generalization, and whether they support your points effectively.

Precedents are examples taken from the past. Often, historical precedents can strengthen your argument for a particular present-day action. For example, if a friend transferred to an out-of-town school and then greatly improved his grades, you could argue to your parents that his case sets a precedent supporting such a move. Before including a precedent in your argument, however, ask yourself how closely the precedent relates to your point, whether the situations are really similar, and how timely the precedent is. A precedent from too long ago — or from a time or place very different from the one you are discussing — may not be effective.

Narratives are stories you tell to help readers understand the logic of your argument. When you plan to include a narrative, ask yourself whether it really supports your thesis and whether its importance will be obvious to your audience. You should also be sure to have other good reasons or pieces of evidence that support your thesis; in general, you do not want a narrative to carry the main burden of proving your argument. Finally, be aware that using too many personal narratives can make you appear too focused on yourself.

Authority and testimony

Another way to support an argument logically is to cite an authority. Indeed, authorities are often cited in research writing or writing about literature. You will often have a choice of authorities to include in your argument. Some authorities are, of course, more effective than others in supporting a particular idea. Before including the words of any expert in your argument, ask yourself whether the authority is timely, whether the authority is really an expert on your topic, and whether the authority will be known and respected by readers (or whether you can identify the authority sufficiently to make his or her expertise obvious).

Testimony is the evidence an authority presents in support of a claim. Make sure that any testimony you cite is timely, supportive, accurate, and reliable.

Causes and effects

Showing that one event is the cause — or the effect — of another can help in supporting an argument. Tracing causes often lays the groundwork for an argument, particularly if the effect is one the audience would like to see changed. If you find, for example, that a number of people got sick after eating meat tainted with bacteria, you could try to trace the cause of the tainting in order to argue for changes that would prevent similar poisonings in the future.

Be careful of asserting too much too definitely, however: cause-and-effect arguments can be very difficult to establish beyond a doubt. If, however, you can make a credible cause-and-effect case, this type of appeal can be very effective.

Inductive and deductive reasoning

Inductive and deductive reasoning are ways of thinking that allow you — and your audience — to draw conclusions. Inductive reasoning involves making a generalization on the basis of specific instances. If, for example, you drank coffee after dinner five times last month and each time had trouble sleeping at night, you would probably draw the inductive conclusion that coffee after dinner keeps you awake.

Deductive reasoning, in contrast, moves from general principles to specific instances; it is often used with inductive reasoning. Traditionally, deductive reasoning involves *syllogisms*, three-part statements containing a major premise (a general principle), a minor premise (a specific instance), and a conclusion.

MAJOR PREMISE	Coffee after dinner keeps me awake.
MINOR PREMISE	I had a cup of coffee with dessert tonight.
CONCLUSION	I will not sleep well tonight.

The problems with syllogisms are that they are often too rigid to work well in arguments that do not have absolute answers and audiences may not find them very appealing.

Another type of deductive reasoning is the *enthymeme*, which asks the audience to supply an implied major premise.

MINOR PREMISE	An energy-efficient refrigerator uses less electricity than a standard model.
CONCLUSION	Our next refrigerator should be an energy-efficient model.

The unstated major premise here, which an audience is likely to supply, is something such as this: "Using less electricity is a good idea."

You can also use the Toulmin system to state the parts of a deductive argument. Here is the argument about conserving electricity, this time in the Toulmin framework.

CLAIM	Our next refrigerator should be an energy-efficient model.
REASON	An energy-efficient refrigerator uses less electricity than a standard model.
WARRANT	Using less electricity is a good idea.

Notice that the warrant—the assumption that is often unstated—in Toulmin's approach serves the same purpose as the unstated major premise in the enthymeme.

Emotional appeals (11g)

Because most successful arguments appeal to our hearts as well as to our minds, good arguments supplement logical appeals with emotional appeals. Three effective ways to engage your audience's emotions include using description and concrete language, using figurative language, and shaping your appeal to your audience.

Description and concrete language

Vivid descriptions and concrete language can work like photographs to bring a moving immediacy to any argument. For example, the statement "Nonnative species of insects may have devastating effects on an area where they have no natural enemies" may be true, but it has little emotional appeal. This revised version paints a much more specific and evocative picture of the devastation: "The Asian longhorn beetle, an invader from abroad, slowly kills maple trees whose brilliant foliage makes New England so glorious in the fall and whose sap gives us maple syrup; nothing can save a tree once the beetles have infested it, and nothing kills the beetles other than cutting down the tree and chipping it."

Figurative language

Figurative language (otherwise known as figures of speech) is an important element in the kind of detailed, vivid writing that evokes readers' emotions and helps them understand — and agree with — your position. A figure of speech compares something the audience knows well with something unfamiliar, thereby making the unfamiliar easier to comprehend. A striking comparison can help readers visualize your point and identify with your argument.

Common figures of speech include metaphors, similes, and analogies. A *metaphor* compares two things directly: "You are the sunshine of my life" is one example. A *simile* compares things using *like* or *as*: "My love is like a red, red rose." An *analogy* is an extended metaphor or simile that uses a well-known idea or process to make an unfamiliar one easy to understand — for example, "An email is like a postcard that allows many people to read its message, while an encrypted message that is used for sending credit card information online is like a letter in an envelope, protected from prying eyes."

As you use figurative language to add emotional impact to your argument, be careful not to overdo it. Emotional appeals that are overly dramatic or unfair diminish an argument's appeal.

Shaping your appeal to your audience

As is the case with an ethical or logical appeal, an emotional appeal is effective only insofar as it moves a particular audience. It is therefore essential to tailor your emotional appeals appropriately. Suppose you were trying to rally support for a farmers' market for your community. You would have to think about the emotional appeals that would work in support of the issue — such as appeals promoting good health, the bounty of nature, energy efficiency (because the produce would not need to be shipped long distances), compassion for farmers, and stronger community ties. You would then need to consider how to tailor your appeals specifically to each of the groups involved — farmers themselves, potential consumers, and community officials whose approval would be needed.

Shaping your appeal to a specific audience calls for careful attention to the language you use. After deciding what emotions your specific audience would be most responsive to, look for appropriate descriptive and figurative language to carry out such an appeal. Appealing to farmers and shoppers might call for folksy language, and targeting community leaders might require more formality. Plan carefully to get the maximum value from your choice of words when shaping an emotional appeal.

Using visuals in an argument (11e, 11f, 11g)

Visuals can make powerful arguments; they can also greatly enhance verbal arguments. (Consult Chapter 9 to find out more about visual arguments.) Like verbal arguments, visual arguments can make various kinds of appeals, including ethical, logical, and emotional appeals.

- *Visuals that make ethical appeals* add to your credibility and fairness. Visuals can reflect authority, as when the president of the United States poses in front of the presidential seal. Universities, nonprofit groups, and government agencies today are often visually represented by carefully designed graphics that are meant to streamline and enhance the organizations' images. A visual that adds to your authority or to the authority of a source can enhance your argument.

- *Visuals that make logical appeals* present factual information that can be taken in at a glance. For example, visual representations of statistics, such as graphs and tables; visual aids to understanding, such as maps and charts; and visual proof, which might include photographs or other images, can often explain information more clearly and quickly than words alone can.

- *Visuals that make emotional appeals* can add substance to your argument as well — or even make arguments all by themselves if the images are striking enough (as were the pictures of ash-covered New Yorkers walking across the Brooklyn Bridge, away from the wreckage of the World Trade Center on September 11, 2001). Test visuals with potential members of your audience. Make sure that the visuals do not strike readers as too manipulative or as so tragic — or so hilarious — that they detract from what you are trying to say.

Organizing and designing an argument (11i, 11j)

Once you have assembled good reasons and evidence in support of your thesis, you must organize the material and design your document in order to present the argument convincingly. Numerous organizational possibilities exist; you may find it useful to use either the classical system or the Toulmin system.

- The classical system begins with an *introduction* that states your thesis, provides *background* information, lays out your *lines of argument*, considers *alternative arguments*, and ends with a *conclusion* that sums up your argument and appeals to your audience again. Under the classical system, logical, ethical, and emotional appeals can be used in any of these steps to add to your believability, present support for your thesis, and win over your readers.

• A simplified form of Toulmin's system for developing an argument calls for you to make a *claim; qualify the claim* if necessary; *present good reasons* in support of the claim; explain the *warrants*, or underlying assumptions, that connect the claim and the reasons; and *provide additional evidence*, including logical, ethical, and emotional appeals, as needed to support the claim.

EXERCISE 10.1   RECOGNIZING ARGUABLE STATEMENTS

NAME _____ **DATE** _____

Indicate which of the following sentences are arguable statements of opinion and which are factual. Be ready to explain your choices.

    EXAMPLE   Some premium channels on cable television fund original programming. _factual_

    EXAMPLE   HBO has the best original programming of any cable network today. _opinion_

1. The island of Manhattan lies between the Hudson and East rivers. _____

2. Volunteer Park is a wonderful place to spend a warm spring afternoon. _____

3. At the wedding reception, the best man toasted the bride and groom and wished them much happiness in the future. _____

4. During a national security crisis, the president of the United States should have the power to conduct domestic surveillance without authorization from Congress. _____

5. The best way to solve the problem of illegal immigration is to secure the country's borders.

   _____

6. Every prisoner on death row in this country should have access to DNA testing to attempt to prove his or her innocence. _____

7. In spite of its nickname, Chicago is not the windiest city in the United States. _____

8. Handgun accidents kill children every year. _____

9. The laws in this state require the use of seat belts. _____

10. Economists forecast slow but steady growth for the next six months. _____

EXERCISE 10.2 FORMULATING AN ARGUMENTATIVE THESIS

NAME _____ **DATE** _____

A. In each of the following items, a claim and a category (the parenthetical words) are provided. Fill in the blank with information about the category that makes the claim true for you. Then complete the reason, beginning with "because," to form an arguable thesis. Make the reason as clear and specific as you can.

> **EXAMPLE**   Smoking (activity) should be banned in all public buildings in town
>
> because secondhand smoke is dangerous to everyone who breathes it.   .

1. I believe that _____ (name of product) should be banned from college classrooms

    because _____.

2. _____ (title of a specific book) is an excellent book

    because _____.

3. _____ (type of animal) make good pets

    because _____.

4. Children under twelve should see _____ (name of movie)

    because _____.

5. _____ (two- to four-word description of an event) changed my life

    because _____.

B. For each arguable thesis you created in part A, write a warrant that links the reason and the claim.

Warrant for thesis 1: _____

_____

Warrant for thesis 2: _____

_____

Warrant for thesis 3: _____

_____

Warrant for thesis 4: _____

_____

Warrant for thesis 5: _____

_____

....

EXERCISE 10.3   SUPPORTING YOUR THESIS

A. After each of the following brief arguments, identify the type of ethical appeal being used: demonstrating knowledge, establishing common ground, or demonstrating fairness.

> **EXAMPLE**   Students and administrators all want the campus to be as safe as it can be.
>
> Type of ethical appeal: establishing common ground _____

1. Based on a survey of 135 students who commute to campus, 95 percent believe that parking fees should not be raised.

   Type of ethical appeal: _____

2. While it is true that state lotteries raise revenue for important public services without requiring an increase in taxes, such lotteries do not serve the public interest because, with the odds of winning being so low, they encourage the poorest citizens to waste their money based on false hopes.

   Type of ethical appeal: _____

3. The number of automobile accidents at the corner of Spruce and Pine — ten in March, eight in April, and eleven last month — suggests that a traffic signal is needed at that intersection.

   Type of ethical appeal: _____

4. No one wants to be considered a poor driver.

   Type of ethical appeal: _____

5. Lots of kids in high school have this idea that nothing really bad can happen to somebody their age, so they don't really get the idea that it's important to stop a friend who's too wasted to drive from getting behind the wheel of a car.

Type of ethical appeal: _____

B. After each of the following brief arguments, identify the type of logical appeal being used: example, precedent, or narrative; authority/testimony; cause and effect; or inductive/deductive reasoning.

> **EXAMPLE**   My older sister skipped a grade in junior high school and felt lost and friendless until she went to college. I don't want my son to skip a grade.
>
> Type of logical appeal: <u>example, precedent, or narrative</u>

1. Frequent exams — as opposed to a single midterm and a final — encourage students to study steadily throughout the term. Instructors should encourage such good study habits. Therefore, instructors should administer frequent exams.

Type of logical appeal: _____

2. The lives of working parents would benefit greatly if employers offered "paid leave for personal illness or that of a family member," if "high-quality child care" were available, and if we developed "a new approach to our social insurance system," according to Karen Kornbluh, director of the Work and Family Program of the New America Foundation.

Type of logical appeal: _____

3. Competitive sports programs often discourage average young athletes, who are likely to drop out of the program. Even players with good physical skills may lack the self-confidence to perform well in a highly competitive environment. As a result, teams often lose members who, with encouragement and practice, might be able to excel.

Type of logical appeal: _____

4. After an equipment problem at the power plant allowed the release of a small amount of radioactive steam, the Nuclear Regulatory Commission investigated the power plant thoroughly before it was allowed to come back online. The NRC report concluded that the plant was being run safely.

Type of logical appeal: _____

5. Sara Milius learned to read at three years of age, and she knew the multiplication tables up to twelve by the time she entered kindergarten. But Sara lives in a district with the worst public schools in the state, and her mother could not afford to send her to a private school. Sara's interests were overlooked and her talents ignored as her teachers struggled to control

undisciplined and sometimes dangerous pupils. Sara Milius illustrates the reason that low-income families need access to school vouchers.

Type of logical appeal: _____

C. After each of the following brief arguments, identify the type of emotional appeal being used: description/concrete language, figurative language, or an appeal shaped to the audience.

> **EXAMPLE**   As president of the student council, Darla Chang is working with community organizations in the hope that next year student ID cards will get you discount admissions to art museums, low-cost gym memberships, and half-price meals at neighborhood restaurants. Please reelect Darla!
>
>   Type of emotional appeal: <u>appeal shaped to the audience</u>

1. An emaciated tiger, its fur mottled with grime, paces the length of its too small cage, back and forth past an empty water bowl.

   Type of emotional appeal: _____

2. The hungry children swarmed around us crying for food like baby birds.

   Type of emotional appeal: _____

3. Local parents should be aware that the chains on the swing set in the King Park playground are rusting and the plastic seats are buckling, allowing potential injury to children playing there.

   Type of emotional appeal: _____

4. The shaggy brown puppy caresses every nearby human with its warm little tongue as it begs the shelter volunteers to give it a real home; meanwhile, four fluffy blue-eyed kittens watch both dog and humans with intense curiosity.

   Type of emotional appeal: _____

5. Flowers were beacons of welcome outside the new rehabilitation center.

   Type of emotional appeal: _____

EFFECTIVE LANGUAGE

"A word is dead
When it is said,
Some say.

I say it just
Begins to live
That day."
— EMILY DICKINSON

PREVIEW QUESTIONS

These questions are designed to help you decide what you need to study. (Answers to preview questions are at the back of the book.) On the line after each sentence, write *T* if the statement is true and *F* if it is false.

1. Readers in every culture admire writing that gets directly to the point. _____
2. A writer today can safely assume that most readers share his or her cultural values. _____
3. A writer should not assume that all members of a group think and behave in similar ways. _____

Put an *X* next to any sentence that uses language that is inappropriate for a college essay.

4. My research into the effect of television on babies requires tons of statistics.
5. Low-income housing has seldom been a priority for government spending.
6. Anyone who has studied this author's work in detail can see that he's just wrong.

Underline any words in the following sentences that seem incorrectly used or inappropriate within the context. Write in the correct word if there is an error. Write *C* on the line after the sentence if there is no error.

7. Woody Allen eludes to T. S. Eliot in his short stories. _____
8. A herd of wild bulls scampered along the narrow cobblestone streets. _____
9. The cafeteria line was so long that I was literally dying of hunger when I got my lunch. _____
10. This wine complements the meal perfectly. _____

Respond to these questions about roots and suffixes.

11. List two words for each of the following roots:
    a. -port- to carry (Latin) _____
    b. -bio- life (Greek) _____
12. Identify one suffix that indicates that a word is an adverb.

Use your dictionary to answer the following questions.

13. What is the origin of the word *coddle*, and what is its meaning? _____

14. Give at least two synonyms for *marriage*.
15. How many meanings does *constitution* have?

Find and correct any misspellings in the following sentences.

16. Their always telling us when they're going to have us over.
17. When her parents seperated, she began to loose interest in her schoolwork.
18. He herd the bells ringing; then he developped a headache.
19. I use to babysit for a neighbor who's daughter is now in preschool everyday.
20. My professer does not beleive that crop circles are created by aliens.

Writing to the World

11

As part of a "global village," you are able to communicate instantly by means of the Internet with people in different cultures, language groups, and countries. You probably also experience greater local diversity than ever before. Thus, like all writers today, you must become a *world writer*, sensitive to cultural differences and able to revise your writing appropriately. Whether you are writing for academic, business, or personal reasons, your goal is effective communication. Whether your writing is going to be read in your town or halfway around the world, you want your message to be understood.

WRITING TO THE WORLD IN EVERYDAY USE

You have probably read material written by someone from a culture other than your own. If you can understand another language, chances are you have read texts written in that language. If English is your only language, you still may have read a translated novel by Leo Tolstoy, chatted online with a student in Japan, corresponded with a French pen pal, or visited a Web site created by an Egyptian. List two or three instances in which you read a work written by someone from another culture. What differences in communication style could you detect between the writer's culture and your own? How did these differences make you feel?

Thinking about what seems "normal" (26a)

Is it normal for you to avoid disagreements at all costs, or do you relish a good argument? Do you make eye contact when talking to a stranger, or do you avert your gaze? How loudly do you speak in everyday conversation? Do you automatically defer to someone who is older or more experienced than you? Do you expect others to do the same? Think about the style of communicating that you consider "normal." Most people consider "correct" behavior to be the behavior that they are used to. But what is considered correct in one community or culture may seem outrageous in another. To communicate effectively with people who are not from your culture, you must learn something about the norms of their culture. You also must be aware about your assumptions of what constitutes "normal" communication.

- Don't assume that a particular style of communication is "right" and that other styles are "wrong."
- Don't assume that people in different cultures communicate in the same ways that you do. Styles of communication differ widely from culture to culture.
- Don't assume that others will adapt to your style of communication. Instead, observe the ways others communicate, and then be flexible enough to adapt your own style so that your message can be received as effectively and warmly as possible.
- Don't assume that all people in a particular culture are alike. Many Americans eat McDonald's cheeseburgers; other Americans are vegans. Some Americans wouldn't dream of missing an episode of *Survivor*; other Americans choose not to even own a television. Just as Americans have different values and tastes, so do other people. Remember: no one wants to be reduced to a stereotype.

Clarifying meaning (26b)

You already know that some words have different meanings in different contexts. A discussion about "programming" means one thing in a media studies class and something else entirely in a computer science course. Words also can vary in meaning when used in different languages and cultures. When communicating with a world audience, remember these tips:

- Listen closely for variations in meaning.
- Ask people to explain or repeat key points if you are not sure you understand what you heard or read.
- Be sure that your own meaning is clear. One way to do this is to ask for a response: ask whether others are understanding you.

Authority, audience expectations, evidence, organization, and style (26c, 26d, 26e, 26f, 26g)

A world audience may have expectations that differ from those of people in your own culture. Considering different expectations of how writers present themselves, of the types and amounts of evidence writing should contain, of how writing is organized, and of the style writing should follow increases the likelihood that your writing will be effective cross-culturally. There are no foolproof rules, but here are some tips for writing to the world:

- In the United States and elsewhere, readers expect a writer, even a student, to establish authority, to get to the main point directly, and to articulate that point unambiguously. In some other cultures, however, sounding authoritative can be considered rude or immodest. In those cultures, writers might aim for indirectness or deference, allowing audience members to "read between the lines."

- Americans tend to give great weight to factual evidence, and American readers expect writers to present fact-based arguments. In other cultures, however, first-hand experience, personal authority, religious argument, and figurative language such as metaphor, allusion, and analogy are expected as evidence.

- Many American teachers value explicit writing that follows a straightforward organization: introduction and thesis, background, overview of parts to follow, presentation of evidence, consideration of other viewpoints, and conclusion. Students in other cultures, however, are taught to follow more elaborate organizational patterns, ones that digress from their main points, are elliptical rather than linear, and repeat points. Writers in such cultures value indirection and subtlety and sometimes view American writing as overly direct and obvious.

- In general, the culture of the United States values informality. American advertisers use sentence fragments for a conversational tone, and Americans tend to address each other in person and in print by first names. Such informality appeals to many audiences, but it may offend some — both within and outside mainstream U.S. culture. If your audience is older or from another culture, and if you cannot be sure that audience members will appreciate a light or informal manner, choose a more formal style in which you avoid slang, sentence fragments, and contractions and address people by their titles and last names. You also may need to consider other stylistic considerations — such as sentence length and use of ornamental writing — in order to make the impression you desire on your audience.

How do you discover the expectations of your specific world audience? You can consult experts online or through books. If you happen to have friends or acquaintances from the same culture as the audience to which you are writing, you can ask questions. You could also read examples (in translation, if necessary) of writing that is highly valued in that culture, paying careful attention to claims of authority, types of evidence, organization, and style. Once you have some insight into how to present yourself and your ideas, you can tailor your work to the audience you want to reach.

EXERCISE 11.1 "NORMAL" COMMUNICATION

A. Using your own paper, answer the following questions.

1. Write a paragraph describing a recent situation in which you had to communicate by phone with someone from another culture — perhaps someone at a help desk, the parent of a classmate, or a foreign professor. Were there any misunderstandings? If so, what caused them? Describe the differences in communication that gave rise to any misunderstanding. Did you find a way to bridge those differences?

2. Write a short paragraph explaining how the situation described in question 1 would have been different if the person had been from your own culture. What does this paragraph tell you about your "normal" style of communication?

B. Make a list of assumptions that you think people from other cultures have about people from your culture. Which of these assumptions are true of you? Which are not?

EXERCISE 11.2   AUDIENCE'S EXPECTATIONS

NAME _____ **DATE** _____

A. Find a short text (perhaps one assigned by your instructor) written by someone new to the United States or by someone who has never resided in the United States. The writer must come from a culture that is not part of the U.S. mainstream, or, if you consider your-self to be from a nonmainstream U.S. culture, choose a text from a culture that is not your own. After reading the text, describe its organization, its style, the kinds of evidence the writer uses, and the level of authority that the writer assumes. How does each feature match the expectations you had for this text?

B. In a paragraph, explain how you have adapted your writing style to suit your audience's culture.

Language That Builds Common Ground

12

When you write, you want your final product to be understood by your readers. Any number of factors can derail effective communication, including the use of offensive words and stereotyping. Avoidance of stereotyping and careful word choice are particularly important whenever you are writing to persuade others. In such writing situations, choosing words carefully can make a tremendous difference in your readers' responses.

Obviously offensive language is easy to identify and revise. Terms, such as *slob* and *dummy*, that are meant to hurt and to insult have no place in academic writing. Other terms just as offensive to readers might be harder to identify. For example, some older readers object to being called "elderly" or to being labeled "the elderly." Such phrasing suggests infirmity, and many older readers lead active lives. *Senior citizens* and *seniors* are more neutral terms, but some find even these terms annoying.

How can you avoid offending members of your audience? The simplest way is to ask members of your reading audience how they prefer to be identified. Be aware that these preferences change over time and that using an old term can be just as offensive as using an intentionally malicious one. Thus *colored people* is now an offensive term; it is better to choose *African American*. In a similar vein, the Native American peoples once referred to as "Eskimos" now prefer "Inuit."

COMMON GROUND IN EVERYDAY USE

A visiting uncle says to his three-year-old niece, "How's my baby?" The little girl responds angrily, "I'm not a baby anymore. I'm a *big* girl!" Even small children may object to labels that they find inaccurate or disrespectful, no matter how well meaning the person making the comment may be. At times, you may not be sure of how to address or describe someone of a different age, race, religion, or sexual orientation without giving unintentional offense. To get some tips, pay attention to the ways people who do not know each other well interact considerately. Listen carefully to co-workers, professors, and peers, or to television and radio interviews, and make note of instances in which speakers make an effort to build common ground and treat each other with respect.

When you draft, and especially when you revise, pay attention to your phrasing and word choice. Keep these questions in mind:

- Is this writing respectful of the ideas and feelings of others?
- Does this writing treat people as unique human beings, or does it unfairly or inaccurately stereotype them?
- Might any individual phrasings or identifications offend readers?

Stereotypes and generalizations (27a)

Stereotyping is assuming that all the members of a group are exactly the same. It ignores individual human differences, and readers might find it inaccurate or offensive. To avoid stereotyping, speak to readers in the way that you yourself want to be spoken to. No one enjoys being insulted or unfairly judged.

When you read an assertion such as "College students are wasting their time; they don't live in the real world," you know that such a sweeping statement fails to do justice to college students and their lives. Similarly, statements such as "Kids are irresponsible" or "Kids don't know what it means to work" assume that it's possible to group all "kids" together and then accurately characterize them. Any readers (of any age) who identify with "kids" might find this stereotyping offensive, and if they discover it in a piece of writing, they are likely to respond with hostility. In fact, in this context, many readers may find the word *kids* itself offensive. Here, both stereotyping and individual word choice provoke anger rather than agreement.

As you work to build common ground with your readers and to avoid offending them, and as you reread your early drafts, pay particular attention to

- assumptions about gender
- assumptions about race, ethnicity, religion, and geographic area
- assumptions about age, class, sexual orientation, and physical ability

Despite your best intentions, your assumptions can prove troublesome.

Assumptions about gender (27b)

These days, nearly all readers are troubled by language that makes unnecessary or sexist references to gender. The principle here is quite simple: use language acknowledging that most human activities are just that, human activities and not gender-specific ones. Nurse, doctor, teacher, engineer, secretary, garbage hauler, choir director, minister—all these occupations are held by women and men. In the past century, commonplace sexist language seemed to limit certain occupations to men: *policeman, fireman, chairman, congressman.* And formerly it was commonplace usage to refer to the entire human race as *man* or *mankind.* Old texts often used *he* to refer to a representative of an entire group, as in "A doctor must know his medicine, and a teacher must know her students." Such usage clearly makes the assumptions that all doctors are men and that all teachers are women — assumptions that were never accurate and that are offensive today. Readers are also offended by usages such as *woman doctor* and *male nurse*, terms implying that the persons described are oddities.

You can avoid sexist usage such as that appearing in the sentence below by using any of the three listed revision methods:

SEXIST USAGE	*A judge* must consider the evidence carefully before *he* arrives at a decision.
REVISION 1	*Judges* must consider the evidence carefully before *they* arrive at a decision. [*Use plural forms.*]
REVISION 2	*A judge* must consider the evidence carefully before arriving at a decision. [*Eliminate the pronoun.*]
REVISION 3	*A judge* must consider the evidence carefully before *he or she* arrives at a decision. [*Use* he or she *or* him or her.]

Beyond those simple revisions, ask yourself whether gender and gender-related characteristics are actually relevant. If you are writing a news story about Dr. Shirley Clark's research, is her marital status relevant? What about the color of her hair or her physical appearance? Does information about these characteristics enhance readers' understanding of Dr. Clark's research? If you were writing about Dr. Charles Clark, would you identify him as the husband of Shirley Clark, and would you mention the fact that he is the father of three children? Would you note that he's a handsome blond (assuming he hasn't gone bald)? If your subject is the research itself, such details are not relevant and should be omitted.

Here is a checklist of questions to help you identify and revise sexist language:

- Have you used *man* or *men* or words containing them to refer to people who may be female? If so, substitute a term that is gender free.

  fireman → firefighter

  manpower → personnel

  anchorman → anchor

- Have you used terms that assume a task is performed by only one gender? For example, have you used *mothering* when what you really mean is *parenting*?
- Have you used pronouns that assume a task or occupation is performed by only one gender? If so, eliminate the sexist assumption by making your terms plural. Thus *A good cook knows how to adjust her recipe* becomes *Good cooks know how to adjust their recipes.*

Assumptions about race, ethnicity, religion, and geographic area (27c, 27d)

When referring to race or ethnicity, do so in ways that the people referred to would find acceptable; be particularly careful not to use such references to minimize or eliminate individual differences. And as with gender-related descriptions such as marital status or physical appearance, ask yourself whether references to race or ethnicity are truly necessary and relevant. Does it matter that John Kowalski is the *Polish* minister who preached last Sunday? Why is it important to mention that a newscaster is *Asian American*? If the reference isn't crucial, omit it.

In addition, be careful not to offend your readers by confusing ethnicity and religion. For example, *Arab* generally refers to people of Arabic-speaking descent. But *Arab* is not the same as *Muslim*, since many Muslims (believers in Islam) live in non-Arab areas (Iran and Pakistan, for example).

Be sensitive to the ways in which you refer to residents of particular areas, and use terms they would find acceptable. For example, many residents of Scotland and Wales would prefer not to be called English. Similarly, it is inaccurate to use *American* to refer exclusively to the United States. Canada, Mexico, Peru, Brazil, and Chile (to name but five) are also American countries.

Assumptions about age, class, sexual orientation, and physical ability or health (27d)

Be wary of age-related terms that might offend or seem condescending — *teenybopper, well-preserved, geriatric set*, and the like. If age is specifically important to your point, report it in years.

Some terms have obvious class overtones — *aristocrat*, for instance, or *peasant*. And some terms have overtones that can easily alienate those to whom they refer. So be careful of expressions such as *yuppie, redneck*, and *blue blood*.

Like any other label, reference to sexual orientation should be included only when it is directly relevant. Would you report sexual orientation regardless of what that orientation is? Would you, for example, say *heterosexual police officer*? If the reference to sexual orientation is unnecessary, omit it.

Also be sensitive to current usage regarding physical ability and health. For example, persons born with the genetic code for Down syndrome are no longer referred to as Mongoloid. And many of those who have suffered accidents resulting in impairments to full physical functioning may object to euphemisms such as *physically challenged*. If you feel the disability needs to be made clear, identify the person first and then the disability. Thus you would say *Stevie Wonder, a singer who is blind*, not *blind singer Stevie Wonder*. Again, as a writer you should ask yourself whether such references are even necessary. If they are not obviously and directly relevant, omit them.

EXERCISE 12.1   STEREOTYPES

NAME _____   **DATE** _____

Each of the sentences below stereotypes a person or a group. Underline the word or phrasing that identifies the stereotyped person or group. In each case, be ready to explain why the language may be offensive, demeaning, or unfair.

1. Why would those white-collar suburban types care about health benefits for factory workers?

2. Mr. Lantana surprised his neighbors in the retirement community when he clearly explained how hedge funds work.

3. Asians get a high percentage of the scholarships here because they are so good at math and science.

4. Dropouts become juvenile delinquents.

5. Politicians care more about their reelection than the concerns of average Americans.

EXERCISE 12.2   OFFENSIVE REFERENCES OR TERMS

Review the sentences below for offensive references or terms. If a sentence seems acceptable as written, write *C* on the line below the sentence. If a sentence contains unacceptable terms, rewrite it on the lines provided.

EXAMPLE   Elderly passengers on the cruise ship *Romance Afloat* will enjoy swimming, shuffleboard, and nightly movies.

REVISION   Passengers on the cruise ship *Romance Afloat* will enjoy swimming, shuffleboard, and nightly movies.

1. A good nurse needs to use her medical training as well as her skills working with people.

_____

_____

2. After the plane took off, the female pilot welcomed everyone aboard.

_____

_____

3. Rolling up to the podium in his wheelchair, Dr. Franklin Benton addressed the organization on regional historical research.

_____

_____

4. My lesbian sociology professor assigns unbelievable amounts of homework.

_____

_____

5. Even after writing dozens of books about space travel, the atheist Isaac Asimov was afraid to fly on airplanes.

_____

_____

6. A male kindergarten teacher heads the school's outreach program.

_____

_____

7. Every union member is expected to take his complaints to the shop steward.

_____

_____

8. Teenagers who listen to rap music probably don't spend much time at the ballet.

_____

_____

9. A West Point cadet must keep his record clean if he expects to excel in his chosen career.

_____

_____

10. Acting as spokesman and speaking with a southern drawl, Cynthia McDowell, attractive mother of two, vowed that every elementary school teacher in the district would take her turn on the picket line until the school board agreed to resume negotiations.

_____

_____

_____

Language Variety

13

The English language contains an amazing diversity of regional and cultural expressions, as well as words and phrases borrowed from other languages. Consider, for example, the various ways people refer to their parents. *Mama, mom, madre, matriarch, mater, ma, mum,* and *mommy* all refer to mothers. *Papa, dad, padre, sire, pater, pa, pop,* and *daddy* all refer to fathers. These words are more than synonyms; each one suggests a different social, ethnic, geographic, or cultural group. *Madre* and *padre* are Spanish; if you use them to refer to your parents, your language reflects a Spanish or Hispanic influence. Similarly, the use of *mama* is more common in southern states, less common in the Northwest. And *ma* and *pa* sound more rural than urban. Each of these usages is appropriate in some context.

LANGUAGE VARIETY IN EVERYDAY USE

When you listen to the radio, you are likely to hear many different kinds of English (and perhaps other languages) on different stations and at different times of day. You might hear a network anchor reading the news, a song containing non-English phrases (or a song entirely in another language), the jokes and comments of a "shock jock," the regionalisms of talk-show callers from Wisconsin and Boston, or an interview with a foreign speaker (overlaid with the voice of a translator) on National Public Radio. You have probably heard different kinds of language on the radio for years, and you are probably quite good at interpreting what you hear.

Take note of the different varieties of language that you hear as you listen. What kinds of English (and other languages) can you identify? What is the purpose of each? How do different types of English affect you as a listener? Explain what your observations reveal to you.

Varieties of language in academic writing (28a)

Sometimes you may wish to use words or short phrases from languages other than English. For instance, in "Black *and* Latino," an essay about his own heritage, Robert Santiago argues against the tendency to categorize people according to easy distinctions. He explains how his dark skin color and the fact that he was of Puerto Rican descent confused other people and confused him, too. Most of Santiago's essay is written in standard English, but he does bring in some Spanish to illustrate what he means: "My lighter-skinned Puerto Rican friends were less of a help in this department. 'You're not black,' they would whine, shaking their heads. 'You're a *boriqua* [slang for Puerto Rican], you ain't no *moreno* [black].'" Notice that Santiago translates words (in brackets immediately following the original term) when he thinks some members of his audience may not understand.

You too may find college writing situations in which you can decide to include more than just standard English. Using ethnic, occupational, or regional varieties of English, or importing words or phrases from other languages, should be something you do to make a particular point. Used carefully and not haphazardly, these other kinds of English will enrich your prose.

Standard varieties of English (28b)

The language that this book teaches — the language of college writing and communication — is often called **standard English**. You can read standard English in magazines such as *Time* and *Newsweek*, and you can hear it whenever you listen to nationally broadcast news. Standard English is the language of most of the textbooks you will read (although these books may also introduce you to highly specialized language). Standard English is also the language of most business communication — reports, proposals, and letters — reason enough for you to learn how to use it effectively. And finally, standard English is the language most of your college teachers expect when they ask you for your explanation or your opinion.

As you think about standard English, remember that what you are really considering is a set of **conventions** — rules that educated people agree to follow. In the United States, for example, there is general agreement that c-o-l-o-r is a correct spelling; in England, Canada, and other places where British English is used, the correct spelling is c-o-l-o-u-r. Similarly, most delis in the United States sell sliced turkey at so much per pound, but across the border in Canada, turkey is sold at so much per one hundred grams. Knowing standard English means knowing — and using — a set of widely understood language conventions, as well as realizing that what constitutes the "standard" in one place or country may not do so in another.

Ethnic and regional varieties of English and other languages (28c, 28d, 28e)

The conventions of standard English are probably not the only ones that you use or have experienced: the English that you speak among your friends, for example, is probably not the English that you use in the classroom. In any job you've held, you have no doubt been exposed to English used in different ways and have used specialized terms. In addition, you have probably experienced many different ethnic varieties of English — Chinese, African American, Mexican, Southeast Asian, Polish, Italian, Jewish, Native American, and Polynesian, not to mention regional dialects from English speakers in Boston, Brooklyn, the South, or southern California. Your own heritage may have exposed you to some of this same richness of English. Most academic writing situations ask you to set this ethnic or regional richness aside. But you will find some occasions when you can draw on your knowledge of the many varieties of English, particularly when you want to let your readers hear that language and that voice. Capturing some of that language and using it inside a larger block of academic prose can lead to some startling and effective contrasts.

Sometimes you can simply quote the ethnic, occupational, or regional English that you want to use. For example, suppose you were asked to write an analysis of Flannery O'Connor's autobiographical essay "The King of the Birds," which discusses how her family raised peacocks in Milledgeville, Georgia. In your analysis, you might write about how O'Connor varies her language, sometimes using quite formal standard English and sometimes using the words her family actually spoke. One paragraph begins by introducing a visitor. The language here is formal: "A man selling fenceposts tarried at our place one day and told me that he had once had eighty peafowl on his farm. He cast a nervous eye at two of mine standing nearby." This prose reads as the controlled, rather formal academic English that it is. But when the man begins to discuss what it meant to have eighty such birds on the farm, the language changes: " 'In the spring, we couldn't hear ourselves think,' he said. 'As soon as you lifted your voice they lifted their'n, if not before.' " Strictly speaking, this is not quite standard academic English. The phrase *we couldn't hear ourselves think* is really a cliché, and *their'n* is not standard usage. However, this is certainly powerful English; listening to it, we can begin to visualize the person who said it. In addition, careful readers notice the contrast. It surprises them a little bit to hear such informal, everyday speech inside more formal prose. The contrast makes readers pay attention.

In her essay "Mother Tongue," Amy Tan, author of the novel *The Joy Luck Club*, discusses the way her Chinese mother speaks English. For Tan, her mother's speech is "vivid, direct, full of observation and imagery." And even from that brief quotation, you can see that Amy Tan's essay itself is a good example of standard English. But Tan's point is that standard English isn't the only English that can be meaningful or persuasive, even though Tan was often called on to translate her mother's speech or to speak on her behalf. Tan illustrates the contrast between standard English and her mother's speech by relating an occasion when a stockbroker had failed to send her mother a promised check. Her mother expressed her complaint this way: "Why don't he send me check, already two weeks late. So mad, he lie to me, losing me money." In speaking on her mother's behalf, Tan "translated" this complaint: "Yes, I'm getting rather concerned. You had agreed to send the check two weeks ago, but it hasn't arrived."

Amy Tan's point in her essay is that in writing *The Joy Luck Club* she wanted to capture her mother on paper. In Tan's words, "I wanted to capture what language ability tests can never reveal: her intent, her passion, her imagery, the rhythms of her speech and the nature of her thoughts." To do this, Tan consciously decided to "use all the Englishes I grew up with," including her mother's "broken" English as well as standard English.

EXERCISE 13.1 STANDARD ENGLISH

NAME _____ **DATE** _____

Working individually or in a small group, consider the differences between the language you hear at home, the language you associate with college, and the language you associate with an occupation. Begin by making a list of six words or phrases that describe the language you hear at home, a second list describing the language of college, and a third describing the language used in a job you have had or know well.

LIST A. THE LANGUAGE OF HOME

_____

_____

_____

_____

_____

_____

LIST B. THE LANGUAGE OF COLLEGE

_____

_____

_____

_____

_____

_____

LIST C. THE LANGUAGE OF WORK

_____

_____

_____

_____

_____

_____

Compare your lists. Do you generally feel that the language you hear at home and at work is close to the language of college, or do the languages seem different? Write four or five sentences that explain your comparison.

_____

_____

_____

_____

_____

_____

EXERCISE 13.2   ETHNIC AND REGIONAL VARIETIES OF ENGLISH

NAME _____   **DATE** _____

Working individually or in a small group, read the following examples by authors using ethnic and regional varieties of English. Using your own paper, write out the sentences, and then see if you can "translate" each of them into standard English.

Watts and Hilda sat and talked while I ate. "Wish you would join me."

"We've ate," Watts said. "Cain't beat a woodstove for flavorful cookin'."

He told me he was raised in a one-hundred-fifty-year-old cabin still standing in one of the hollows. "How many's left," he said, "that grew up in a log cabin? I ain't the last surely, but I must be climbin' on the list."

Hilda cleared the table. "You Watts ladies know how to cook."

"She's in nursin' school at Tennessee Tech. I went over for one of them football games last year there at Coevul." To say *Cookeville*, you let the word collapse in upon itself so that it comes out "Coevul."

— William Least Heat-Moon, *Blue Highways*

. . . Looking at the ceiling [Salzman] devoutly exclaimed, "Yiddishe kinder, what can I say to somebody that he is not interested in high school teachers? So what then you are interested?"

Leo flushed but controlled himself.

"In what else will you be interested," Salzman went on, "if you not interested in this fine girl that she speaks four languages and has personally in the bank ten thousand dollars? . . .

"If she's so wonderful, why wawsn't she married ten years ago?"

"Why?" said Salzman with a heavy laugh. "— Why? Because she is *partikiler*. This is why. She wants the *best*."

— Bernard Malamud, "The Magic Barrel"

Once you have your translated sentences, write a paragraph (in standard English) that discusses the differences you see between standard English and the ethnic or regional examples and the effects that are achieved by using each variety of English. In your paragraph, quote at least one of these examples.

EXERCISE 13.3 OTHER LANGUAGES

NAME _____ **DATE** _____

Working individually or in a small group, see if you can come up with five words or phrases familiar to you that are either English words or phrases heavily influenced by another language (as Amy Tan's mother uses English) or words or phrases from a language other than English (as in Robert Santiago's essay). Write out the five words or phrases and then "translate" them into standard English. Once you have done this, use your own paper to write a paragraph that explains to a stranger the differences between the originals and the translations. Write this paragraph in standard English, but make sure that you quote from your first list.

WORDS OR PHRASES

1. _____

2. _____

3. _____

4. _____

5. _____

MEANINGS

1. _____

2. _____

3. _____

4. _____

5. _____

Word Choice

14

Choosing words carefully (29a)

Choosing appropriate **diction** for college essays means choosing vocabulary and grammar that your intended readers will recognize and readily understand. In addition to avoiding regionalisms and dialects, college prose tends to avoid colloquial language and slang. Colloquial language (*snooze, a lot, nukes*) is informal; slang (*phat, dawg, wack*) is both informal and often understandable only to a few. The unconscious or haphazard use of either colloquial language or slang in college writing suggests that the writer has not thought hard about what is being said to whom. Colloquial language or slang undermines an essay's credibility.

WORD CHOICE IN EVERYDAY USE

Restaurant menus provide good examples of word choice at work. See how two very different menus describe fried chicken.

Crispy-tender, finger-licking, soul-satisfyin' good chicken. Choose regular or extra spicy.

Succulent poulet frit, with a subtle hint of garlic. Presented with steamed snow peas and potatoes lyonnaise.

Write a brief paragraph explaining what the different word choice tells you about the two restaurants. What do you think each of them would be like?

When we speak about levels of language (sometimes also called **registers**), we acknowledge the differences between the writing of a hastily written note to a roommate and the writing of a job application letter. Three levels of language — familiar, informal, and formal — are discussed here. Most college writing uses the formal level, but you should also be able to recognize and use the other levels.

Familiar language

Familiar language — the language of nicknames, nonstandard grammar, regionalisms, slang, and sentence fragments — is almost exclusively spoken. It is sometimes the language of special groups. For instance, armed forces personnel serving in Vietnam had an intricate "second language" unique to that time and place. "In country" was their term for South Vietnam; "the world" was everywhere else but especially the United States.

Consider this bit of talk:

> Skoochies we hit about nine. Dead. Nothing. Tried Eighty-Second but too many blue lights. Makes ya nervous, ya know. And Jimmy wanting to crash. So we bailed out.

Translated into more formal language, it might read like this:

> We arrived at Skoochies, a dance club, about 9 P.M. Since the dance floor was virtually empty, we decided to try driving up and down Eighty-Second Avenue. When we got there, we noticed several police cars. Just seeing police cars made us nervous. All this time, Jimmy kept saying that what he wanted to do was go home and sleep. With nothing more to do, we finally just went home.

Although the first version is terse and somewhat dramatic, not everyone will be able to follow it. The second, more formal version is less exciting, but it is also more understandable to more readers. Familiar language appears in print almost exclusively in the pages of fiction, in song lyrics, and in personal letters or diaries. Because familiar language excludes anyone not within its circle of intimacy, it is rarely appropriate for college writing.

Informal language

The use of **informal language** still implies a fairly close relationship between writer and reader: we use informal language for much of our everyday conversation. Informal language typically includes contractions (*won't*) rather than full phrasings (*will not*), abbreviations (*L.A.* instead of *Los Angeles*), and colloquialisms (*a bunch* rather than *many*).

Some college writing situations appropriately call for informal language. An assignment to write a play review for a college newspaper might stipulate college students as its audience. That review will probably be more informal than an essay examining the dramatic structure of Shakespeare's *Romeo and Juliet*. When in doubt about the appropriate tone for a given piece of writing, consult the person who assigned the writing or your readers.

Formal language

Formal language establishes a courteous, friendly relationship with readers without being fanatical or chummy. It avoids slang, regionalisms, and nonstandard grammar, and it uses contractions sparingly. Since writers using formal language usually wish to maintain an objective and impersonal stance toward their topic, they tend to avoid the use of *I*. This is not a matter of modesty so much as it is a wish to focus readers' attention on the subject at hand rather than on the writers themselves.

There are notable exceptions to this tendency; reviews, narratives, and personal essays may all use formal language *and* speak in the first person. If you have a question about a particular college writing assignment and the use of *I*, ask your instructor.

Formal language is typically the language of explanation. It should be specific, often literal, and may include description, brief narratives, or quotations. Even within formal language, there is room for considerable variation. For example, the explanations in this workbook should be formal enough to be understandable to a wide variety of readers yet not so formal that they seem stuffy or coldly impersonal.

■ *Writing Formal Language*

Some college writers feel uncomfortable using formal language. One strategy here is to write formally from the very beginning of the writing process. Use formal language as you make notes. Try freewriting using formal language, and use that same language as you complete a rough draft and begin to revise.

Or you could postpone the question of language level until you have completed note-taking, brainstorming, and drafting. Writing a review, you might begin freewriting this way:

> I think this movie was dull, boring, and visually a yawner. For one thing, the lead actor was really miscast. For another thing, all the camera angles were the ones you'd expect, and besides, the story kept jumping around. It was really confusing.

This writer will consider tone only at the revision stage. At this stage, he or she may decide to focus on the movie itself and so eliminate the use of *I*. The writer might also realize that readers need more explanation of *dull, boring,* and *visually a yawner;* these terms may also seem too informal and may actually encourage readers to conclude that the review itself is offhand or rushed. Thus the freewriting might be revised in this way: *Due to miscasting of the leading actor, uninspired camera work, and a confused and confusing story,* Sherlock *is a disappointment.*

Getting used to writing formal language may take some time, but the effort is worth it. Once you have become comfortable writing in formal language, you will feel confident that you can handle almost any writing challenge — from a letter to a friend to a job application letter to a sales presentation.

Denotation and connotation (29b)

Obviously, as a writer, you want to choose words that accurately convey the meaning you intend. There are at least two ways in which a word can carry meaning, and it's important to be aware of both as you make your verbal choices. **Denotations** are the straightforward dictionary meanings, and every word has at least one. Many words also carry certain **connotations** — suggestions of associated meanings. Connotations may be trickier to master, but they are potentially a writer's resource. By carefully choosing words for both kinds of meaning, you can communicate your meaning with precision and depth.

Unlike denotations, connotations are not often found in the dictionary; words gather connotative meanings through the ways in which they are customarily used. And words with similar denotations may carry different connotations. Think of the nouns *smell*, *odor*, and *aroma*. All refer to the same thing: that quality of an object that you can perceive through your nose. But different associations are attached to each because of the way people habitually use them. You might write, for instance, *I awoke to the smell of coffee*. There is nothing wrong with this; it's straightforward and efficient. Now compare it to *I awoke to the aroma of coffee*. The connotations of *aroma* suggest delight when you woke up, anticipation of that delicious first cup. In comparison, the first sentence seems to say that you simply, neutrally noticed the smell upon waking. Now try this: *I awoke to the odor of coffee*. Something seems off-key. Do you dislike coffee? *Odor* seems to carry a subtle but real connotation of distaste, and unless that is what you want to express, the word is a less-than-perfect choice. By the same token, you might not write *The aroma of my roommate's unwashed gym socks*, unless you are trying purposely for humorous effect.

Writers or speakers who aim to persuade their readers to do something — to buy a product or to take a position on an issue — often choose words to take advantage of connotative meanings. Consider the difference between *The Democrats are planning a new education bill* and *The Democrats are conspiring on a new education bill*. One might assume the second sentence was written by someone unsympathetic to the Democrats. Connotative meanings can make the difference between a nearly right word and the exactly right word, but they can also, as here, convey harsh judgments and convince a reader that the writer is not being fair-minded.

Writers often make denotative or connotative errors when using words with which they are not completely familiar — and that includes every writer sooner or later. If writers restricted themselves to words they were sure of, they would never expand their vocabularies. When you write a rough draft, be willing to reach for new words, and be willing to check the words you are uncertain about, either in a dictionary or with readers or other writers.

General and specific language (29c)

General words refer to or identify broad categories, classes, or groups of things. *Tree*, *book*, *house*, *emotion* — these are general words. *Elm*, *hymnal*, *bungalow*, and *anger* are specific words. Most good writing balances general and specific words to make its content clear. Imagine the span from general to specific as a continuum:

GENERAL	→	LESS GENERAL	→	SPECIFIC	→	MORE SPECIFIC
plant		flower		rose		tropicana rose
writing		article		online article		"Hip-Hop's Murky Whodunit"

Weak writing often depends too heavily on words at one end of the continuum. For example, some writers forget that they are writing to readers who do not yet share their experiences or ideas. The result is prose full of summary and judgment. Here are three sentences long on general and abstract diction and short on specifics: *That ride is scary. The equipment looks old, and the ride operators seem oblivious to safety concerns. We got in, and before we could feel comfortable, the first car started moving.*

These sentences give readers emotion (*scary*) and judgment (*equipment looks old, operators . . . oblivious to safety concerns*). The only people named, *the ride operators*, are shown in only the most general terms. Readers do not get to see any of the sensory information that yields the feeling *scary* except *looks old*. Do the words *looks old* mean that the equipment needs a paint job, that it has bent supporting rods, or that bolts are missing or very rusty? What is it about those ride operators that makes them seem *oblivious to safety concerns*? What exactly do those ride operators do (or not do)? Presumably, the writer of the passage could easily answer these questions. By not answering them, the writer actually excludes the reader from the experience he or she seeks to describe.

Writers can also err in the direction of too many specifics, particularly if the details are presented in what seems like random fashion. College essays should provide readers with both a general context and the specifics to illustrate it; the general statements raise questions, and the specific statements answer those questions.

GENERAL	Tenants complain that their apartments are decrepit and unsanitary. [*Readers' questions: What have the tenants complained about? What are the apartments really like?*]
SPECIFIC	Tenants complain repeatedly by phone and by letter that their windows will not seal and some of the window panes are cracked and loose, so the rooms are drafty, and the older tenants especially find their health jeopardized. They complain that the oil heater has been malfunctioning for months and has never been properly fixed; that the bathroom plumbing leaks consistently whether you shower, use the sink, or flush the toilet; . . . [*Readers will wish that this writer would get to the point.*]
GENERAL + SPECIFIC	Tenants complain that their apartments are decrepit and unsanitary, with windows that will not seal, heaters that have never been repaired, and bathroom plumbing that leaks every time it is used. In an effort to force the owner to make repairs, the tenants have filed a suit in county court.

Figurative language (29d)

Often, **figurative language** also plays a crucial role in conveying a writer's meaning and tone. For example, few of us would really grasp the force of an ocean wave hitting a rocky outcropping if that force were expressed simply as "extreme." But we can quite readily understand the statement that the waves hit with the impact of a truck driven into a brick wall at eighty miles per hour. That comparison is one type of figurative language.

Metaphors, similes, and analogies

Metaphors describe one thing as though it were another: *The street is a carnival.* **Similes** claim that one thing *is like* another, and they make the comparison obvious by including the words *like*, *as*, or *as if: The ball rolled toward the hole as if drawn by a magnet.*

Metaphors and similes appear inside single sentences. **Analogies** extend the comparison to several sentences:

> Looked at in these ways, capital punishment amounts to state-sponsored murder. After all, capital punishment is the premeditated taking of another life. Like the act of a murderer, capital punishment argues that human beings have the right to deny life; it argues that human beings know how and when to exercise this right.

Metaphors, similes, and analogies help us look at things in surprising, interesting new ways. Instead of saying, *We were all bored watching that movie*, a writer might say *Consider* Shoot 'Em Up III *a sleeping pill*. Metaphors such as that one carry considerable punch. Of course, no movie is actually a sleeping pill. What the writer means is that both movie and sleeping pill have the same effect. The use of metaphor turns an unremarkable thought into a fresh, amusing statement, the tone of which is very different from *We were all bored watching that movie.*

Avoiding clichés

Phrases such as *true blue*, *quick as a wink*, *slow as molasses in January*, and *scarce as hen's teeth* are **clichés**. So are *beyond the shadow of a doubt*, *have a nice day*, *dyed in the wool*, *climb the ladder of success*, *explore new horizons*, *have a sneaking suspicion*, *flagrant violations*, *unexpected development*, *raging fire*. Such phrases have been overused to the point that they have lost their original sparkle or wit. They have become so commonplace that readers find them boring and quickly lose interest in your writing if you use them often.

Avoiding mixed metaphors

Mixed metaphors are comparisons that go in two or more directions at once. Instead of creating a clear impression, they confuse the reader by pitting one image against another. The following sentence would be better off without its second comparison:

> Wilhelm is a well-rounded player with many facets.

Allusions

Allusions, indirect references to cultural works, people, or events, bring a wide range of associations to the minds of readers who recognize them. Allusions can be drawn from history, literature, current events, the Bible, or common wisdom. If you say "Your shirt gets two big thumbs up!" your friend knows you are alluding to a common movie-rating system and are giving the shirt your approval.

EXERCISE 14.1   LANGUAGE APPROPRIATE TO COLLEGE ESSAYS

NAME _____   **DATE** _____

The sentences below contain regional, colloquial, or slang terms. Revise the sentences to make them more acceptable for college essays.

EXAMPLE   Some Soviet and American nukes were junked in compliance with recent treaties.

REVISION   <u>Some Soviet and American nuclear weapons were destroyed in compliance with</u> <u>recent treaties.</u>

1. Moby Dick's humongous size was matched only by Ahab's obsessive desire to wipe him out.

   _____

   _____

2. The experiment was a major flop because the cruddy old equipment in the physics lab did not work properly.

   _____

   _____

3. Both teams were trash-talking.

   _____

4. After the big test, Sean blew off the party and went back to his crib to crash.

   _____

   _____

5. Baseball players and fans have gotten into it both on and off the playing field throughout the history of the sport.

   _____

   _____

EXERCISE 14.2   IDENTIFYING FAMILIAR AND INFORMAL LANGUAGE

NAME _____ **DATE** _____

What characteristics of this passage lead you to describe it as familiar or informal? Underline any particular words or phrases that reflect these characteristics. Then write a paragraph discussing these characteristics, using brief quotations to illustrate your points. Do you believe that the passage is appropriate as college writing? Why, or why not?

The jerk who runs the pizza joint on Broadway doesn't seem to care a bit about customer satisfaction. I mean, this guy is a real flake. Last Tuesday he sits in the corner booth watching the cable sports channel while people wait in line to give their orders. Then, instead of helping out, he gets up and pokes his finger in the pizza dough. Ugh. Would you believe? Then he ticks off the two pizza makers by bad-mouthing them while the line gets longer. We had to wait half an hour just to order, thanks to Mr. Jerko. Then, almost an hour later, when the pizza was finally ready, he yells at the server to take it over to us. She has three other pizzas ready to take to customers. But he does *nada* to help out. What a manager! If he expects people to come back, he needs to wise up and start taking care of customers instead of sitting around driving the workers crazy.

EXERCISE 14.3   REVISING FAMILIAR AND INFORMAL LANGUAGE

NAME _____ **DATE** _____

In the space below, revise the passage you examined in exercise 14.2 so that it consistently uses formal language to establish a tone appropriate to college writing. Begin by revising the first sentence as follows:

The manager of the pizzeria on Broadway does not seem to care about his customers.

EXERCISE 14.4   VARYING LANGUAGE TO FIT YOUR AUDIENCE

NAME ————————————————————— **DATE** —————

A. The following is an email you received from your friend Nancy Green. After reading it, you called Nancy and urged her to write a formal letter to the bank about this experience. At a loss, Nancy asked for your help. Using your friend's message as a guide, write a more formal letter to the manager of the bank that owns the ATM.

> Hey —
>   What is the deal with the creepy ATM situation in the bank lobby downstairs from me (you know, the one at Broad and 12th)? Have you been there? Last night it was pitch black in the doorway, and the lock on the door is shot, apparently — the thing pulled right open without me putting in my card or anything. Three homeless guys sleeping in there, it turned out. I mean, I'm sorry for them and all, but it totally freaked me out. I walked in and turned right around again — yow! Do I need this? Seriously? The next closest cash machine's miles away, but this place is trouble waiting to happen. Steer clear! Wanna lend me twenty till I can get to another bank? Kidding — talk to you soon —
>
> N.

B. Nancy sent your letter to the bank, which acted immediately to eliminate the dangerous conditions at the ATM — and promised to make a donation to a local homeless shelter. Nancy told her seven-year-old daughter about the letter and its results, and her daughter's second-grade teacher asked Nancy to talk to the class about the problem and how she helped to solve it. Once again, Nancy turns to you for help. Write the story out as you think she should tell it to a young audience.

EXERCISE 14.5   DENOTATION

NAME ———————————————————————— **DATE** ——————

Look for denotative errors in the following sentences, using your dictionary as needed. Underline every error that you find; then examine each error to determine the word intended. Write the correct word in the blank following each sentence. If there are no denotative errors in the sentence, write *C* in the blank. The first sentence has been done for you.

1. Your conscious would tell you that dishonesty is not the best policy.

   conscience ———

2. To try to impress their children, some parents flout their knowledge of slang popular with young adults. ———————

3. Art by Escher contains optical allusions. ———————

4. Carrying elicit drugs on campus is counterproductive.———————

5. The manual did not mention drug testing, inferring a lenient policy. ———————

6. She is an imminent attorney, highly regarded by her opponents in court as well as by her colleagues. ———————

7. Conscientious employees typically expect promotions and regular increases in compensation. ———————

8. When emergency personnel arrived, the victim was conscience and alert. ———————

9. Encyclopedias often feature both biographical and geographic entries. ———————

10. The mother and father of our son's best friend are, respectfully, a doctor and a lawyer.

   ———————

11. She seemed completely disinterested in everything I told her about my family.

   ———————

12. Don't let the judges effect the way you feel about yourself. ———————

EXERCISE 14.6   CONNOTATION

NAME _____ **DATE** _____

A. Write a sentence that accurately uses the connotations associated with each word in the following pairs of similar words. If you are unsure of the connotations of a particular word, check a good dictionary.

EXAMPLE   disturbing: The stranger in the diner had a disturbing stare, and my friend left soon after he fixed it on her.

distressing: The plight of the homeless is distressing to any feeling person.

1. cute: _____

_____

elegant: _____

_____

2. pleased: _____

_____

ecstatic: _____

_____

3. crazy: _____

_____

psychotic: _____

_____

4. cheap: _____

_____

inexpensive: _____

_____

5. insult: _____

_____

critique: _____

_____

B. The sentences that follow contain words with strongly judgmental connotative meanings. Underline these words; then revise each sentence to make it sound more neutral.

EXAMPLE   The current NRA <u>scheme</u> appeals to patriotism as a <u>smokescreen to obscure the real issue</u> of gun control.

REVISION   <u>The current NRA campaign appeals to patriotism instead of responding directly to gun control proposals.</u>

1. Under the guise of free speech, the civil-liberties zealots prefer so-called equal access to pornography to protecting the safety of innocent children surfing the Web.

_____

_____

2. The self-serving lecturer made unseemly appeals to the captive audience to buy his book and to harangue friends and family to purchase it also.

_____

_____

3. Only philistines would want the pristine woodland to go to a motel chain rather than to a community nature center

_____

_____

4. Her demented grandfather took saying grace on Thanksgiving perilously close to a droning lecture.

_____

_____

5. A mob of thugs skulked around the concert hall.

_____

_____

6. The fast-talking sales clerk conned me into shelling out for an extended warranty on the washing machine.

_____

_____

7. Ignorant voters signed that outrageous petition.

_____

_____

EXERCISE 14.7 GENERAL AND SPECIFIC LANGUAGE

NAME _____ **DATE** _____

The following excerpt from a college newspaper article contains some writing that is too specific and some that is not specific enough. Considering the general audience, circle the troublesome phrases or sentences, and then rewrite the paragraph on a separate piece of paper with any additions or deletions you feel are necessary.

Last night University President Martha Majors held a press conference in Shanklin Hall, located at 732 Waverly Place in the town of Millvale, Texas, in the United States of America. President Majors, forty-eight years of age with blond hair, spoke to a crowd of more than three thousand students and teachers. Her speech touched upon many important topics. One student, who was wearing a very attractive red cotton shirt from Saks Fifth Avenue, asked President Majors about her proposed cutbacks in financial aid. After she smiled, took a sip of water from a glass on the podium nearby, and placed the glass back down, Majors answered the question. She said cutbacks were only a last resort. She then outlined the university's options other than cutbacks. Before she left, something very funny happened.

EXERCISE 14.8 FIGURATIVE LANGUAGE

NAME _____ **DATE** _____

A. Most of the sentences that follow contain some figurative language. In the space provided, identify the type of figurative language each sentence uses. If a sentence contains no figurative language, write *none* in the space.

> **EXAMPLE**   By the end of her summation, Ms. Ashford had the jury following her as an orchestra follows a conductor. simile_____

1. It's well written, but it's not exactly "To be, or not to be." _____

2. My kitchen is a sanctuary where I quietly contemplate recipes. _____

3. Like huge matchsticks on the horizon, the tinder-dry pines flared one by one as the flames reached them. _____

4. The dog sat on the wooden floor and wagged his tail, a jazz drummer improvising his solo. _____

5. The summer heat settled over the people on the porch like a down comforter that could not be thrown aside. _____

6. "The face of the water, in time, became a wonderful book — a book that was a dead language to the uneducated passenger, but which told its mind to me without reserve, delivering its most cherished secrets as clearly as if it uttered them with a voice. And it was not a book to be read once and thrown aside, for it had a new story to tell every day." (Mark Twain, *Life on the Mississippi*) _____

7. She walked to the stage for the award as gracefully as a swan and as proud as a peacock. _____

8. The lecturer struck a spark that flooded the students' appetite for the unusual. _____

B. On your own paper, write sentences to illustrate each of the figures of speech you identified in part A (four altogether).

EXERCISE 14.9   CLICHÉS

Circle all the clichés you can find in the following employee evaluation. There are twenty-three in all.

Sam Byrd has been keeping his nose to the grindstone here for six years now, and, after working his fingers to the bone, he has become a shining light of the human resources department. When a problem rears its ugly head, Sam dives in headfirst to find a solution. For instance, when our willing and able receptionist Greta Shoemaker threw in the towel after thirty years of loyal service, Sam threw caution to the winds and searched high and low for a suitable candidate to replace her. He did not merely use tried-and-true methods to find the perfect receptionist; he thought outside the box and looked for a candidate who might be a diamond in the rough. At the end of the day, his hiring of Howard Solkowski, who was fresh out of cooking school and might have seemed at first glance to lack the necessary experience, has proved that Sam's gut instincts remain true to form. While Sam's gruff bedside manner can occasionally rub others here the wrong way, everyone knows that beneath the rough exterior lies a heart of gold with a real nose for business.

Dictionaries, Vocabulary, and Spelling

15

Many years ago, the famous baseball player Dizzy Dean injured his leg sliding into second base. After examining the leg, the trainer announced with a serious expression that it looked as if the leg was fractured. "Fractured, hell!" cried Dean. "The damned thing's broken!" If *fractured* wasn't a part of Dizzy Dean's active vocabulary before then, he surely figured it out quickly. So it is with all of us, for we meet new words every day. With the help of context, word roots, and dictionaries, we figure them out and make them ours.

DICTIONARIES, VOCABULARY, AND SPELLING IN EVERYDAY USE

Spell checkers have largely replaced dictionaries as the writer's primary weapon against spelling errors. However, the spell checker may suggest bizarre substitutes for many proper names and specialized terms (even when you spell them correctly) and for certain typographical errors, thus introducing wrong words into your paper if you accept all suggestions without thinking. For example, a student who had typed "fantic" — instead of "frantic" found that the spell checker's first choice was to substitute "fanatic" — a replacement word that made no sense in context. Wrong-word errors are the most common surface error in college writing today, and spell checkers are partly to blame. So be careful not to take a spell checker's recommendation without paying careful attention to the replacement word.

Information in dictionaries (30a)

Dictionaries help writers check spelling, meaning, and syllabic divisions, as well as various other things. Suppose that you are working on a rough draft and quoting a speaker who said, "That should appeal to the *hoypoloy*." You underline *hoypoloy* because you are unsure of its spelling and its meaning. In revising, you come upon *hoypoloy* and decide to look it up.

How do you look up a word that you have heard but never seen in print? First, figure out the letter combinations that could produce the word's opening sound. The first syllable could be spelled *hoy* (as in *boy*) or *hoi* (as in *noise*). Using a college dictionary, you look first under *hoy* but find nothing. Looking under *hoi*, however, gives you the entry. The word (really a phrase, as it turns out) appears this way: **hoi pol·loi**. Now you know how to spell the term and how to divide it into syllables. The phrase means "the general populace; the masses." So in effect, your speaker was saying, "That should appeal to the masses."

Dictionary entries vary slightly from publisher to publisher and may provide as many as a dozen separate kinds of information. Most entries include at least the first six of the following items.

1. *Spelling*, including alternate spellings, if they exist.
2. *Word division*, with syllables separated by bars or dots, showing where to break a word at the end of a line.
3. *Pronunciation*, including alternate pronunciations, if any. Keys indicating the sounds of the phonetic spellings are typically found in a dictionary's front matter and at the bottom of every page.
4. *Grammatical functions and irregular forms*, including plurals of nouns, principal parts of verbs, and comparative and superlative forms of adjectives and adverbs.
5. *Etymology*, the language and words that the word comes from. Knowing a word's origin can often help writers choose among several words that mean roughly the same thing.
6. *Meanings*, usually given in order of either development or frequency of use.
7. *Examples* of the word in the context of a phrase or sentence.
8. *Usage labels and notes* telling readers that some or all meanings of a word may not be appropriate in certain contexts. For example, the use of the word *mart* to mean "a fair" might be called *archaic* to indicate that this meaning is no longer in common use. Other common usage labels include *obs.*, meaning obsolete; *colloq.* or *coll.*, meaning colloquial; *informal*; and *slang*.
9. *Field labels*, indicating that a word has a specialized meaning in a particular field of knowledge.
10. *Synonyms* and *antonyms*.
11. *Related words* and their grammatical functions.
12. *Idioms*, conventional phrases in which the word appears, and their meanings.

Figure 15.1 shows the *American Heritage Dictionary* entry for the word *compose*.

Figure 15.1 A Standard Dictionary Entry

Types of dictionaries (30b)

Abridged and unabridged dictionaries

If you are purchasing a dictionary, you will likely buy one of the more popular **abridged** dictionaries, such as the *American Heritage Dictionary* (published by Houghton Mifflin) or *Merriam-Webster's Collegiate Dictionary* (published by Merriam-Webster). If you need more extensive information, you might consult an unabridged dictionary. Unabridged, or "unabbreviated," dictionaries typically contain more than twice as many entries as an abridged dictionary. Often multivolumed and quite expensive, unabridged dictionaries are most easily found in libraries. The most famous unabridged dictionary is the *Oxford English Dictionary*, often referred to simply by its initials, OED. An OED entry provides a complete historical account of a word, indicating not just its spelling but also the evolution of its meaning.

Specialized dictionaries

In addition to general-use abridged and unabridged dictionaries, there are many dictionaries designed for specific uses. *Longman's Dictionary of American English* provides considerable grammatical and usage information not often found in other dictionaries. For example, this dictionary identifies nouns as countable (*dime* is a countable noun) or uncountable (*honesty* is an uncountable noun). Non-native speakers find this dictionary particularly helpful.

Other dictionaries of usage address the appropriate use of specific words. Is it possible, for example, for something to be *more unique* than something else? That is a usage question. Among the better-known usage dictionaries are H. W. Fowler's *Dictionary of Modern English Usage*, Bergen and Cornelia Evans's *Dictionary of Contemporary American Usage*, and Margaret M. Bryant's *Current American Usage*.

Probably the most commonly used of the specialized dictionaries is the thesaurus. Providing synonyms and antonyms, a thesaurus can help a writer choose the precise word for a particular context. Under *anger*, for example, writers might find *rage, resentment, annoyance*, and *pique* as synonyms and *patience, love*, and *charity* as antonyms.

Other specialized dictionaries are "spelling dictionaries" (entries are common misspellings, followed by correct spellings) and thematic dictionaries (such as a dictionary of musical terms or a dictionary of American slang). Your library and campus bookstore probably have a wide selection of such reference books.

Vocabulary building blocks (30c)

Most words possess long histories; before they became the English words we recognize, they may have been French (*ensign*, for example) or Spanish (*armadillo*) or African (*banjo*). Many English words come from Latin and Greek. Thus the Latin words for mother (*mater*) and father (*pater*) are the **root words** (or simply *roots*) for *maternal* and *paternal*, respectively.

Readers familiar with common Latin and Greek roots often find that they can determine the meaning of an unfamiliar word. Thus if you know the Greek roots *-biblio-* (meaning "book") and *-phil-* (meaning "love"), you can figure out that a *bibliophile* is a book collector—someone who loves books.

Here is a list of some common Latin and Greek roots:

ROOT	MEANING AND EXAMPLES
-audi- (L)	to hear: *audible, auditorium*
-bene- (L)	good, well: *benevolent, benefit*
-bio- (G)	life: *biology, biography*
-duc-, -duct- (L)	to lead: *induct, conducive*
-gen- (G)	race, kind: *gene, genealogy*
-geo- (G)	earth: *geologist*
-graph- (G)	to write: *graphic, biography*
-jur-, -jus- (L)	law: *justice, jury*
-log-, -logo- (G)	word, thought: *logical, biology*
-luc- (L)	light: *translucent*
-manu- (L)	hand: *manufacture*
-mit-, -mis- (L)	to send: *mission, submit*
-path- (G)	to feel, to suffer: *empathy*
-phil- (G)	love: *philosopher, bibliophile*
-photo- (G)	light: *photograph, telephoto*
-port- (L)	to carry: *portable, transport*
-psych- (G)	soul: *psychology*
-scrib-, -script- (L)	to write: *scribble, manuscript*
-sent-, -sens- (L)	to feel: *sensitive, sentiment*
-tele- (G)	far away: *telegraph, telepathy*
-tend- (L)	to stretch: *extend, tendency*
-terr- (L)	earth, ground: *territory*
-therm- (G)	heat: *thermometer, thermal*
-vac- (L)	empty: *evacuate, vacuum*
-vid-, -vis- (L)	to see: *envision, video*

Prefixes and suffixes

Sets of letters attached to the front of a root word are called **prefixes**, and sets of letters following a root word are called **suffixes**. Prefixes act like modifiers, altering the original meaning. Suffixes typically change the word's part of speech.

Knowing the meaning of a particular prefix or suffix can help you puzzle out an unfamiliar variation of a familiar word. Suppose that you know that *practice* means, in general, to do something, as in *to practice medicine*. Then, if you know that the prefix *mal-* means something bad or wrong, you can guess that *malpractice* means "wrong-practice," a wrong action. The following lists provide the meanings of some commonly used prefixes and suffixes. Although in some cases the lists show the same meaning for more than one prefix or suffix, those prefixes and suffixes are *not* interchangeable: we say *hemisphere* but not *semisphere, bicycle* but not *dicycle*. If you are in doubt about the prefixes that can be attached to a specific noun, consult a good college dictionary by looking under the prefix. If you are in doubt about suffixes, consult your dictionary by looking under the word itself.

PREFIXES INDICATING NEGATION OR OPPOSITION

a-, an-	without, not: *amoral, anemia*
anti-, contra-	against: *antidote, contradict*
de-	from, take from: *decontaminate, deduct*
dis-	part, away: *disappear*
il-, im-, in-, ir-	not: *illogical, immature, inconclusive, irrelevant*
mal-, mis-	wrong, bad: *maladjusted, misjudge*
non-, un-	not: *nonsense, unfortunate*

PREFIXES INDICATING QUANTITY

bi-, di-	two: *bicycle, dichotomy*
milli-	thousand: *millimeter*
omni-	all: *omnivorous, omnipotent*
poly-	many: *polysyllabic*
semi-, hemi-	half: *semicircle, hemisphere*
tri-	three: *tripod, triplicate*
uni-, mono-	one, single: *unicycle, monotone*

PREFIXES INDICATING TIME AND SPACE

ante-, pre-	before: *antechamber, prejudice*
circum-	around: *circumnavigate*
co-, col-, com-, con-, cor-	with, together: *coequal, collaborate, commiserate, construct, correlate*
e-, ex-	out of: *emit, exhale*
hyper-	over, more than: *hyperventilate*
hypo-	under, less than: *hypodermic*
inter-	between: *interrupt, intercoastal*
mega-	large, enlarge: *megaphone*
micro-	tiny: *microscope*
neo-	recent, new: *neoconservative, neonatal*

post-	after: *postscript*
re-	again, back: *rewind*
sub-	under, below: *submarine*
super-	over, above: *superscript*
sym-, syn-	with, together, at the same time: *sympathy, synchronize*
trans-	across, over: *transmit*

SUFFIXES INDICATING NOUNS

-acy	state or condition of: *piracy, democracy*
-al	act of: *refusal*
-ance, -ence	state or quality of: *maintenance, dependence*
-dom	place or state of being: *fiefdom, freedom*
-er, -or	one who: *trainer, investor*
-ism	doctrine or belief: *Catholicism*
-ist	one who: *soloist*
-ment	condition of: *entertainment*
-ness	state of being: *cleanliness*
-ship	position held: *professorship*
-sion, -tion	state of being or action: *confusion, constitution*

SUFFIXES INDICATING VERBS

-ate	cause to be: *regulate*
-en	cause to be or become: *enliven*
-ify, -fy	make or cause to be: *amplify*
-ize	make, give, or cause to become: *popularize*

SUFFIX INDICATING ADVERBS

| *-ly* | way or manner: *slowly* |

SUFFIXES INDICATING ADJECTIVES

-able, -ible	capable of: *assumable, edible*
-al, -ial	pertaining to: *regional, proverbial*
-ful	having a notable quality of: *colorful*
-ious, -ous	of or characterized by: *nutritious, famous*
-ish, -ive	having the quality of: *clownish, conductive*
-less	without, free of: *relentless*

Vocabulary in context (30d)

Here are four suggestions to help you become a more active reader and thus build your vocabulary:

- *Increase the amount of time you spend on pleasure reading.* Do not confine reading to schoolwork; save some time for reading material that interests *you* — news-magazines, general science magazines, specialty sport or craft magazines. If you do not read a daily newspaper, start doing so. Read novels or biographies. Even the busiest schedule can accommodate twenty minutes a day for such reading.
- *Pay close attention to word choice as well as meaning.* Reading in this way will inevitably slow your reading speed somewhat, but part of your purpose is to increase the number of words you recognize and can use.
- *Underline or otherwise note any word you are not familiar with.* You may be able to guess at some of the words you note from their context; others may be entirely baffling.
- *Copy new words into a vocabulary journal.* Make sure that your entry contains space for a brief definition and for a sentence using the word correctly. There is no need to complete the entries as you read. Simply enter the words; then, after you finish reading, use a dictionary to check definitions and to help you write sample sentences. Here is a typical entry:

WORD	DEFINITION	USE
obdurate	hardened, unyielding	The tenants were obdurate in their decision to resist eviction.

Note that you are doing considerably more than simply consulting a dictionary; you are writing definitions and composing examples. Keeping such a journal during a time when you are also required to do considerable writing will increase your working vocabulary.

Remember, reading and writing go hand in hand. To increase your writing vocabulary, you need to be reading and writing.

Context analysis

Knowing roots, prefixes, and suffixes will certainly help you determine the meanings of new words. But even if a word is entirely unknown to you, the words around it will give you clues about its meaning. We call those clues **context clues**. Consider the following sentence: *The clown's long face and lugubrious manner brought laughs from the crowd.* Whatever *lugubrious* means, it has something to do with laughter and with a long face. In fact, the *American Heritage Dictionary* says it means "mournful or doleful, especially to a ludicrous degree."

Checking spelling (30e)

A number of techniques will help you improve your spelling.

Spelling tip 1: Change your writing habits

As you draft, underline every word that you are not sure how to spell, even if you believe you have remembered it correctly. Later, look up all the underlined words at once. It is easy, after you have written a word and gone on to something else, to forget that you may have misspelled it; underlining as you go will help you remember to check. You can look up words in any standard dictionary. If you draft on a computer, you should use your word processor's spell checker. These programs are helpful for spotting *some* misspellings, but they are not a substitute for careful proofreading of your own work. For example, a spell checker will not catch typographical errors such as *form* for *from* or *king* for *kind*, nor will it know that you wrote *herd* instead of *heard* or *loose* instead of *lose*, because these misspellings spell words that are correct in other contexts.

Spelling tip 2: Learn to proofread for spelling errors

A final proofreading of anything you have written is essential if you want to catch your own spelling errors. The best way is to proofread sentence by sentence from the end to the beginning. Underline any questionable word as you go along. Pay little attention to content; force your eyes to study each word.

Spelling tip 3: Master commonly misspelled words

Research on college writing by the authors of *The St. Martin's Handbook* has identified the fifty words most commonly misspelled. Chances are that at least a few of these words give you trouble:

1. their/there/they're	14. affect/-s	27. necessary
2. too/to	15. cannot	28. sense
3. a lot	16. separate	29. therefore
4. noticeable	17. success	30. accept/-ed
5. receive/-d/-s	18. through	31. heroes
6. lose	19. until	32. professor
7. you're/your	20. where	33. whether
8. an/and	21. successful/-ly	34. without
9. develop/-s	22. truly	35. business/-es
10. definitely	23. argument/-s	36. dependent
11. than/then	24. experience/-s	37. every day
12. believe/-d/-s	25. environment	38. may be
13. occurred	26. exercise/-s/-ing	39. occasion/-s

40. occurrences	44. categories	48. against
41. woman	45. final/-ly	49. before
42. all right	46. immediate/-ly	50. beginning
43. apparent/-ly	47. roommate/-s	

Spelling tip 4: Recognize homonyms and similarly confusing words

Many words are **homonyms**: they have the same sound but different spellings and meanings. *Deer* are wild animals; *dear* often begins a letter. *Cereal* is a breakfast food; *serial* is an adjective for things in a series. Other words sound so similar that they are often confused. Here is a list of homonyms and frequently confused words; familiarizing yourself with these words may help you become more sensitive to this kind of spelling problem.

accept/except	desert/dessert	plain/plane
advice/advise	device/devise	principal/principle
affect/effect	die/dye	quiet/quite
allusion/illusion	elicit/illicit	rain/rein/reign
are/our	eminent/immanent/imminent	right/rite/write
bare/bear	fair/fare	road/rode
board/bored	forth/fourth	seen/scene
brake/break	hear/here	than/then
breath/breathe	heard/herd	their/there/they're
buy/by	its/it's	threw/through/thorough
capital/capitol	know/no	to/too/two
choose/chose	later/latter	waist/waste
cite/sight/site	lead/led	weak/week
coarse/course	loose/lose	wear/where/were
complement/compliment	meat/meet	weather/whether
conscience/conscious	passed/past	who's/whose
council/counsel	peace/piece	your/you're
dairy/diary	personal/personnel	

In some instances, terms may be written as two words or combined to make a single word, depending on the intended meaning. Here is a list of commonly confused terms; check your dictionary for differences in meaning.

all ready/already	every day/everyday	may be/maybe
all ways/always	every one/everyone	no body/nobody

Writers also commonly misspell *a lot* and *all right*: these words are never combined. *Cannot*, in contrast, is always spelled as one word.

Spelling tip 5: Be wary of linking spelling and pronunciation

Spelling words according to their sounds often leads to trouble (consider a word such as *enough*). Even when words are spelled the way they sound, we sometimes mispronounce them and so misspell them. We may say "reconize" when we mean "recognize," and we may carry the inaccurate pronunciation over onto the page. Here are some additional examples; in each case, the correct spelling is italicized.

artic *arctic*	nucular *nuclear*	use to *used to*
goverment *government*	strickly *strictly*	wich *which*
liberry *library*	suppose *supposed*	

To remember the spelling of words with unpronounced or unstressed letters or syllables, try to picture the words in your mind. Or create an alternate pronunciation that allows you to hear every letter and syllable. For example, remember *drastically* by saying to yourself "dras-tic-al-ly"; similarly, *Wednesday* becomes "Wed-nes-day." Here is a list of frequently misspelled words of this kind, with their unpronounced or unstressed letters or syllables italicized:

can*d*idate	fo*r*eign	pro*b*ably
condem*n*	gove*r*nment	quan*t*ity
diffe*r*ent	inte*r*est	rest*au*rant
drastic*al*ly	ma*rr*iage	We*d*nesday
Feb*r*uary	mu*sc*le	

Words such as *definite* contain unstressed vowels, making it hard to hear whether the last syllable should be spelled *-ite* or *-ate*. Sometimes picturing the word helps; remembering a related word (such as *define*) should help you locate *definite* in the dictionary.

Spelling tip 6: Take advantage of spelling rules

■ Remembering "i before e"

- *I* before *e*, except after *c* or when sounds like "ay" as in *neighbor* and *weigh*.
  i before *e*: *achieve, believe, grief, friend, piece, relieve*
  except after *c*: *receive, ceiling, deceit*
  or when sounds like "ay": *neighbor, weigh, sleigh, inveigh, heinous, their*
  EXCEPTIONS: *either, neither, foreign, forfeit, height, leisure, efficient, seize, seizure, weird, science, ancient, nonpareil, conscience*

■ Adding Prefixes and Suffixes

A prefix is a set of letters added to the front of a word; a suffix is a set of letters added to the end of a word. Sometimes the original word is spelled the same when a prefix or suffix is added to it, but many times the word changes by dropping, altering, or doubling a letter. These changes, with a few exceptions, tend to follow predictable patterns. Learning these patterns can help you spell many seemingly tricky words.

- When attaching a prefix, merely add it; do not change the spelling of the original word.

  contaminate + prefix *de-* = *decontaminate*
  moral + prefix *a-* = *amoral*
  spell + prefix *mis-* = *misspell*

- To add a suffix for a word ending in silent *e*, keep the *e* if the suffix begins with a consonant; drop the *e* if the suffix begins with a vowel.

  snare + *-ing* (suffix begins with vowel; drop *e*) = *snaring*
  care + *-ful* (suffix begins with consonant; keep *e*) = *careful*
  EXCEPTIONS: *acreage, mileage, judgment, acknowledgment, wholly*

The silent final *e* is retained after a soft *c* (*service* + *-able* = *serviceable*) or soft *g* (*courage* + *-ous* = *courageous*). Sometimes the silent *e* is dropped when it is preceded by another vowel: in *true* + *-ly*, the silent *e* is preceded by the vowel *u*; hence, *true* + *-ly* = *truly*. The *e* is also retained occasionally to prevent confusion with other words (*dye* + *-ing* = *dyeing*).

- When adding *-ally* or *-ly*, use *-ally* if the word ends in *ic*; use *-ly* if the word does not end in *ic*.

  basic + *-ally* = *basically*
  slow + *-ly* = *slowly*
  EXCEPTION: *public* + *-ly* = *publicly*

- When adding a suffix to a word ending in *y*, keep the *y* when it follows a vowel and whenever adding *-ing*; change the *y* to *i* when the *y* follows a consonant.

  play + *-ful* (*y* follows vowel; keep *y*) = *playful*
  play + *-ing* (adding *-ing*; keep *y*) = *playing*
  beauty + *-ful* (*y* follows consonant; change *y* to *i*) = *beautiful*
  beauty + *-fy* (*y* follows consonant; change *y* to *i*) = *beautify*
  beautify + *-ing* (adding *-ing*; keep *y*) = *beautifying*
  EXCEPTIONS: Keep the *y* in some one-syllable base words: *shy* + *-ness* = *shyness*.
  Change the *y* to *i* in some one-syllable base words: *day* + *-ly* = *daily*. Keep the *y* if the base word is a proper name: *Kennedy* + *-esque* = *Kennedyesque*.

Sometimes adding a suffix means doubling the final consonant of a word (*pin* + *-ed* = *pinned*), and sometimes it does not (*shower* + *-ed* = *showered*). Knowing when to double depends on your ability to identify the number of syllables in a word and your ability to hear where the stress falls when a word is pronounced correctly.

For suffixes beginning with a vowel:

- When adding suffixes to words of one syllable that end in consonants, double the final consonant only when a single vowel precedes that final consonant.

  pin + *-ing* (final consonant preceded by single vowel; double consonant)
  = *pinning*
  flip + *-ed* (final consonant preceded by single vowel; double consonant)
  = *flipped*

> *stream* + *-er* (final consonant preceded by two vowels; do not double)
> = *streamer*
>
> *curl* + *-ing* (final consonant preceded by consonant; do not double)
> = *curling*

- In words of more than one syllable, double the final consonant when a single vowel precedes the final consonant *and* the sounded stress falls on the last syllable of the original word.

> *recall* + *-ed* (final consonant preceded by consonant; do not double) = *recalled*
>
> *begin* + *-er* (final consonant preceded by single vowel, and sounded stress falls on last syllable of original word; double final consonant) = *beginner*
>
> *invent* + *-ing* (final consonant preceded by consonant; do not double) = *inventing*
>
> *shower* + *-ed* (final consonant preceded by single vowel, but sounded stress does not fall on last syllable of original word; do not double) = *showered*

■ Adding the Endings -sede, -ceed, and -cede

The ending pronounced "seed" can be spelled in three ways.

- *-sede*: The only word in which this occurs is *supersede*.
- *-ceed*: The only words in which this occurs are *exceed, proceed,* and *succeed.*
- *-cede*: The ending pronounced "seed" is spelled this way in all other English words.

■ Making Words Plural

- Form the plurals of most nouns by adding *-s*, as in *papers, clouds,* and *dimes.*
- Form the plurals of nouns ending in *s, ch, sh, x,* or *z* by adding *-es*, as in *churches, bosses, brushes,* and *faxes.*
- Form the plurals of nouns ending in *y* preceded by a consonant by changing the *y* to *i* and adding *-es*, as in *countries* (from *country*), *luxuries* (from *luxury*), and *scarcities* (from *scarcity*).
- Form the plurals of nouns ending in *f* or *fe* by changing the *f* or *fe* to *v* and then adding *-es*, as in *leaves* (from *leaf*), *loaves* (from *loaf*), and *knives* (from *knife*).
- Form the plurals of nouns ending in *o* by adding *-s* if the *o* is preceded by a vowel (as in *radios*) or by adding *-es* if the *o* is preceded by a consonant (as in *potatoes* or *heroes*).
EXCEPTIONS: *sopranos, pros, pianos, hippos, pimentos*

Some words taken from other languages use the plurals from those languages: *phenomenon/phenomena, datum/data, medium/media, locus/loci, radius/radii.*

Spelling tip 7: Use a personal spelling chart

Spelling errors are not deliberate errors: no one sets out to use inaccurate spelling. Constructing, using, and evaluating the data from a personal spelling chart will help you see the pattern of your particular spelling problems. When you know the pattern, you will be able to identify the specific kinds of words that give you trouble. You can then begin to anticipate which words you will need to underline (during either drafting or proofreading) and then look up. And you will also be able to concentrate on learning the appropriate rules.

Here is the format for a personal spelling chart:

WORD (SPELLED CORRECTLY)	INACCURATE VERSION	LETTERS OR SYLLABLES INVOLVED	TYPE OF MISSPELLING
1. due	do	ue/o	homonym
2. receiving	recieving	ei/ie	letter reversal
3. response	reponse	s	missing letter
4. nastiest	nastyest	i/y	suffix rule
5. supreme	supream	e/ea	long vowel sound
6. language	langauge	ua/au	letter reversal
7. flue	flew	ue/ew	homonym
8. definite	definate	i/a	unstressed vowel
9. snoring	snoreing	e	suffix rule
10. compiling	compilling	l	suffix rule

If words such as the ten listed here appeared on your own spelling chart, you would be able to see that homonyms, letter reversals, and suffix rules consistently cause trouble. If you keep such a chart over the course of a term, you will see patterns in the errors you make. Armed with such knowledge, you will become an even more effective proofreader of your own writing.

EXERCISE 15.1 BASIC DICTIONARY ENTRIES

Consult a college dictionary to confirm spelling and to determine the syllabic divisions of each of the following words. Some of the words may be spelled incorrectly; consider possible variants before you give up! On your own paper, write the correctly spelled word, placing asterisks between the syllables. At the top of your paper, write the name of the dictionary you are using.

> **EXAMPLE**   disterbution: dis*tri*bu*tion

1. rememberance
2. renaisance
3. paradime
4. mispelling
5. obnoctious
6. melencollie
7. precede
8. taranchola
9. prestigeous

Next, find two or three synonyms for each of the following words. Use definitions from the dictionary to help you.

> **EXAMPLE**   fair: just, equitable, impartial

10. rigor
11. command
12. lonely
13. flourish
14. angry
15. rip
16. illuminate
17. slide
18. clear

Finally, look up the following words. For each word, write out each pronunciation provided, indicate the grammatical functions, and briefly summarize all meanings. Note that many words have more than one meaning. Follow the format of the example.

> **EXAMPLE**   conduct
> Pronunciations: kən-dukt' (v.), kon'dukt (n.)
> Grammatical Function Labels: v. — tr. (transitive verb), n. (noun)
> Meanings: (v.) to direct the course of, lead, or manage; (n.) the way a person acts, behavior, management

19. raven
20. intimate
21. sanction
22. advocate
23. increase
24. either
25. concrete
26. delegate
27. strengthen

EXERCISE 15.2 USING A THESAURUS

NAME _____ **DATE** _____

Use a thesaurus to find five synonyms for each of the italicized words in the phrases that follow. If you do not own a thesaurus, your reference librarian should be able to help you find one in the library or online. List the synonyms, and be ready to discuss the shades of meaning and tone that distinguish one synonym from another.

> **EXAMPLE** a *savvy* politician
> Synonyms: <u>shrewd, perceptive, wise, understanding, experienced</u>

1. She was *entranced* by the film.

   _____

   _____

2. a *peculiarly* interesting topic

   _____

   _____

3. to *confirm* the results

   _____

   _____

4. to *placate* an angry boss

   _____

   _____

5. the *strength* of her argument

   _____

   _____

6. the *scared* child

_____

_____

7. She *explored* the issue.

_____

_____

8. a *stigma* attached to the neighborhood

_____

_____

9. the *happiness* he felt in Mexico

_____

_____

10. The howling outside was *terrifying.*

_____

_____

11. She *hates* that place.

_____

_____

12. a *busy* shopping center

_____

_____

EXERCISE 15.3   USING A DICTIONARY OR A THESAURUS

NAME _____ **DATE** _____

Use a dictionary or a thesaurus to replace the underlined words in the following passage. Select words that have about the same meaning as the words used but are more commonly known and more likely to be clear to a general reader. Write your selections in the space above each underlined word.

My <u>inaugural</u> job, washing dishes in a cafeteria, began when I was a sophomore in high school and in need of <u>capital</u>. I wanted to buy a car, and my parents <u>spurned</u> my <u>entreaty</u> that they pay for the insurance, so I went to work. Convinced that the <u>enterprise</u> would not be too <u>arduous</u>, I cheerfully scrubbed <u>cutlery</u> and <u>crockery</u> in the steamy kitchen on my first day. Another dishwasher <u>discerned</u> my <u>ebullience</u> and pulled me aside. He wanted to know the <u>impetus</u> for my happiness, which apparently <u>vexed</u> him. He also told me that the cafeteria's owner had <u>queried</u> whether I was taking <u>intoxicants</u> because no other dishwasher had ever smiled so much. He <u>reproached</u> me for having a positive attitude. After a few days of dishwashing, my cheery smile was no longer a factor. At that point, my <u>preeminent</u> thought was, "I need to find another way to make my insurance payments!"

EXERCISE 15.4   USING SPECIAL DICTIONARIES

At your local library, find special dictionaries in the reference area (ask your reference librarian for help if you need it) or online. Select three of them. For each, on your own paper, provide the types of information shown in the example below.

EXAMPLE

Title: *The Oxford Dictionary of English Christian Names*
Author or Editor: E. G. Withycombe, ed.
Publisher: Oxford University Press
Year of Publication: 1977
Information Provided: 310 pages of first names together with their meanings and origins
Sample Entry (from p. 235): OSWIN (m): Old English *Oswin*, compound of *os* 'a god' and *wine* 'friend.' It remained in use until the 14th C. and was occasionally revived in the 19th C.

Next, consult a dictionary of usage, and briefly answer the following questions. Indicate the name, all authors or editors, and the publisher of the dictionary you consult.

EXAMPLE

What is the difference, if any, between *further* and *farther*?
Fowler's *Modern English Usage* says that *farther* is now common only where distance is concerned. *Further* "has gained a virtual monopoly of the sense of *moreover*, both alone and in the compound *furthermore*."

A Dictionary of Modern English Usage, by H. W. Fowler, 2nd ed., revised by Sir Ernest Gowers. New York: Oxford University Press (paperback), 1983, p. 190.

1. What is the difference between *predilection* and *bias*?

2. Is it permissible to *ellude* to someone by name?

3. What is the difference between *mendacity* and *mendicity*?

4. What is the difference between *eminent, immanent*, and *imminent*?

5. What is the proper past tense of *hang*?

EXERCISE 15.5   USING WORD ROOTS

NAME _____ **DATE** _____

The following paragraph uses many words with Greek and Latin roots. Review the list of roots earlier in this chapter; then read the paragraph, and circle each root-based word you recognize. Next, write out which root each word uses, and write in parentheses the meaning of the root.

EXAMPLE   The (photographers) took portraits of the (biographers.)

photo (light) graph (write), bio (life) graph (write) _____

   Although no one as yet has evidence that extraterrestrial beings are trying to contact the earth, scientists are conducting a thorough search of the universe. Researchers use special telescopes to search for radio waves that might be transmitted by alien beings. Whenever audible signals appear, these scientists try to transcribe and translate them to find any lucid messages. Some people envision someday establishing communication with beings whose biological and genetic makeup is different from our own. The mission, if successful, might benefit humankind, or it might have logical but unanticipated consequences that we cannot yet deduce. Most scientists who are searching for signs of life in the vacuum of space sense that discovering aliens would teach us a great deal about science— and about ourselves.

EXERCISE 15.6   DETERMINING MEANINGS FROM CONTEXT

NAME _____ **DATE** _____

Try to determine the meanings of the following underlined words by studying the context of the sentences they are in. Write out what you think each word means. Then look each one up in your dictionary, and see how close you came.

1. The cold weather and gray skies of February contributed to my <u>lethargy</u>.

   _____

2. Delighted to see the <u>harbingers</u> of spring, I welcomed the robins and daffodils.

   _____

3. Unlike the vivacious young man, the young woman on the blind date seemed <u>despondent</u>.

   _____

4. In stories by Charles Dickens, young children are often punished with a <u>ferule</u>.

   _____

5. The <u>pestilence</u> of the Middle Ages took a great toll in lives.

   _____

6. As the sun rose over Istanbul, the streets around the mosque rang with the voice of the <u>muezzin</u> calling the people to prayer.

   _____

7. The first and second levels were finished; then came the <u>tertiary</u> level.

   _____

8. The ocean water <u>undulated</u> toward the shore.

   _____

9. The accused man was <u>exonerated</u> when another person confessed to the crime.

   _____

10. Dr. King urged his fellow marchers to keep their <u>equanimity</u> even in the face of violence.

   _____

EXERCISE 15.7   PREFIXES AND SUFFIXES

A. Drawing from the prefixes listed in this chapter and the list of common roots in this exercise, construct five new words. If you are not sure your word is in fact an English word, consult your dictionary. Write the words on a separate page, and indicate the literal meaning and the common meaning. Then use the word in a short sentence. See the example following the list of common roots. (Number your words from 1 to 5.)

COMMON ROOTS AND MEANINGS

-dict-, to say	*-phon-*, sound	*-vid-, -vis-*, to see
-vene-, to come	*-graph-*, to write	*-duct-*, to lead
-scrib-, to write	*-ped-*, foot	*-mit-, -mis-*, to send

> **EXAMPLE**   transmit   Literal meaning: *across + to send*   Common meaning: *to send across*
> Sentence: *A radio tower transmits radio waves.*

B. Attach an appropriate noun suffix to each of the following root words. Then write two sentences. Use the original word in the first sentence. Use the new word in the second sentence. Consult your dictionary as necessary.

> **EXAMPLE**   king: *Henry VIII is a famous British king.*
> kingdom: *The daily changing of the guard reminds Britons that they still live in a kingdom.*

6. child   **7.** patient   **8.** professor

C. Add an appropriate verb suffix or adjective suffix to each of the following root words. Then follow the instructions in part B.

9. use   **10.** fat   **11.** fate   **12.** poison

EXERCISE 15.8 NOTING YOUR SPELLING WEAKNESSES

NAME _____ **DATE** _____

Working either individually or in a small group, read over the following list of words. Some words are spelled correctly, but others are not. Without consulting a dictionary, decide whether a word is accurately spelled. Mark *OK* beside the words you think are correct. If you think a word is incorrect as printed, write your own spelling in the space provided. When you are finished, check your dictionary to see how often you identified the spellings accurately. Which words surprised you? Finally, write three or four sentences explaining the methods you use to make sure your spelling is accurate.

atribute _____   embarrass _____

atitude _____   Febuary _____

congradulations _____   awfull _____

allright _____   benefit _____

cemetary _____   necessary _____

congragate _____   occurr _____

deterrent _____   disterb _____

enviroment _____   professer _____

individuel _____   solatude _____

drasticly _____   wierd _____

When you write a paper, how do you make sure that your spellings are accurate?

_____

_____

_____

_____

EXERCISE 15.9   PROOFREADING FOR SPELLING ERRORS

NAME _____ **DATE** _____

Proofread the following passage. Underline misspelled words or words you do not know how to spell. Check all of them, and then, in the space below, list the misspellings you found and the correct spelling of each word.

Constructing any thing takes knowlege, time, and patients. Wether you are sewwing a dress, desining a cabinet, or useing your culinery skills to make a grate omlet, chances are that your product will not be prefect the first time. So plan on makeing that first dress for youself and giving the second one as a gift; plan on staying at the workbench longer than you woud like and on hanging that first cabanet in the garage; and plan on consumeing that first omlet in privite. In this way, your expectted mistakes hurt no one. Keepping your patience, maintaning high stanards, controling your tempter — these things aren't easy. However, if you can make mistakes and lern from them, your work will improove and so wil your one estimateion of your talence.

EXERCISE 15.10 COMMONLY MISSPELLED WORDS

NAME _____ **DATE** _____

Reread the list of commonly misspelled words. From the list, identify five words that have given you trouble. Indicate how you misspelled the word, and then use that word (correctly spelled) in a sentence. Use the space below for this exercise.

EXAMPLE   Word: apparently
In the past, I've misspelled this word by adding an extra *r*.
Sentence: Apparently, I forgot to finish the assignment last night.

EXERCISE 15.11 HOMONYMS AND OTHER SIMILAR-SOUNDING WORDS

NAME _____ **DATE** _____

Twelve pairs of words are given below. For each word, write a sentence that uses the word correctly.

EXAMPLE   **a.** witch   **b.** which

    a. The wicked witch wore ruby slippers.
    b. I cannot decide which one of these movies to rent tonight.

1. **a.** breath   **b.** breathe

2. **a.** than   **b.** then

3. **a.** here   **b.** hear

4. **a.** affect   **b.** effect

5. **a.** quiet   **b.** quite

6. **a.** chose   **b.** choose

7. **a.** accept   **b.** except

8. **a.** there   **b.** their

9. **a.** its   **b.** it's

10. **a.** personal   **b.** personnel

11. **a.** too   **b.** to

12. **a.** brake   **b.** break

EXERCISE 15.12 USING *I* BEFORE *E* AND SUFFIX RULES

NAME _____ **DATE** _____

Read the following ten sentences carefully. Circle any misspelled words, and write the correct spelling above each misspelling.

EXAMPLE   ~~Basicly~~, ~~procedes~~ of the fund-raising activities will be used to rebuild the ~~nieghbor's~~ house.
[corrections written above: Basically proceeds neighbor's]

1. Twelve-step programs such as Alcoholics Anonymous or Overeaters Anonymous are designed to help individuals succede in overcomming problems common to the group.

2. Individuals enroled in twelve-step programs beleive that they can control their negative behaviores by faceing problems personaly and by supportting one another.

3. To sucede in these programes requires each individual to make a wholley honest acknowledgment that he or she has a problem.

4. Faceing a community of others with the same problem, members of twelve-step programs often feel releived to stop pretendding that nothing is wrong.

5. After admiting that they need help, members must spend time atoneing for any deciet or cruellty committed in the past.

6. A new member's crys for help are often answered by others who have been struggleing with their own addicttions for years and can wiegh in with good advice.

7. Members meet anonymousally and introduce themselfs by thier first names only.

8. In such waies, members of Alcoholics Anonymous carfuly procede through that program's twelve steps.

9. Many other programs have acheived success with basicly the same approach useing group meettings and following steps.

10. People meeting in churches, town halls, and other gatherring places all over the country have managed to come to terms with their innability to control drinking, eating, and gambleing and to turn their lives around.

EXERCISE 15.13 ADDITIONAL SUFFIX RULES

NAME _____ **DATE** _____

Recalling the suffix rules discussed in this chapter, determine the proper spelling of the following new words, and state the rule you applied.

EXAMPLE *coin + -ed* Correct spelling: coined
Rule: In words of one syllable, double the final consonant only when a single vowel precedes the final consonant.

1. *repel + -ent*

2. *hate + -ful*

3. *specific + -ly*

4. *beauty + -ful*

5. *outrage + -ous*

6. *bet + -ing*

7. *finance + -ial*

8. *convert + -ible*

9. *employ + -er*

10. *bark + -ing*

11. *refer + -ing*

12. *satisfy + -ed*

EXERCISE 15.14 PERSONAL SPELLING CHART

NAME _____ **DATE** _____

Following the format given in this chapter (see spelling tip 7), begin your own personal spelling chart. Use anything you have written recently (a term paper or a letter or a list). Find and list at least ten words you have misspelled, and fill out the other three columns of the chart for each of those words. If your draft does not contain ten misspellings, complete your chart with words you have misspelled in the past. Finally, identify and list any misspelling patterns you see in your chart. What kinds of words should you look at more carefully the next time you are proofreading your writing for spelling errors?

WORD (SPELLED CORRECTLY)	INACCURATE VERSION	LETTERS OR SYLLABLES INVOLVED	TYPE OF MISSPELLING

SENTENCE GRAMMAR

"We learn a great deal about grammar from reading — and not grammar books but newspapers, novels, poetry magazines, even the labels on cereal boxes."
— LYNN Z. BLOOM

PREVIEW QUESTIONS

These questions are designed to help you decide what you need to study. Read each sentence; then underline the word or words specified in parentheses, or underline the correct word of the two provided within the sentence. (Answers to preview questions are at the back of the book.)

1. In the novel, the surgeon, Henry Perowne, has a very busy Saturday. (nouns)
2. The mother watched with pride as her only daughter won the gold in Torino, Italy. (nouns)
3. I would have wished on a star if I had seen one. (verbs)
4. José might speak to his father about the ball game. (verbs)
5. Everyone who rode the school bus stayed home the day of the blizzard, but some who walked were able to get to school only to find it shut. (pronouns)
6. Whose life is this anyway? (pronouns)
7. In the refrigerator, Silvio found a jar of spaghetti sauce that was fuzzy with mold, so he threw it into the garbage can. (prepositions)
8. Denny and (I, me) are cousins.
9. The press corps did not know (who, whom) to interview first — the gunman or the victim.
10. (Who, Whom) do you expect to win?
11. (Her, She) and Sara went to the movie with (him, he) and his brother.
12. Please speak to Steve or (me, I) if you can't attend the meeting.
13. I (be, am) a marvelous cook.
14. That woman (don't, doesn't) want anyone to help her.
15. My father has (gone, went) to the store, but he will be home soon.
16. She told the dog to (lay, lie) down and be quiet.
17. If I had done better, (will, would) you be satisfied?
18. Neither I nor anyone else (want, wants) trouble.
19. The class assembled at (its, their) usual time.
20. Each student should bring (his, a) notebook to class.
21. The mob began to shake (its, their) fists.
22. The members of my family (has, have) much in common.
23. The news (is, are) always on at six o'clock.
24. His new haircut looked (bad, badly).
25. Mom left us two cookies, and Julio grabbed the (bigger, biggest) one.
26. He took a (real, really) hard exam.
27. She is the (most helpful, helpfullest) librarian at the school.

On a separate sheet of paper, list at least one of each of the following, taken from any of the sentences listed above: a complete subject, a complete predicate, a direct object, an indirect object, a possessive pronoun, a linking verb, a past-tense verb, a future-tense verb, and a compound subject. Check your answers against the material presented in the next five chapters. If you need help, ask your instructor.

Grammatical Sentences

16

The parts of speech are the building blocks of language. English has eight different parts of speech: **verbs**, **nouns**, **pronouns**, **adjectives**, **adverbs**, **prepositions**, **conjunctions**, and **interjections**. Native speakers of English learn these parts of speech and sentence patterns as young children, intuitively saying "The bright red cardinal surprised me" rather than "Cardinal bright the surprised me red." Although you use the parts of speech each time you speak or write, reviewing them can help you speak and write more skillfully.

GRAMMATICAL SENTENCES IN EVERYDAY USE

Perhaps more than any other subject, grammar is something we learn almost automatically, without even being aware of it. Listen in, for instance, on this conversation between two six-year-olds:

> Charlotte: My new bike that Grandma got me has a red basket and a really loud horn, and I love it.
>
> Anna: Can I ride it?
>
> Charlotte: Sure, as soon as I take a turn.

This simple exchange features sophisticated grammar—subordination of one clause to another, a compound object, a series of adjectives—all used effortlessly.

Listen to a conversation, and transcribe a few sentences as done above. Do the sentences seem grammatical to you? Think about how you decide if a sentence seems correct or not.

Verbs

Verbs describe action (*run*, *sleep*, *scratch*) or occurrence (*become*, *happen*) or a state of being (*be*, *live*). The verb is underlined in these sentences:

The cat <u>scratches</u> with its paw.

A tadpole slowly <u>becomes</u> a frog.

Mrs. Byron <u>is</u> Sadek's teacher.

Verbs are often combined with words called **auxiliary verbs** to indicate time or obligation. The most common auxiliaries are forms of *be, can, do, have, may, must, shall,* and *will.* A verb combined with an auxiliary is called a **verb phrase**. The verb phrase is underlined in these sentences.

Josh <u>will go</u> to the store for bread.

Yukiko <u>has finished</u> her letter.

Tonight I <u>must get</u> some sleep!

A verb is the key word in the part of a sentence called the predicate. In a complete sentence, the **subject** tells what the sentence is about and the **predicate** asserts or asks something about the subject. For more information about subjects and predicates, see the next major section in this chapter, "The Parts of a Sentence: Subjects and predicates." In addition, Chapter 17 provides a complete discussion of the forms and functions of verbs, and Chapter 18 provides a discussion of subject-verb agreement.

Nouns

Nouns name things or places or people or ideas or concepts. The following words are nouns: *cup, wood, paper, St. Louis, lake, Einstein, Jordan, love, gravity, justice.* **Proper nouns** name specific people or places (such as *Einstein* and *St. Louis*); their first letters are capitalized (for more on capitalization, see Chapter 37).

■ Plural Nouns

Most nouns that are *not* proper nouns can be changed from **singular** form (one) to **plural** form (more than one) by adding *-s* (*lake, lakes; paper, papers*) or *-es* (*church, churches; lunch, lunches*). Some nouns, however, form plurals in other ways (*child, children*). **Noncount nouns** name things that cannot be easily counted and so cannot be made plural (*dust, peace, tranquillity*).

■ Possessive Nouns

Nouns use a **possessive** form to show ownership. You form the possessive of many nouns by adding *'s* (for more on using apostrophes, see Chapter 34). For example, if you wished to talk about an idea that was unique to Einstein, you would refer to it as *Einstein's idea.*

■ Articles Preceding Nouns

Nouns are often preceded by **articles** (sometimes called determiners): *a, an,* and *the.* Nouns always follow these words, as in *a dime, an apple, the bank.*

REVIEW

- Nouns name things, places, people, ideas, or concepts.
- Proper nouns name specific people or specific places.

- Possessive nouns indicate ownership, often by adding *'s*.
- Articles are always followed by nouns.

Pronouns

Pronouns are used in place of nouns, making repetition unnecessary. In practice, we use pronouns frequently. Consider this sentence: *Marion lost the watch, but she found ten dollars.* The word *she* is a pronoun referring to *Marion*. Without a pronoun, the sentence would read this way: *Marion lost the watch, but Marion found ten dollars.* Pronouns usually refer to specific earlier nouns, called **antecedents**. In the example, *Marion* is the antecedent of the personal pronoun *she*.

There are many types of pronouns. *She* is a **personal pronoun** because it refers to a person. Personal pronouns take different forms depending on how they are used in sentences. For now, you should simply be able to recognize the personal pronouns:

I, me, my, mine, we, us, our, ours

you, your, yours

she, her, hers, he, him, his, one, it, its, they, them, their, theirs

There are quite a few other kinds of pronouns. **Reflexive pronouns** refer to the subject:

Aimee talks to *herself*.

Bert prepared *himself* for the interview.

Myself, ourselves, yourself, yourselves, himself, herself, itself, and *themselves* are reflexive pronouns.

Indefinite pronouns do not indicate a specific individual:

Everyone saw the winning play.

Nobody likes going to the dentist.

All, another, any, anybody, anyone, anything, both, each, either, everybody, everyone, everything, few, most, much, neither, nobody, none, no one, one, somebody, someone, and *something* are indefinite pronouns. (Some of these words can also be used as adjectives.)

Demonstrative pronouns single out or point to some particular thing:

That was a mean trick!

These are my best sneakers.

This, that, these, and *those* are demonstrative pronouns.

Interrogative pronouns are used to ask questions:

Which is your favorite pizza topping?

What do you think?

Who, whom, which, what, and *whose* are interrogative pronouns.

Relative pronouns introduce dependent noun or adjective clauses (more about clauses later in this chapter):

The day *that* it rained I caught a cold.

Who, whom, whose, which, that, and *what* are relative pronouns.

Note that several pronouns (*who, whom, whose, which, that, what*) appear in more than one list. How these pronouns are used determines their particular classification. (Further information about correct pronoun use is provided in Chapter 19.)

Adjectives

Adjectives modify nouns—that is, they describe or limit them. In the following pairs, the underlined word is an adjective, and the second word is the noun is modifies:

red ball	crowded store
sleepy man	empty bucket
beautiful sunset	aged man

Note also that nouns may act as adjectives and modify other nouns. Although the underlined words in the next examples function as adjectives, they are still considered nouns:

Styrofoam cup	tuna sandwich
Sunday clothes	peace symbol

(For more on using adjectives, see Chapter 20.)

Adverbs

Adverbs describe or limit verbs, adjectives, other adverbs, or (rarely) entire sentences. Many adverbs end in *-ly,* but some common adverbs, such as *always, soon, rather, very, not, never,* and *well,* do not. The adverbs are underlined in the following examples:

Tamar walked quickly toward me. [*adverb modifies verb* walked]

She seemed unusually glad to see me. [*adverb modifies adjective* glad]

She had not really wanted to take the class. [*adverb* not *modifies adverb* really, *which modifies verb phrase* had wanted]

Apparently, she hopes to borrow my notes on Mondays. [*adverb modifies whole sentence*]

Prepositions

Prepositions indicate specific relationships between nouns or pronouns in a sentence. Often, but not always, prepositions define direction, location, or time. Prepositions are used with nouns (and their adjectives) to form **prepositional phrases**. *Under the stairs, with the boxes,* and *of old clothes* are prepositional phrases. In each case, the preposition begins the phrase. Here is a list of common one-word prepositions:

about	as	beyond	inside	out	under
above	at	by	into	over	until
across	before	down	like	past	up
after	behind	during	near	regarding	with
against	below	except	of	since	without
along	beneath	for	off	through	
among	beside	from	on	to	
around	between	in	onto	toward	

Some prepositions themselves are phrases:

according to	except for	in place of	next to
because of	in addition to	in spite of	out of
due to	in front of	instead of	with regard to

A prepositional phrase always has at least one noun or pronoun as the object of the preposition. In the following examples, the entire prepositional phrase is underlined:

According to your recent letter, the orders never arrived. [*The preposition is* according to; *the noun* letter *is the object of the preposition;* your *and* recent *are adjectives modifying the noun.*]

The coffee chain has opened new stores at my school, near my house, and in the train station. [*This example shows three prepositional phrases in a row.*]

For us, twenty dollars is a lot of money. [*The pronoun* us *is the object of the preposition.*]

→ **COMMON ERROR: WRONG OR MISSING PREPOSITION**

Many prepositions are small words, and when working quickly, we may not pay much attention to them. This is probably why a wrong or missing preposition is a very common student writing error.

MISSING PREPOSITION	Mo went the store. [*missing* to]
WRONG PREPOSITION	I took that part *out in* the story.
WRONG PREPOSITION	I took that part *out from* the story.

To check for incorrect prepositions, slowly reread your draft to be sure that each preposition you used is appropriate (*I went* to *Texas* rather than *I went at Texas*; *I took that part* out of *the story* rather than out in *the story*). To check for missing prepositions, read your draft aloud. Reading silently, we often mentally supply words that are not actually on the page. But reading *Mo went the store* aloud makes it obvious that something has been omitted.

Conjunctions

Conjunctions link words, phrases, and clauses. In so doing, conjunctions indicate logical relationships. For example, the conjunction *but* indicates a reversal or a contradiction, whereas *and* indicates an addition. There are four kinds of conjunctions. (The use of conjunctions to join clauses is discussed later in this chapter.)

Coordinating conjunctions and correlative conjunctions link grammatically equivalent words, phrases, or clauses. The most common coordinating conjunctions are *and, but, for, nor, or, so,* and *yet.*

> In sixth grade, I ate tuna *and* pickle sandwiches for lunch. [*The conjunction* and *links two modifying nouns* — tuna *and* pickle — *which both modify* sandwiches.]
>
> She would have been happy with a trip to California *or* a cruise. [*The conjunction* or *links two nouns.*]
>
> Susan enjoys softball, *but* basketball is her favorite sport. [*The conjunction* but *works with a comma to link two independent clauses.*]

Correlative conjunctions join equal elements and come in pairs. The most common correlative conjunctions are *both . . . and, either . . . or, neither . . . nor, not only . . . but also,* and *whether . . . or.*

> *Both* Monica *and* Suki will graduate this term. [*The correlative conjunctions link two nouns.*]
>
> *Either* I mow the lawn now, *or* I take a nap. [*The correlative conjunctions work with a comma to link two independent clauses.*]

Subordinating conjunctions introduce dependent clauses and link them to independent clauses. A dependent clause has a subject and a predicate but cannot stand alone as a sentence; an independent clause can stand alone (see "Clauses," later in this chapter). The most common subordinating conjunctions are these:

after	even though	since	unless
although	if	so that	until
as	in order that	than	when
because	once	that	where

I understood the material *once* I reread it carefully. [*The subordinating conjunction* once *introduces a dependent clause.*]

Although I enjoy writing, I also find it hard work. [*The subordinating conjunction* although *introduces a dependent clause.*]

Some words — *before*, *since*, and *until*, for example — can function as prepositions. When they introduce whole clauses, they are functioning as subordinating conjunctions. When they precede only nouns (plus any adjectives) or pronouns, they are functioning as prepositions. Compare these examples:

After the lecture, I understood the material more clearly. [After *is a preposition here;* lecture *is the object of the preposition;* After the lecture *is a prepositional phrase.*]

After I heard the lecture, I understood the material more clearly. [After *is a subordinating conjunction here; it introduces the dependent clause* After I heard the lecture.]

In contrast to subordinating conjunctions, **conjunctive adverbs** link independent clauses, each of which could stand alone as a sentence. These conjunctions act as adverbs, describing or limiting the second independent clause. Here are some common conjunctive adverbs:

besides	moreover	similarly
finally	nevertheless	then
however	next	therefore

Pokey is an outside cat; *nevertheless*, she greets me at the front door each evening.

The political struggle pitted North against South; *however*, economic factors brought the South to a crisis.

The political struggle pitted North against South; economic factors brought the South to a crisis, *however*.

Notice that the two clauses joined by a conjunctive adverb must be separated by a semicolon, not just a comma. In addition, unlike other conjunctions, conjunctive adverbs can be moved to different positions within a clause.

Interjections

Interjections express emotions or exclamations. They often stand alone. Even when they are part of a sentence, interjections are not grammatically related to the rest of the sentence. Common interjections are *Oh! No! Hey!* and *Yeah!* Interjections are most frequently used in informal writing and dialogue:

> "*Hey!* Wait for me!"

> "Ouch!"

The parts of a sentence: Subjects and predicates (31a, 31c)

As you have seen, every word in a sentence can be talked about as a part of speech. The words of a sentence can also be talked about according to how they function in that sentence. But before we go further, we need a definition of the word *sentence*.

→ **COMMON ERROR: FAULTY SENTENCE STRUCTURE**

What is a sentence? A **sentence** is a grammatically complete group of words that expresses a thought. To be grammatically complete, a sentence must contain at least two structural parts: a **subject**, which identifies what the sentence is about, and a **predicate**, which asserts or asks something about the subject. A subject and a predicate that combine to express a complete thought can also be called an **independent clause**.

The simplest sentences consist of a one-word subject and a one-word predicate—for example, *Marcellus sneezed*. Here the subject is *Marcellus*, and the predicate is *sneezed*. By now you recognize that *Marcellus* is a noun and *sneezed* is a verb. In this sentence, then, *Marcellus* is a **simple subject**—a noun acting as the sentence subject—and *sneezed* is a **simple predicate**—a verb acting as the sentence predicate.

Of course, most sentences contain more than two words. Consider a sentence such as this one: *The drawing shows her latest design*. The nouns are *drawing* and *design*. *Shows* is the verb. You should also be able to identify *the drawing* as the subject of the sentence and *shows her latest design* as the predicate.

SUBJECT	PREDICATE

The drawing shows her latest design.

A predicate that contains more than a verb, such as *shows her latest design*, is a **complete predicate**. Similarly, a **complete subject** contains more than a simple, one-word subject. It might be *the drawing on the north wall by the door* instead of just *the drawing*.

Marcellus sneezed is a complete sentence, but the simple subject–simple predicate pattern of *Marcellus sneezed* does not always present a complete thought or action. *The train was* and *Abby caught* follow the same pattern as *Marcellus sneezed*, but clearly we need more information in order to make the thought, idea, or action complete.

Four grammatical elements can be added to the predicate to complete the meaning of a sentence. They are subject complements, direct objects, indirect objects, and object complements.

A **subject complement** is a noun, noun phrase, adjective, or adjective phrase that is used with a linking verb to describe the subject of the sentence (more about linking verbs later in this section). In the compound sentence *The train was an express, but it was late*, both the noun phrase *an express* and the adjective *late* act as subject complements.

A **direct object** receives the action of the verb. In *Abby caught the ball*, the direct object is *the ball*; it is the thing that is *caught*. Direct objects typically answer the question *what?* or *whom?* (*What* was caught? *The ball* was caught.) *Edward slapped Mark.* (Edward slapped *whom*? Edward slapped *Mark.*)

An **indirect object** receives the action of the verb indirectly. It is used along with a direct object — never without one — when subject, verb, and direct object do not tell the whole story. In the sentence *Rafael made Lisa breakfast*, *Lisa* is the indirect object of *made*, and *breakfast* is the direct object. Without *Lisa*, this sentence would tell a different story.

An **object complement** relates to the object in a sentence the way a subject complement relates to the subject: it describes the object, particularly with respect to the state of being that the verb establishes. Consider the sentence *Rafael's thoughtfulness made Lisa very happy. Very happy* is the object complement of *Lisa*; it describes the effect resulting from the action of the verb.

Common sentence patterns

The sentences you have just read follow patterns that are used over and over in English. The patterns are as follows:

subject + verb + subject complement

subject + verb + direct object

subject + verb + indirect object + direct object

subject + verb + direct object + object complement

Not all sentences you write are required to follow these patterns; however, it may help you to refer to them during revision of your own writing if you have trouble deciding whether a sentence is complete or if you question whether you have arranged sentence elements in the correct order. Be aware, for example, that indirect objects and object complements are always used with direct objects, never by themselves. (*Rafael's thoughtfulness made Lisa* and *Rafael made very happy* are not complete sentences.)

The common patterns, and the patterns of most complete English sentences, boil down to subject + verb + information to complete and specify the action of the verb. Thus, in our earlier examples, *late* and *an express* both answer the question *the train was what?* and *the ball* answers the question *Abby caught what?* The *type* of verb used in a sentence often determines, at least in part, which of the four predicate elements (subject complement, direct object, indirect object, and object complement) must follow it.

Verb type and sentence structure

A verb can be classified as one of three types: linking, transitive, and intransitive. **Linking verbs** generally require subject complements, **transitive verbs** generally require direct objects, and **intransitive verbs** generally require neither (intransitive verbs are the ones used in the sentence pattern subject + verb; *sneezed* in *Marcellus sneezed* is an intransitive verb). Let us look at these types of verbs and how they help to determine sentence structure.

■ Sentence Structures Using Linking Verbs

Linking verbs act exactly as their name implies: they link a subject with a subject complement.

> The actress *was* Selma Hayek.
>
> Coffee *is* a beverage.

In each case, the subject complement (*Selma Hayek, a beverage*) is a noun or noun phrase that renames the subject (*the actress, coffee*). Nouns used in this way are called **predicate nouns**.

When the subject complement describes rather than renames the sentence subject, we call it a **predicate adjective**:

> The actress was *beautiful*.
>
> Coffee is *hot*.

Those examples use *is* or *was*—forms of the verb *be*. Other verbs, such as *feel*, *look*, *taste*, *seem*, *appear*, and *become*, can also function as linking verbs. These verbs can almost always be interchanged with a *be* verb without substantially affecting sentence meaning. For example, *The actress looked beautiful* can become *The actress was beautiful*.

■ Sentence Structures Using Transitive and Intransitive Verbs

Consider this sentence: *The door opened slowly.* You should be able to identify *the door* as the subject of the sentence and *opened* as the verb. You should also be able to identify *slowly* as an adverb modifying the verb *opened*.

Now consider this sentence: *Reynaldo opened the door.* Here, *Reynaldo* is the subject, and *opened* is the verb. But what is *the door*? It is the direct object of the verb *opened*. In this second sentence, *opened* is a transitive verb. The action implied in the word *opened* is transferred to something, in this case, *the door*. Transitive verbs transfer their action to a noun other than the sentence subject. That other noun is called the direct object of the verb.

In the following sentences, transitive verbs are underlined once, and direct objects are underlined twice. Remember, direct objects typically answer the question *what?* or *whom?*

> Stevie replaced the ink cartridge. [*replaced what? the* cartridge]
>
> The elms dropped their leaves. [*dropped what? their* leaves]

Sergio <u>kissed</u> <u>Abigail</u>. [*kissed whom?* Abigail]

How does *opened* function in the sentence *The door opened slowly?* There, *opened* is an intransitive verb. It does not take an object. It cannot transfer its action to the noun *door* because that noun is already the sentence subject.

Next, consider this sentence: *The lioness gave her cubs food.* You should be able to identify *lioness* as the noun subject and *gave* as the verb—in this case, a transitive verb. What did the lioness give? She gave *food*; *food* is the direct object. Who received the food? *Her cubs.* In this example, *cubs* is the indirect object of the verb *gave.* Note that if a sentence contains both a direct object and an indirect object, these elements appear in a typical order: subject, verb, indirect object, direct object.

Look at another example:

SUBJECT	VERB	INDIRECT OBJECT	DIRECT OBJECT
John	sent	Kate	a birthday card.

There, *a* and *birthday* modify the direct object, *card.* Indirect objects in such sentences can easily be converted to prepositional phrases. For example, *John sent Kate a birthday card* becomes *John sent a birthday card to Kate.* In the second sentence, *Kate* is the object of the preposition *to.* One way to identify the indirect object is to see whether the sentence can be rephrased so that the possible indirect object becomes the object of a preposition.

Because pronouns frequently replace nouns, pronouns can also act as direct objects and indirect objects:

SUBJECT	VERB	INDIRECT OBJECT	DIRECT OBJECT
You	should give	me	that.

Direct objects and indirect objects are never parts of a prepositional phrase:

SUBJECT	VERB	PREPOSITIONAL PHRASE	PREPOSITIONAL PHRASE
They	flew	to Africa	for a vacation.

Phrases

A **phrase** is a group of words that are associated in some grammatical way but lack both a subject and a predicate. There are six types of phrases: noun phrases, verb phrases, prepositional phrases, verbal phrases, absolute phrases, and appositive phrases.

A **noun phrase** consists of a noun and all its modifiers. *The blue sweater, an exciting day,* and *a moderately priced air conditioner* are noun phrases. (For more on noun modifiers, see the earlier section on adjectives.)

A **verb phrase** consists of a verb and its auxiliaries. (For more on auxiliaries, see the earlier section on verbs.) *Are composed, must arrive,* and *should have been explained* are all verb phrases.

A **prepositional phrase** consists of a preposition plus one or more nouns or pronouns and their modifiers. (For more on prepositions and prepositional phrases, see the earlier section on prepositions.) The preposition comes first, and the nouns (or pronouns) plus any modifiers complete the phrase: *to Grady's store, beneath her, for the next assignment, after our supper.*

Prepositional phrases act as either adjectives or adverbs, depending on what they modify. Consider this example: *In the morning, she will call.* The prepositional phrase *in the morning* modifies the verb *will call*, specifying when this action will take place. Because it modifies a verb, this prepositional phrase acts as an adverb. Now, consider this example: *Your directions to the store were clear.* The prepositional phrase *to the store* modifies the noun *directions*, specifying which directions. Since it modifies a noun, this prepositional phrase acts as an adjective.

Verbal phrases are phrases made from verbs that function as nouns, adjectives, or adverbs. The three types of verbal phrases are infinitives, gerunds, and participles.

Infinitive phrases are made by adding *to* before the verb. Thus *to run, to sleep,* and *to enjoy the ball game* are infinitive phrases. Here are some more examples:

> *To sleep late on Saturdays* is a habit at our house. [*This infinitive phrase includes a prepositional phrase; the entire infinitive phrase functions as a noun and acts as the subject of the sentence.*]

> *To draw plans* is a good way *to begin.* [*This example contains two infinitive phrases. The first functions as a noun and acts as the subject of the sentence. The second modifies the noun* way *and so acts as an adjective.*]

> She coughed a little *to clear her throat.* [*Here, the infinitive phrase modifies the verb* coughed *and so acts as an adverb.*]

Be careful to distinguish infinitives from prepositional phrases. The word *to* is used to introduce them both. In a prepositional phrase, *to* is followed by a noun or pronoun; in an infinitive, *to* is followed by a verb.

> Though busy, Harry found time *to run.* [*infinitive as adjective modifying* time]

> Sam ran *to the store.* [*prepositional phrase*]

Gerunds are formed by adding *-ing* to a verb for use as a noun. (When the *-ing* form of a verb acts as an adjective, it is called a participial phrase; more on participles in a moment.) A **gerund phrase** consists of a gerund and its modifiers. Since gerunds and gerund phrases always act as nouns, they may occur in any sentence position that nouns would occupy. Here are examples:

> *Running every other day* is good exercise. [*The gerund phrase acts as the subject of the sentence.*]

> Alicia enjoys *running every day.* [*Now the gerund phrase is functioning as the direct object of the verb* enjoys. *Enjoys what? Enjoys* running every day.]

Participial phrases may be either in the present tense or in the past. **Present participles** are formed by adding *-ing*; **past participles** are usually formed by adding *-ed* or *-en*. Some past participles (*gone*, for example) have irregular forms. All participles function as adjectives. Note that the present participial form and the gerund form are identical: both are made by adding *-ing* to the verb. What differentiates gerunds and participles is their function. Gerunds always act as nouns; participles always act as adjectives. Here are examples of both past and present participles:

> *Tired by a long hike*, the dog slept before the fire. [*The past participial phrase acts as an adjective modifying* dog.]

> The stereo *blaring next door* made sleep difficult. [*The present participial phrase acts as an adjective modifying* stereo.]

Note that participial phrases may either precede or follow the nouns they modify.

An **absolute phrase** is formed by combining a noun or pronoun and a participial phrase. Absolutes modify an entire sentence and are always set off from the rest of the sentence by commas. Here are two examples:

> The big cat waited, *its nostrils flaring slightly.*

> *Feet aching*, I finally crossed the finish line.

Absolute phrases can often be moved in the sentence without destroying the meaning: *Its nostrils flaring slightly*, the big cat waited.

An **appositive phrase** is a noun phrase that renames the noun that precedes it. An appositive phrase is always set off by commas. Here are two examples:

> Victor Atiyeh, *a former governor*, lives in Portland. [*This appositive phrase consists of a noun*, governor, *its article*, a, *and its modifying adjective*, former.]

> The police officer fed Scarlet, *the station-house mascot.*

Clauses

There are two types of clauses: **independent clauses**, which can stand alone as sentences, and **dependent clauses**, which cannot stand alone. Clauses always have subjects and predicates. *The weather forecast calls for snow* and *I'll start the fire* are both independent clauses; they are also sentences. *Although the weather forecast calls for snow* and *that I'll start the fire* are both dependent clauses, but they are not sentences.

By themselves, dependent clauses are sentence fragments; they do not express a complete thought. Some dependent clauses are introduced by subordinating conjunctions:

> *After the snow stops*, Deddrick and I will shovel the driveway. [*dependent clause introduced by the subordinating conjunction* after]

Whenever we go outside, the neighbor's dog barks at us. [*dependent clause introduced by the subordinating conjunction* whenever]

(For more on subordinating conjunctions, see the section on conjunctions in this chapter.) Other dependent clauses are introduced by **relative pronouns** such as *who*, *which*, and *that*. (For more on relative pronouns, see the section on pronouns in this chapter.)

The dog *that I chose at the pound* has become a member of the family. [*dependent clause introduced by* that *and acting as adjective modifying the subject* dog]

Dependent clauses may also function as nouns, adjectives, or adverbs. Here are some examples:

We have agreed *that we should arrive early*. [*dependent clause introduced by* that *and acting as a noun — in this case, the direct object of the verb* agreed]

Everyone *who works here* has trouble getting a good Internet connection. [*dependent clause introduced by* who *and acting as an adjective modifying the noun* everyone]

When I am confident, tests do not bother me. [*dependent clause introduced by the subordinating conjunction* when *and acting as an adverb modifying the main verb* do not bother]

When I am confident that I will pass, tests do not bother me. [*Here are two dependent clauses, one embedded inside another.* When I am confident that I will pass *is an adverbial clause modifying the main verb* do not bother. *Within that adverbial clause is another adverbial clause,* that I will pass, *which modifies the predicate adjective* confident.]

Dependent clauses must be coupled with independent clauses in order to make a complete sentence.

REVIEW

- Dependent clauses are always introduced by a subordinating word.
- Dependent clauses always contain a subject and a predicate.
- Dependent clauses must be combined with an independent clause to form a full sentence.

Classifying sentences (31d)

Sentences can be classified according to both function and form. There are four basic sentence functions: **declarative sentences** state facts or opinions, **interrogative sentences** ask questions, **imperative sentences** give commands, and **exclamatory sentences** express strong feeling.

Most of the sentences in this book are declarative sentences. [*declarative sentence*]

Why is English such a curious language? [*interrogative sentence*]

Think of language as a set of tools. [*imperative sentence*]

At last I am beginning to understand this language! [*exclamatory sentence*]

Sentence form is determined by the type and number of clauses in a sentence. (For more on clauses, see the preceding section.) A sentence that consists of a single independent clause (*Jack sneezed*) is a **simple sentence**.

A **compound sentence** consists of two or more simple sentences—that is, two or more independent clauses: *Jack sneezed, and the dog jumped.* The independent clauses that make up a compound sentence are linked by commas and coordinating conjunctions (see also Chapter 31) or by a semicolon (see also Chapter 32).

A **complex sentence** consists of one independent clause and at least one dependent clause. When the dependent clause opens the sentence (as it does in this one), a comma is used to separate it from the independent clause. No comma is necessary when the dependent clause follows the independent one (as in this sentence).

A **compound-complex sentence** contains at least two independent clauses and at least one dependent clause.

REVIEW

The independent clauses are underlined.

- Simple sentence (one independent clause):

  A flicker sometimes sings in our yard.

- Compound sentence (two or more independent clauses):

  A flicker sometimes sings in our yard, and the neighbor's cat watches it.

- Complex sentence (one independent clause + at least one dependent clause):

  Some afternoons a flicker sings in our yard while the neighbor's cat watches.

- Compound-complex sentence (more than one independent clause + at least one dependent clause):

  When the sun comes out, I open the windows, and fresh air fills the rooms.

To understand the form of a question, convert the question into a statement. Once you have done so, the clauses will be easy to identify. Here is an example:

EXAMPLE   Will Ann pick me up after her racquetball lesson is over?

REVISED AS A STATEMENT	Ann will pick me up after her racquetball lesson is over.
INDEPENDENT CLAUSE	Ann will pick me up
DEPENDENT CLAUSE	after her racquetball lesson is over

The original question is a complex sentence.

EXERCISE 16.1   VERBS

NAME _____ **DATE** _____

A. **Underline the verbs in the following sentences.**

  1. We <u>enjoyed</u> ourselves in Boston.
  2. The weather <u>was</u> glorious in Palm Beach.
  3. I <u>choose</u> broccoli over asparagus.
  4. The alarm clock on the dresser <u>rings</u> at 6:15.
  5. My mother <u>hung</u> the clothes on the line.
  6. <u>Call</u> the building superintendent before dark.

B. **Underline the verbs and their auxiliaries in the following sentences.**

  1. People <u>have moved</u> south in record numbers.
  2. They <u>may prefer</u> a milder salsa.
  3. My, how your tomatoes <u>have grown</u>!
  4. The next match <u>will be</u> more challenging.
  5. The cleaning crew <u>has not washed</u> the floor.
  6. Nobody in my class <u>can understand</u> this story.

EXERCISE 16.2 NOUNS

NAME _____ **DATE** _____

Underline all the nouns in the short paragraph below; remember not to confuse nouns and pronouns. The first noun has been underlined for you.

In the <u>middle</u> of a cold night in February when Siobhan was twelve years old, she awoke to the sound of fire engines and the smell of smoke. Her father rushed into the room she shared with her sister, Angela, and told them to get up. "The building is on fire," he said hoarsely. Angela, a nine-year-old, began to cry, so Siobhan helped her find her kitten, who had been sleeping on the bed. They rushed down the stairway, which fortunately was not blocked by smoke or flames. The whole family — Siobhan, Angela, their parents, and the kitten — reached the safety of the cold, dark street. As it turned out, the building did not burn down, and only two apartments were damaged. Siobhan and her family were back in their home a few days later. However, Siobhan never forgot how afraid she had felt that night, and when she moved to her own apartment seven years later, she installed smoke detectors in every room.

.3

EXERCISE 16.3   PRONOUNS

NAME _____ **DATE** _____

First, underline all the pronouns in each of the following sentences. Then, in parentheses after each sentence, use the following symbols to indicate the types of pronouns being used: PER for personal; REF for reflexive; IND for indefinite; DEM for demonstrative; INT for interrogative; REL for relative. The first sentence has been done for you.

1. That cup, which you found on the coffee table, is mine. (DEM, REL, PER, PER)

2. He ran for office because somebody asked him to. (PER, IND, PER)

3. Some of them made huge donations. (IND, PER)

4. My son, who is a vegan himself, can suggest restaurants for you and your family. (REL, REF, PER)

5. To whom is she speaking? (REL, PER)

6. Everyone told him to ignore the problem, but he could not keep his concerns to himself. (IND, PER, PER, PER, REL) REF

7. Nobody saw the bear, but the ranger said it was dangerous. (IND, PER)

8. Which of these should I choose? (INT, DEM, PER)

9. Our paper was assigned on Monday. (PER)

10. Her supervisor evaluated her work after six weeks on the job. (PER, PER)

11. The recorded voice repeated itself, saying, "Your call is important to us." (REF, PER, PER)

12. Terri felt tired after she worked that double shift. (PER, DEM)

217

EXERCISE 16.4   ADJECTIVES

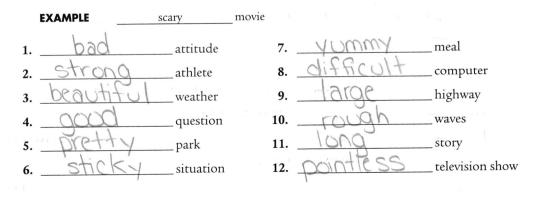

NAME _____   **DATE** _____

Provide an appropriate adjective for each noun below.

EXAMPLE _____ scary _____ movie

1. _____bad_____ attitude
2. _____strong_____ athlete
3. _____beautiful_____ weather
4. _____good_____ question
5. _____pretty_____ park
6. _____sticky_____ situation

7. _____yummy_____ meal
8. _____difficult_____ computer
9. _____large_____ highway
10. _____rough_____ waves
11. _____long_____ story
12. _____pointless_____ television show

EXERCISE 16.5 ADVERBS

NAME _____ **DATE** 8/17/13

Underline the adverbs in the following passage.

Psychologists have (long) suggested that the pace of our lives has quickened <u>dramatically</u>. This (extremely) busy pace means we have little time to deal with normal daily emotions. Instead, we finish one task so that we can <u>quickly</u> move to the next. Our workdays often become <u>increasingly</u> frantic efforts to cross off another task on our lists of things to do. If we spend all week at such a hectic pace, we probably have trouble truly relaxing on weekends. Instead of <u>leisurely</u> taking that long walk, we find ourselves walking at an <u>uncomfortably</u> brisk pace as we replay the little slights and angers and frustrations of the week. But since this makes us uncomfortable, when we get home we get busy again, keeping ourselves so <u>fully</u> absorbed in the present that we don't notice how rushed our lives have become. The solution to this, psychologists repeatedly suggest, lies in learning to pay attention to now, to find some pleasure and joy in the process of whatever we're doing.

NAME _____ **DATE** _____

Underline the prepositional phrases in the following paragraph. Circle the prepositions. The first phrase has been done for you.

Our newspapers and magazines often report problems (with) elementary education. Some of these articles argue that because class sizes have increased, teachers give attention only to disruptive students. Even students who are working below grade level may not get enough help from the overloaded teacher. Other writers believe that schools located in areas where poverty and crime and joblessness set the tone cannot by themselves overcome such problems. When students arrive in the morning without breakfast, when they go home to crowded living conditions that make doing homework difficult, and when the adults in their lives have little interest in education, then, ask these writers, how can we expect a single teacher to succeed?

EXERCISE 16.7 CONJUNCTIONS AND INTERJECTIONS

NAME _____ DATE _____

Read the following sentences. Underline conjunctions once and interjections twice. Write COORD (for coordinating), CORREL (for correlative), or SUBORD (for subordinating) in parentheses after each sentence to indicate the types of conjunctions being used. The first sentence has been done for you.

1. Hey! Unless you turn the oven on, the cake won't bake! (SUBORD)

2. Before the meeting begins, we need a strategy to enlist volunteers.

3. Whoops! I broke a cup and saucer.

4. Even though I've had a driver's license for forty years, I didn't drive regularly until recently.

5. Neither the manager nor the assistant manager approved the new schedule.

6. He not only made my problems worse but also laughed at my predicament.

7. While I was traveling with my banjo on my knee, I met Susannah, and Clementine joined us later.

8. Dee is arranging her schedule so that she can chair next week's meeting.

9. The receptionist was friendly, but he did not know if I got the job.

10. Howard left the company and got a teaching degree, for he wanted to help children.

11. You performed last night and still passed the test? Wow!

12. When she asked the former mayor about his plans, he admitted a wish to run for president.

EXERCISE 16.8   THE PARTS OF SPEECH

Identify the part of speech of each underlined word as it functions in the sentence.

> **EXAMPLE**   The <u>car</u> <u>door</u> slammed <u>into</u> the utility pole.
>
> car: adjective   door: noun   into: preposition

1. Advertisers both reflect <u>what</u> Americans want and <u>try</u> to convince <u>us</u> to want <u>things</u>.

   _____

   _____

2. Today's ads insist that Americans <u>long</u> to be <u>young</u> and cool.

   _____

   _____

3. And as the <u>frequency</u> of <u>movie</u> ads and music ads <u>suggests</u>, we <u>also</u> <u>want</u> entertainment and relief <u>from</u> stress.

   _____

   _____

4. Advertisers try to accommodate us <u>by</u> offering films with attractive stars and <u>very</u> <u>little</u> plot.

   _____

   _____

5. <u>In</u> addition, advertisements suggest <u>that</u> we <u>consistently</u> worry about <u>our</u> health.

   _____

   _____

6. <u>So</u> we buy the <u>latest</u> herbal extract or the latest all-natural vitamin <u>supplements</u> and ask our doctors about <u>prescription</u> drugs we've seen advertised.

   _____

   _____

7. If you believe the automobile advertisements, Americans also have a great desire to drive up cliffs and through wilderness areas.

_____

_____

8. On commercial television, America appears to be populated with sexy, cool young people driving expensive vehicles in the middle of nowhere as they consume soft drinks and beer and take prescription medicine for their allergies.

_____

_____

9. Thinking about all these ads makes one wonder.

_____

_____

10. How many people have learned to want things from watching commercials, and how many are as happy as the people in the ads once they get the product?

_____

_____

EXERCISE 16.9 SUBJECTS AND PREDICATES

NAME _____ **DATE** _____

Underline the subject of each sentence once and the predicate twice.

> **EXAMPLE**   <u>Life</u> <u><u>is just a bowl of cherries</u></u>.

1. Everyone needs someone to lean on.

2. Some developers, fearing nature lovers, set aside acres to be forever wild.

3. America's ability to prepare a new generation of scientists and mathematicians remains to be seen.

4. Migratory butterflies born in northern climates travel to their ancestors' southern homes in late summer.

5. Bad spellers such as my uncle are thankful for computer programs that can check spelling.

6. Even writing a celebrated novel, which may well be forgotten by future generations, is no guarantee of lasting fame.

7. Television talk shows have become as popular as soap operas.

8. Cookie crumbs all over the floor marked the end of Anthony's experiment with the Atkins diet.

9. Television shows may be the United States's most successful export.

10. Schoolchildren need safe classrooms in which to learn.

EXERCISE 16.10 DIRECT AND INDIRECT OBJECTS

NAME _____ **DATE** _____

A. Underline each direct object once and each indirect object twice. If a sentence has no direct or indirect object, leave the sentence as is. The first sentence has been done for you.

1. Luis poured his <u>coffee</u> into a <u>flamingo pink cup</u>.

2. Jelly beans give Louise hives.

3. The reporter asked a difficult question.

4. The stranger tossed me his overcoat.

5. The personnel department will give them information on Monday about possible layoffs.

6. His voice drives me crazy.

7. Digital technology gives listeners almost flawless sound.

8. My eighteen-year-old niece whined and sulked throughout her entire visit.

9. That new haircut suits you.

10. Jennie gave the dog Mike's dinner.

11. Information about internships was sent to all business majors at the beginning of the semester.

12. The service never picked up my package for next-day delivery.

B. Using the verbs provided, construct pairs of sentences, one sentence containing an indirect object and one converting that indirect object to the object of a preposition.

> **EXAMPLE** Verb: sent
> **a.** _indir. obj._ The president sent his secretary a memo. _____
> **b.** _obj. of prep._ The president sent a memo to his secretary. _____

1. Verb: gave

   a. _indir. obj._ _____

   _____

   b. _obj. of prep._ _____

   _____

2. Verb: sang

   a. *indir. obj.* _____

   _____

   b. *obj. of prep.* _____

   _____

3. Verb: owed

   a. *indir. obj.* _____

   _____

   b. *obj. of prep.* _____

   _____

4. Verb: wrote

   a. *indir. obj.* _____

   _____

   b. *obj. of prep.* _____

   _____

5. Verb: offered

   a. *indir. obj.* _____

   _____

   b. *obj. of prep.* _____

   _____

EXERCISE 16.11 LINKING VERBS AND SUBJECT COMPLEMENTS

NAME _____ **DATE** _____

A. Using the subjects provided, construct sentences containing linking verbs followed by predicate adjectives. Use the linking verbs *is, are, was, were, feel(s), taste(s), look(s), seem(s),* **or** *become(s)*. **Do not use any verb more than once.**

EXAMPLE   cup   The cup was broken. _____

1. skyscraper _____

_____

2. taxes _____

_____

3. complaints _____

_____

4. bagel _____

_____

5. apartment _____

_____

B. Using the subjects provided, construct sentences containing linking verbs followed by predicate nouns. The predicate nouns may be modified by adjectives.

EXAMPLE   sand wedge   A sand wedge is a golf club. _____

1. this MP3 _____

_____

2. the shoes _____

_____

227

3. my morning wake-up call _____

_____

4. those dogs _____

_____

5. two children _____

_____

EXERCISE 16.12   LINKING, TRANSITIVE, AND INTRANSITIVE VERBS

NAME _____ **DATE** _____

A. The following items consist of a subject and a verb. Complete the thought of each by adding an indirect object and a direct object. Underline the direct object once and the indirect object twice.

EXAMPLE   The school sent   The school sent <u>Mary</u> <u>her grades</u>   .

1. The jury awarded _____.

2. The crossing guard gave _____.

3. The chef made _____.

4. An old woman told _____.

5. The dog brought _____.

6. Masio passed _____.

7. The catcher tossed _____.

8. My friend promised _____.

9. The children make _____.

10. The host served _____.

B. Indicate whether the underlined verb in each sentence is transitive, intransitive, or linking.

EXAMPLE   The race <u>started</u> with a pistol shot. intransitive _____

                             This lasagna <u>tastes</u> delicious. linking _____

                             You should <u>wear</u> a coat today. transitive _____

1. Out on the lake, the loon <u>called</u> for a long time. _____

2. Franklin <u>felt</u> sorry about their breakup. _____

3. My boss <u>requested</u> a meeting with me today. _____

4. Her roommate <u>built</u> those bookshelves. _____

5. You <u>seem</u> distracted this morning. _____

6. The mice <u>rustled</u> in the attic over my head. _____

7. This building <u>is</u> the oldest on the block. _____

8. The rubber duck <u>floated</u> in the water. _____

9. The committee <u>drafted</u> the new bill late last night. _____

10. The sales manager <u>has considered</u> your report very useful. _____

NAME _____ **DATE** _____

Add a prepositional phrase to each of the following sentences. Circle the phrase you add, use an arrow to indicate the word your phrase modifies, and indicate whether the phrase functions as an adjective or an adverb.

EXAMPLE   Carrie slept.

(After dinner,) Carrie slept. (adverb)

1. The medical information was not accurate.

_____

2. We made a U-turn.

_____

3. Hamid felt ill.

_____

4. The plumbers will repair that leak.

_____

5. I read the comics daily.

_____

6. Strict diets are troublesome.

_____

7. Luciano fell asleep.

_____

8. Traveling solo offers both rewards and dilemmas.

_____

9. Make sure you close the door.

_____

10. The sun sets early here.

_____

EXERCISE 16.14 INFINITIVES, GERUNDS, AND PARTICIPLES

NAME _____ **DATE** _____

Add the specified phrase to the given sentence.

    EXAMPLE   I discovered the book _____. (Add a past participial phrase with
                  hide to modify *book*.)
                  I discovered the book hidden under the couch. _____

1. _____ is to live. (Add an infinitive phrase with *run*.)

   _____

2. My cousins always enjoyed _____ . (Add a gerund phrase with *play*.)

   _____

3. The dog _____ is the liveliest. (Add a present participial phrase with *bark*.)

   _____

4. My family believes in _____ . (Add a gerund phrase with *recycle*.)

   _____

5. _____ , I arrived just as class began. (Add a present participial form of
   hurry to modify the subject *I*.)

   _____

6. Mira expects _____ . (Add an infinitive phrase with *win*.)

   _____

7. He wanted to go to medical school _____ . (Add an infinitive phrase with *make*.)

   _____

8. His favorite pastime was _____ . (Add a gerund phrase with *play*.)

   _____

9. _____, Zelda left the party. (Add a past participial phrase with *annoy.*)

_____

10. The baby, _____, must have been miserable. (Add a present participial phrase with *cry.*)

_____

11. _____, the house looked brand new. (Add a past participial phrase with *build.*)

_____

12. _____ made the politician smile. (Add a gerund phrase with *win.*)

_____

EXERCISE 16.15 PHRASES

NAME _____ **DATE** _____

Combine or add to the following sentences as specified.

> **EXAMPLE** Monica phoned Harold. (Add an infinitive phrase.)
>
> Monica phoned Harold to ask him for a date.

1. Liang emailed Randi. (Add only a prepositional phrase.)

   _____

   _____

2. Roshan finished his essay exam before the hour was over. (Add a present participial phrase.)

   _____

   _____

3. Contestants must think quickly under pressure. (Add an infinitive phrase.)

   _____

   _____

4. Olivia drives a minivan. She dislikes it. (Combine using a gerund phrase as a direct object.)

   _____

   _____

5. Havre, Malta, and Glasgow were named by the railroad. All these towns can be found in Montana. (Combine using a past participial phrase.)

   _____

   _____

6. Raccoons and skunks are common carriers of rabies. They tend to live close to human homes. (Combine using an appositive phrase.)

   _____

   _____

7. We saw a huge bear. (Add a prepositional phrase with a gerund as the object of the preposition.)

   _____

   _____

8. My ears were ringing, and my legs were aching. I left the concert and headed for my car. (Combine using an absolute phrase.)

   _____

   _____

9. Ned Hashim is a surgeon. He specializes in cardiology. He delivered a fascinating lecture. (Combine using an appositive phrase that contains a present participial phrase.)

   _____

   _____

10. Carlos plays Mozart. He loves the intricate pieces. (Combine using a gerund as a direct object.)

    _____

    _____

EXERCISE 16.16 DEPENDENT CLAUSES

NAME _____ **DATE** _____

Underline the dependent clauses in the following passages. The first dependent clause has been underlined for you.

Sometimes I wish <u>that I had gone to college right after high school</u>. I decided to work for a while instead, and after I started a job, I stayed there for fifteen years. When I was laid off after the dot-com boom ended, I chose to finally continue my education. I can't pretend that the adjustment was an easy one. For one thing, I had a husband and a twelve-year-old son who were counting on me. For another, I discovered that working was easier than going to school because at work someone had always told me what to do and when to do it. Although being older than most other students was often difficult, it also helped somewhat: I was more patient than in the past, and my business experience helped me excel in certain classes. Finally, I managed to get an associate of arts degree, which made me very proud.

Journal writing means quick writing. When I sit down to add something to my journal, I have no idea what I'll say. Maybe I'll praise the sunshine after days of fog. After another phone call requesting money or trying to sell me something, maybe I'll complain about that for two or three sentences. As I read over old entries, I see that in the last month I've talked about airplane travel, music that I like to listen to, my frustration with technology that doesn't work, the sound of rain on the roof at night, and the people who ride my bus. Although most writing takes time and effort, journal writing is quick, and I don't usually revise it.

235

EXERCISE 16.17 FUNCTION AND FORM

NAME _____ **DATE** _____

Underline each independent clause once and each dependent clause twice in the following sentences. Then identify each sentence according to function and form.

> **EXAMPLE**   Will you take me to the store <u><u>when I get home from school?</u></u>
>
> Function: interrogative _____
> Form: complex _____

1. You can make me go to the concert, but you can't make me like it!

   Function: _____

   Form: _____

2. Jason finally scored a goal!

   Function: _____

   Form: _____

3. Has Sylvie heard the news that the Starlight Drive-In closed?

   Function: _____

   Form: _____

4. On Halloween night, the streets of my neighborhood are filled with miniature goblins.

   Function: _____

   Form: _____

5. Although the region had heavy snow this winter, the total is still below average.

   Function: _____

   Form: _____

6. While we were sleeping, Alec went to the store for us, and he even fixed us dinner!

   Function: _____

   Form: _____

7. I can still taste the delicious Cajun chicken that you prepared for us last night.

   Function: _____

   Form: _____

8. Try low-fat cheese instead.

   Function: _____

   Form: _____

9. The grocery store burned to the ground during the winter, and now the nearest market is miles away.

   Function: _____

   Form: _____

10. Ignore the protesters, or you won't be hired.

    Function: _____

    Form: _____

11. If the feeling moves me, I will go to the jeweler and I will buy a ring.

    Function: _____

    Form: _____

EXERCISE 16.18 CLAUSES

NAME _____ **DATE** _____

A. **Determine whether each of the following clauses is dependent (DEP) or independent (IND). Then make a sentence by adding a clause of your own.**

EXAMPLES   when lightning hit the roof DEP_____
(Make into a complex sentence.) Every bulb in the place blew out when lightning hit
the roof._____
the alarm sounded IND_____
(Make into a compound sentence.) The burglar shattered the window, and the alarm
sounded._____

1. choosing a major is difficult _____

   (Make into a compound sentence.) _____

   _____

2. the song that you suggested _____

   (Make into a complex sentence.) _____

   _____

3. when the police arrived _____

   (Make into a compound-complex sentence.) _____

   _____

4. the leaves fell _____

   (Make into a compound sentence.) _____

   _____

5. no public restrooms were available anywhere _____

   (Make into a complex sentence.) _____

   _____

6. the eggs all had cracks _____

   (Make into a compound sentence using any coordinating conjunction except *and*.) _____

   _____

7. the manager turned on the alarm system _____

(Make into a complex sentence.) _____

_____

8. before I had finished the test _____

(Make into a complex sentence.) _____

_____

9. because the new boy was too shy to speak _____

(Make into a compound-complex sentence.) _____

_____

10. the cat had vanished _____

(Make into a complex sentence.) _____

_____

B. Select six of the ten sentences you wrote in part A (all declarative sentences). Convert two of them to interrogative sentences, two to imperative sentences, and two to exclamatory sentences. You may shorten your original sentences to single independent clauses.

EXAMPLE   The burglar shattered the window, and the alarm sounded. [declarative sentence]

imperative sentence:

Tell me what time the burglar shattered the window.
_____

1. interrogative sentence:

_____

2. interrogative sentence:

_____

3. imperative sentence:

_____

4. imperative sentence:

_____

5. exclamatory sentence:

_____

6. exclamatory sentence:

_____

Verbs 17

Verbs identify action, occurrence, or state of being. They are crucial to our understanding of experience, and using them well is central to mastering English grammar. We use verbs to tell what we do: *sleep, wake, yawn, eat, talk*. We use them to tell what is or was or will be: *The sunshine* is *warm. The rain showers* felt *refreshing. The weekend* will be *partly cloudy*. As these examples indicate, we change a verb's form to make the verb agree grammatically with its subjects and to indicate tense, voice, and mood. Understanding how verbs work will allow you to select the form that communicates your meaning precisely.

VERBS IN EVERYDAY USE

Choose some kind of text that you read regularly—perhaps the sports section, a cookbook, a magazine, email, or a piece of your own writing—and have a look at the verbs. Jot down some interesting examples that convey lively action.

Verb forms (32a)

Verb mistakes are very common. They take many forms and represent any number of confusions about verb use that trouble the writers who make them. Some of the material that follows may be new to you, some of it may be things you once knew but have forgotten, and some of it will help you to become more sure of yourself as a verb user.

Except for *be*, all English verbs have five forms (*be* has eight). Examples of regular verbs follow (*be* and other irregular verbs deviate from this pattern and are discussed later in this chapter):

BASE FORM	-S FORM	PRESENT PARTICIPLE	PAST TENSE	PAST PARTICIPLE
cheer	cheers	cheering	cheered	cheered
type	types	typing	typed	typed
discuss	discusses	discussing	discussed	discussed

The **base form** is the form listed in the dictionary. Writers use this form to indicate action that is happening now—in the present. The base form (without *-s* or

-es) is used whenever the subject is a plural noun or the pronouns *I, we, you,* or *they.* Here are two examples:

Dogs *howl.* [*plural noun subject,* Dogs]

I *howl.* [*pronoun subject,* I]

The *-s* form is the base form plus *-s* or *-es.* The *-s* form is used whenever the subject preceding it is a singular third-person noun, as in *The dog howls.* (For spelling rules indicating whether to add *-s* or *-es,* see Chapter 15.) The *-s* form is also used with many indefinite pronouns (*everyone* and *someone,* for example). The *-s* forms are italicized in the following chart:

	SINGULAR	PLURAL
FIRST PERSON	I wish	we wish
SECOND PERSON	you wish	you wish
THIRD PERSON	he/she/it *wishes*	they wish
	the child *wishes*	children wish
	everyone *wishes*	

Some speakers use the base form instead of the *-s* form with a third-person singular subject. However, in all but the most informal writing, and especially in college writing, readers will expect the *-s* form with third-person singular subjects; when it is not present, they will assume the writer made a mistake.

DIALECT	She *live* in a high-rise apartment.
ACADEMIC	She *lives* in a high-rise apartment.

The **present participle** is made by adding *-ing* to the base form of a verb. By itself, a present participle is a verbal that can function as a modifier or as a noun (see the discussion of participial phrases and gerunds in Chapter 16). A participle can also be combined with an auxiliary verb (often some form of *be* or *have*) to indicate continuing or prolonged action. Here are two examples:

Barking all night, the dogs disturbed the neighbors. [*The present participle* barking *is a verbal; it modifies the dogs.*]

Those dogs *were barking* all night. [*The present participle* barking + *the auxiliary verb* were *form the main verb of the sentence.*]

The **past tense** indicates action that happened in the past, as in *Dogs barked.* As you can see, the past-tense form of regular verbs is made by adding *-ed* (again, more on regular and irregular verbs later in this chapter).

The **past participle** of regular verbs is identical to the past-tense form; irregular verbs have different past participles. Like present participles, the past participle is a verbal when used alone (see Chapter 16). Consider this example:

Encouraged by her own success, Erin *encouraged* Mary Lou and Jeanette to study harder.

The first *encouraged* is a past participle and a verbal; it modifies *Erin*. The second *encouraged* is the past-tense verb of the sentence; it tells us what Erin did.

Now consider this example:

Erin's parents *were encouraged* by her success.

Here the past participle *encouraged* is combined with the auxiliary verb *were* to form the main verb of the sentence (more on auxiliary verbs later in this chapter).

Using the verbs *be* and *have*

The verbs *be* and *have* are commonly used as auxiliaries and have several unexpected forms, so they require special attention.

The verb *be* has eight different forms:

BASE FORM	-S FORM	PRESENT PARTICIPLE	PAST TENSE	PAST PARTICIPLE
be	am	being	was	been
	are		were	
	is			

The verb *be* is one of two English verbs (the other is *have*) whose *-s* form does not consist of the base form plus *-s* or *-es*. This verb has three present-tense forms: *am, are,* and *is.*

	SINGULAR	PLURAL
FIRST PERSON	I *am* a Cubs fan.	We *are* Cubs fans.
SECOND PERSON	You *are* a Cubs fan.	You *are* Cubs fans.
THIRD PERSON	She *is* a Cubs fan.	They *are* Cubs fans.

Be also has two different past-tense forms: *was* and *were*:

	SINGULAR	PLURAL
FIRST PERSON	I *was* a Cubs fan.	We *were* Cubs fans.
SECOND PERSON	You *were* a Cubs fan.	You *were* Cubs fans.
THIRD PERSON	She *was* a Cubs fan.	They *were* Cubs fans.

The verb *have* presents fewer complications than *be*. The forms of *have* are as follows:

BASE FORM	-S FORM	PRESENT PARTICIPLE	PAST TENSE	PAST PARTICIPLE
have	has	having	had	had

Except in the third-person singular (notice the unexpected *-s* form *has*), the present tense is regular:

	SINGULAR	PLURAL
FIRST PERSON	I *have* an idea.	We *have* an idea.
SECOND PERSON	You *have* an idea.	You *have* an idea.
THIRD PERSON	She *has* an idea.	They *have* an idea.

Auxiliary verbs (32b)

We combine **auxiliary verbs** (also known as *helping verbs*) with other verb forms to create a variety of verb tenses and to indicate other meanings. The most common auxiliaries are forms of *be*, *have*, and *do*, as well as *shall* and *will*.

I *am working* hard. [*present progressive tense*]

Candice *has been working* hard. [*present perfect progressive tense*]

Carlo *will approve* of that concept. [*simple future tense*]

Aaron *does* not *enjoy* wearing a tie. [*simple present tense to form a negative*]

You *will have seen* your present by this time on Friday. [*future perfect tense*]

One commissioner *did* not *agree*. [*simple past tense to form a negative*]

Some speakers use the base form *be* as an auxiliary, but this usage is generally not appropriate in academic or formal writing. In addition, speakers sometimes leave out the auxiliary when academic or formal writing requires it:

DIALECT	I *be working* hard today.
	I *working* hard today.
ACADEMIC WRITING	I *am working* hard today.

In academic or formal writing situations, you should also be careful to distinguish between the contractions *doesn't* and *don't*. Use *doesn't* only with third-person singular subjects; use *don't* with everything else.

DIALECT	The character *don't understand* her situation.
ACADEMIC WRITING	The character *doesn't understand* her situation.
	The characters *don't understand* their situation.

A group of auxiliaries called **modal auxiliaries** are used to indicate necessity, obligation, or possibility. The most common modal auxiliaries are *can, could, may, might, must, ought, should,* and *would*.

I *could* not *work* harder.

Deshon *can substitute* for me.

The government *must address* issues of poverty.

The Mets *ought* to *win* tonight. [*The preposition* to *almost always accompanies* ought.]

The Mets *should have won* last night.

Regular and irregular verbs (32c)

Most English verbs are **regular verbs**: they form their past tense and past participle by adding *-d* or *-ed* to the base form. Several hundred English verbs do not follow this pattern. These **irregular verbs** are special cases to be memorized or looked up in a dictionary.

As you look over the following list of common irregular verbs, you will notice several patterns. Some irregular verbs change form by altering an interior vowel (as in *begin, began, begun*). Other irregular verbs do not change at all (as in *hurt, hurt, hurt*). Still others make quite radical changes (as in *go, went, gone*). For convenience, only the base form, past tense, and past participle are listed.

BASE FORM	PAST TENSE	PAST PARTICIPLE
arise	arose	arisen
awake	awoke/awaked	awoke/awoken/awaked
be	was/were	been
beat	beat	beaten
become	became	become
begin	began	begun
bite	bit	bitten/bit
blow	blew	blown
break	broke	broken
bring	brought	brought
build	built	built
burn	burned/burnt	burned/burnt
buy	bought	bought

choose	chose	chosen
come	came	come
cost	cost	cost
dive	dived/dove	dived
do	did	done
draw	drew	drawn
drink	drank	drunk
drive	drove	driven
eat	ate	eaten
feel	felt	felt
fly	flew	flown
forget	forgot	forgotten/forgot
freeze	froze	frozen
get	got	gotten
give	gave	given
go	went	gone
grow	grew	grown
have	had	had
hear	heard	heard
hide	hid	hidden
hurt	hurt	hurt
keep	kept	kept
know	knew	known
lead	led	led
let	let	let
lose	lost	lost
mean	meant	meant
meet	met	met
pay	paid	paid
put	put	put
ride	rode	ridden
ring	rang	rung
run	ran	run
say	said	said
see	saw	seen
set	set	set
shake	shook	shaken
shoot	shot	shot
shrink	shrank/shrunk	shrunk/shrunken
sink	sank	sunk

sleep	slept	slept
speak	spoke	spoken
spend	spent	spent
spread	spread	spread
spring	sprang/sprung	sprung
stand	stood	stood
swim	swam	swum
swing	swung	swung
take	took	taken
teach	taught	taught
tear	tore	torn
tell	told	told
think	thought	thought
throw	threw	thrown
wear	wore	worn
write	wrote	written

Lay and *lie*, sit and *set*, raise and *rise* (32d)

Does the book *lie* on the table or *lay* on the table? Do you *sit* that record on the stack or *set* it on the stack? Does the sun *rise* in the sky or *raise* in the sky? To use these words correctly, you need to distinguish between transitive and intransitive verbs.

To review, if a verb is **transitive**, it can take an object. *Kicked* is a transitive verb, as in *Wally kicked the empty can*. Kicked what? Kicked the can. The object of the verb *kicked* is *can*. In the pairs of verbs under discussion, *lay*, *set*, and *raise* are transitive verbs; they take objects.

> I *lay* the plate on the table. [Lay *means "to put or place."*]
>
> I *set* the plate on the stack. [Set *means "to put or place."*]
>
> I *raise* the fork off the plate. [Raise *means "to lift or bring up."*]

As you might guess, if a verb cannot take an object, it is an **intransitive** verb. *Lie*, *sit*, and *rise* are intransitive verbs; they do not take objects.

> I *lie* on the bed. [Lie *means "to recline."*]
>
> I *sit* in the chair. [Sit *means "to be seated."*]
>
> The bird *rises* into the air. [Rise *means "to go up."*]

One other complication with these pairs of verbs is that they are irregular. Here are their principal parts:

BASE FORM	-S FORM	PRESENT PARTICIPLE	PAST TENSE	PAST PARTICIPLE
lie	lies	lying	lay	lain
lay	lays	laying	laid	laid
sit	sits	sitting	sat	sat
set	sets	setting	set	set
rise	rises	rising	rose	risen
raise	raises	raising	raised	raised

The forms of *lie* and *lay* are likely to be the most confusing. The base form of *lay* is the same as the past tense of *lie*. You should also be careful to distinguish between *lie* meaning "to recline" and *lie* meaning "to tell a falsehood." When used to indicate a falsehood, as in *Eric lied to his friend*, the verb is regular, and its forms are as follows:

BASE FORM	-S FORM	PRESENT PARTICIPLE	PAST TENSE	PAST PARTICIPLE
lie	lies	lying	lied	lied

Verb tenses (32e)

→ **COMMON ERROR: UNNECESSARY SHIFT IN VERB TENSE**

Verb tense is important. Using the different tenses correctly allows writers to tell readers exactly when things occur in relationship to one another. If you have studied verb forms, you have already begun to study verb tenses. The following material examines in detail how to tell one tense from another and how to know when to use each one.

Tenses are verb forms that indicate when the action named by the verb takes place. Here is a list of tenses, illustrated by the regular verb *talk* (the tenses of an irregular verb may be formed differently):

SIMPLE PRESENT	talk *or* talks
SIMPLE PAST	talked
SIMPLE FUTURE	will talk
PRESENT PROGRESSIVE	is talking *or* are talking
PAST PROGRESSIVE	was talking *or* were talking
FUTURE PROGRESSIVE	will be talking
PRESENT PERFECT	has talked *or* have talked

PAST PERFECT	had talked
FUTURE PERFECT	will have talked
PRESENT PERFECT PROGRESSIVE	has been talking *or* have been talking
PAST PERFECT PROGRESSIVE	had been talking
FUTURE PERFECT PROGRESSIVE	will have been talking

Present-tense forms

■ *Simple Present*

The **simple present tense** can show action happening at the time of speaking or writing:

> Hannah *loves* her sisters.
>
> He *shoots*! He *scores*!

It is also used for habitual actions, for actions likely to be true at all times, and in discussions of literary or artistic works:

> Jeremy *expects* everyone to wait on him.
>
> I *work* at a radio station.
>
> Water *boils* at 100 degrees centigrade.
>
> Hamlet *hesitates* to kill his uncle.

The simple present tense may indicate a scheduled event in the future, if a time is indicated:

> We *move* in on October 16.

■ *Present Progressive*

The **present progressive tense** shows action that is ongoing or repeated at the time it is being written or spoken about:

> I *am pushing* on the brake, but the car *is* not *stopping*.
>
> She *is running* five miles a day.

It can also be used to indicate a scheduled event in the future:

> We *are going* to New York this summer.

■ *Present Perfect*

The **present perfect tense** shows an action begun in the past and either completed at some unspecified time or continuing into the present:

> I *have painted* my masterpiece.

> She *has talked* about her boyfriend so much I can't stand it anymore.

■ *Present Perfect Progressive*

The **present perfect progressive tense** shows an ongoing or repeated action begun in the past and continuing into the present:

> I *have been thinking.*

> He *has been eating* here for years.

As you can see, a knowledge of verb tenses enables you to specify a wide variety of time relationships.

Past-tense forms

The past tenses all discuss events that are over. Understanding the various relationships of these past tenses will allow you to present events in their proper time order.

■ *Simple Past*

The **simple past tense** shows completed action:

> Last night I *dreamed* about flying.

> The United States *bombed* Hiroshima on August 6, 1945.

Note that the simple past tense shows actions that occurred at a specific time and do not continue into the present, unlike the present perfect tense.

■ *Past Progressive*

The **past progressive tense** shows ongoing or repeated actions occurring in the past:

> I *was wondering* what to do until you came along.

> Clyde *was smoking* two packs a day.

■ *Past Perfect*

The **past perfect tense** shows actions completed in the past before the occurrence of some other action also in the past:

> I *had tried* everything; then a new idea struck me.

> She looked around and saw that the other *had vanished*.

■ *Past Perfect Progressive*

The **past perfect progressive tense** shows ongoing or repeated action occurring in the past and continuing up until the point of some other action also in the past:

> We *had been driving* for six hours when we ran out of gas.

> When the escapee surrendered, he *had been hiding* for nearly twenty years.

Future-tense forms

The future tenses discuss events that have not yet occurred. As with the present and past tenses, understanding the full variety of future tenses allows writers to indicate time relationships accurately.

■ *Simple Future*

The **simple future tense** shows action still to occur:

> The store *will open* next week.

(Note: The auxiliary *shall* is still occasionally preferred over *will* with the first-person-pronoun subjects *I* or *we* in formal and academic writing. Most American usage, however, now accepts *will* everywhere.)

■ *Future Progressive*

The **future progressive tense** shows ongoing action to occur in the future:

> As the population ages, we *will be paying* more for health care.

■ *Future Perfect*

The **future perfect tense** shows action that will be completed before some other action in the future:

> I *will have eaten* by the time you get here.

■ *Future Perfect Progressive*

The **future perfect progressive tense** shows a continuing action that will be completed by some specified time in the future:

This June, Sherman *will have been going* to college for three years.

Verb tense sequence (32f)

Writers frequently need to indicate a particular sequence of actions. They often do so by using dependent clauses or verbals. The simplest sequence involves actions happening at the same time: *Debbie looked at me, and I looked at her.* The two actions were happening in the past. Whenever two actions happen at the same time (whether in the present, past, or future), the tenses of the verbs or verbals are the same.

The matter gets more complicated when sentences describe actions that happened at different times. In such sentences, the tense of the main verb often differs from the tense of the verbs in dependent clauses. In general, you may use whatever tense you need in order to communicate your meaning, as long as your tense sequences stay logical and reasonable. Study the following examples.

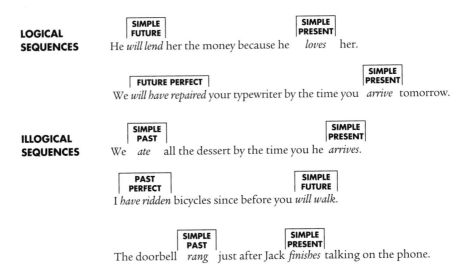

LOGICAL SEQUENCES

> SIMPLE FUTURE SIMPLE PRESENT
> He *will lend* her the money because he *loves* her.

> FUTURE PERFECT SIMPLE PRESENT
> We *will have repaired* your typewriter by the time you *arrive* tomorrow.

ILLOGICAL SEQUENCES

> SIMPLE PAST SIMPLE PRESENT
> We *ate* all the dessert by the time you he *arrives*.

> PAST PERFECT SIMPLE FUTURE
> I *have ridden* bicycles since before you *will walk*.

> SIMPLE PAST SIMPLE PRESENT
> The doorbell *rang* just after Jack *finishes* talking on the phone.

Infinitives and participles also play an important role in communicating time relationships to readers. There are two infinitive forms: the **present infinitive** (the base form of the verb plus *to*, as in *to swim*) and the **perfect infinitive** (the past participle plus *to have*, as in *to have appeared*). These infinitive forms are used as follows:

- The **present infinitive** indicates an action occurring *at the same time as* or *later than* the main verb.

Alec and Frank like *to play* double solitaire. [*The liking and the playing occur at the same time.*]

Kyrie will decide *to hire* a specialist. [*The decision comes first, then the hiring.*]

- The **perfect infinitive** indicates action occurring *earlier than* the main verb.

  He was reported *to have left* his fortune to his bulldog Jake. [*The leaving of the fortune came before the report.*]

The three participial forms indicate different times in relation to the main verb. The use of these participles is illustrated next.

- The **present participle** (formed by adding *-ing* to the base form of the verb) indicates action occurring at the same time as the action of the main verb.

  Trying to see over the crowd, Ariel stood on her chair. [*The trying and the standing occur at the same time.*]

  Seeking shelter from the hail, we ran to the porch. [*The seeking and the running occur at the same time.*]

- The **present perfect participle** (formed by combining the auxiliary *having* with the past participle) indicates action occurring before the action of the main verb.

  Having finished her finals, she decided to take a long nap. [*The finishing of finals occurs before the decision to nap.*]

  Having predicted rain, the forecaster was embarrassed by the sunshine. [*The prediction comes before the embarrassment.*]

- The **past participle** (formed by adding *-d* or *-ed* to the base form of the verb) indicates action occurring either before or at the same time as the action of the main verb.

  Surprised by the first question, I decided to move on to the next one. [*The surprise comes before the decision.*]

  Flown by an expert pilot, the plane turned to a northerly course. [*The flying and the turning happen at the same time.*]

Voice (32g)

Minnesota Fats pocketed the last ball with a two-cushion bank shot.

The last ball was pocketed by Minnesota Fats with a two-cushion bank shot.

In the first of these two sentences, a person is doing something. The person is Minnesota Fats, a legendary pool player. He is the subject of the first sentence. Since Minnesota Fats is performing the action, we can say that the first sentence is written in the **active voice**.

In the second sentence, the subject is not Minnesota Fats; it is the word *ball*. The verb is *was pocketed*. In the second sentence, Minnesota Fats is the object of the preposition *by*. This sentence is written in the **passive voice**: something is done to the subject; the subject does not act but instead is acted upon.

All the examples used so far in this chapter to indicate tense and verb sequence are written in the active voice. The passive voice is formed by using the appropriate auxiliary verb (some form of *be*) with the past participle of the main verb. In the Minnesota Fats example, the auxiliary is *was* and the past participle is *pocketed*. To compare active and passive voice, see the following:

	ACTIVE	PASSIVE
SIMPLE PRESENT	She reads the paper.	The paper is read by her.
PRESENT PERFECT	She has read the paper.	The paper has been read by her.
SIMPLE PAST	She read the paper.	The paper was read by her.
PAST PERFECT	She had read the paper.	The paper had been read by her.
SIMPLE FUTURE	She will read the paper.	The paper will be read by her.
FUTURE PERFECT	By noon, she will have read the paper.	By noon, the paper will have been read by her.

In considering the merits of either active or passive voice, writers must recognize several points. Even a quick glance at the comparison chart shows that writing in the active voice produces shorter, more direct sentences. In many kinds of writing, readers appreciate this directness. Sentences in the active voice are also livelier.

The difference between active voice and passive voice is partly a matter of emphasis. In the active voice, the subject of the sentence performs the action; both the performer (the subject) and the action (the verb) receive emphasis. In contrast, in the passive voice, the originator of the action is not the sentence subject. In fact, in passive voice, the originator of the action can be omitted altogether, as in this example:

The last ball was pocketed with a two-cushion bank shot.

Here the *action* receives the emphasis; the force responsible for the action receives no mention at all. Passive constructions of this sort are common and appropriate in scientific reporting. A paragraph describing experimental procedures should rightly focus on the procedures themselves rather than on the lab assistants who performed them.

Measurements of water temperature were taken every three minutes for one hour. These temperatures were then compared to measurements taken during phase one.

Passive constructions, however, make it impossible for readers to learn who or what is responsible for the actions reported. Consider this example:

The monthly rate for day care has been increased another $50.

Who is responsible for implementing this increase? To whom should you complain? The passive voice allows those responsible to remain unnamed.

- To change from active voice to passive voice, convert the object of the verb into the subject of the sentence.

  ACTIVE   Tom chased the cat. [The *object of the verb is* cat.]

  PASSIVE   The cat was chased by Tom. [Cat *has become the subject.*]

- To change from passive voice to active voice, convert the subject of the verb into a direct or indirect object, and identify the performer of the action described by the verb.

  PASSIVE   The cake was baked for forty minutes. [Cake *is the subject.*]

  ACTIVE   Scott baked the cake for forty minutes. [Cake *is the direct object, and* Scott *is identified as the baker.*]

Mood (32h)

The **mood** of a verb reflects how the message expressed by that verb is conceived by the writer.

The most common mood is the **indicative mood**, which is used to convey facts or ask questions. Nearly all of this workbook is written in the indicative mood. All the examples of tense and voice given earlier in this chapter are written in the indicative mood.

The second most common mood is the **imperative mood**, which is used to express commands or requests. Many of the exercise directions in this workbook are written in the imperative mood. Such directions omit *you*, the sentence subject, and use the base form of the verb, as in *Analyze the following sentences.*

The **subjunctive mood** may be used to express requirements, requests, desires, suggestions, or conditions contrary to fact. The subjunctive is used primarily in clauses beginning with *if*, *that*, *as if*, or *as though*. See the forms and examples that follow.

The **present subjunctive** uses the base form of the verb. The present subjunctive of the verb *be* is simply *be*.

Contest rules require that you *be* present to win. [*subjunctive expressing a requirement*]

The teacher asked that one volunteer *stay* after school. [*subjunctive expressing a request*]

Note: Third-person singular present subjunctive verbs — such as *stay* in the second sample sentence — do not end in *-s* like third-person singular verbs in other moods.

The **past subjunctive** is the same as the past tense except for the verb *be*, which uses *were* for all subjects.

> If I *were* you, I would vote for the other candidate. [*subjunctive expressing a condition contrary to fact*: If I were you (but I am not you) . . .]

> The chimp scratched its head as if it *were* human. [*subjunctive expressing a condition contrary to fact*: . . . as if it were human (but it is not human, it is a chimpanzee); *notice the as if, which requires the subjunctive in formal writing*]

> We wished we *were* in Texas. [*subjunctive expressing a desire*]

Note: Because the subjunctive mood often creates a formal tone, some writers and speakers substitute the indicative mood in less formal writing or speaking situations. However, for academic writing, you should use the subjunctive whenever required.

> **INFORMAL**   That commercial says that if I *was* a real man, I'd own a truck.
>
> **ACADEMIC**   That commercial implies that if I *were* a real man, I would own a truck.

EXERCISE 17.1   FORMS OF *BE* AND *HAVE*

NAME _____ **DATE** _____

Circle the appropriate form of *be* or *have* in each of the following sentences.

1. Grandma Berry am/be/is the oldest living member of the family.

2. I was/were thinking about her this afternoon.

3. We has/have a lot in common in spite of our age difference.

4. She has/have memories of events I can only imagine.

5. Her maiden name is/be/am Boone.

6. Daniel Boone been/was/were her great-great-grandfather.

7. Like their famous ancestor, the Boones been/was/were all adventurous and capable.

8. Grandma Berry is/be/am a good shot with a rifle, and she has/have kept her farm running for seventy years.

9. She is/be/am the mother of six children, the grandmother of fifteen, and the great-grandmother of twelve.

10. About having a large family, she said once, "At least you was/were never bored."

11. Her descendants be/are her proudest achievement, she says.

12. I hope that I is/be/am as wise in my old age as Grandma Berry is/be/am.

EXERCISE 17.2   AUXILIARY VERBS

NAME _____ **DATE** _____

Underline the auxiliary and main verb in each sentence below. If an incorrect auxiliary has been used, pencil in the correct auxiliary above it. If a needed auxiliary has been left out, pencil it in. If the sentence is correct, write *C* next to the number of the sentence.

1. She be abusing the office of president.

2. When the snow stops, we must shovel the driveway.

3. If you is applying for a job, you should reviewing answers to challenging interview questions.

4. In the spring, Bryan will been planning the trip for two years.

5. The players on our team running out of time to regain the lead.

6. If I been watching, I wouldn't be in this mess.

7. I chosen to work for a semester before returning to school.

8. They must have realized that the pup had been following them all over town.

9. Since Toulon got his job, he don't watch much television.

10. Jesse does not want to go inside for lunch yet.

EXERCISE 17.3   VERB FORMS

NAME _____   **DATE** _____

Using the subjects and verbs provided, write the indicated sentences.

> **EXAMPLE**   subject: *Bernie*   verb: *touch*
>
> sentence using a present form: Bernie touches the soft fur. _____
> sentence using the auxiliary verb *had*: Bernie had touched a squid before. _____

1. subject: *nurse*   verb: *speak*   sentence using a past-tense form: _____

   _____

   sentence using an auxiliary verb + the present participle: _____

   _____

2. subject: *elephants*   verb: *walk*   sentence using a present-tense form: _____

   _____

   sentence using an auxiliary verb + the past participle: _____

   _____

3. subject: *llamas*   verb: *be*   sentence using a past-tense form: _____

   _____

   sentence using an auxiliary verb + the present participle: _____

   _____

4. subject: *waiter*   verb: *pour*   sentence using a present-tense form: _____

   _____

   sentence using the auxiliary verb *had* + the past participle: _____

   _____

5. subject: *housekeeper*   verb: *dust*   sentence using a past-tense form: _____

_____

sentence using the auxiliary verb *was* + the present participle: _____

_____

6. subject: *grandfather*   verb: *amuse*   sentence using a present-tense form:_____

_____

sentence using an auxiliary verb + the past participle: _____

_____

7. subject: *rice*   verb: *steam*   sentence using a past-tense form: _____

_____

sentence using an auxiliary verb + the present participle: _____

_____

8. subject: *kites*   verb: *soar*   sentence using a past-tense form: _____

_____

sentence using an auxiliary verb + the present participle: _____

_____

9. subject: *pizza*   verb: *taste*   sentence using a present-tense form:_____

_____

sentence using an auxiliary verb + the past participle: _____

_____

10. subject: *hiccups*   verb: *bother*   sentence using a past-tense form: _____

sentence using an auxiliary verb + the present participle: _____

_____

EXERCISE 17.4   IRREGULAR VERBS

NAME _____ **DATE** _____

Consult the list of irregular verbs, and write sentences as specified. Use auxiliary verbs as needed.

> **EXAMPLE**   a sentence using *they* as its subject and the past participle form of *go* as its main verb. [Remember that past participles are combined with auxiliary verbs.]
>
> By the time we arrived, they had gone for supplies.

1. a sentence using *we* as its subject and the past tense of *bring* as its main verb

_____

2. a sentence using *you* as its subject and the past tense of *hurt* as its main verb

_____

3. a sentence using *customer* as its subject and the past participle of *break* as its main verb

_____

4. a sentence using *children* as its subject and the past participle of *ride* as its main verb

_____

5. a sentence using *I* as its subject and the past participle of *hear* as its main verb

_____

6. a sentence using *we* as its subject and the past tense of *think* as its main verb

_____

7. a sentence using any appropriate noun as its subject and the past tense of *lead* as its main verb

_____

8. a sentence using *they* as its subject and the past participle of *feel* as its main verb

_____

9. a sentence using any appropriate noun as its subject and the past participle of *wake* as its main verb

_____

10. a sentence using any appropriate noun as its subject and the past tense of *swim* as its main verb

_____

EXERCISE 17.5 *LAY* AND *LIE, SIT* AND *SET, RAISE* AND *RISE*

Underline the correct verb in each of the following sentences. The first one is done for you.

1. She wanted to <u>lie</u>/lay on the beach all afternoon.

2. The negotiator lied/lay/laid his cards on the table.

3. Emmett couldn't remember where he had sat/set his glass.

4. The class began to fidget because they had sat/set so long.

5. The bear rose/raised its head up and peered over the tall grass.

6. Kevin finished dinner while I sat/set the table.

7. He turned on the television and lied/lay/laid down on the couch as soon as he came home from work.

8. We will take a blanket to the park and lie/lay it on the grass.

9. Once the blanket is on the grass, we will lie/lay down for a snooze.

10. Sit/Set still while the doctor examines your knee.

11. As house prices rose/raised, we figured we could never afford to move.

12. The dough bubbles as it rises/raises.

EXERCISE 17.6   PRESENT-TENSE FORMS

NAME _____ **DATE** _____

For each specified verb and tense, write a sentence. If the verb is irregular, you may need to consult the list of irregular verbs or a good dictionary.

> **EXAMPLE**   *run*, present perfect   <u>The new car has run every day without fail.</u>

1. *regret*, present progressive _____

_____

2. *lose*, present perfect _____

_____

3. *astonish*, simple present _____

_____

4. *build*, present perfect progressive _____

_____

5. *lie* (tell an untruth), present progressive _____

_____

6. *sit*, present perfect _____

_____

7. *discuss*, present progressive _____

_____

8. *drink*, present perfect progressive _____

_____

9. *decide*, simple present _____

_____

10. *feel*, present perfect progressive _____

_____

11. *test*, simple present _____

_____

12. *dream*, present progressive _____

_____

EXERCISE 17.7 PAST-TENSE FORMS

NAME _____ **DATE** _____

For each specified verb and tense, write a sentence. If the verb is irregular, you may need to consult the list of irregular verbs or a good dictionary.

EXAMPLE   *swim*, past perfect progressive   <u>I had been swimming for years before the injury.</u>

1. *howl*, simple past _____

_____

2. *write*, past perfect _____

_____

3. *eat*, past perfect _____

_____

4. *drive*, past perfect progressive_____

_____

5. *jog*, past progressive_____

_____

6. *take*, simple past _____

_____

7. *protest*, past perfect progressive _____

_____

8. *conclude*, past progressive _____

_____

9. *break*, past perfect _____

_____

10. *choose*, simple past _____

_____

11. *expect*, past perfect progressive _____

_____

12. *enlighten*, past progressive _____

_____

EXERCISE 17.8   FUTURE-TENSE FORMS

NAME _____ **DATE** _____

For each specified verb and tense, write a sentence. If the verb is irregular, you may need to consult the list of irregular verbs or a good dictionary.

EXAMPLE   *swim*, future perfect   You will have swum thirty laps by the time I wake up.

1. *trek*, future progressive _____

_____

2. *try*, simple future_____

_____

3. *write*, future perfect_____

_____

4. *save*, future perfect progressive_____

_____

5. *think*, future progressive _____

_____

6. *visit*, future perfect progressive_____

_____

7. *leave*, future perfect_____

_____

8. *regret*, simple future _____

_____

9. *sing,* future perfect _____

_____

10. *celebrate,* future progressive _____

_____

11. *vote,* future perfect progressive _____

_____

12. *sleep,* simple future _____

_____

EXERCISE 17.9   VERB TENSE SEQUENCE

NAME _____ **DATE** _____

Read the following sentences carefully, and provide the specified information. If a sentence uses a logical sequence of tenses, write *L* on the lines provided. If the sentence uses an illogical sequence of tenses, rewrite the sentence so that your new version is logical. You may find that you need to review the portion of this chapter that identifies the various tenses.

EXAMPLE   Mitch Williams threw a curve even though the catcher will signal a fast ball.

main verb: <u>threw</u>

tense of main verb: <u>past</u>

dependent clause verb: <u>will signal</u>

tense of dependent clause verb: <u>future</u>

<u>Mitch Williams threw a curve even though the catcher signaled a fast ball.</u>

1. The students had reviewed their notes thoroughly before they took the exam.

   main verb: _____

   tense of main verb: _____

   dependent clause verb: _____

   tense of dependent clause verb: _____

   _____

   _____

2. As the light changed to green, the pickup truck crumples the passenger side of my Toyota.

   main verb: _____

   tense of main verb: _____

   dependent clause verb: _____

   tense of dependent clause verb: _____

   _____

   _____

269

3. Will you have finished your dissertation by the time your deadline arrives?

    main verb: _____

    tense of main verb: _____

    dependent clause verb: _____

    tense of dependent clause verb: _____

    _____

    _____

4. When she notices her son's report card, she fainted.

    main verb: _____

    tense of main verb: _____

    dependent clause verb: _____

    tense of dependent clause verb: _____

    _____

    _____

5. Tyler will have milked the cows before the sun came up.

    main verb: _____

    tense of main verb: _____

    dependent clause verb: _____

    tense of dependent clause verb: _____

    _____

    _____

6. Joanna has been studying Italian for years, and her accent has finally improved.

    main verb: _____

tense of main verb: _____

dependent clause verb: _____

tense of dependent clause verb: _____

_____

_____

7. I had intended to cook dinner until my boss asks me to work overtime.

main verb: _____

tense of main verb: _____

dependent clause verb: _____

tense of dependent clause verb: _____

_____

_____

8. He has planned the best way to propose before he reached the restaurant.

main verb: _____

tense of main verb: _____

dependent clause verb: _____

tense of dependent clause verb: _____

_____

_____

9. Mark bought two shirts that were on sale.

main verb: _____

tense of main verb: _____

dependent clause verb: _____

tense of dependent clause verb: _____

_____

_____

10. Brad was just beginning to do his Spanish assignment when he has dropped his book.

main verb: _____

tense of main verb: _____

dependent clause verb: _____

tense of dependent clause verb: _____

_____

_____

EXERCISE 17.10   VERB TENSES IN LOGICAL SEQUENCE

NAME _____ **DATE** _____

Read each sentence below. If the sequence of tenses is logical, write *L* on the line following the sentence. If the sequence of tenses is illogical, rewrite the sentence on the lines provided.

> **EXAMPLE**   When the family cat got hungry, she decides to climb the window screen and look inside.
>
> When the family cat got hungry, she decided to climb the window screen and look inside.

1. Chaunta has surgery last month and hopes to begin training again next week.

   _____

   _____

2. The hermit was rumored to live on nuts and berries until his death in 1970.

   _____

   _____

3. Accepting the stranger's gift, I could not then turn down her request for assistance.

   _____

   _____

4. The evergreens began to grow where the meadow grass ended.

   _____

   _____

5. The herb garden began to take shape as I work on it all day long.

   _____

   _____

6. Ashley opened her first present as the guests began to have sung "Happy Birthday."

   _____

   _____

273

7. Before we started to have eaten dinner, we emptied the dishwasher.

_____

_____

8. Libby will bake you a cake if you will have ordered one early enough.

_____

_____

9. The coach announced the team's travel schedule after the players finish practice.

_____

_____

10. Staying up all night to finish his lab report, Noah was exhausted during the final exam the next morning.

_____

_____

11. She wishes to be born rich and pampered.

_____

_____

12. Having been warned not to drink the punch, I was the only person sober enough to drive the guests home.

_____

_____

EXERCISE 17.11   IDENTIFYING ACTIVE VOICE AND PASSIVE VOICE

NAME _____ **DATE** _____

A. Underline the main verb in each sentence, and indicate whether it is active or passive.

> **EXAMPLE**   The azalea blossoms <u>nod</u> in the wind. active_____

1. This paper argues for the existence of extraterrestrial life. _____

2. The report on fat and heart disease was highlighted on the first page of the newspaper. _____

3. The study was commented on by many scientists. _____

4. The lead investigator defended the experimental design. _____

5. Other variables may have contributed to the unexpected finding. _____

6. We were tormented by mosquitoes during the entire boat ride. _____

7. Are you going to change your diet? _____

8. Everything in print about diets might be discredited. _____

9. Within hours, snow drifted across the field and against the fence. _____

10. Michael has regretted his rudeness for weeks. _____

11. The morning weather report predicts a high of 86 degrees. _____

12. The final grades will be submitted on Friday. _____

B. The following paragraph contains five examples of the active voice and six of the passive voice. Circle each example, and mark *A* for active or *P* for passive over each one.

    Martin Scorsese makes wonderful films. Each frame is shot carefully, and each set includes the smallest of details. That is because Scorsese demands excellence from his crew. And the crew is expected to fulfill their filmmaker's vision. Each actor is directed by Scorsese with sensitivity and skill. The director choreographs every move, every word. Yet it is all made to appear completely natural. That is the mark of a truly great director, and that is why his work is treasured by moviegoers and critics alike. The movies that are made by Scorsese will surely distinguish themselves for many years to come.

EXERCISE 17.12   USING ACTIVE VOICE AND PASSIVE VOICE

NAME _____ **DATE** _____

Below is the paragraph from part B of Exercise 17.11. Rewrite it on your own paper, changing the active voice to passive voice and vice versa. Underline each verb in your rewritten version. As you rewrite, pay attention to which voice you think sounds better for each sentence. Which voice do you think holds the reader's interest more?

Martin Scorsese makes wonderful films. Each frame is shot carefully, and each set includes the smallest of details. That is because Scorsese demands excellence from his crew. And the crew is expected to fulfill their filmmaker's vision. Each actor is directed by Scorsese with sensitivity and skill. The director choreographs every move, every word. Yet it is all made to appear completely natural. That is the mark of a truly great director, and that is why his work is treasured by moviegoers and critics alike. The movies that are made by Scorsese will surely distinguish themselves for many years to come.

EXERCISE 17.13   IDENTIFYING VERB MOOD

Read the following short paragraph from a letter. Above each underlined verb, pencil in the mood of that verb. The mood of the first verb has been identified for you.

indicative

You <u>may have</u> many different reasons for liking the music that you <u>prefer</u>. <u>Think</u> about your favorite music for a moment. What <u>makes</u> it worth listening to? Perhaps you feel that a good dance beat <u>is</u> essential, or maybe you <u>want</u> clever lyrics or a political sensibility. Perhaps you <u>can be convinced</u> to buy music once in a while just because the artist is cute. Although you may know people who <u>identify</u> with only one kind of music, most people choose different styles based on what they <u>are doing</u> at the time. Suppose that you <u>were asked</u> to choose one type of music to take to a desert island. What music would end up in your collection? <u>Remember</u> that you might have to live with your choices for a long, long time.

EXERCISE 17.14   USING VERB MOOD

NAME _____ **DATE** _____

Circle the correct form of the verb to be used, and indicate in the blank whether the mood of the verb is indicative, imperative, or subjunctive.

EXAMPLE   Whenever he sees a cat, our Doberman bark /barks. _indicative_____

1. His parents now insist that he tells/tell them where he is going. _____

2. Lemurs climb/climbs trees much better than gorillas. _____

3. Whenever that screen door close/closes, it slams. _____

4. Earning an attendance award requires that you are/be on time every day. _____

5. If Lamont were/is/was here, he would know what to do. _____

6. Just puts/put the groceries on the counter. _____

7. Your cooperation is/were requested at the hearing. _____

8. I am asking that the winner share/shares the bonanza with all of us. _____

9. Opens/Open your test booklets now. _____

10. She wished she was/were on vacation. _____

Subject-Verb Agreement

18

Just as friends agree about going to a favorite restaurant, you and your boss agree about your responsibilities at work, and countries agree to honor a treaty, so must subjects and verbs agree in **number** (singular or plural) and in **person** (first, second, or third). Similarly, pronouns must agree with their antecedents in number, person, and **gender** (feminine, masculine, or neuter). This grammatical accord, or **agreement**, allows readers to associate subjects with verbs correctly (and thereby to understand correctly what writers intend to say). Lack of agreement in these word relationships often leaves readers confused and irritated. Studying the points presented in this and the next chapter should help if you find agreement a difficult skill to master. This chapter focuses on agreement between subject and verb; Chapter 19 deals with agreement between pronoun and antecedent.

SUBJECT-VERB AGREEMENT IN EVERYDAY USE

Subjects and verbs are at work in almost every statement you make, and you make them "agree" effortlessly most of the time. Look, for instance, at three sentences from a recent broadcast of a baseball game. The subjects and verbs are italicized.

Guzman powers another blistering curveball over the plate.

The Yanks move on to Milwaukee tomorrow.

The duel of the no-hitters *continues* into the eighth.

Listen to someone reporting an event—perhaps a play-by-play announcer or an on-the-scene reporter. Then jot down some of the subject-verb combinations used by this person. Do you find any that don't sound right, that might not "agree"?

The general rule for subject-verb agreement is simple: singular subjects take singular verbs, and plural subjects take plural verbs. Most often, you make a verb singular by adding -s or -es to the base form. See the examples in the sections that follow.

Verbs with third-person singular subjects (33a)

In the present tense, a singular noun subject takes a verb ending in *-s* or *-es*. The third-person pronoun subjects *he*, *she*, and *it* also take verbs ending in *-s* or *-es*. (Note that the verbs *be* and *have* are exceptions to this rule. See Chapter 17 for a discussion of these verbs.)

EXAMPLES   A Madras shirt fade<u>s</u> when washed. [Shirt *is the singular noun subject of the verb.*]

The projectionist watch<u>es</u> the movie. [Projectionist *is the singular noun subject of the verb.*]

She swim<u>s</u> every other day. [She *is the third-person singular pronoun subject of the verb.*]

The *-s* or *-es* endings are not always easy to hear in speech and are not a part of some spoken American dialects of English. However, writers using standard written English should always use these endings. (Of course, subjects that are not third-person singular do not require an *-s* or *-es* ending. Be careful to write *we swim* and *you swim* rather than *we swims* and *you swims*, for instance.)

Subjects and verbs separated by other words (33b)

Do not let words that come between subject and verb confuse subject-verb agreement. In the following example, the noun nearest the verb is *baskets* (plural). However, *baskets* is not the sentence subject; the subject is *contestant*.

RIGHT   The contestant who makes the most baskets wins four free pizzas.

WRONG   The contestant who makes the most baskets win four free pizzas.

In that example, a dependent clause comes between the subject and the verb.

Sometimes the intervening words are other sentence elements, such as prepositional phrases, as in this example:

RIGHT   One of his bodyguards accompanies him at all times.

WRONG   One of his bodyguards accompany him at all times.

Occasionally a sentence's meaning appears to conflict with its actual grammar. This is especially true when a sentence subject is followed by a phrase beginning with *as well as, along with, together with, in addition to,* or similar expression. In such sentences the meaning becomes plural, though grammatically the sentence subject stays singular. Here is an example:

Senator Kutz, along with her aides, travels the state in a large van.

The grammatical subject (*Senator Kutz*) is in the third-person singular and so takes a singular verb (*travels*).

Even though that sentence is grammatically correct, it may sound awkward to you. To eliminate such awkwardness, some writers would revise the sentence in this way: *Senator Kutz and her aides travel the state in a large van.* The subject becomes *Senator Kutz and her aides*; it is grammatically plural and takes a plural verb, *travel*. (More on such compound subjects appears below.)

When you proofread to check on subject-verb agreement, reducing the sentence to its subject and verb should make any errors easy to spot.

The cook who baked these pizzas knows what he's doing. [cook . . . knows]

The coach, together with the team members, arrives in Salt Lake City at 9:36 P.M. [coach . . . arrives]

Verbs with compound subjects (33c)

Even though you may well understand the general rule that singular subjects take singular verbs and plural subjects take plural verbs, you still may have some difficulty deciding when a subject is singular and when it is plural. Consider this example:

Jack and Jill run up the hill.

The word *Jack* by itself is singular; so is *Jill*. Yet the sentence has the two people running up a hill. This sentence has a **compound subject**: two subjects (or more) joined by *and*. As you see from the following rule, most of the time sentences with compound subjects take plural verbs.

- Subjects joined by *and* are usually plural and take plural verbs. However, if two or more parts of a subject form a single idea or refer to one person, those parts are considered to be singular and take a singular verb.

    EXAMPLES   Jack and Jill *run* up the hill. [*Subjects joined by* and *take a plural verb.*]

    Bacon and eggs *is* the most commonly ordered breakfast. [*Subjects combine to form a single item; thus the verb is singular.*]

- If the adjective *each* or *every* precedes a compound subject, the verb following that subject is usually singular.

    EXAMPLE   Each bud and flower *is* a sign of spring.

Now look at several other agreement rules.

- Compound subjects joined by *or* or *nor* take singular verbs if they are both singular, plural verbs if they are both plural.

  EXAMPLES   Neither the lifeguard nor the instructor *is* responsible for providing towels. [*singular subjects, singular verb*]

  Either the pool employees or the parents *are* responsible for providing towels. [*plural subjects, plural verb*]

- When one part of a subject joined by *or* or *nor* is singular and the other part is plural, the verb agrees with the part of the subject closest to it. (Common practice is to place the plural part of the subject last in these constructions, making the verb also plural.)

  EXAMPLE   Typically, either rain or cold temperatures *ruin* March weekends.

- When the parts of a subject differ in person, the verb agrees with the nearer subject.

  EXAMPLES   Either Trent or you *were* lying.

  Either you or Trent *was* lying.

  Since sentences of this sort often sound awkward, writers often split the subjects, giving each its own verb: *Either Trent was lying or you were.*

Verbs with collective nouns or indefinite-pronoun subjects (33d, 33e)

Collective nouns also cause some writers trouble when it comes to agreement because these nouns (such as *family* and *team*) are singular in form even though they refer to collections of many people or things. Should such nouns be considered singular or plural? Should they take singular or plural verbs? The answers to these questions hinge on the writer's intentions.

Commonly used collective nouns are *family, team, audience, group, jury, crowd, band, class, flock,* and *committee.*

- When used as subjects, collective nouns take singular verbs when they refer to the group as a whole; they take plural verbs when they refer to parts of the group.

  EXAMPLES   My family generally *eats* dinner at six o'clock. [family *as one unit: singular verb*]

  That committee *makes* the policy decisions. [committee *as a unit: singular verb*]

My family *were* all born in the United States. [*individual family members: plural verb*]

By their nature, **indefinite pronouns**—pronouns that do not refer to specific things or persons—cause writers trouble when it comes to agreement. Often these pronouns can be used as both singular and plural, and some sound plural but are considered grammatically singular. Here is a list of pronouns that are singular in meaning and thus take singular verbs:

another	either	neither	other
anybody	everybody	nobody	somebody
anyone	everyone	no one	someone
anything	everything	nothing	something
each	much	one	

EXAMPLES   *Neither* of the children *enjoys* broccoli. [Of the children *is a prepositional phrase; therefore,* children *cannot function as the grammatical subject of* enjoys.]

Another of the Barlows *enters* school next year.

Something about his voice and delivery *seems* particularly convincing.

Other indefinite pronouns are always plural. These include *both, few, many, others,* and *several.*

Several of the graduates *take* vacations after their graduation ceremony. [*Several is plural; hence, the plural verb* take.]

Still other indefinite pronouns—*all, any, enough, more, most, none,* and *some*—may be singular or plural, depending on the noun they refer to.

Most of the members *are* satisfied. [Members *is plural; thus* most *is considered plural.*]

Most of the cake *is* gone. [Cake *is singular; thus* most *is considered singular.*]

Verbs with antecedents of *who, which,* and *that* (33f)

So far, the discussion of subject-verb agreement has focused mostly on simple sentences. Now it is time to shift attention to sentences that contain dependent clauses introduced by **relative pronouns** (*who, which,* or *that*). Often (though not always) these relative pronouns act as subjects of the clauses they introduce.

By themselves, relative pronouns are neither singular nor plural; the singular form of *who* is no different from the plural form. Thus writers must determine what the pronoun refers to in order to decide whether the verb should be singular or plural.

- Relative pronouns (*who, which, that*) used as subjects of dependent clauses take the same verb form as their antecedents, the independent-clause nouns to which they refer.

EXAMPLES   Writers who start early are likely to be successful. [*The subject of the dependent clause* who start early *is the relative pronoun* who. *Since* who *refers to the plural word* writers, *the verb* start *is also plural.*]

The writer who starts early is likely to be successful. [*Now* who *refers to the singular word* writer; *thus the verb* starts *is also singular.*]

Cups that hold coffee are often made of Styrofoam. [*Here the dependent clause is* that hold coffee. *Since* that *acts as the subject of this clause and since it refers to the plural word* cups, *the verb* hold *takes the plural form.*]

Note that relative pronouns do not always act as the subjects of the clauses they introduce. In the sentence *The books that she wants arrive tomorrow*, for example, the relative pronoun *that* introduces the dependent clause *that she wants*. Since the subject of this clause is *she*, the verb *wants* agrees with *she* rather than with *books*.

When the phrase *one of* precedes the relative pronoun, take special care to determine whether the relative pronoun refers to *one* or to another word. Consider these two examples:

A. Christopher is one of those students who <u>meet</u> /meets every obligation.

B. Christopher is the only one of those students who meet/<u>meets</u> every obligation.

The differences between these two sentences are subtle but important. In example A, the sentence implies that several students meet every obligation and that Christopher is one of them. In example B, the sentence quite specifically indicates that Christopher is the only student who meets every obligation. In example A, *who* refers to *students*; the verb is therefore plural — (*students*) *who meet*. In example B, *who* refers to *one*; the verb is therefore also singular — (*one*) *who meets*.

Linking verbs and their subjects (33g)

Here writers need only remember that verbs agree with their *subjects* and not with the **complements** that describe or rename those subjects.

EXAMPLES   Her favorite breakfast is bagels and cream cheese. [*subject,* breakfast, *is singular; hence, singular verb,* is]

The committee's preference is soft drinks rather than alcoholic ones. [*subject,* preference, *is singular; hence, singular verb,* is]

Verbs with singular subjects ending in -s, titles, and words used as words (33h, 33j)

Words such as *gymnastics, aesthetics, news,* and *politics* end in *-s* and so look plural; however, their meaning is singular. When used as subjects, such words take singular verbs.

> Politics is a human constant, like death and taxes. [*politics as a human activity*]

> Statistics remains a mystery to most of us. [*statistics as a mathematical science*]

Note that some of these words can be used in either a singular or a plural sense. In such cases, verb agreement depends on the meaning of the sentence.

> The statistics were nonsignificant. [*statistics as numbers*]

In addition, titles of works or words named as words always take singular verbs even if those titles or words are themselves plural.

> *The Corrections* tells the story of a dysfunctional American family.

> *Concerns* is a synonym for *worries.*

Verbs with subjects that follow them (33i)

In most English sentences, the subject precedes the verb. Occasionally writers change this word order to emphasize the subject (by placing it last) or to ask questions. Whenever you change the customary word order, remember to make sure that the verb agrees with the subject.

> |VERB|| **COMPOUND SUBJECT** |
> At the top of the stairs were a coat rack and an umbrella stand.

The more normal word order there would be *A coat rack and an umbrella stand were at the top of the stairs.*

> |VERB| |SUBJECT|
> Near her teddy bears is a catcher's mitt.

The more normal order there would be *A catcher's mitt is near her teddy bears.* Notice that the "normal" word order reduces the impact of this sentence.

|VERB| |SUBJECT|

Is   a duck-billed platypus a mammal?

As a declarative sentence, the word order would be *A duck-billed platypus is a mammal.*

Writers working on rough drafts commonly use another kind of sentence inversion. These sentences typically begin with *there*, followed by a form of the verb *be*. In such cases, the subject follows the verb. *There* never acts as the subject of a sentence.

> There are many Vietnam veterans who are still haunted by their war experience.
> [*The verb* are *agrees with the subject* veterans.]

Sentences beginning with *there are* bury their most important content in dependent clauses. A more forceful wording would be *Many Vietnam veterans are still haunted by their war experience.*

EXERCISE 18.1 SUBJECT-VERB AGREEMENT

NAME _____ **DATE** _____

Read the following paragraph. Then go back and look at each sentence. Circle sentence subjects, and underline main verbs. (Ignore dependent clauses.) If the sentence subject and verb do not agree, write in the correct verb. The first sentence has been done for you. (Remember that sentence subjects cannot be the objects of prepositions.)

continue

(Computers) <u>continue</u> to change business practices. The use of photographs are one example. Before computers, the process worked something like this. A news photographer take a picture of an athlete. The photograph captures the essence of determination and hard work. Several of the competing newspapers decides to buy the picture for their Sunday editions. In each case, the photographer sells only one-time reproduction rights. Thus each of these sales generate new income. Now, however, many photographs have been digitized and stored online. Anyone who downloads the photo now also own it. The question that arises are this: how do photographers make sure that they receive fair payment?

EXERCISE 18.2 VERBS WITH COMPOUND SUBJECTS

A. Read the following sentences. Circle each subject, and underline each verb. If subjects and verbs agree, write C on the line below the sentence. If they do not agree, write a corrected version.

EXAMPLE Neither the (lawyer) nor her (clients) <u>shows</u> any worries about winning the case.

Neither the lawyer nor her clients show any worries about winning the case. _____

1. Neither the witnesses nor the police officers was able to identify the hit-and-run driver

   positively. _____

   _____

2. Every doctor and nurse were diving for cover when the patient went berserk.

   _____

   _____

3. Neither the father nor his children were prepared for the long drive. _____

_____

4. Either a teacher or an editor are responsible for your mastery of English composition. _____

_____

5. Either he or you is on vacation — not both. _____

_____

B. Below you are provided with compound subjects and the base forms of verbs. Use them to write a sentence in the present tense, taking particular care that subjects and verbs agree.

> **EXAMPLE**   subject: *budding flowers and freshly cut lawns*   verb: *remind*
>
> Budding flowers and freshly cut lawns remind me of spring. _____

1. subject: *robins and finches*   verb: *fly*

_____

_____

2. subject: *each fruit and vegetable*   verb: *provide*

_____

_____

3. subject: *my friend and esteemed colleague*   verb: *help*

_____

_____

4. subject: *he and his wife*   verb: *raise*

_____

_____

5. subject: *neither her lawyer nor her accountants*   verb: *tell*

_____

_____

EXERCISE 18.3   SUBJECT-VERB AGREEMENT WITH COLLECTIVE NOUNS OR INDEFINITE-PRONOUN SUBJECTS

NAME _____ **DATE** _____

In each sentence below, circle the subject, and underline the main verb. Indicate whether the subject is a collective noun or an indefinite pronoun. If the subject and verb agree, write C on the line below the sentence. If the subject and verb do not agree, rewrite the sentence so that the verb agrees with its subject.

EXAMPLE   (None) of the people is interested in leaving the co-op.

Subject is an indefinite pronoun.

None of the people are interested in leaving the co-op.

1. A group of twelve students in my apartment building form a grocery shopping co-op.

   Subject is _____

   _____

2. Of the students' two original goals, creating a neighborhood market for fresh food and offering bulk prices, both is still important to us.

   Subject is _____

   _____

3. Most of our purchases each month reflects the best produce buys available that season.

   Subject is _____

   _____

4. All of the fruits and vegetables come from nearby farms.

   Subject is _____

   _____

5. Each of the people involved in these shopping trips volunteer at least four hours a month.

   Subject is _____

   _____

6. Everyone in the co-op take a turn shopping so that we don't all have to shop every month.

Subject is _____

_____

7. Anyone with strong preferences has a choice of several different vegetables.

Subject is _____

_____

8. Some of us likes having the chance to try many new things, so we take whatever the shoppers can get.

Subject is _____

_____

9. All of the members is responsible for picking up a carton on Saturday afternoon.

Subject is _____

_____

10. The group are happy to save money and to get a variety of fresh food.

Subject is _____

_____

EXERCISE 18.4 VERBS WITH ANTECEDENTS OF *WHO*, *WHICH*, OR *THAT*

NAME _____ DATE _____

Underline the correct verb form in each of the following sentences. In each case, be ready to explain your choice.

> **EXAMPLE** Tom is one of those dogs that <u>bark</u>/barks at bees or cars or the neighbor's radio.
> *[Many dogs bark; Tom is just one of them.]*

1. The only one of Steven Soderbergh's films that I disliked was/were *Full Frontal*.

2. Firefighters and police officers who protects/protect the public has/have earned my respect.

3. She is one of those comedians who make/makes audiences laugh out of embarrassment.

4. He is one of the people who work/works at the front desk.

5. Each of the members who vote/votes have/has a duty to keep the ballot a secret.

6. Which pup in the litter seem/seems the most affectionate?

7. The candidate who insists/insist on making public restrooms available downtown will get my vote.

8. Any student in this class who does/do not expect to work hard should consider studying another subject instead.

9. Days that is/are as foggy as today make driving difficult.

10. Only one of the tenants disagree/disagrees with the new parking rules.

EXERCISE 18.5   CHECKING SUBJECT-VERB AGREEMENT

NAME _____ **DATE** _____

A. Read the paragraph below carefully, and underline the verbs. If a verb does not agree with its subject, cross out the verb and write the correct form above it. You may need to review earlier sections of this chapter. The first two verbs have been underlined for you.

Increasingly, smokers and nonsmokers <u>find</u> themselves in disagreement about which group <u>have</u> the right to a congenial environment. Among the problems with cigarette smoke are its potential to cause disease and its odor. A waitperson or bartender who works in a smoky restaurant inhale a lot of smoke on the job, and this secondhand smoke is known to be damaging. Everyone do not agree about the best way to solve this problem, however. Some cities in this country is banning smoking in all indoor public areas. But people who owns bars worry that their business will suffer if smokers cannot light up indoors, and many a nonsmoking bartender wonders if a ban is a good idea if it will result in a loss of income. Which are more important, good money or good health? And do a smoker's preference count more than a nonsmoker's preference? The only certain thing are that making everyone happy will be difficult.

B. Read the paragraph below, and fill in each blank with a verb that agrees with its subject.

Fast-food restaurants _____ become more popular in America in recent years. Groups of people _____ to burger and chicken places each day by the millions. Often, on one strip of road, there will be five or six places that _____ hungry customers. Each and every restaurant _____ a member of a larger chain that _____ the raw products and materials. Prices _____ also controlled by the parent company. Of all the foods on the menus, hamburgers consistently _____ more than any other item. That is because American customers _____ hamburgers more than almost any other food. The nutritional value of these foods _____ not the highest possible, but the food tastes so good that most people _____ happy to eat fast-food often. Besides, nobody_____ nutrition to convenience all the time.

EXERCISE 18.6   REVIEWING SUBJECT-VERB AGREEMENT

NAME _____ **DATE** _____

Read each sentence below. If all subjects and verbs agree, write _C_ on the line below the sentence. If there are errors of agreement, rewrite the sentence on the lines provided.

1. The hurricanes that hit the Carolina coast is one cause of beach erosion.

   _____

   _____

2. The last show of the television series reveal the identity of the killer.

   _____

   _____

3. Janie Crawford tell the story in *Their Eyes Were Watching God*.

   _____

   _____

4. Fruit juice and seltzer makes for a thirst-quenching drink in August.

   _____

   _____

5. The strike committee agree to further negotiations.

   _____

   _____

6. My photographs of the lynx and the cougar proves the presence of wildcats in this area.

   _____

   _____

7. Learning to write letters are a challenge for most children.

_____

_____

8. In our family, discussing politics lead to trouble.

_____

_____

9. Neither the waiters nor the customers was injured when the tablecloth caught fire.

_____

_____

10. Neither I nor my friend have been able to get tickets.

_____

_____

11. Your memories of your childhood forms a part of who you are.

_____

_____

12. Physics were taught by one of my favorite professors.

_____

_____

13. The audience always applaud after this scene.

_____

_____

14. Novels based on historical fact interest me.

_____

_____

15. The intricate designs on kalamkari cloth attract viewers' eyes and hands.

_____

_____

16. The jack-o'-lantern's eyes and nose was beginning to collapse.

_____

_____

17. Each of the biographies tell the story of a famous scientist.

_____

_____

18. Down from the hills come a bear in need of food and water.

_____

_____

19. No one present during the argument are able to pinpoint who started it.

_____

_____

20. Our group in history class have been assigned the 1960s.

_____

_____

Pronouns

19

Denied the use of pronouns, writers would have to use the same nouns over and over; the result would be dull repetition. In a description, for example, the name of the person or thing described would have to be repeated. A dog would scratch the *dog's neck* instead of *its neck*, and Robert would put on *Robert's raincoat* instead of *his raincoat*. Fortunately, we can use pronouns. But, every time we do so, we need to be careful so that readers will understand each pronoun's antecedent. The **antecedent** is the noun or noun phrase to which the pronoun refers. Writers must make sure that pronouns and their antecedents agree in *gender, number,* and *person.*

PRONOUNS IN EVERYDAY USE

Look — or listen — for pronouns in some everyday places. Look at the frequently asked questions on a favorite Web site, listen to an explanation of how to work on office machines, read a story in a supermarket tabloid, or focus on pronouns in some other situation. Record what you find. If you wish, compare written and spoken directions to see how pronouns are used differently and whether writers are more careful than speakers.

Pronoun case (34a)

Most of us generally know that some sentences require *I* instead of *me* or *they* instead of *them.* When we distinguish between these pronoun forms, we are distinguishing between *cases.* Intuition, unfortunately, does not always help us choose the correct pronoun. Should we say "Mike and him went skiing" — or "Mike and he"? Should it be "I invited Paul and her" — or "Paul and she"? Should "us fans" or "we fans" support our favorite team? In addition, many writers have trouble recalling the distinctions between *who* and *whom.* Fortunately, if you know enough grammar to identify subjects, predicate nouns, and objects, you can use that knowledge to determine correct pronoun usage. (For an introduction to pronouns and to basic sentence grammar, see Chapter 16.)

In general, pronouns take different forms to indicate singular and plural and to function as subjects, objects, or possessives. This chapter discusses each of these cases — called subjective, objective, and possessive. The one pronoun not much discussed here is the pronoun *you.* This pronoun is easy to use because it stays the same whether it is singular or plural, in both subjective and objective cases.

Subjective case

When pronouns function as subjects, they take the **subjective case**. Here are the forms for personal pronouns used in the subjective case:

SINGULAR	PLURAL
I	we
he, she, it	they

Subjective-case pronouns can appear in a variety of grammatical constructions; examples follow:

PRONOUNS AS SUBJECTS OF SENTENCES AND CLAUSES

Excited and eager, *we* drove to the hospital. [*In this simple sentence with one independent clause,* we *acts as the subject of the verb* drove.]

Although *they* were tired, the chorus sang well. [*In this complex sentence with one dependent and one independent clause,* they *acts as the subject of the verb* were.]

PRONOUNS AS SUBJECTS OF SUBORDINATE CLAUSES

Nobody knew that *she* had arrived. [*subject of noun clause*]

When *he* arrived, the store had already closed. [*subject of adverb clause*]

Irwin returned the book that *he* had borrowed. [*subject of adjective clause*]

Subject complements follow linking verbs and rename the subject. Because they rename the subject, they traditionally take the subjective case, although this usage is often not preserved in spoken English.

PERSONAL PRONOUNS AS SUBJECT COMPLEMENTS

The only students who didn't get the flu were Sofia and I. [Sofia *and* I *are predicate nouns renaming the subject,* students.]

Objective case

When pronouns function as objects of a verb, a verbal (an infinitive, gerund, or participial word or phrase), or a preposition, they take the **objective case**. The objective case forms for personal pronouns are as follows:

SINGULAR	PLURAL
me	us
him, her, it	them

Here are examples of pronouns used as objects:

PRONOUNS AS DIRECT OBJECTS OF VERBS

Daniel caught the ball and threw *it* to Jacob. [It *acts as the object of the verb* threw.]

Jamal asked Debbie and *me* to go to the party. [Me *acts as one of the objects of the verb* asked.]

PRONOUNS AS INDIRECT OBJECTS OF VERBS

Thursday's unexpected blizzard gave *us* an unscheduled holiday. [Us *acts as the indirect object: the blizzard gave what?* holiday *(direct object); gave a holiday to whom?* us *(indirect object)*]

PRONOUNS AS OBJECTS OF VERBALS

It has taken me years to know *him* well. [Him *acts as the direct object of the infinitive* to know.]

Wishing *us* luck, Professor Decker said we could begin the final exam. [Us *acts as the indirect object of the participle* wishing.]

In helping *us* this way, Professor Ede showed real concern for students. [Us *acts as the direct object of the gerund* helping.]

PRONOUNS AS OBJECTS OF PREPOSITIONS

Andre handed the graphite racquet to *her*. [Her *acts as the object of the preposition* to.]

With *him* and Jack, no two hunting trips were ever the same. [Him *acts as one of two objects of the preposition* with.]

Possessive case

The **possessive case** indicates ownership or possession. Possessive pronouns take one form when they are used alone to replace nouns and a separate form when they are used as adjectives to modify nouns. The possessive-case forms of personal pronouns are as follows:

SINGULAR		PLURAL	
Noun Form	**Adjective Form**	**Noun Form**	**Adjective Form**
mine	my	ours	our
yours	your	yours	your
his, hers, its	his, her, its	theirs	their

Note: The possessive pronoun *its* is often confused with the contraction *it's*. Keep in mind that *it's* is a shortened form of *it is*.

■ *Possessive Forms Functioning as Adjectives*

The adjectival forms are used only before a noun or a gerund, as in these examples:

Her yoga class is the most advanced. [Her *precedes the noun* class.]

Your shoes are worn, especially at the heels. [Your *precedes the noun* shoes.]

Their sleeping late caused them to miss the train. [Their *precedes the gerund* sleeping.]

Be careful to distinguish between gerunds and participles. Gerunds always act as nouns, so when pronouns precede gerunds, they always take the possessive case. But the same word may function as a gerund in one sentence and as a participle in another. Consider this example: *I remember his singing well.* Here, *singing* is a gerund; it functions as a noun and is the direct object of the verb *remember.* Thus the possessive pronoun *his* is accurate. The singing is *his.* The original sentence could be arranged in this way without changing its meaning: *I well remember his singing.* After all, *well* is an adverb, and adverbs cannot modify nouns.

Now consider this example: *I remember him singing well.* Only one word has changed, but the pronoun *him* creates a sentence with a very different meaning. Now the adverb *well* must modify the participle *singing.* Here we know the quality of his song: he sang well.

■ *Possessive Forms Functioning as Nouns*

When functioning like the nouns they replace, possessive pronouns may also be used by themselves, often appearing in sentences using some form of the verb *be.* Here are two examples:

Theirs was the toughest schedule in the league. [*possessive noun as subject*]

The one coat left must be *hers.* [*possessive noun as subject complement*]

Who, whoever, whom, and *whomever* (34b)

Who or *whom* in a question

In everyday speech, we often do not preserve the distinction between *who* and *whom,* but formal and academic writing still does. Thus *who* and *whom* often give writers trouble. The rule is simple enough: use *who* as a subject, and use *whom* as an object. That rule, however, is sometimes difficult to apply when the sentence is a question. Should you write *Whom did the consultant interview?* or *Who did the consultant interview?*

You can determine which pronoun to use by constructing a possible answer for the question and using a personal pronoun in that answer. The case of that personal pronoun will tell you the case of the interrogative pronoun. This sounds confusing, but the following examples should help:

Who/Whom is a good teacher? [*Answer:* He *is a good teacher.* He *is the subject; therefore, the pronoun must be the subjective form:* who.]

Who/Whom did the consultant interview? [*Answer: The consultant interviewed* her. Her *is the object; therefore, the pronoun must be the objective form:* whom.]

Who/Whom should I send this report to? [*Answer: I should send this report to* her. Her *is the object of the preposition* to. *Therefore, the pronoun must be the objective form:* whom. *In a formal writing situation, this sentence would probably be reordered to read* To whom should I send this report?]

Who, whoever, whom, or whomever in a dependent clause

The pronouns *who, whoever, whom,* and *whomever* are called **relative pronouns**; often they begin dependent clauses. How the pronoun functions *inside that clause* determines which form should be chosen.

If the pronoun is the subject of the dependent clause, use the subjective form *who* or *whoever*.

I'll award a prize to *whoever* can recall the name of the first Russian cosmonaut.

How can you tell that *whoever* is the subject in that subordinate clause? One way is to write out the subordinate clause. Doing that gives you *whoever can recall the name of the first Russian cosmonaut.* The verb in this clause is *can recall*; the subject of that verb must be the subjective-case pronoun *whoever*.

Another way to identify the correct form of a relative pronoun is to isolate the subordinate clause and then substitute a personal pronoun in place of the relative pronoun:

She identified the clerk _____ had given her the wrong change.

Here, the relative pronoun is the subject of the verb *had given*. By itself, the subordinate clause reads _____ *had given her the wrong change.* Substituting the objective pronoun *him* makes the clause read *him had given her the wrong change.* Clearly the objective case *him* is incorrect in this clause, so the correct choice here is the subjective form: *who.*

The objective forms of the relative pronouns *who* and *whoever* are *whom* and *whomever*. The same methods and criteria apply for identifying the correct use of these pronouns. The function of the pronoun within the dependent clause determines the choice. If the relative pronoun functions as an object, the correct choice is either *whom* or *whomever*.

At the party, Emma talked to _____ she found interesting.

By itself, the subordinate clause reads _____ *she found interesting.* This is a somewhat awkward word order; a more normal word order would yield *she found _____ interesting.* The accurate personal pronoun here would be *them*, which is the objective form. Thus the correct relative pronoun here is the objective *whomever*.

Case in compound structures (34c)

You will often encounter personal pronouns used as **compound subjects** (two or more subjects that have the same verb, generally joined by a coordinating conjunction such as *and* or *or*) or **compound objects** (two or more objects of a verb, a verbal, or a preposition, also generally joined by a word such as *and* or *or*). If you simply drop the other half of the compound, you should have no trouble determining the correct pronoun case. For example, take the sentence *Margaret and her went to the movie.* Keep the pronoun, drop the other half of the compound subject, and you have this sentence: *Her went to the movie.* That sounds wrong, and it is wrong. You now know that the correct case is the subjective: *Margaret and she went to the movie.*

You may find a pronoun as part of an **appositive**, a noun or noun phrase that renames a preceding noun. When this happens, the pronoun takes the case of the noun it renames. Here are two examples:

> Two great fishermen, my father and me/I, were skunked again today. [*The appositive phrase is* my father and me/I. *This phrase renames the noun* fishermen. *Since* fishermen *is the subject of this sentence, the pronoun in the appositive must also be the subjective form.* I *is the proper choice.*]

> That one coastal cedar defeated two great tree climbers, Beth and I/me. [*The appositive phrase is* Beth and I/me. *This phrase renames the noun* climbers. *Since* climbers *is the direct object of the verb* defeated, *the pronoun in the appositive must also be the objective form.* Me *is the proper choice.*]

Case in elliptical constructions (34d)

Elliptical constructions are sentence patterns in which one or several words are omitted because the writer assumes that readers will understand what is meant without them. Such constructions are used often; if we never left any words out, our writing would be very repetitive indeed. Leaving out words, however, can make it easier to make mistakes, especially with pronoun usage.

Consider this sentence: *Jason is younger than me.* Is the pronoun *me* used correctly? To find out, you must determine which words have been left out of the sentence and put them back in: *Jason is younger than me am.* Clearly that sounds incorrect. *Me* is an objective-case pronoun; we never hear it used as the subject of a verb, so it sounds unnatural. The correct pronoun to use in this sentence is the subjective-case pronoun *I*—*Jason is younger than I (am)*—because this pronoun is the subject of the dependent clause *than I am.*

Using the correct pronoun case in elliptical constructions is often crucial to your readers' understanding of your sentence meaning. Consider these two sentences:

> I like Chen better than he. [*If fully written out, this sentence would read* I like Chen better than he likes Troy.]

> I like Chen better than him. [*If fully written out, this sentence would read* I like Chen better than I like him.]

As you see, changing the pronoun from *he* to *him* alters the meaning considerably.

We and *us* before a noun (34e)

When you want to use a pronoun before a noun for emphasis, how do you decide whether to say "*We* psychology majors understand what makes people tick" or "*Us* psychology majors understand what makes people tick"? How do you choose between "The players owe it to *we* fans" and "The players owe it to *us* fans"? The simple way to make the choice is to drop the noun and see which pronoun fits. This trick will probably prove to you that "*We* psychology majors understand what makes people tick" and "The players owe it to *us* fans" sound best.

Pronoun-antecedent agreement (34f)

Often, pronoun-antecedent agreement is easy to achieve, and we manage that agreement without giving it a thought. But some special cases are confusing and give even experienced writers difficulty. Let us look at these cases now.

→ **COMMON ERROR: LACK OF PRONOUN-ANTECEDENT AGREEMENT**

Compound or collective-noun antecedents

A **compound antecedent**, two or more nouns or noun phrases joined by *and*, usually requires a plural pronoun.

> **EXAMPLE** It was such a hot afternoon that Beth and Jane left their coats at school. [Their *refers to* Beth and Jane.]

However, note two exceptions:

1. If *each* or *every* precedes a compound antecedent, the indefinite pronoun acts as an antecedent, and the following pronoun is singular.

> **EXAMPLES** Each undergrad and grad student carries his or her own student ID. [His or her *refers to the singular pronoun* each.]
>
> Every mother and daughter should fill out her own questionnaire. [Her *refers to the singular pronoun* every.]

2. If a compound antecedent joined by *and* refers to a single thing or person, the following pronoun is singular.

> **EXAMPLE** This writer and student has achieved his success through discipline and diligence. [His *refers to one person*, this writer and student.]

When two or more antecedents are connected by *or* or *nor*, the pronoun should agree with the part of the antecedent closest to it.

EXAMPLES   Either one novel or several short stories are assigned each week. [*Pronoun* each *agrees with* chapters.]

Neither the suitcase nor the golf clubs were recovered in their original condition. [*Pronoun* their *agrees with* clubs.]

Note: In the second example, the plural noun antecedent *clubs* follows the singular noun antecedent *suitcase*. This reflects the common practice of putting the plural antecedent second, nearer the verb.

Compound antecedents of different genders can pose problems for writers. Consider this sentence: *Either Dave or Holly will bring _____ own guitar.* What pronoun should go in the blank? Using *her* would seem to eliminate Dave; using *his* would seem to eliminate Holly. Using *their* would imply that they own one guitar jointly, and perhaps they do. But if the sentence means to indicate that both Dave and Holly own separate guitars, no single pronoun will fit in that blank. The best solution here is to rewrite the sentence: *Either Dave will bring his guitar, or Holly will bring hers.*

Agreement problems arise for some writers when they use **collective nouns**, nouns that are singular in form but refer to collections of things or people. These nouns include words such as *army, audience, committee, crowd, class, family, group,* and *team.* Collective nouns with singular meanings take singular pronouns; collective nouns with plural meanings take plural pronouns. When you are referring to a group as a single unit, use the singular pronoun. When you are referring to individual members of that group, use the plural pronoun.

EXAMPLES   The crowd erupted with applause as it demanded an encore. [Crowd *as a single unit takes the singular pronoun* it.]

After the encore, the crowd drifted away to their cars. [Crowd *focusing on its members is plural in meaning and takes the plural pronoun* their.]

Indefinite-pronoun antecedents

If you have already worked through Chapter 18 of this book, you may recall that some **indefinite pronouns** are always singular (*anybody, each,* and *someone* are examples), some are always plural (*many, few, several*), and some are either singular or plural depending on context (*all, more, some*). Pronouns referring to indefinite-pronoun antecedents must agree in number with their antecedents. See the examples that follow.

Each of the women in the bridal party wore a dress that *she* herself made. [Each *is the singular pronoun subject of this sentence.* She *is singular and refers to* each.]

Many of the visiting swimmers won *their* races. [Many *is a plural indefinite pronoun;* their *is also plural and refers to* many.]

All of the remaining sale items should be returned to *their* original storeroom locations. [*Since* all *refers to* items, *it is considered plural; hence, the plural pronoun* their.]

Not *all* of the recovered oil could be cleansed of *its* impurities. [*Here* all *refers to an uncountable quantity,* oil; *hence,* all *is considered singular.* Its, *a singular pronoun, refers to* all.]

Sexist pronouns (34g)

Indefinite pronouns such as those discussed in the preceding section often present problems of sexist usage. Consider this example:

> An usher stood at the front of the movie theater and asked, "If *anyone* here is a doctor, would *he* please come forward?"

This sentence uses the masculine pronoun *he* generically to refer to people of either sex. Though grammatically acceptable, today this usage is often criticized because it seems to ignore or exclude half the human race. The best remedy for sexist usage is rewording:

> "If *anyone* here is a doctor, would *he or she* please come forward?"

> "Will *anyone* who is a doctor please come forward?"

Sometimes a sentence originally phrased in the singular can be rephrased in the plural, thereby allowing use of the pronoun *they*. Thus a sentence such as *Each student must do his own homework* becomes *All students must do their own homework*.

Sometimes you will not know the gender of a pronoun antecedent. Consider this sentence:

> *Someone* from the main office left *their* coat on the back of this chair.

Although the sentence avoids sexism, it also connects a singular antecedent, *someone*, with a plural pronoun, *their*. Informally, we often speak this way, and some readers now view this construction as acceptable even in formal, academic writing. However, many other readers find it unacceptable, so you should be careful about using it in your writing. The sentence can be revised in at least two ways:

> *Someone* from the main office left a coat on the back of this chair.

> *Someone* from the main office left *his or her* coat on the back of this chair.

Ambiguous pronoun references (34h)

→ **COMMON ERROR: VAGUE PRONOUN REFERENCE**

When used effectively, pronouns speed readers along; when used ineffectively or inaccurately, pronouns may actually stop the reading process by forcing readers to work backward to track down unclear references. This portion of the chapter looks carefully at pronoun reference, one of the most common sources of error in student writing. Vague pronoun reference occurs when a pronoun does not clearly refer to an **antecedent**, a specific noun or pronoun appearing elsewhere in the sentence or in a preceding sentence. Pronoun reference also is vague if a pronoun seems to refer to more than one antecedent or if the antecedent is not specifically stated.

Matching pronouns clearly to one antecedent

Sometimes writers inadvertently provide readers with two possible antecedents, as in this sentence: *Mary asked Cathy if she was responsible for the car accident.* Here, *she* could refer to Cathy or to Mary; readers cannot tell for sure who may be responsible for the car accident. The writer knows the intended meaning, but readers are forced to guess.

To improve such a sentence, your first impulse may be to try to change a word or two to clarify the pronoun reference. However, this strategy is not likely to work. On a piece of scratch paper, try to revise the sample sentence by changing just a word or two.

In most cases, a sentence such as *Mary asked Cathy if she was responsible for the car accident* will need to be recast in order to clarify the pronoun reference. One solution would be to quote directly: *Mary asked Cathy, "Are you responsible for the car accident?"* or *Mary asked Cathy, "Am I responsible for the car accident?"*

Here is another example:

UNCLEAR	The dolphins raced the sailboats across the harbor, and Marion thought they looked beautiful.
REVISED	Marion thought the dolphins looked beautiful racing the sailboats across the harbor.

Keeping pronouns and antecedents close together

Distancing pronouns from nouns also makes for difficult reading. Such separations usually force readers to stop and retrace the references. As a reader, you may remember instances of such frustration. When you discover this problem in your own prose, sometimes the best alternative is to repeat the original noun (thus eliminating the pronoun). If a pronoun does seem appropriate, make sure the pronoun and its antecedent are close together.

REMOTE REFERENCE

What seems to unite the lives and careers of several seemingly disparate graduates might be called the concept of useful work. Mike B. served for two years in the peace corps and is now an obstetrician who spends an afternoon a week at a free clinic; Alison R. easily passed her CPA exams and now works mainly with nonprofit arts organizations. A physicist in college, Joanna K. now holds a management position in an engineering firm that specializes in the cleanup of toxic waste sites. *It* seems to unite *them* because, one way or another, their careers, while personally challenging and often mone-tarily rewarding, also acknowledge some obligation to society as a whole.

What does *it* refer to? If you backtrack far enough, you find that *it* refers to "the concept of useful work." You would know that only because the verb *unite* is repeated and thus serves as a pointer back to that first sentence. The most immediate referent for *them* is *toxic waste sites* — clearly not what the passage really means to say. Revising this example means repeating the original nouns.

REVISION FOR CLEARER REFERENCE

What seems to unite the lives and careers of several seemingly disparate graduates might be called the concept of useful work. Mike B. served for two years in the peace corps and is now an obstetrician who spends an afternoon a week at a free clinic; Alison R. easily passed her CPA exams and now works mainly with nonprofit arts organiza-tions. A physicist in college, Joanna K. now holds a management position in an engineer-ing firm that specializes in the cleanup of toxic waste sites. *The concept of useful work* seems to unite *these graduates* because, one way or another, their careers, while personally challenging and often monetarily rewarding, also acknowledge some obligation to soci-ety as a whole.

Vague use of *it, this, that,* and *which* (34i)

In some situations, writers use the pronouns *it, this, that,* or *which* to refer not to a par-ticular noun but rather to some concept or situation mentioned in an earlier clause, sentence, or paragraph. For example, look at the pronoun *that* as used in this sen-tence: *Grace felt tired after the racquetball game, and that is why she went to bed early.* The antecedent for *that* is not one noun. Instead, *that* refers to the entire clause *Grace felt tired after the racquetball game.* This is but one example of **broad reference**.

When carefully used, broad reference presents few problems. However, broad reference can become problematic whenever reader confusion is possible. Writers should be particularly wary of starting sentences with *this* or *that.* Here is an example of such unclear use of broad reference:

UNCLEAR	For dinner that evening, two of us ate leftover tuna casserole, while the rest of us ate leftover salmon loaf. That must have made Jack sick. [*What does* that *refer to? Did Jack eat the tuna or the salmon loaf?*]
REVISED	For dinner that evening, two of us ate leftover tuna casserole, while the rest of us ate leftover salmon loaf. The tuna must have made Jack sick.

As a writer, you should be sure that the antecedents of clauses introduced by the relative pronouns *which* and *that* are clear. The sentence *Jack drove his new truck to the dance, which his grandparents bought him* says literally that Jack's grandparents bought him a dance. Eliminating such confusion is easy: put the relative pronoun directly after the noun it refers to. Sometimes a sentence may need to be reworded: *Jack drove to the dance in his new truck, which his grandparents had bought him.* Now *which* clearly refers to *truck.*

Inappropriate use of *who*, *which*, and *that* (34j)

Writers conventionally use *who, which,* and *that* in the following ways:

- *Who* refers to people and to animals with personalities or names.

    EXAMPLES   Megan is the girl *who* lives next door.

    Matsumi, *who* likes to fly paper airplanes, wants to be a pilot.

    Our dog Tom, *who* scares the meter readers, is completely harmless.

    The pony *who* nibbled my ear became my favorite companion.

- *Which* refers to inanimate objects and to animals without personalities or names.

    EXAMPLES   Dogs, *which* must be on leashes, are permitted in this park.

    I lost my favorite mitt, *which* my father gave me on my last birthday.

- *That* can refer to animals and things and occasionally to anonymous persons or people treated collectively.

    EXAMPLES   The beach house *that* my parents rented no longer exists.

    The deer *that* has been feeding in the backyard appeared again last night.

    People *that* drink and drive should be required to visit hospital emergency rooms.

Indefinite use of *you*, *it*, and *they* (34k)

Sometimes, when speaking informally, we use pronouns to refer to nouns that are implied, rather than mentioned directly. Consider this sentence: *During registration, they gave me the wrong forms.* In that sentence, *they* does not refer to any named people. Perhaps the writer doesn't know who gave out those wrong forms. The sentence should be revised to read *During registration, someone gave me the wrong forms* or *During registration, a person at the Biology Department table gave me the wrong forms.*

You is also sometimes used in this informal, vague way: *Whenever you go down-town after ten o'clock, you're taking your life in your hands.* To whom does *you* refer? In the context of a conversation, the referent might be clear. But in academic or formal writing, clarity demands that the *you* be replaced with a more specific referent: *People who go downtown after ten o'clock risk harassment, assault, or worse.* As you can see, the informal, vague construction has been replaced by clearer phrasing; readers now know more precisely what this writer means.

The guideline here is simple: make your antecedents specific nouns whenever you can.

UNCLEAR	We went to the Old World for a pint of Bellhaven and a wedge of short-bread, but they were hosting a concert, so we did not stay.
REVISED	We went to the Old World for a pint of Bellhaven and a wedge of short-bread, but the pub was hosting a concert, so we did not stay.

Implied antecedents (34l)

Examine this sentence: *In Professor Ede's class, she requires weekly papers.* To whom does *she* refer? We can only assume that *she* refers to Professor Ede. Yet in that sentence, *Professor Ede's* functions as a possessive adjective modifying the noun *class.* Although the reference may be clear enough (and acceptable in conversation), many formal or academic readers find this construction unacceptable. Remember, pronouns refer only to nouns or to other pronouns. The sentence can be revised in either of two ways:

Professor Ede requires weekly papers in her class.

In her class, Professor Ede requires weekly papers.

Here is another example:

INACCURATE	After Elvis Presley's death, he was still reportedly appearing to fans.
REVISED	Elvis Presley was still reportedly appearing to fans after his death.

EXERCISE 19.1   SUBJECTIVE AND OBJECTIVE PRONOUNS

NAME _____ **DATE** _____

Read each of the following sentences, and decide if the underlined word or words are in the subjective or objective position. Write *S* on the line after the sentence if the word or words are subjective; write *O* if the word or words are objective. Then choose the correct pronoun to replace the word or words, and write it above the underlined word(s).

> **EXAMPLE**   *he*
>   Jack and <u>George</u> visited the new science library.   *S*

1. Whenever <u>Jeri, David, and Sean</u> went to the beach, the weather was bad. _____

2. Chris was a better tennis player than <u>Al</u>. _____

3. <u>Jody, Juan, Scott, and I</u> were the only people still in the building. _____

4. Maya wonders whether James is smarter than <u>Maya</u>. _____

5. Mrs. Markle was upset because no one had told <u>Mrs. Markle</u> about the wedding. _____

6. We earned very little money, but our poverty did not really bother <u>Michel and me</u>. _____

7. Justin, Paolo, and I have a great time whenever <u>Justin, Paolo, and I</u> get together. _____

8. Sport-utility vehicles may not be any safer than cars, but people feel safer in <u>sport-utility vehicles</u>. _____

9. The professor asked Martin and <u>Jimmy</u> to hand out the exams. _____

10. The woman wondered where <u>the woman</u> could find a supermarket nearby. _____

NAME _____ **DATE** _____

Several of the following sentences use pronouns incorrectly. Identify and correct the incorrect sentences. If the sentence is already correct, write *C* on the line beside it.

EXAMPLE   Whenever we go into that store, the clerk asks ~~we~~ our names. _____
                                                                                      us

1. The waiter finally seated Kim, Sidney, and I. _____

2. After dinner with my mother, she suggested that I write my paper. _____

3. Jarrett and her delivered meals to older people who could not cook. _____

4. Everyone in the office except she had contributed money for Jana's gift. _____

5. The day was perfect, so him and I decided to skip class. _____

6. For Bill, Ubijo, and I, cycling thirty miles a day was our training for the triathlon. _____

7. Talking through our differences keeps my mother and I from fighting. _____

8. Though even the idea of hang gliding made her nervous, she gave it a try. _____

9. Harry called she before him left the house. _____

10. The memo bothered Sara and I because the boss assumed that we would cover up the problem. _____

EXERCISE 19.3 SUBJECTIVE-, OBJECTIVE-, AND POSSESSIVE-CASE PRONOUNS

NAME _____ **DATE** _____

Substitute pronouns for the nouns in parentheses after each blank.

> **EXAMPLE** The basketball team made _____its_____ (the team's) way onto the court.

On the first play, Micki and Jenni tightly guarded (1) _____ (Micki and Jenni's) two opponents. Micki shadowed the opposing player so that (2) _____ (Micki) could keep the other team from shooting. That forced Melanie to pass the ball to (3) _____ (Melanie's) teammate, Rosie. (4) _____ (Rosie) dribbled around (5) _____ (Rosie and Melanie's) opposing guards and passed to Carrie. Wide open, Carrie received (6) _____ (Rosie's) pass. Now it was up to Carrie to make the shot, so (7) _____ (Carrie) took time to set up before shooting. The ball followed (8) _____ (the ball's) usual perfect arc. Carrie did what (9) _____ (Carrie) did best. (10) _____ (Carrie) sank (11) _____ (Carrie's) shot. All the team members shouted (12) _____ (the members') delight, and the people in the stands shouted (13) _____ (the people's). As the fans jumped and shouted in the stands, (14) _____ (the fans) all knew that (15) _____ (the fans') team would be hard to beat in playoffs. Everyone watching the women would remember (16) _____ (the women's) performance that night.

NAME _____ **DATE** _____

Work through the following sentences to determine whether to use a subjective or an objective relative pronoun. The first sentence has been done for you.

1. Matthew said he would be glad to speak to _____ showed up to listen.

   The clause that contains the blank is <u>showed up to listen</u>   .

   Inserting a personal pronoun (he/she/him/her/they/them) yields
   <u>he showed up to listen</u>   .

   Does this personal pronoun act as the subject or as an object? <u>subject</u>   .

   Thus the correct relative pronoun in this sentence is <u>whoever</u>   .

2. I yelled at _____ was calling me and making obscene remarks.

   The clause that contains the blank is _____ .

   Inserting a personal pronoun (he/she/him/her/they/them) yields

   _____ .

   Does this personal pronoun act as the subject or as an object? _____ .

   Thus the correct relative pronoun in this sentence is _____ .

3. I did not know _____ had thrown the snowball.

   The clause that contains the blank is _____ .

   Inserting a personal pronoun (he/she/him/her/they/them) yields

   _____ .

   Does this personal pronoun act as the subject or as an object? _____ .

   Thus the correct relative pronoun in this sentence is _____ .

4. The neighbor with _____ she spoke said they would attend the town meeting.

   The clause that contains the blank is _____ .

   Inserting a personal pronoun (he/she/him/her/they/them) yields

   _____ .

Does this personal pronoun act as the subject or as an object? _____ .

Thus the correct relative pronoun in this sentence is _____ .

5. _____ she waves to usually waves back.

The clause that contains the blank is _____ .

Inserting a personal pronoun (he/she/him/her/they/them) yields

_____ .

Does this personal pronoun act as the subject or as an object? _____ .

Thus the correct relative pronoun in this sentence is _____ .

6. The teacher shared the lesson plan with those _____ she trusted.

The clause that contains the blank is _____ .

Inserting a personal pronoun (he/she/him/her/they/them) yields

_____ .

Does this personal pronoun act as the subject or as an object? _____ .

Thus the correct relative pronoun in this sentence is _____ .

7. _____ you want as mayor never seems to win.

The clause that contains the blank is _____ .

Inserting a personal pronoun (he/she/him/her/they/them) yields

_____ .

Does this personal pronoun act as the subject or as an object? _____ .

Thus the correct relative pronoun in this sentence is _____ .

8. Many whistle-blowers _____ want to protect consumers put themselves at risk.

The clause that contains the blank is _____ .

Inserting a personal pronoun (he/she/him/her/they/them) yields

_____ .

Does this personal pronoun act as the subject or as an object? _____ .

Thus the correct relative pronoun in this sentence is _____ .

EXERCISE 19.5 *WHO, WHOEVER, WHOM, AND WHOMEVER*

NAME _____ **DATE** _____

Underline the correct pronoun choice in each of the following sentences, and briefly explain the reason for your choice.

> **EXAMPLE**   The woman who/<u>whom</u> I met is, I discovered today, the sales manager.
>
> _Whom functions as the object of the verb met._ _____

1. Who/Whom finished the biography of Adams?

   _____

2. Surgeons may choose whoever/whomever they want as their nurses.

   _____

3. Larry complained that he had no idea who/whom to root for.

   _____

4. Whoever/Whomever leaked the report should confess.

   _____

5. The doctor who/whom you recommended doesn't accept new patients.

   _____

6. Callers who/whom phone during dinner and cannot pronounce my name do not get my full attention.

   _____

7. Whoever/Whomever he asked told him that his son's teacher was excellent.

   _____

8. Who/Whom did you invite to the dance?

   _____

9. Who/Whom will be our designated driver Friday night?

   _____

10. To who/whom should I make out this check?

   _____

EXERCISE 19.6 PRONOUN CASE

In each of the following sentences, underline the pronoun form that should be used. The first sentence is done for you.

1. To we/<u>us</u> New Englanders, hurricanes are a bigger worry than tornadoes.

2. The two newcomers, Vivian and I/me, found the subway station without any trouble.

3. When we/us classmates gather on Saturday, we'll be celebrating our fifth anniversary since graduation.

4. The infomercial features an actor my brother and I/me loved when we/us were kids.

5. Sara did better than I/me on the test.

6. The sound of him/his snoring kept she/her awake.

7. The casting director chose two unknowns, Alexi and I/me, for the new speaking roles.

8. That laptop is Ava's, and this one is your/yours.

9. Forget about dating Julie or she/her if you don't like obsessive people.

10. Two families, the Cohens and they/them, won't join the protest.

EXERCISE 19.7   PRONOUNS WITH COMPOUND OR COLLECTIVE-NOUN ANTECEDENTS

NAME _____   **DATE** _____

Identify the pronouns and their antecedents in each of the sentences below. If the pronouns are used inaccurately, rewrite the sentence to correct the errors. If the sentence is correct, write C on the line below the sentence.

EXAMPLES   Whenever Leigh and Jack go out, Taylor stays with their children.

Pronouns/antecedents: <u>their/Leigh and Jack</u>

<u>C</u>

The goat and the two sheep have cropped that pasture right down to their roots.

Pronouns/antecedents: <u>their/pasture</u>

<u>The goat and the two sheep have cropped that pasture right down to its roots.</u>

1. The committee needs to find more evidence if they are ever going to sway the mayor.

   Pronouns/antecedents: _____

   _____

2. My infant daughter and son, twins, sleep in their crib curled up together.

   Pronouns/antecedents: _____

   _____

3. The team decided that it would continue to hold practices on Sundays.

   Pronouns/antecedents: _____

   _____

4. Each Oscar nominee is grateful for the publicity they receive.

   Pronouns/antecedents: _____

   _____

5. Neither an urban setting nor a rural one inspired me to make them my home.

   Pronouns/antecedents: _____

   _____

6. This husband and father knows not to upset the women in his family.

   Pronouns/antecedents: _____

   _____

7. Jeremy or Lawrence wore their snowshoes after being told not to.

   Pronouns/antecedents: _____

   _____

8. Every restaurant in town would like to improve their revenue Monday through Thursday.

   Pronouns/antecedents: _____

   _____

9. The contractor and the subcontractors always showed up when they said they would.

   Pronouns/antecedents: _____

   _____

10. Either Dr. John Adams or Dr. Carla Delacruz will give me their analysis of my health.

    Pronouns/antecedents: _____

    _____

EXERCISE 19.8 SEXIST PRONOUNS AND PRONOUNS WITH INDEFINITE-PRONOUN ANTECEDENTS

NAME _____ **DATE** _____

Some of the sentences in the following paragraph use pronouns that unnecessarily identify the gender of an antecedent and thereby seem to exclude one sex. Some sentences may also contain errors of agreement between pronouns and indefinite-pronoun antecedents. In either case, circle the incorrect or sexist pronoun and write the correct one above it. If you need to alter the antecedent or any other words, feel free to do so. If the sentence does not need revision, write C next to it.

EXAMPLES

Doctors study   *their*
A doctor studies for years in order to provide the best care for (his) patients.

their rounds
All golfers should be finished with (his or her) round by 5:30.

Many people choose a doctor because of his credentials, and they may keep him if he has a good bedside manner. However, one more criterion factors into people's opinions of their doctor's office: the nurse who works there. A nurse usually spends more of her time with patients than a doctor does. She may well be the person patients talk to most often. A nurse checks vital signs and notes patient complaints, reporting her concerns and impressions to the doctor so that he can take appropriate action. She may also dispense medication and perform some examinations. A competent nurse can make their patients feel well cared for even if the doctor is sometimes busy or abrupt. A patient may even base their positive feelings about their doctor's office more on the treatment the nurse gives them than on anything the doctor does. If a doctor is smart, he will pay attention to hiring a good nurse, for she can keep patients happy — and keep them coming back.

EXERCISE 19.9   CONFUSING PRONOUN USAGE

NAME _____ **DATE** _____

Many of the sentences that follow contain potentially confusing pronoun usage. Rewrite the sentences to clear up any such confusion. If a sentence is clear as written, write C on the line below the sentence.

    EXAMPLE   Keiko trusted Nicole because she had worked for her before.

    REVISION   Keiko trusted Nicole because she had worked for Nicole before.

1. After Marjorie published a self-help book along with Emily, she became a household name.

   _____

   _____

2. The union representative called me last night at home and asked me if I was ready to go on strike today; I told him I still wasn't sure.

   _____

   _____

3. Don and Margie visited Fran for the weekend, but she spent a lot of time shopping at the outlets.

   _____

   _____

4. Of the novels by the three Brontë sisters — Anne, Charlotte, and Emily — I like her novels the most.

   _____

   _____

5. The exercise instructor talked about gymnastics versus yoga, and she stressed that it was beneficial for people of all ages.

   _____

   _____

6. When tennis matches are televised, with all the top players competing, I like watching them.

_____

_____

7. My great-aunt told a secret to my aunt, but then she told it to my cousin.

_____

_____

8. Janice and Michael went to Janice's cousins for the weekend, and they were overly formal.

_____

_____

9. Because the mayoral race between Jensen and Wilson was so close, the debates forced him to state his position on airport expansion.

_____

_____

10. Marco invited Mario to dinner before he went away on vacation.

_____

_____

EXERCISE 19.10 VAGUE, AMBIGUOUS, OR WORDY PRONOUN USAGE

NAME _____ **DATE** _____

A. This paragraph from a letter written by a first-year college student to a school board member has been altered to include several kinds of pronoun errors. Underline all problematic pronouns. Then rewrite the letter to eliminate problems of pronoun usage. Use the space below or a separate sheet of paper.

I am a former student of Hoover High School that is now attending Valley University as a first-year student in engineering physics. Several friends which graduated in my class are also attending VU and are having a hard time with their classes. To graduate from high school, they took the bare minimum requirements, and they are not enough to prepare them for college. After all, most college classes build on what you have already learned. And if they don't already know the foundations, it is going to be hard to pass the class. One example is Chemistry 204. It is a class that starts off with the basics, but after two weeks, they are two hundred pages into the book. Without a good high school chemistry class as background, they're lost. It is important that each school board member consider his duty to students and look into this lack of preparation. Action is needed to improve new students' chances for success in college.

B. Underline any pronoun errors in the following paragraph. Then rewrite the passage, using specific and concise language.

Nuala and her sister Rena love to play marathon games of Monopoly, and they can keep going until very late at night. Nuala tells Rena that she should get out the game board, and the sisters set out the "Get Out of Jail Free" cards and the brightly colored hundred-dollar bills. They sit down and arrange them in front of them. Rena argues with Nuala about her using the shoe playing piece. The sisters buy railroads and streets and put little green and red buildings on them. Nuala tells Rena that she needs to play more carefully. After she puts a hotel on the Boardwalk and another on Park Place, it is an expensive place for her sister to land. Rena admits that she always wins but she still enjoys playing.

EXERCISE 19.11 CLEAR PRONOUN REFERENCE

NAME _____ **DATE** _____

Read the sentences below. If a sentence already uses pronouns in clear, concise, and unambiguous ways, write *C* on the line below the sentence. Revise any sentences that use pronouns in vague, wordy, or ambiguous ways. Make sure your revision is clear, concise, and unambiguous.

EXAMPLE	When Sherri discussed wages with Mari, she understood she would get a raise.
ACCEPTABLE REVISIONS	When Sherri discussed wages with Mari, Sherri understood Mari would get a raise.
	When Sherri discussed wages with Mari, Sherri promised her a raise.

1. He is driving his van past Dry Creek Reservoir, which has given him problems in the past.

   _____

   _____

2. The legislature discussed one bill to increase funding for highways and another to support mass transit; at the end of the session, they passed it.

   _____

   _____

3. After examining the horse's hoof, he offered it a carrot.

   _____

   _____

4. The neighborhood teenagers painted a mural covering the graffiti on the wall that offended local residents.

   _____

   _____

5. When the guests arrive, please show them into the living room.

   _____

   _____

6. When Marla wrapped the new scarf around my neck, it looked soft and beautiful.

_____

_____

7. The Broadway show has been canceled that you liked.

_____

_____

8. The landscape design program that you are interested in has four openings next year; that makes it a competitive program.

_____

_____

9. Negotiators reached a settlement after fifteen weeks that included two holidays and new provisions for vacation time.

_____

_____

10. As she stared out of the rain-streaked window, Hannah found it depressing.

_____

_____

EXERCISE 19.12   *WHO, WHICH, THAT, YOU,* AND *THEY*

NAME _____**DATE** _____

Read the following sentences, and pay particular attention to pronoun usage. If a sentence uses pronouns in clear and appropriate ways, write C on the line below the sentence. If pronouns are used in vague or inappropriate ways, revise the sentence.

EXAMPLE		Most college classes require homework. They complain about it, but they do it.
REVISION		Most college classes require homework. Students complain about it, but they do it.

EXAMPLE		The pilot whale who beached itself yesterday swam back out to sea this morning.
REVISION		The pilot whale that beached itself yesterday swam back out to sea this morning.

1. Dogs who sleep during the day may be getting ready for a night on the town.

   _____

   _____

2. On the college Web site, they tell you about the new entrance requirements.

   _____

   _____

3. Do indoor cats who never get to explore the great outdoors lose their instincts?

   _____

   _____

4. In the faculty lounge they were deeply divided about the tuition increase.

   _____

   _____

5. The actress who plays Salome is a wonderful dancer.

   _____

   _____

6. Doctors should consider their own reactions to bad news when giving their patients a frightening diagnosis.

_____

_____

7. My cousin which is in medical school has always been a good student.

_____

_____

8. On this winding two-lane road, someone in a hurry always tries to pass you illegally.

_____

_____

9. Whenever you walk into that stereo store, they come right up to you rather than letting you browse.

_____

_____

10. Are you the singer that will perform before me?

_____

_____

Adjectives and Adverbs

20

Writers use adjectives and adverbs to describe, limit, qualify, and specify. Without these modifiers, we would find it hard to say precisely what we want to say: instead of *medium-rare steak*, it would be just *steak*; instead of *fresh New England–style clam chowder*, it would be just *chowder*. Without adjectives and adverbs, we would not be able to do justice to the fascinating and necessary details of our lives. (Note: This chapter does not discuss verbals used as adjectives or adverbs, nor does it discuss prepositional phrases functioning as adjectives or adverbs. For discussion of these matters, see Chapter 16.)

ADJECTIVES AND ADVERBS IN EVERYDAY USE

Adjectives often carry indispensable shades of meaning. When you're looking at a catalog, you know there's an enormous difference between *cowboy boots* and *motorcycle boots*, between a *bathing suit* and a *pin-striped suit*, and between a *rugby shirt* and a *Hawaiian shirt*. In each case, the difference is in the adjectives. Look in a newspaper or magazine for examples of adjectives that carry significant meaning in an activity or subject that you know well. Make notes about what you find. Which adjectives add vividness to the writing, and which provide essential information?

Distinguishing adjectives from adverbs (35a)

Adjectives modify nouns (blue *marble*, desperate *clients*, sleazy *proposal*) and pronouns (Stylish *and* confident, *he arrived for the trial*). Some adjectives are formed by adding endings to nouns or verbs. These endings include *-al*, *-ive*, *-ish*, *-able*, *-less*, and *-ful*:

form (noun)	formal (adjective)
act (noun or verb)	active (adjective)
style (noun)	stylish (adjective)
comfort (noun)	comfortable (adjective)
rest (noun or verb)	restless (adjective)
rest (noun or verb)	restful (adjective)

A few adjectives are formed by adding the *-ly* ending to a noun (as in *lovely*, *earthly*, *ghostly*). Regardless of how they are formed, adjectives usually answer one of these questions: *which*, *how many*, or *what kind?*

Adverbs modify verbs, adjectives, and other adverbs:

The cat *patiently* waited for its dinner. [*modifies verb* waited]

Phil waited for an *especially* hungry fish to take the bait. [*modifies adjective* hungry]

After dinner, the cat rested *quite* comfortably on the sofa. [*modifies adverb* comfortably]

Occasionally adverbs modify whole clauses, as in this sentence: *Garcia said that, regrettably, he would be late.* Here, *regrettably* modifies the clause *he would be late*.

The most common way of forming adverbs is by adding *-ly* to adjectives. However, quite a number of adverbs do not have the *-ly* ending. Examples include *very*, *quite*, *here*, *fast*, *there*, *now*, *then*, *often*, *soon*, and *late*. Regardless of how they are formed, adverbs usually answer one of these questions: *how*, *when*, *where*, or *to what extent?*

REVIEW

- Adjectives modify nouns and pronouns.
- Adverbs modify verbs, adjectives, other adverbs, and (occasionally) entire clauses.

Adjectives after linking verbs (35b)

As you have seen, a word may have both an adverbial and an adjectival form. Consider *bright*, for example. The word *bright* is an adjective. Adding *-ly* makes the adverb *brightly*. Partly because informal speech often does not distinguish between these two forms, writers sometimes have trouble deciding which form to use in a given sentence. The only certain way to choose correctly between *bright* and *brightly* is to identify the part of speech of the word being described. If the word is a noun or a pronoun, the modifier must be an adjective, *bright*. If the word (or phrase or clause) functions as a verb, as an adjective, or as an adverb, the modifier must be an adverb, *brightly*.

The sun shone *brightly* through the window. [*adverb modifies the action verb* shone]

The *bright* sun shone through the window. [*adjective modifies the noun subject* sun]

Adverbs can often change position in a sentence without destroying its meaning:

The sun shone *brightly* through the window.

The sun shone through the window *brightly*.

Adjectives, by contrast, usually either precede closely the nouns or pronouns they modify (*rainy* morning, *yellow* paper) or follow linking verbs. If they follow linking verbs, they are called predicate adjectives. Recall that **linking verbs** are various forms of the verb *be* (*is, are, was, were, will be*, and so on), as well as verbs such as *look, sound, become, appear, taste, feel, seem, smell, remain*, and *prove*. In general, if you can replace a verb with some form of *be* without substantially changing the sentence meaning, the verb is probably a linking verb.

Consider the sentence *The doughnuts tasted delicious.* Is the verb *tasted* a linking verb? If we substitute a past-tense plural form of *be*, we get this sentence: *The doughnuts were delicious.* The test works; *tasted* functions here as a linking verb. But how do we determine whether the word *delicious* should be an adjective or whether it should be the adverbial form *deliciously*? The rule is simple:

- Modifiers following a linking verb modify the sentence subject and must therefore be adjectives.

CORRECT	After three hours in a warm keg, the beer tastes *flat*.
INCORRECT	After three hours in a warm keg, the beer tastes *flatly*.

CORRECT	Sorenson felt *angry* that the elevator was broken again.
INCORRECT	Sorenson felt *angrily* that the elevator was broken again.

Good and *well*, bad and *badly*, real and *really* (35c)

These adjectives and adverbs can cause writers trouble because common speech often blurs the distinctions between them. When you are writing dialogue or quoting someone speaking informally, you may also blur those distinctions. But when you are writing in a formal or academic setting, you should be careful to observe the distinctions outlined here.

- *Good, bad, well,* and *real* are adjectives and may follow linking verbs. (Note that *well* here means "in good health.")

Our June weather has been *good.* [Good *describes the subject,* weather.]

This leftover tuna smells *bad.* [Bad *describes the subject,* tuna.]

After treatment, the patient felt *well* again. [Well *describes the subject,* patient.]

That pearl looks *real.* [Real *describes the subject,* pearl.]

Remember that some linking verbs can also act as action verbs, as in *I looked really carefully at the fine print.* Here *looked* functions as an action verb; *carefully* is an adverb modifying *looked*; *really* is an adverb modifying *carefully*.

- *Well* may also function as an adverb to modify a verb, an adjective, or another adverb. (Note that when functioning as an adverb, *well* has nothing to do with health.)

  A chef for over eight years, she cooks *well*. [Well *modifies the verb* cooks.]

- *Badly* and *really* are adverbs and should be used to modify verbs, adjectives, or other adverbs.

  A chef for over eight years, she cooks *really* well. [Really *modifies the adverb* well.]

  They bungled that first experiment *badly*. [Badly *modifies the verb* bungled.]

Comparatives and superlatives (35d)

Most adjectives and adverbs have three forms. The **positive** form is the simple dictionary form:

  The mouse is a *small* mammal.

  Alyce arrived *early*.

The **comparative** form is made by adding the ending *-er* or by adding *more* or *less* (intensifiers). The comparative form literally compares the modified thing with some other thing:

  The mouse is *smaller* than the hedgehog. [*comparative form of the adjective* small]

  Hank arrived *earlier* than she did. [*comparative form of the adverb* early]

The **superlative** form is made by adding the ending *-est* or by adding *most* or *least* (intensifiers). The superlative form compares the modified thing with at least two others and declares it to be the most extreme:

  Of the mouse, the hedgehog, and the wildebeest, the mouse is the *smallest*. [*superlative form of the adjective* small]

  Josie arrived *earliest* of all. [*superlative form of the adverb* early]

How do you know when to add an ending (*-er* or *-est*) and when to use an intensifier (*more, most, less, least*)? The *-er* and *-est* endings are used for most—though not all—one- and two-syllable adjectives. Longer adjectives and most adverbs use the intensifiers (*more/less, most/least*). Sometimes intensifiers are used with short adjectives; the effect is greater emphasis and formality.

POSITIVE	COMPARATIVE	SUPERLATIVE
tall	taller	tallest
early	earlier	earliest
imposing	more imposing	most imposing

Some two-syllable adjectives do not take *-er* or *-est* (*careful, honest,* and *scattered,* for instance). If you are not sure whether a particular adjective or adverb has *-er* and *-est* forms, look up the positive form in a college dictionary. If the *-er* and *-est* forms exist, they will be listed following the positive form.

- When comparing two things, use the comparative form.

When speaking informally, we are often tempted to use the superlative; however, formal or academic writing normally requires the correct comparative form.

CORRECT	The painting is taller than I am. [*comparison of two things: a painting's height and the speaker's height*]
INCORRECT	Of woodworking and painting, painting is the most difficult. [*comparison of two things: the difficulty of painting and the difficulty of woodworking*]
CORRECT	Of woodworking and painting, painting is the more difficult.

- Use the superlative when comparing three or more things and to indicate that the modified word is the most extreme—the largest or smallest, best or worst, most intense or least intense—of those things.

Of all the dogs we know, we like Tom the *best.*

My personal opinion is that *The Shining* is Stephen King's *best* novel. [*King has written more than two novels.*]

Consider this example:

Elise was least interested in art history and most interested in mathematical group theory.

Are only two things being compared? If so, the example is incorrect as given. If Elise is interested in several things, the sentence is technically correct as written; it is also open to misinterpretation by readers. The solution? Rewrite the sentence to clarify the terms of the comparison.

Of all her college courses, Ling was least interested in art history and most interested in mathematical group theory.

Of her two courses that term, Elise was less interested in art history and more interested in mathematical group theory.

Recognizing irregular forms

Note the following irregular forms for some commonly used adjectives and adverbs.

POSITIVE	COMPARATIVE	SUPERLATIVE
good	better	best
well	better	best
bad	worse	worst
ill	worse	worst
little [quantity]	less	least
little [size]	littler	littlest
many	more	most
some	more	most
much	more	most

As you can see, the comparative and superlative forms of some adjectives and adverbs are identical. Thus it is accurate to write *Serena Williams played better today than she played yesterday* (*better* here functions as an adverb modifying the verb *played*), and it is also accurate to say *She feels better today than she did yesterday* (*better* here functions as a predicate adjective following the linking verb *feels* and modifying the subject *she*).

Selecting adjectives and adverbs when using comparative forms

REVIEW

- Adjectives modify nouns or pronouns.
- Adverbs modify verbs, adjectives, or other adverbs; sometimes adverbs modify whole clauses.

When we talk, we frequently blur the distinction between comparative adverbs and comparative adjectives. Thus we might say, "I finished this marathon easier than the last one." In that sentence, *easier* is an adjective incorrectly modifying the verb *finished*. Writers should preserve the adjective-adverb distinction, making the sentence read, "I finished this marathon more easily than I finished the last one."

Checking for double comparatives and superlatives

Do not use an intensifier with an *-er* or *-est* ending.

INCORRECT   Helen is more smarter than I am. [*double comparative*]

REVISED   Helen is smarter than I am.

INCORRECT	Tran is the most quietest student in the class. [*double superlative*]
REVISED	Tran is the quietest student in the class.

Making comparisons complete

In the shared context of everyday speech, we may often make ourselves clear without completing the second half of a comparison. For example, if you and your spouse are shopping for a used car, one of you might walk up to the fourth car you've looked at and say, "This looks better to me." Such statements are not effective in writing. The reader can only wonder, "Better than what?" The context of your shared experience with the earlier three cars would probably make that comparison clear. But in formal or academic writing (or whenever a reader or listener does not share your experience), the audience can easily misunderstand. Thus it is important to make the terms of your comparisons absolutely straightforward.

INCOMPLETE	Some people argue that the deterrent effect of capital punishment is more important. [*more important than what?*]
COMPLETE	Some people argue that the deterrent effect of capital punishment is more important than the moral argument against the taking of human life.

EXERCISE 20.1 ADJECTIVES AND ADVERBS

NAME _____ **DATE** _____

Rewrite each of the sentences below, adding your own words to modify various elements. Indicate after the sentence whether you added an adjective or an adverb.

> **EXAMPLES** Teresa sang last night. (Modify the verb *sang*.)
>
> Teresa sang loudly last night. (adverb)
> _____
>
> I like that car. (Modify the noun *car*.)
>
> I like that yellow car. (adjective)
> _____

1. Information is useful in an emergency. (Modify the noun *Information*.)

   _____

2. Imagine that you are driving your car along the highway to get to an appointment. (Modify the verb *driving*.)

   _____

3. A sound tells you that you have a flat tire. (Modify the noun *sound*.)

   _____

4. After you pull out of the traffic, you rummage through the glove compartment looking for the manual. (Modify the noun *traffic*; modify the verb *rummage*.)

   _____

   _____

5. On page 55, you see a diagram that shows where the jack is stored. (Modify the noun *diagram*; modify the verb *shows*.)

   _____

   _____

6. After you block the wheels as the instructions direct, you begin jacking up the car. (Modify the verb *block*.)

   _____

   _____

7. The manual proves helpful as it tells how you should proceed. (Modify the adjective *helpful*; modify the clause *how you should proceed*.)

   _____

8. After fifteen minutes, you finish removing the tire and attach your spare. (Modify the noun *tire*; modify the noun *spare*.)

_____

9. The information in the manual saves you money and time by teaching you to change a tire by yourself. (Modify the verb *saves*; modify the phrase *money and time*.)

_____

_____

10. The manual's illustrations and explanations have told you what you needed to know. (Modify the noun *illustrations*; modify the noun *explanations*.)

_____

_____

....

EXERCISE 20.2 *GOOD, WELL, BAD, BADLY, REAL,* AND *REALLY*

Underline the correct adjective or adverb in each of the following sentences. Be ready to explain your choices.

    EXAMPLE   I felt <u>bad</u>/badly when I lost my job.

1. Speak real/really forcefully when you give your oral presentation.
2. After a layoff, you may feel bad/badly and not want to start job hunting right away.
3. Writing a novel may be real/really difficult for some people.
4. Performing bad/badly at a concert will not help your career.
5. Spelling good/well is a basic requirement for a proofreader.
6. Sitting on the beach with a cold drink feels real/really good/well.
7. Try to dress good/well for a date.
8. Some animals try to look real/really colorful to ward off predators.
9. Will a former employer's recommendation be good/well enough to get you into graduate school?
10. I want to go to the Coachella music festival bad/badly.

EXERCISE 20.3 ADJECTIVE-ADVERB ERRORS

NAME _____ **DATE** _____

The following paragraph contains several errors in the usage of adverbs and adjectives. Underline those errors, and write in the correct forms. The first error has been underlined and corrected for you.

       valuable
Diamonds are considered very <u>valuably</u>; they are one of the rarest gems in the world. Diamonds are remarkable similar, so it is only sometimes possibly to tell where a diamond comes from. However, knowing the origin of a particularly diamond may be more importantly than most customers realize. According to the United Nations, some diamonds may be used to fund internationally terrorists. Gems known as "conflict diamonds" are smuggled out of countries, usual in Africa, and sold as quick as possible in legitimate markets. Then the money goes back to the smugglers, who are frequent trying to overthrow a government or making murderously attacks on civilians. Conflict diamonds can be real profitable, earning smugglers millions of dollars. But while identifying such diamonds cannot be done easy, scientists are trying to find ways to "fingerprint" diamonds chemically to prevent conflict diamonds from being sold as if they were obtained legal.

EXERCISE 20.4 COMPARATIVE AND SUPERLATIVE FORMS

In each case below, you are given an adjective or an adverb and a specified form. Write a sentence using the specified form correctly. Make sure that your sentences distinguish appropriately between adjectives and adverbs and that the terms of any comparisons are complete.

    EXAMPLES   *blue*, superlative form

               The sky this afternoon is the bluest that I've ever seen.

               sleepy, comparative form

               I'm sleepier today than I was yesterday.

1. tedious, comparative form

   _____

   _____

2. *scintillating*, superlative form

   _____

   _____

3. *seriously*, comparative form

   _____

   _____

4. *many*, superlative form

   _____

   _____

5. *elegantly*, superlative form

   _____

   _____

6. *uplifting*, superlative form

   _____

   _____

7. *well*, comparative form

   _____

   _____

8. *bad*, comparative form

   _____

   _____

9. *ill*, superlative form

   _____

   _____

10. *quick*, comparative form

   _____

   _____

EXERCISE 20.5 COMPARATIVE AND SUPERLATIVE FORMS

NAME _____ **DATE** _____

The sentences that follow contain various comparisons. In each case, determine what is being compared and whether the correct form of adjective or adverb has been used. If the sentence is correct as written, write C in the space after the sentence. If the sentence is incorrect, underline the incorrect form and write in the correct form. Use a dictionary if you need to check a comparative or superlative form.

> **EXAMPLE**   Compared to Pizza Gallery's crust, Dumbo's was <u>thickest</u>. _____*thicker*_____

1. Three local pizza restaurants — Dumbo's, Pizza Gallery, and the Downtowner — try to outdo

   one another in making the most perfect pizza. _____

2. Dumbo's and Pizza Gallery both deliver, but Dumbo's gets its pizzas out quicker.

   _____

3. Pizza Gallery, however, has more handsomer delivery people. _____

4. The Downtowner, offering at least six veggie specials in addition to the choices on the regu-

   lar menu, is the restaurant better loved by vegetarians. _____

5. Meat lovers will be happier with Pizza Gallery's excellent sausage than with anything at the

   Downtowner. _____

6. Although the prices were comparable at all three restaurants, Pizza Gallery's were more

   reasonable. _____

7. The Downtowner is more friendlier than Dumbo's, which is dark and smells like stale beer,

   but Dumbo's appeals to a college crowd. _____

8. Between Dumbo's and the Downtowner, Dumbo's sauce is the most rich. _____

9. I am not certain which of the three restaurants I would give more points — I like them all.

   _____

10. With three really good pizza places to choose from, pizza lovers in our town are the luckiest

    ones in the county. _____

SENTENCE CLARITY

"When you start writing — and I think it's true for a lot of beginning writers — you're scared to death that if you don't get that sentence right that minute it's never going to show up again. And it isn't. But it doesn't matter — another one will, and it'll probably be better."
— TONI MORRISON

PREVIEW QUESTIONS

These questions are designed to help you decide what you need to study. (Answers to preview questions are at the back of the book.)

1. Some of these sentences may contain unnecessary or confusing shifts in person, number, tense, mood, subject, or voice. Mark *C* for correct or *I* for incorrect.
   a. We waited in stunned silence, and you just didn't know what would happen next.
   b. Parents must write notes explaining their children's absences.
   c. Everyone in the room should turn in your exam papers now.
   d. We planned to go by bus, but then it was decided that the subway would be quicker.

2. Some of these sentences may not use parallel structures correctly. Mark *C* for correct or *I* for incorrect.
   a. The car jumped the curb and hit a fire hydrant, it then hit a tree.
   b. I am, have been, and always will be a lover of meat loaf.
   c. Freedom is justice, and justice is exactly the same thing as freedom.
   d. The determination to succeed against all odds, a willingness to forge his own path, courage, these are the things that make this man a great father, mayor, and he is a great golfer.

3. Some of these independent clauses may not be correctly joined. Mark *C* for correct or *I* for incorrect.
   a. We loved weekend guests, but we also needed time alone.
   b. I entered a contest online, I don't expect to win.
   c. The rain made driving treacherous, however, this area has been suffering during the recent drought.
   d. The door was closed; my brother came in anyway.

4. These examples may contain sentence fragments. Mark *C* for correct or *I* for incorrect.
   a. Some people are pathological liars. Not I.
   b. I think we could get there in an hour. If we hurry.

5. Some of these sentences may use modifiers incorrectly. Mark *C* for correct or *I* for incorrect.
   a. Sworn to secrecy, her husband knew better than to ask the FBI agent for the latest news of the investigation.
   b. After calling the doctor, I took the pills.
   c. The report was full of mistakes that I gave my manager.

6. Some of these sentences may have garbled grammatical structures. Mark *C* for correct or *I* for incorrect.
   a. It is no secret that in small towns everyone knows everyone else's business.
   b. The tourists flocked to see the autumn leaves made the hillsides an explosion of color.
   c. The professor said that in most of our papers showed too little attention to detail.
   d. The fruits and vegetables at the farmers' market are wonderful, and the cheese is first rate too.

Shifts

21

A novel may shift from present to past, from dialogue to narrative, or from the author's voice to a character's dialect. Readers accept—even welcome—such changes when they make sense, help develop the characters or plot, or otherwise advance the story. Whenever readers notice any abrupt change or shift in what they are reading, however, they should be able to recognize the reason for that change. Some changes — shifting from active to passive voice, for example — can be useful, even necessary. But sometimes writers make inadvertent shifts that only confuse readers. This chapter focuses on such inadvertent or confusing shifts.

SHIFTS IN EVERYDAY USE

Dramatic or even outrageous shifts are a staple of comedians and humor writers who often jump from the serious to the commonplace. If you have a favorite humor writer, comedian, or comic strip, look for such shifts in tone in the writer's or comic's work, and jot down some examples. What role do these shifts play in making you laugh?

Shifts in tense (36a)

→ **COMMON ERROR: UNNECESSARY SHIFT IN VERB TENSE**

As Chapter 16 discussed, writers use **verb tenses** to identify time relationships—for example, *After I go* (present tense) *to the bank, I will pay* (future) *you back.* Here the sentence meaning makes the shift in verb tense clear and necessary. However, sometimes writers carelessly or inadvertently shift tenses, and it is hard for readers to make sense of the sentences these shifts yield. To avoid such confusion, keep verb tenses consistent unless there is clear reason to do otherwise. Consider these examples:

CONFUSING TENSE SHIFT

PAST	PRESENT	FUTURE
After I studied chemistry	and go to the bank,	I will pay you back.

REVISION ELIMINATING SHIFT

PRESENT	PRESENT	FUTURE
After I study chemistry	and go to the bank,	I will pay you back.

Besides paying attention to verb tenses within sentences, writers should make sure that verb tenses are consistent from sentence to sentence.

CONFUSING TENSE SHIFT	First she set up her camera. Then she walked entirely around the table with its plate of fettuccine. Finally, she adds a scattering of sliced olives, adjusts the lights, checked the exposure, and began to take the pictures that were scheduled to appear in the Sunday food section of the paper.
REVISION ELIMINATING SHIFT	First she set up her camera. Then she walked entirely around the table with its plate of fettuccine. Finally, she added a scattering of sliced olives, adjusted the lights, checked the exposure, and began to take the pictures that were scheduled to appear in the Sunday food section of the paper. [*Observe that the past tense is used throughout.*]

When referring to events in literary works, use the present tense:

In *Beloved*, Sethe *escapes* from slavery.

Shifts in mood and voice (36b, 36c)

As discussed in Chapter 16, writers use verbs in the indicative mood to report facts or to ask questions; the imperative mood to convey orders, instructions, or requests; and the subjunctive mood to state wishes or conditions contrary to fact. Shifting from one mood to another without good reason confuses readers. Here is an example:

CONFUSING SHIFT	My car repair company always requests that a customer *call* for a [SUBJUNCTIVE] service appointment and then *brings* the car in promptly at eight o'clock. [INDICATIVE]
REVISION ELIMINATING SHIFT	My car repair company always requests that a customer *call* for a [SUBJUNCTIVE] service appointment and then *bring* the car in promptly at eight o'clock. [SUBJUNCTIVE]

Writers may also make unnecessary shifts in verb voice. You already know that in the **active voice** the subject performs the action of the verb (*Our dog Freckles chases cars*) and in the **passive voice** something is done to the subject (*Cars are chased by our dog Freckles*). Sometimes, shifting from passive to active (or vice versa) is justified and useful, as in this sentence: *Professor Emberson asked* (active) *for the papers, and, as they were being passed* (passive) *forward, he gave* (active) *the new assignment.* Switching voices here keeps the sentence focused on Professor Emberson's actions, not on the actions of his students. However, such shifts are sometimes unnecessary and may be confusing if the performer of the action goes unnamed. Here are some examples:

CONFUSING SHIFT	*ACTIVE* Lisa *called* the children, and	*PASSIVE* the groceries *were brought* to her.

REVISION ELIMINATING SHIFT	*ACTIVE* Lisa *called* the children, and	*ACTIVE* they *brought* her the groceries.

UNNECESSARY SHIFT	*PASSIVE* After the minutes *were read* by Harry,	*ACTIVE* he *turned* to the first item on the agenda.

REVISION ELIMINATING SHIFT	*ACTIVE* After Harry *read* the minutes,	*ACTIVE* he *turned* to the first item on the agenda.

Shifts in person and number (36d)

→ **COMMON ERROR: UNNECESSARY SHIFT IN PRONOUN**

Writers should not shift between **first person** (*I, we*), **second person** (*you*), and **third person** (*she, he, it, one, they*) unless there is good reason to do so. Be particularly careful about such shifts inside a sentence.

UNNECESSARY SHIFT	*One* ought to be careful about alcohol consumption, especially if *you* plan to drive. [*The sentence begins with the third person* one *but ends with the second person* you.]

REVISIONS ELIMINATING SHIFT	One ought to be careful about alcohol consumption, especially if one plans to drive. [*consistently third person*]
	You should be careful about alcohol consumption, especially if you plan to drive. [*consistently second person*]

Remember that the pronoun *you* should not be used in a vague or indefinite way. (For more on the vague or indefinite use of *you*, see Chapter 18.) Perhaps the clearest solution lies in replacing the problematic pronoun with a noun:

People ought to be careful about alcohol consumption, especially if they plan to drive.

Here is another example:

UNNECESSARY SHIFT	Golfers should try the new course, but you should beware of those long holes on the back nine. [*Here* you *is being used as an incorrect substitute for* they.]

REVISION	
ELIMINATING	Golfers should try the new course, but they should beware of
SHIFT	those long holes on the back nine.

Shifts from singular to plural (or vice versa) can also be confusing: *A city dweller* (singular) *may feel that they* (plural) *are moving in slow motion in a small town.* To whom does *they* refer? The sentence should read: *City dwellers may feel that they are moving in slow motion in a small town.* As you can see, many shifts in person and number are actually problems with pronoun-antecedent agreement. (For more on such agreement, see Chapter 19.)

Shifts in tone and diction (36f)

Writers establish a relationship with readers by maintaining a tone in their writing. In part, **tone** indicates the goal a writer has for a particular piece of writing. If you want readers to laugh, you try to set a humorous, lighthearted tone. If you want readers to think about some idea or experience, you try to set a more serious, perhaps reflective, tone. The tone of a textbook should be straightforward without being stuffy. A workbook should be deliberate and trustworthy. You are not likely to find in this book (except by way of example) a sentence such as *OK, you mules, listen up!* A book with a hostile and arrogant tone would be a novelty for a few paragraphs; then the tone would simply be annoying.

As you may recall from Chapters 12, 13, and 14, **diction** refers to word choices and to the level of formality or technicality that writing possesses. *Formal* diction is appropriate for many kinds of academic writing; *technical* diction is appropriate for scientific and research writing; *informal* diction is the language of normal talk and may be appropriate for personal essays. In addition, *slang* is usually the language of banter between friends.

FORMAL	We loaded the truck with a larger cargo than it was designed to carry.
TECHNICAL	The vehicle was loaded 112 pounds in excess of its maximum recommended weight.
INFORMAL	We loaded that truck until the springs groaned.
SLANG	We stuffed that rig until it near croaked.

Shifts in tone and diction can be sources of richness and surprise. However, when inappropriately used, such shifts may indicate that a writer is inexperienced or perhaps not entirely in control of the writing. In general, when we talk, we mix levels of diction without creating problems. Body language and facial expression help us to do so. But readers, who have access only to sentences on a page, must be convinced that any shifts in tone or diction are controlled and purposeful.

MIXED TONE AND DICTION OF ACTUAL SPEECH

Whoa there! Hold it! This is my land, and you have no permission to drive all over it willy-nilly with total impunity and rank disregard for native plant species.

CONSISTENT TONE AND DICTION OF A WRITTEN COMPLAINT

When I came upon Mr. Jones, he was behind the wheel of a Jeep in the middle of a field that contains one of the few remaining undisturbed populations of a rare species of wild rose. I asked Mr. Jones to stop his vehicle, and I expressed my irritation with his disregard for the local ecology and for the borders of private property.

NAME _____   **DATE** _____

The sentences that follow make up a paragraph. Underline the verbs. If a sentence is correct as written, write *C* on the line below the sentence. If a sentence needs revising to eliminate confusing tense shifts, rewrite the sentence on the lines provided.

EXAMPLE   The barn swallows <u>return</u> about the same time that school <u>recessed</u> for spring break.

REVISION   <u>The barn swallows return about the same time that school recesses for spring break.</u>

1. World War II ended slowly in Europe as the Allies win major victories on different fronts.

   _____

   _____

2. In the spring of 1944, a large part of the Nazi military is occupied on the eastern front, for the Germans had underestimated the Soviet will to fight.

   _____

   _____

3. On the French coast, General Eisenhower is leading a massive landing of American, British, and Canadian troops.

   _____

   _____

4. The invasion, which was called Operation Overlord but now was known as D-Day, takes place on June 6, 1944.

   _____

   _____

5. During the six months when the operation has been in the planning stages, an Allied bombing campaign weakened the German air force.

   _____

   _____

351

6. Well over 150,000 Allied soldiers crossed the English Channel and land on five beaches.

_____

_____

7. Omaha Beach sees such heavy Allied casualties that General Omar Bradley almost pulled the troops out.

_____

_____

8. Some paratroopers arrive at the same time as the beach invasions but missed their targets.

_____

_____

9. However, historians now suggest that the scattered paratroopers actually made it more difficult for the Nazis to fight back effectively.

_____

_____

10. The D-Day victory was opening up Europe to Allied troops, which begin working their way toward Germany.

_____

_____

11. At the same time, Soviet forces were slowly driving the German troops out of Eastern Europe.

_____

_____

12. The German surrender is signed May 8, 1945, and ended the war in Europe.

_____

_____

EXERCISE 21.2   SHIFTS IN MOOD AND VOICE

NAME _____ **DATE** _____

Underline the verbs in the following sentences and pay particular attention to any shifts in mood or voice. If those shifts appear confusing or unnecessary, rewrite the sentence. If a sentence unnecessarily employs both the active and the passive voice, convert the passive verbs to active. If a sentence is clear and well written in its original form, write C on the line below the sentence. See the examples in the text, as well as those provided here.

EXAMPLE   Ms. MacNaught <u>read</u> the plans carefully, and they <u>were approved</u> by her. [*unnecessary shift from active to passive*]

REVISION   Ms. MacNaught read the plans carefully, and she approved them.

EXAMPLE   The dinner <u>was prepared</u> and <u>was delivered</u> by Fast Catering Co. [*no shift here*]
C

EXAMPLE   On race day, <u>drive</u> slowly, and you <u>should be careful</u> of the competitors. [*unnecessary shift from imperative to indicative*]

REVISION   On race day, drive slowly, and be careful of the competitors.

1. Find a way to lose weight, and you must stick to it.

   _____

   _____

2. Guido's delivers dairy products on Monday, and fruits and vegetables are delivered by Guido's on Wednesday.

   _____

   _____

3. The designer recommends that the sweater be turned inside out for washing and that liquid, not powdered, soap is used.

   _____

   _____

4. Holiday traffic congested the highway and delayed the wedding party's arrival by more than an hour.

   _____

   _____

5. Town hall asks that each resident fill out the census form and returns it within ten days.

_____

_____

6. If she was not winning at poker, Sheila would be full of self-hate.

_____

_____

7. I insist that she speak to me before accepting the offer.

_____

_____

8. The hikers set off, and the great outdoors was enjoyed by all.

_____

_____

9. When the committee leaves the conference room, put away unused supplies, and you should turn off the lights.

_____

_____

10. The president asked that each citizen demonstrate patriotism and makes a sacrifice.

_____

_____

EXERCISE 21.3   SHIFTS IN PERSON AND NUMBER

NAME _____   **DATE** _____

Many of the following sentences contain unnecessary shifts in person and number. Rewrite the sentences to eliminate those unnecessary (and potentially confusing) shifts. If a sentence is accurate as written, write C on the line below the sentence.

EXAMPLE   Zoo patrons should be sure to visit the aviary, and you shouldn't miss the elephant house, either.

REVISION   Zoo patrons should be sure to visit the aviary, and they shouldn't miss the elephant house, either.

1. One must behave appropriately when you attend a state dinner at the White House.

   _____

   _____

2. Sports fans always want to see his or her team win.

   _____

   _____

3. If you live around here, you see flocks of wild turkeys almost every day, and people also spot deer, foxes, and an occasional bear.

   _____

   _____

4. A doctor always has their own stethoscope.

   _____

   _____

5. Reporters have to work hard and gain experience before getting his or her byline on a story.

   _____

   _____

6. When amateur photographers take pictures, he or she often enjoys the activity as much as the finished pictures.

_____

_____

7. Lewis and Clark both kept journals, even though they wrote under less-than-ideal conditions.

_____

_____

8. A weekend runner is a prime candidate for running-related injuries, especially if they get no exercise during the week.

_____

_____

9. While he was answering the telephone, we slipped out the door.

_____

_____

10. Whenever newspaper carriers go on vacation, you should make sure that you have arranged for a substitute to take over your route in your absence.

_____

_____

EXERCISE 21.4 SHIFTS IN TONE AND DICTION

NAME _____ **DATE** _____

A. Each of the following sentences is identified as being at a particular level of diction. Rewrite each sentence using the type of diction indicated. You may have to create details for some rewrites.

> **EXAMPLE**   Some jerkwater salesman sold me an empty box! (slang; write an informal version)
>
> **REVISION**   An out-of-town salesman sold me an empty box.

1. Which non-Western country produces an abundance of vibrant films with visual richness and musical invention that delight cinema admirers around the globe? (formal; write an informal version)

   _____

   _____

2. We spent a boring afternoon in that smallish room looking through a trick mirror and watching white mice to see if they could remember which button to hit in order to get some of those food pellets. (informal; write a technical version)

   _____

   _____

3. The truck skidded for a bit and then struck the wall. (informal; write a technical version)

   _____

   _____

4. A hundred-square-foot exterior takes sixteen gallons of high-gloss, fast-drying latex. (technical; write an appropriately formal version)

   _____

   _____

5. For ages, people have called us washed-up old hippies whose music has nothing new to say, so we just keep proving those folks wrong. (informal; write a more formal version)

   _____

   _____

6. Attention: Remember to take personal belongings when you exit the bus at your stop. (formal; write an informal or slang version)

_____

_____

7. I beg your pardon, ladies and gentlemen, but please collect your litter, and deposit it properly in the designated receptacle. (formal; write a slang version)

_____

_____

8. In days to come, I would appreciate your not conversing at such great volume with your acquaintances on your cell phone. (inappropriately formal; write an informal version)

_____

_____

9. Your cousin busted a potted plant in the rec room, and it's a mess in there. (informal/slang; write a more formal version)

_____

_____

10. Cease these cacophonous histrionics; I have no intention of capitulating to your demand for a lollipop. (inappropriately formal; write an appropriately informal version)

_____

_____

B. Read the following paragraph carefully. Most of it employs a reasonably formal, informative tone and level of diction. Underline any sentences or phrases that strike you as inappropriate in tone or diction. Then, on your own paper, rewrite the paragraph so that its tone is consistently appropriate.

Teenagers are the most sought-after customers in the world of advertising. A TV show that is watched by only a small bunch of teenagers may not get very high ratings, but, boy, can the network move ads — even expensive ads — for a show like that. The rationale for this apparently incoherent behavior among advertisers is a theory that states that teenagers have not yet developed "brand loyalty." Advertisers hope to suck teenagers in and instill in them a lifelong habit of buying a particular brand. Madison Avenue types also claim that kids have all of this disposable income just burning a hole in their pockets. The problem with the theory that teens are the perfect consumers is that it simply isn't true. According to new research, middle-aged people show less brand loyalty than teenagers, who tend to freak if they drink the wrong cola or wear the wrong shoes. Plus, teenagers generally have less money for discretionary spending than baby boomers do. If the ad guys were really so smart, they would be pitching their wares to the moms and dads of those high school and college students.

EXERCISE 21.5 RECOGNIZING AND REVISING INAPPROPRIATE, UNNECESSARY, OR CONFUSING SHIFTS

NAME ——————————————————— **DATE** ————————

The following passage contains several shifts of the kind discussed in this chapter. Read the passage carefully, and underline any shifts you believe inappropriate, unnecessary, or confusing. Then, on your own paper, rewrite the passage to eliminate these shifts.

Employees ought to follow these company guidelines whenever dealing with customers:

First, if you can't understand what some bozo is saying, you shouldn't say, "Huh?" Say instead, "Pardon me" or "I'm sorry." If one is receiving a phone order, say, "We seem to have a bad connection; could you repeat that, please?"

Second, if one believes a customer's choice of apparel is inappropriate, one should not register disapproval. You ain't there to raise folks' fashion consciousness; you're there to provide courteous service.

Third, if you are sick and could not come to work that day, he or she should have called the store manager. One employee went home early before they told anyone. That was wrong too. Such absences result in customers who feel neglected and other employees who felt frustrated because of your absence from the sales floor.

Fourth, if you were obligated by store policy to say no to some big spender, follow your no with a yes. For example, if you say that a credit purchase has not been approved, make sure you said that the store welcomed personal checks, or say, "We will gladly set this merchandise aside for you."

Following these four guidelines will help ensure that customers returned to our stores. And repeat customers (and solid sales figures) made for a stable and remunerative employer-employee relationship.

Parallelism

22

Why do we remember (and use) maxims, or clichés, such as *A bird in the hand is worth two in the bush* or *Take it or leave it*? Such succinct sayings are easy to remember because of their **parallelism**: they express comparable ideas in the same grammatical form.

| NOUN | + | PREPOSITIONAL PHRASE | | | NOUN | + | PREPOSITIONAL PHRASE |
A bird   in the hand   is worth   two   in the bush.

| VERB | + | OBJECT | | VERB | + | OBJECT |
Take   it   or leave   it.

As a writer, you need to be wary of clichés, but you need to be aware of the effectiveness of parallel constructions. Writers can employ parallel words, parallel phrases, or parallel clauses. Such constructions can make prose more concise, more graceful, and more readable. Many writers also carry parallel structures from sentence to sentence to create tighter, more emphatic passages.

PARALLELISM IN EVERYDAY USE

Jot down some examples of parallel structures that you find in everyday use — on bumper stickers, on T-shirts, in song lyrics, in advertising jingles, and so on. To explore why messages of this sort are often written in parallel form, revise one of the parallel structures you find to make it *not* parallel. Does one version more effectively catch your attention and stick in your mind?

Parallel structures in series (37a)

Listing items in groups of three creates one common parallel construction:

> I did not take my mother to that movie because it contains *nudity, profanity,* and *graphic violence.*

Notice that the italicized items are all nouns or noun phrases. By the time readers have read *nudity, profanity, and . . .* , the parallel structure has led them to expect that third noun phrase.

Occasionally, writers unconsciously or inadvertently break this pattern of expectation, resulting in confusion for readers:

> I did not take my mother to that movie because it contains nudity, profanity, and the violence is graphic.

The confusion may not be particularly dramatic if it occurs only once. However, if writers consistently misuse parallel structures in a series, readers (particularly academic readers) will react with frustration and impatience.

Parallel structures to pair ideas (37b)

Consider this sentence:

> Some psychologists argue that genetics dictates our personalities, but experience is what other researchers claim is the major factor.

The two independent clauses have different constructions, so a reader may think that in the second clause the writer is changing the subject. When the clauses are made parallel, however, it becomes clear that they present versions of a single idea—psychologists' differing opinions on what dictates our personalities.

To make such a sentence parallel, use the same grammatical structure in both parts of the sentence; often, you will be able to use the same words:

> Some psychologists *argue that* genetics dictates our personalities, but other researchers *argue that* experience is the major factor.

Notice that the coordinating conjunction *but* joins the two parts of that sentence. The other **coordinating conjunctions** (*and, or, nor, yet, for,* and *so*) serve the same grammatical function.

Some parallel structures are nested inside pairs of **correlative conjunctions** such as *either . . . or, both . . . and, neither . . . nor,* and *not only . . . but also*. When correlative conjunctions are used, the structures following each conjunction must be grammatically parallel.

NONPARALLEL	Either I will take a nap, or going swimming would be nice.
PARALLEL	Either I will take a nap, or I will swim.
NONPARALLEL	She hopes to both play on the basketball team and the softball team.
PARALLEL	She hopes to play on both the basketball team and the softball team.

Including all necessary words (37c)

Look at the following sentence:

> After work, *I might* stop by to see my mother, or *I might* go grocery shopping.

Suppose that you decided to omit the second *I might*, figuring that such repetition is unnecessary. The resulting sentence would be

> After work, I might stop by to see my mother or go grocery shopping.

Remember that *or* is a coordinating conjunction and that coordinating conjunctions are to be used to join words, phrases, or clauses that are parallel in structure. What is *or* joining in the example? *Mother* is the object of the infinitive *to see*. The phrasing *mother or* leads readers to expect a compound object, but the sentence does not provide one. Thus, leaving out *I might* is likely to mislead readers.

Be careful about omitting repeated words in parallel constructions. Repeat words whenever necessary to ensure clear and grammatically correct sentences, particularly in formal or academic prose.

NAME _____ **DATE** _____

Read each sentence below. If a sentence has accurate parallel structures, underline these structures and write "parallel" on the lines provided. If a sentence does not have accurate parallel structures, write a parallel revision. Do not worry if your revision changes the content of the original. Your goal is to write sentences with accurate parallel structures.

EXAMPLES   Some kids love reading, and for others it's soccer that they love.
Some kids love reading, and others love soccer.
_____

Take it or leave it.
parallel _____

1. After watching a movie featuring the Hannibal Lecter character, do people really conclude that serial killers are intelligent, they have exquisite taste, and an appreciation of fine wine?

_____

_____

2. When someone you're dating either takes you for granted or looking at others while supposedly listening to you, you know the end is in sight.

_____

_____

3. I have always and will always love traveling.

_____

_____

4. Reasonable prices, late hours, and the staff is friendly — these are what students liked about BLT Café.

_____

_____

5. This company not only designs and manufactures superior hardware but also provides first-class customer service.

_____

_____

6. The Empire State Building offers views west to New Jersey; New York Harbor in the south; north to upper Manhattan, the Bronx, and Westchester County; and on the east to Long Island.

_____

_____

7. The test officials asked for quiet and that students not start the exam until told to do so.

_____

_____

8. Many New England towns divide power among selectmen, boards, then there is the town manager.

_____

_____

9. He was tempted to cheat on the test but worrying about getting caught.

_____

_____

10. Following in her mother's footsteps meant skipping college and to go straight to Hollywood.

_____

_____

NAME _____ **DATE** _____

Read the passage that follows, and pay particular attention to any sentences that could use parallel structures but do not. Remember that combining sentences will sometimes yield useful parallel structures. Underline any sentences that you want to revise to achieve parallelism. Then revise the passage, and copy your best version onto your own paper. The sentences are numbered for easy reference.

(1) In some parts of the country, summer brings sunshine, heat, and thunderstorms are possible. (2) The appearance of a thunderhead cloud can warn that a storm is forming. (3) Inside these very tall clouds, particles either become positively charged or negatively charged. (4) When the electrically charged particles move up and down inside the cloud, they run into each other or colliding with other charged particles from the ground. (5) The spark from these collisions is what people see as lightning. (6) Lightning is classified by the locations between which the charges move: cloud to ground, ground to cloud, cloud to air, or moving between two clouds. (7) Another method of categorization is shape; for example, lightning can resemble a fork, streak, chain, or the kind that looks like a ribbon. (8) The heat of the lightning makes air molecules move, they bounce, and collide in the air, producing the sound of thunder. (9) The time between seeing the lightning and the sound of the thunder indicates how far away the storm is. (10) In a storm that is moving closer, the length of time between lightning and thunder decreases; the time interval is increased when the movement is away. (11) When a storm is approaching, people who are outdoors should come inside, seek shelter in an outbuilding, or should lie down on flat ground away from trees. (12) From a safe place, a thunderstorm appears powerful and causes awe, but the same storm can be deadly from an unprotected location.

EXERCISE 22.3   EVALUATING SENTENCES FOR PARALLELISM

Each item below consists of three statements of a single idea. Some versions use parallelism; others do not. On your own paper, indicate whether each version uses parallel structure.

1. **a.** The new vegetable cutter from Veggo doesn't need batteries, and the cook doesn't need to replace its blade. Also, using it simplifies cutting vegetables quickly into different shapes.
   b. When you need to cut vegetables quickly into different shapes, Veggo's exciting new vegetable cutter works without batteries, without new blades, and without complications.
   c. Veggo's Vegetable Cutter. No batteries. No new blades. No complications.

2. **a.** At the rodeo, the calf roping was skillful, the steer wrestling was energetic, and watching the clowns do their tricks was a classic example of slapstick comedy.
   b. The calf roping was skillful. The steer wrestling was energetic. The clowns did great tricks.
   c. With skillful calf roping, energetic steer wrestling, and funny clown tricks, the rodeo is sure to be exciting.

3. **a.** I thought that the dogs in the competition were adorable; my boyfriend thought that they looked silly.
   b. To me, the dogs were adorable. Silly — that's what my boyfriend thought of them.
   c. Either the dogs were adorable, or they were silly.

4. **a.** Joe wants a big house and a fast car. Joe wants nice landscaping and a built-in swimming pool. Joe wants a lot of things.
   b. Joe wants a big house, a fast car, nice landscaping, and a built-in swimming pool; Joe wants a lot of things.
   c. Joe wants a big house. You should see the car he wants to buy. Nice landscaping is important to him, too. After he has all of that, the next thing on his list of things to buy is a built-in swimming pool. An awful lot of things is what Joe wants.

5. **a.** The film failed, I thought, as a work of art. When I consider the movie as entertainment, I would say this movie was a success.
   b. I thought the film failed as a work of art. I would say it did succeed as entertainment.
   c. The film failed as a work of art, but as entertainment it succeeded.

6. **a.** In my neighborhood, the blizzard of 2006 was marked by a mother pulling her son to church on a sled, deli workers having a snowball fight, and the sounds of city streets were muffled.
   b. During the blizzard, twenty-first-century photographers captured pictures of nineteenth-century city life: a mother pulled her son to church on a sled; workers at a deli had a snowball fight; the streets were devoid of cars.
   c. A mother pulled her son to church on a sled, workers at a deli had a snowball fight, and cars did not make a sound.

7. **a.** We have to decide where we want to go for our vacation. We could ski in Colorado, dive in Florida, or camp in New Mexico.

   b. For our vacation we could either ski in Colorado, go diving in Florida, or another option is camping in New Mexico.

   c. Do you want to ski in Colorado, or do you want to dive in Florida, or would you like to go to New Mexico to go camping?

8. **a.** Watson and Crick received a Nobel Prize for discovering the structure of DNA. They were working in the lab for a long time, and finally the structure of the DNA molecule was discovered.

   b. After years of research, scientists Watson and Crick discovered the structure of DNA. For their work, the men shared a Nobel Prize.

   c. Watson and Crick worked in their lab for a long time. They discovered the structure of DNA. They shared a Nobel Prize.

Comma Splices and Fused Sentences

23

Suppose that you are writing about summer visits to your grandmother's house. During brainstorming, you jot down some of your memories about her lilacs.

> I recall Grandma's lilacs, they had been planted under the kitchen window. Grandma always kept that kitchen window open the fragrance of those flowers filled the room. I remember the light through the leaves.

Because you are brainstorming, your concern is to record your ideas — not necessarily to write complete sentences. When you look back at your notes, you see that you wrote one comma splice and one fused sentence. The grammatical terms in the preceding sentence are defined below, after two more examples from a published work.

COMMA SPLICES AND FUSED SENTENCES IN EVERYDAY USE

We certainly pause as we speak in order to mark off our thoughts or to add emphasis, but we do not "speak" punctuation. In fact, everyday conversation may contain many comma splices. In imaginative or journalistic writing, these comma splices are used in dialogue to represent the rhythms of speech. Consider this example:

> "What else do you want to know? His folks live in Boca, he goes there for dinner every other Saturday. He has a younger sister, she's there sometimes. His dad's retired."
> — ELMORE LEONARD, *Maximum Bob*

In this segment of a conversation in which a woman tells a co-worker about her new boyfriend, the comma splices are effective because they suggest the sound of casual conversation. They would not be appropriate or effective in most college writing. Using your own paper, try revising this dialogue to make it sound more formal. You may discover some ways — and reasons — to keep comma splices out of your own writing.

→ **COMMON ERRORS: COMMA SPLICE AND FUSED SENTENCE**

When commas alone — without conjunctions — are used to join two independent clauses, the result is a **comma splice** (two independent clauses "spliced together" with only a comma). Although this construction is occasionally used in journalism and literature, most readers and academicians view comma splices as errors. Do not use only a comma to link two independent clauses.

COMMA SPLICE	I recall Grandma's lilacs, they had been planted under the kitchen window.

When two independent clauses are run together ("fused") without any intervening punctuation, the result is a **fused sentence** (sometimes called a run-on sentence). This construction is incorrect and confusing to readers.

FUSED SENTENCE	Grandma always kept that kitchen window open the fragrance of those flowers filled the room.

Separating the clauses into two sentences (38a)

The simplest way to revise comma splices and fused sentences is to separate the clauses and punctuate them as two sentences.

COMMA SPLICE	Cleaning house has never been one of my favorite activities, I can happily overlook the dirt and clutter for days or even weeks.
FUSED SENTENCE	Cleaning house has never been one of my favorite activities I can happily overlook the dirt and clutter for days or even weeks.
CORRECTED SENTENCE	Cleaning house has never been one of my favorite activities. I can happily overlook the dirt and clutter for days or even weeks.

Revising by making each clause a sentence emphasizes the separate content of each clause. However, if the two clauses are very short, converting them into two sentences may produce choppiness, and another method of revision may be preferable.

Linking the clauses with a comma and a coordinating conjunction (38b)

You can link two independent clauses with a comma and a coordinating conjunction. **Coordinating conjunctions** include *and, but, for, nor, or, so,* and *yet.* To use this method, place the comma after the first clause, and follow this comma with the coordinating conjunction. The pattern looks like this:

[Independent clause], [coordinating conjunction] [independent clause].

Referring to that diagram, we can revise *Margaret had a bad cold. She bought three boxes of tissues.* It would read *Margaret had a bad cold, so she bought three boxes of tissues.*

Linking independent clauses by using a comma and a coordinating conjunction is the best way to show a specific relationship between independent clauses. The conjunction *and* indicates continuation; *but, yet, or,* and *nor* indicate opposition; and *for* and *so* indicate cause and effect. As the next two examples show, the choice of a coordinating conjunction can make a considerable difference in sentence meaning:

Maria felt somewhat uncomfortable, *for* she was the first guest to arrive at the party. [*Maria was uncomfortable because she was the first guest.*]

Maria felt somewhat uncomfortable, *yet* she was the first guest to arrive at the party. [*Maria was uncomfortable but arrived first despite this feeling.*]

Linking the clauses with a semicolon (38c)

Comma splices and fused sentences also may be revised by inserting a semicolon between the two clauses. Using a semicolon in this way suggests that the clauses are equally important.

COMMA SPLICE	In Daytona Beach, the teenagers gathered for their traditional spring break celebration, back at home their parents put their feet up and savored the peace and quiet.
FUSED SENTENCE	In Daytona Beach, the teenagers gathered for their traditional spring break celebration back at home their parents put their feet up and savored the peace and quiet.
CORRECTED SENTENCE	In Daytona Beach, the teenagers gathered for their traditional spring break celebration; back at home, their parents put their feet up and savored the peace and quiet.

By linking two clauses with semicolons, you indicate that the two ideas are very closely related and that you are counting on your reader to understand the relationship without your spelling it out. Here are two examples:

I won't be able to meet you at noon today; I have an appointment at the Financial Aid office. [*cause-effect relationship implied*]

They danced all night; they wanted to dance forever. [*the action; the impulse behind it*]

So far in this chapter, you have seen how to join independent clauses by using a comma with a coordinating conjunction and by using only a semicolon. A third method is to use a semicolon with a conjunctive adverb or transitional phrase.

The test was difficult; *however*, Jason did well.

Jason did well; *on the other hand*, Jonah failed.

Note that a comma follows the conjunctive adverb *however* and the transitional phrase *on the other hand*. The pattern looks like this:

[Independent clause];   or   [independent clause].
[conjunctive adverb], / [transitional phrase],

Here are lists of commonly used **conjunctive adverbs** and **transitional phrases**:

CONJUNCTIVE ADVERBS

also	finally	indeed	nevertheless	subsequently
anyway	furthermore	instead	next	then
besides	however	meanwhile	otherwise	therefore
consequently	incidentally	moreover	still	thus

TRANSITIONAL PHRASES

after all	for example	in other words
as a result	in addition	on the other hand
even so	in fact	

Linking independent clauses with a semicolon and a conjunctive adverb (or a transitional phrase) allows you to specify relationships and to vary tone.

That Simm's Grocery had to raise its coffee prices shouldn't surprise us; *after all*, Mr. Simm's prices have gone up too. [After all *indicates a cause-and-effect relationship; the tone is informal.*]

Sally was a fine golfer; *in fact*, she once shot a hole-in-one. [In fact *indicates that an example follows; the tone is more formal.*]

Common usage sometimes omits the comma after some conjunctive adverbs or transitional phrases. If you are a native speaker, you can probably hear the pause that follows a transitional phrase such as *in addition*, or a conjunctive adverb such as *incidentally*. Conjunctive adverbs such as *then* and *thus* require less of a pause, encouraging writers to omit the comma (for more on commas, see Chapter 31).

Many questions on the test were familiar; *thus* Jason wrote most of the answers quickly.

Recasting two clauses as one independent clause (38d)

Sometimes two spliced or fused clauses may be revised to make a single independent clause. When such revision is possible, the new version is generally shorter and more direct. Consider the following set of examples.

FUSED SENTENCE The word *education* is an elusive one it often means different things to different individuals.

COMMA SPLICE The word *education* is an elusive one, it often means different things to different individuals.

Faced with either incorrect sentence, the writer must decide on a correctly punctuated revision that retains his or her original intention. By now, you are aware of several ways to link spliced or fused clauses. Here is a way to combine them to form one independent clause:

An elusive word, *education* often means different things to different individuals.

In that revision, the first clause has been reduced to an appositive phrase modifying *education*. The resulting sentence is concise and forceful. Is the shorter, concise version necessarily better? That is a question of style. However, the most concise statement often makes the greatest impact.

Recasting one independent clause as a dependent clause (38e)

Chapter 16 discusses dependent clauses and provides a list of subordinating conjunctions. To review, a **dependent clause** is introduced by a subordinating word and contains a subject and a verb but cannot stand on its own as a sentence. Here are two ways to revise the previous example using a dependent clause; the subordinating word in the first case is *since*; in the second case, it is *which*.

Since the word *education* is an elusive one, it often means different things to different individuals.

The word *education*, which is an elusive one, often means different things to different individuals.

Can independent clauses ever be joined with commas?

In working to avoid comma splices and fused sentences, you should now be aware of several options for their revision. Sometimes, however, writers can correctly join independent clauses by using commas.

Three (or more) independent clauses in a series

Suppose that you have a set of directions to convey. There are three parts to these directions: *Crumple the paper, lay the wood, and then light the fire.* Or suppose that you want to describe an accident at Ninth and Monroe: *The bicyclist slowed to make a left turn, the Dodge swerved to avoid the bicyclist, and a garbage truck plowed into the Dodge.* These two sentences are both punctuated correctly, even though they appear to break the rules.

What these sentences have in common is that they come in three distinct parts, three independent clauses. Because they are independent clauses in at least a three-part series, they follow different rules — the ones for punctuation of a series, explained in Chapter 31.

Note that placing three independent clauses in one sentence makes for interesting effects. In the first example, the directions are terse and therefore more easily remembered. In the second example, the cause-effect relationships are clearer than they might otherwise be. The quickness of the sentence also mimics the speed at which the accident actually occurred.

Reversed emphasis clauses (negative, then positive)

In this kind of sentence, the opening independent clause has a negative emphasis and the second independent clause reverses that emphasis. Such independent clauses are appropriately joined by a comma. *The spectators didn't just cheer, they exploded!* In sentences such as this one, the *not* clause leaves readers wondering what happened. The second clause delivers this information quickly. Caution: Do not reverse the emphasis in a sentence such as this one; if you do, the result is a comma splice: *The spectators exploded, they didn't just cheer.*

Using commas with quotations

When writers quote speakers, the result is often a sentence within a sentence: *"We'll plan on seeing the late show," she said.* In such sentences, a comma correctly joins two independent clauses: the quotation and the attribution.

EXERCISE 23.1 REVISING COMMA SPLICES AND FUSED SENTENCES BY SEPARATING THE INDEPENDENT CLAUSES OR BY LINKING THEM WITH A SEMICOLON

NAME _____ **DATE** _____

Read the sentences that follow. Identify comma splices with *CS*, fused sentences with *F*, and correct sentences with *C*. Revise the comma splices and fused sentences either by making the independent clauses separate sentences or by using a semicolon to link them. *Be ready to explain your choice.* **Write in your revisions in the space above each line.**

EXAMPLE <u>CS</u> An unusual thunderstorm dumped over half an inch of rain in less than an hour, /
Several
several area roads flooded.

_____ 1. The Columbus Day parade, a traditional event, aroused some controversy parade organizers clashed with demonstrators who called Columbus a slave trader.

_____ 2. Fashion designing demands a rigorous knowledge of fabric, of the human form, and of changing taste, it also demands daring, intuition, and an eagerness to set fashion rather than follow it.

_____ 3. A classical music program comes on the radio after the news, I can hardly listen to it.

_____ 4. The *New York Times* reported on hotel services for dogs during the Westminster Kennel Show in New York City would you want to sleep in a hotel bed previously slept in by a dog — even a prize-winning dog?

_____ 5. Computers can bring users radio programs broadcast from locations as widely separated as South Africa, Britain, Germany, Brazil, Canada, and Japan.

_____ 6. My sister's newborn daughter was a perfect angel she slept through the night almost from the beginning.

_____ 7. A quilter can create an inventive design while producing a useful household item at the same time other artisans such as weavers also can combine both goals.

_____ **8.** Jamal had been offered more money at another company, but he took the position that allowed him to stay in Philadelphia.

_____ **9.** I love dancing the tango it is such a passionate yet formal dance.

_____ **10.** Several good movies have been made from Elmore Leonard's books, Leonard writes dialogue better than any other popular novelist does.

EXERCISE 23.2 REVISING COMMA SPLICES AND FUSED SENTENCES

NAME _____ **DATE** _____

Underline all comma splices and fused sentences in the following passage (remember the exceptions). Then use the space below to rewrite the passage. You may add coordinating conjunctions, conjunctive adverbs, or transitional phrases as you wish. You may revise by using dependent clauses or by converting two clauses into one. Make sure that your revised paragraph is grammatically correct and accurately punctuated. For each comma splice or fused sentence you rewrite, be ready to explain the reason for the particular revision you propose.

People have always made things. One cool day long ago, swallows migrated dogs got heavier coats snakes went into a kind of hibernation people knitted themselves caps. People without caps and people with too many caps got together and invented money. Having invented money, people went on to pay other people to make parkas and slickers they used money to buy kits and make these things themselves. In the cold, deer sought the densest cover, people built houses with roofs. When cats got cold, they curled into tight little balls. People invented insulation they paid sheep ranchers to provide wool for warm shirts. When caribou got hungry, they had no choice but to seek a new range. When people got hungry, they didn't move eventually they taught themselves how to cook. Yes, people are makers.

EXERCISE 23.3 LINKING INDEPENDENT CLAUSES WITH COMMAS AND COORDINATING CONJUNCTIONS

NAME _____ **DATE** _____

Each of the following numbered items presents two sentences. Join the two sentences with a comma and an appropriate coordinating conjunction. Write your additions between the lines, as the example shows. Rearrange words if necessary. Reread each resulting compound sentence to make sure it sounds correct.

EXAMPLE No biography of Shakespeare was written during his lifetime, and Scholars continue to puzzle over his identity.

1. Jack's employee evaluation was mostly positive. His layoff was due to a shortage of orders.

2. Maybe we should plan on discussing this tomorrow at the staff meeting. Maybe we should call a special meeting with the other working group.

3. The Food and Drug Administration expressed satisfaction with the safety of the meat. Consumers were reluctant to buy any of it.

4. I want a dog badly. I'm afraid of the responsibility.

5. Perhaps this whole thing is just a joke. Then again, maybe it isn't.

6. The letter to the editor irritated my father tremendously. He fired off an angry letter of his own.

7. I'd love to go to Tokyo for a year. I'm afraid it's too expensive.

8. David did not enjoy his history textbook. He did find the class itself stimulating.

9. Marisol picked all of the green tomatoes still on the vine. The weather forecast predicted a hard frost for the next three nights.

10. The instructions for assembling the tricycle were incomprehensible. Martin decided to rely on his common sense.

EXERCISE 23.4 LINKING INDEPENDENT CLAUSES WITH SEMICOLONS AND CONJUNCTIVE ADVERBS OR TRANSITIONAL PHRASES

NAME _____ **DATE** _____

Each of the following numbered items presents two sentences. Join the two sentences with a semicolon and an appropriate conjunctive adverb or transitional phrase. Write your additions between the lines, as the example shows. Rearrange words if necessary. Reread each resulting compound sentence to make sure it sounds correct.

EXAMPLE Students returning to college after years at home or in the workforce are often
; nonetheless,
nervous about the transition. With good academic counseling and with good

support at home, most succeed.

1. I really don't want to see the movie. I have to work tonight.

2. No rain fell in Iowa for more than six weeks. Grain and corn farmers suffered significant

   losses.

3. Tomás has taken on too many responsibilities in addition to his schoolwork this semester.

   He baby-sits for his nephew every Sunday and works two part-time jobs.

4. Many Americans have no love for opera. Opera continues to speak to some Americans.

5. We're supposed to know our own tastes in reading. Many Americans rely on Oprah

   Winfrey's thoughts about books.

6. Our diplomatic efforts failed. War was inevitable.

7. The cost of living in Boston, New York City, and San Francisco is outrageous. Graduates

   looking for careers in theater, publishing, law, and technology keep arriving.

8. The woman in this picture must be your mother. You and your brother bear an amazing resemblance to her.

9. Last month the forwards couldn't seem to shoot straight. They began scoring two or three goals every game.

10. Your lab reports do not explain your procedures in enough detail. The rest of the sections are fine.

EXERCISE 23.5   DISTINGUISHING BETWEEN COORDINATING CONJUNCTIONS
AND CONJUNCTIVE ADVERBS OR TRANSITIONAL PHRASES

NAME _____ **DATE** _____

A. Each item below presents a pair of sentences. Combine the sentences as indicated, with either a comma and a coordinating conjunction or a semicolon and a conjunctive adverb (or transitional phrase). You may wish to review the lists of coordinating conjunctions, conjunctive adverbs, and transitional phrases.

EXAMPLE   The Russian processing ship remained stationary on the horizon. Several Russian trawlers fished for hake. (Combine using an appropriate conjunctive adverb.)

REVISION   The Russian processing ship remained stationary on the horizon; meanwhile, several Russian trawlers fished for hake.

1. Topicality is important to comedians. They count on audiences' familiarity with politicians' and celebrities' current antics. (Combine using an appropriate transitional phrase.)

_____

_____

2. The nights are longer and colder. Winter is almost here. (Combine using an appropriate coordinating conjunction.)

_____

_____

3. Deer are curious animals. They will often run a short distance, stop, and look back. (Combine using an appropriate conjunctive adverb.)

_____

_____

4. Half the staff was home with the flu. Two managers called in sick. (Combine using an appropriate coordinating conjunction.)

_____

_____

5. The term paper in psychology is not due until finals week. The critical reviews are due every other week all semester. (Combine using an appropriate conjunctive adverb.)

_____

_____

6. Her grandmother's house seemed smaller and dimmer than she remembered. She still knew where to find the sugar, the tea, and the box of gingersnap cookies. (Combine using an appropriate coordinating conjunction, conjunctive adverb, or transitional phrase.)

_____

_____

_____

B. Read the following passage, paying particular attention to the words and punctuation marks joining clauses. If a sentence is incorrect, write your corrections between the lines, as the example shows.

EXAMPLE   He could hear traffic noise behind him he could see the white-capped Pacific in front of him.
                                                    ; however,

REVISION   He could hear traffic noise behind him he could see the white-capped Pacific in front
                                          ^
of him.

Meteorologists track obvious weather conditions, such as temperature, rainfall, and wind speed; in addition, they monitor more complex aspects of weather, such as the chemical composition of the air and typical patterns for storm formation. They rely on old-fashioned observation and collection for some of these data but, much meteorological information today comes from computers, weather satellites, and other modern technology. The most up-to-date computer modeling and weather tracking can help meteorologists predict weather more accurately and further in advance than ever before, even so, weather forecasts are far from exact. Most people have experienced a storm that seemed to come out of nowhere; or they may have waited in vain for a giant blizzard. Knowing when to carry an umbrella or wear boots is useful, however, accurate weather information is important for more urgent reasons. Better predictions would save both lives and dollars for the losses due to unexpected weather crises such as tsunamis are unacceptably high.

EXERCISE 23.6   REVISING COMMA SPLICES AND FUSED SENTENCES BY USING DEPENDENT CLAUSES OR BY RECASTING TWO INDEPENDENT CLAUSES AS ONE INDEPENDENT CLAUSE

NAME _____ **DATE** _____

Each item below features a comma splice or a fused sentence. Revise the incorrect sentence in two ways: (a) by making one of the clauses a dependent clause and (b) by converting the two clauses into one independent clause.

EXAMPLE   Twentieth-century-studies courses carry three units of credit they fulfill the requirements for electives in humanities.

a. REVISION USING A DEPENDENT AND AN INDEPENDENT CLAUSE   Twentieth-century-studies courses, which carry three units of credit, fulfill the requirements for electives in humanities.

b. REVISION USING A SINGLE INDEPENDENT CLAUSE   With three units of credit, twentieth-century-studies courses fulfill the requirements for electives in humanities.

1. The drafty windows allow cold air to seep into the house all winter, they should be replaced or sealed more tightly.

   a. _____

   _____

   _____

   b. _____

   _____

2. The cougar had encountered a skunk previously, the big cat turned and ran from the small black-and-white animal.

   a. _____

   _____

   b. _____

   _____

3. The report included recommendations, graphics, and financial projections it was presented Friday morning.

a. _____

_____

_____

b. _____

_____

_____

4. Omar has been living in Detroit for seventeen years he owns a grocery store opened by his father, Abdellah, fifteen years ago.

a. _____

_____

_____

b. _____

_____

_____

5. The committee discussed the zoning variance for thirty minutes, the committee then approved the variance by five to three.

a. _____

_____

b. _____

_____

6. The governor does not want a national post he has decided not to attend the national nominating convention this year.

a. _____

_____

b. _____

_____

7. Computer technology changes rapidly, however few businesses can afford to take advantage of every new advance.

a. _____

_____

b. _____

_____

8. The airline now has a no-smoking policy on all of its flights this policy grew out of consumer demands.

a. _____

_____

b. _____

_____

9. The dandelions, Queen Anne's lace, and cornflowers grow along the side of the road, they appear every year without any help from humans.

a. _____

_____

b. _____

_____

10. The new driver saw a red arrow and panicked, she didn't know the meaning of a red arrow: "turn" or "stop"?

a. _____

_____

b. _____

_____

Sentence Fragments

24

If you pay close attention to advertisements, you will find many sentence fragments like these:

> Effective pain relief.

> Delicious—and nutritious.

> Works overnight.

A **sentence fragment** is some part of a sentence (often a phrase or a dependent clause) that is punctuated so that it looks like a sentence: beginning with a capital letter and ending with a period, exclamation point, or question mark. What is wrong with a sentence fragment? When readers see what *looks* like a sentence, they expect the full meaning that a sentence provides. Although fragments are often used intentionally in advertising and in literature, in academic prose they are usually considered errors.

SENTENCE FRAGMENTS IN EVERYDAY USE

Browse through the advertisements in a few magazines, or look at billboards and other signs, noting the use of fragments. Record a few examples of what you find. What is the effect of each example you noticed? Why do you think fragments are so often used in advertising?

➜ **COMMON ERROR: SENTENCE FRAGMENT**

An occasional sentence fragment may tell readers that the writer did not proofread carefully. Frequent sentence fragments suggest that the writer is not fully aware of what constitutes a grammatical sentence. Many college writers have trouble with sentence fragments. This chapter discusses how to recognize and revise them.

Sentence fragments often occur as a result of the way we think. We write something and put a period at the end of that thought. Then we remember something to add, so we add it. The result might look something like this: *Holly and Anne have definite opinions on education. And the statistics to back them up.* There is nothing at all wrong with writing this in a rough draft; the writer's error here is in failing to recognize and correct the fragment before turning in the final draft. It should read *Holly and Anne have definite opinions on education and the statistics to back them up.*

Perhaps the easiest way to detect sentence fragments is to read your writing backward, from the last sentence of a paragraph to the first. Reading in this way will alert you to your own punctuation.

Phrase fragments (39a)

The kinds of phrases that are most often punctuated as sentences are listed here (for a review of these phrases, see Chapter 16).

- Verbal phrases are made from verb forms that function as nouns or adjectives or adverbs. Infinitives (*to confuse*), present participles (*confusing*), past participles (*confused*), and gerunds (*confusing* [noun]) are all verbals.

FRAGMENT	The team lined up in punt formation. *To confuse their opponents.* [*infinitive-phrase fragment*]
REVISION	The team lined up in punt formation to confuse their opponents.
FRAGMENT	*Confused by the fake punt.* The opposing team allowed our halfback to score. [*participial-phrase fragment*]
REVISION	Confused by the fake punt, the opposing team allowed our halfback to score.
FRAGMENT	*Confusing your opponents.* That is one strategy for successful football. [*gerund-phrase fragment*]
REVISION	Confusing your opponents is one strategy for successful football.

- **Prepositional phrases** consist of prepositions and their objects and associated words. Such phrases do not include subjects or complete verbs.

FRAGMENT	*Because of the color of these walls.* I think we ought to choose a different rug.
REVISION	Because of the color of these walls, I think we ought to choose a different rug.
FRAGMENT	Meet me at 4:30. *Inside the hotel lobby.*
REVISION	Meet me at 4:30 inside the hotel lobby.

- **Noun phrases** consist of nouns and their modifiers. Noun-phrase fragments are often followed by fragments containing verbs but no subjects.

FRAGMENT	*The children who are screaming in the upstairs apartment. Should be disciplined by their parents.* [*two fragments: the first is a noun-phrase fragment*]
REVISION	The children who are screaming in the upstairs apartment should be disciplined by their parents.
FRAGMENT	*The jumper that Donna outgrew last spring. Has been sent to Aunt Lucille for her kids to wear.* [*two fragments: the first is a noun-phrase fragment*]
REVISION	The jumper that Donna outgrew last spring has been sent to Aunt Lucille for her kids to wear.

- **Appositive phrases** consist of nouns and their modifiers. An appositive phrase renames (or describes) an adjacent noun.

FRAGMENT	All Sunday afternoon, the two of them followed Tiger Woods. *The most famous professional golfer in the world.* [*Note that this appositive phrase has a prepositional phrase embedded in it.*]
REVISION	All Sunday afternoon, the two of them followed Tiger Woods, the most famous professional golfer in the world.
FRAGMENT	On the day of William Faulkner's burial, everything else stopped in Oxford, Mississippi. *Faulkner's hometown.*
REVISION	On the day of William Faulkner's burial, everything else stopped in his hometown of Oxford, Mississippi.

As these examples show, eliminating sentence fragments is easy and can be accomplished by combining the fragment with a nearby sentence.

Compound-predicate fragments (39b)

"Compound predicate" is a technical way of saying "two or more verbs." A **compound-predicate fragment** results when the second or last of the verbs (plus any modifiers) is punctuated as a sentence; such fragments lack subjects. Since compound verbs are typically linked with words such as *and, or, then,* and *but,* compound-predicate fragments often begin with these words. Remember that the key to spotting a compound-predicate fragment is the absence of a subject; many perfectly good sentences (with subjects and verbs) begin with *and, or, then,* or *but.*

ACCEPTABLE SENTENCES	Julie ate her lunch. Then she began studying for a midterm.
COMPOUND-PREDICATE FRAGMENT	Julie ate her lunch. *Then began studying for a midterm.* [*The fragment lacks a subject.*]

Eliminating such fragments involves combining the fragment with a nearby sentence or building a new sentence to express the fragment's meaning.

ACCEPTABLE REVISIONS	Julie ate her lunch and then began studying for a midterm.
	Julie ate her lunch. Afterward, she began studying for a midterm.

Dependent-clause fragments (39c)

Dependent clauses begin with subordinating conjunctions, such as *after, even though,* and *if,* and relative pronouns, such as *who, which,* and *that.* Dependent clauses cannot stand alone as sentences. When readers find a dependent clause that is not linked to an independent clause, the result is at least momentary confusion. In such cases, the writer's real message is this: *I didn't catch this fragment.* (For lists of relative pronouns and subordinating conjunctions and for more information about dependent clauses, see Chapter 16.)

FRAGMENT	We shouldn't forget. *That we all have days that seem dark and endless.*
REVISION	We shouldn't forget that we all have days that seem dark and endless.

Dependent-clause fragments are sometimes long, so their length alone may make them seem like sentences. These are often the hardest fragments to catch.

FRAGMENT	*After I arrived at the airport and found that the plane was late leaving Phoenix and would not depart for another hour.* I decided to buy a magazine at the newsstand.
REVISION	After I arrived at the airport and found that the plane was late leaving Phoenix and would not depart for another hour, I decided to buy a magazine at the newsstand.

Using fragments sparingly for special effect

Sometimes writers use fragments for particular stylistic reasons. Two guidelines are crucial here: writers must be sure that they are entirely aware of sentence-building rules before deliberately using fragments to achieve a certain effect, and writers must be sure that their readers will not object to this use of fragments. Many teachers and readers of academic prose consider *any* incomplete sentence to be a fragment. If your teachers or readers object to the stylistic use of fragments, do not use them.

Stylistic fragments do function in some predictable ways. The types of fragments listed here may appear in informal prose but almost never appear in more formal academic prose.

- *Fragments in dialogue.* People often speak in fragments. When such speech is faithfully reproduced on the page, the result is often a sentence fragment.

  "Really?"

  "Yes. Right there in line for the movie."

- *Fragments in answer to questions.* When questions are followed immediately by answers, repeating information presented in the questions often seems unnecessary, particularly in informal writing.

  Does this mean all is lost? Not necessarily.

  What makes this sauce so special, you ask? The garlic.

- *Fragments as exclamations.* By definition, exclamations are not complete sentences.

  That home run traveled more than 450 feet. Amazing!

  The model wore a swimsuit that cost over a thousand dollars. Incredible!

Writers occasionally use sentence fragments in other situations, particularly when describing or telling a story. Award-winning writer Barry Lopez uses fragments rarely but effectively. Here is an excerpt from his book *Of Wolves and Men*; the fragment is underlined.

  We killed hundreds of thousands of wolves. <u>Sometimes with cause, sometimes with none.</u> In the end, I think we are going to have to go back and look at the stories we made up when we had no reason to kill, and find some way to look the animal in the face again.

The preceding paragraph appears on page 199 of Lopez's book; by this time, Lopez has amply demonstrated his skills as a writer.

EXERCISE 24.1   PHRASE FRAGMENTS

NAME _____ **DATE** _____

Several of the short passages that follow contain phrase fragments. Read each passage sentence by sentence. Underline any fragments. Then, using your own paper, revise the passage so that it contains only complete sentences. If a passage is correct as printed, write C beside the number of that passage.

EXAMPLE   The rhododendrons bloomed densely. <u>Outside her window.</u> As she typed, she could see them. Some of the blooms were a deep vermilion. Others were the pale, off-white color. <u>Of piano keys.</u>

REVISION   The rhododendrons bloomed densely outside her window. As she typed, she could see them. Some of the blooms were a deep vermilion. Others were the pale, off-white color of piano keys.

1. Dancing in the rain was something Gene Kelly did in a 1952 movie. Called *Singin' in the Rain*. Besides his and others' engaging performances, this flick wins praise for lively choreography. Also for catchy tunes and hilarious jokes.

2. Going through one's work life with only one career is becoming a thing of the past. Some examples. People who were business journalists become financial planners. Teachers leave the classroom. For editing jobs in book publishing. Architects into artists.

3. Knowing how difficult it is. To train a cat to do tricks. He was thrilled when he succeeded. In getting Sylvester to respond to a whistle.

4. After an unusually warm winter, with little snow. The tick population in the county is at an all-time high. A huge percentage of the ticks are infected with Lyme disease. An illness that can be passed to humans and can become serious if untreated.

5. Police in nineteenth-century London did not understand the potential value of the clue that came in the mail. From someone calling himself Jack the Ripper. With the science of fingerprinting still in its infancy. The bloody handprint on the page seemed a grim joke to them, not a way to find the killer.

6. How do you explain the drop in U.S. enthusiasm for the Olympics as measured by American TV viewership of the games? One commentator on trends claims the drop is due to young people's impatience with time delays. "Why wait for evening TV coverage?" They ask. "When results are immediately posted on the Internet."

7. Over the years. I have wondered whether anyone really has everything he or she wants. Surely no one has the time and energy. To devote to family, career, and hobbies. Without shortchanging something.

8. When Madison decided to buy a car, she asked advice about a fair price. From friends, from family members, and from competing car dealers. She also went to the Internet for more information. In online consumer magazines. And in online car guides. Finally, she depended on her instinct. To see which seller seemed to offer the fairest deal.

9. To search for information online is to make a remarkable discovery. For every Web site filled with facts from impeccable sources, another exists to spread shameless rumors. The Internet may create a global village, but residents must still pay attention to what their neighbors are whispering.

10. The Prospect Heights Environmental Committee is looking for new members who will encourage recycling in the dorms or help assess recycling in campus facilities. Other members need to encourage the campus community. To use recycled products. In order to build a bigger market. For recycled paper and plastic.

EXERCISE 24.2 COMPOUND-PREDICATE FRAGMENTS AND DEPENDENT-CLAUSE FRAGMENTS

NAME _____ **DATE** _____

Read the following paragraph, and underline any sentence fragments. Then revise the paragraph to eliminate the fragments. Write your revision in the space below.

While some people may sit silently absorbing the programs that flow out of the television set. And never talk about them. Others have found a way to express their thoughts. To fellow viewers and to TV programming executives. The Internet gives fans of both popular and obscure shows a way to find one another. Even if they live in different states or different countries. The strangest thing of all is this. That television may become a truly interactive medium as a result of fan involvement. Web sites hosting chats about TV shows are often visited. And closely followed by the people who create the shows. In some cases, television executives are actually paying attention to the obsessive fans. Who spend too many waking hours in front of the television and the computer screen. In a very few instances, the fans have been able to influence the way characters on a show are presented. Or the direction of a story line. Does the Internet really give power to the people who used to be nothing more than targets of advertising for a particular show? If so, fans of cult favorites should pay attention. And realize that they may have a voice in the development of their beloved shows.

NAME _____ **DATE** _____

Read the following passages carefully. Underline every fragment. Then revise the passages on your own paper. You may combine or rearrange sentences in any way you see fit, as long as you retain the original content. You need not eliminate every single fragment. If you decide to keep a fragment, copy it after your revision, and briefly explain why you chose to keep it.

A. How people take tests says something. About them as people. Some individuals worry. And do nothing but worry. They don't revisit reading assignments, they don't review their notes, and they don't discuss major issues with classmates. After all this inaction, they may still be surprised. When the test day arrives and they aren't prepared. Other people worry, but they put that worry to work. These individuals use their worry. As motivation to make study plans. In addition to rereading texts and reviewing notes. These students also try to anticipate test questions. And then construct appropriate answers. In effect, they make and take practice tests. Still another group of people don't worry at all. They don't take tests seriously. And probably don't spend much time in preparation. The most naturally gifted in this group. May still do reasonably well on tests. However, even the most naturally gifted may be cheating themselves. If they don't study. As my grandma used to say, "If you've never worked hard, how do you know how hard you can work?"

B. Because water supplies are limited in many areas. We need to conserve water. In as many ways as possible. Most people who have experienced water shortages have learned to take shorter showers. To avoid wasting water doing dishes, and to save water in other ways. When people do not have plentiful water to drink or to use for bathing and washing. They cannot afford to waste water on their lawns and plants. As a result. Water companies, extension offices, and nurseries encourage gardeners to select low-water plants. Adding large borders of low-maintenance, low-water shrubs and plants to a yard. That is almost all grass. Will save water. In fact, some people have cut their water usage in half. Besides saving water for the most important needs. Such changes also save money. As shown by low water bills. And save time and energy because less grass needs weekly mowing.

Modifier Placement

25

Modifiers are words that act as adjectives or adverbs to describe or limit other words, phrases, or clauses. Modifiers add concrete and vivid details, turning an ordinary pair of jeans into faded jeans dragging on the ground, tight-fitting jeans tucked into boots, or mud-splattered jeans. A modifier is connected to the word it describes or limits by its placement. The importance of placement is clear if you consider the difference between these two phrases: "Linn's silk blouse worn only on Saturday nights" and "Linn's only silk blouse worn on Saturday nights."

MODIFIER PLACEMENT IN EVERYDAY USE

Modifiers play a major role in advertising. A bakery sign doesn't try to sell you just *bread*; it offers *100% whole-wheat bread, freshly baked this morning*. Sometimes modifiers are simple adjectives such as *new* or *deluxe*, and sometimes they are phrases: *in your grocer's freezer, expertly blended, working harder for you*. Jot down some of the modifiers you see around you. Is the primary function of these modifiers to provide information, to make a product sound appealing, or to do something else? Is it always clear to you what words the modifiers are describing?

This chapter discusses misplaced and dangling modifiers. Curing this problem depends first on becoming knowledgeable about it. Once knowledgeable, you should be able to identify such modifiers by carefully rereading your draft. (For background on the use of modifiers, see Chapter 20.)

Misplaced modifiers (40a)

Writers use modifiers to add detail. The sentence *We had a great weekend* becomes more interesting when it becomes more specific: *We had a great weekend waterskiing behind the Lakowskis' blue Chris Craft.* Readers expect modifiers to be positioned next to the words they refer to. When modifiers are misplaced, the result is confusion (or outright gibberish): *We Lakowskis had a blue weekend waterskiing behind the great Chris Craft.* Sometimes the result is funny:

MISPLACED **MODIFIERS**	Roiling and foamy, we stood at the viewpoint and watched the surf. [*As now positioned,* roiling *and* foamy *modify* we.]
CORRECTED	We stood at the viewpoint and watched the roiling and foamy surf.

A **limiting modifier** always comes before the word or words it modifies. Here is a list of limiting modifiers: *almost, even, hardly, just, merely, nearly, scarcely,* and *simply.* Repositioning a limiting modifier can result in an entirely new meaning.

Only crocuses bloom in March. [The one flowering plant in March is the crocus.]

Crocuses *only bloom* in March. [*Crocuses are only blooming, not growing, adding leaves, etc.*]

Crocuses bloom *only in* March. [*Crocuses bloom only during March, not in February or April.*]

Misplaced phrases and clauses

The placement of phrases and dependent clauses follows the same general guideline as that for positioning single-word modifiers: keep the phrase or dependent clause close to the word or words that it modifies. Generally, a phrase at the very beginning of a sentence should modify the subject of the sentence. (For a review of phrases and clauses, see Chapter 16.)

MISPLACED **PREPOSITIONAL** **PHRASE**	*In the refrigerator,* Amelia Bedelia chilled the wine. [*implies that Amelia Bedelia herself is in the refrigerator*]
REVISION	Amelia Bedelia chilled the wine *in the refrigerator.*
MISPLACED **PARTICIPIAL** **PHRASE**	*Newly washed and tumbled dry,* the kids put on their play clothes. [*implies that the kids were washed and tumbled dry*]
REVISION	The kids put on their *newly washed and tumbled-dry* play clothes.
MISPLACED **PARTICIPIAL** **PHRASE**	The warm sun felt good on her legs *streaming through the windows.* [*implies that her legs were streaming through the windows*]
REVISION	The warm sun *streaming through the windows* felt good on her legs.
MISPLACED **DEPENDENT** **CLAUSE**	The tennis racket was no good to anyone *that was broken during the last match.*
REVISION	The tennis racket *that was broken during the last match* was no good to anyone.

MISPLACED DEPENDENT CLAUSE	People should stay away from pet stores *who are allergic to cat hair.*
REVISION	People *who are allergic to cat hair* should stay away from pet stores.

Squinting modifiers

Consider this sentence: *People who swim frequently will improve their physical condition.* Look at that word *frequently.* Does the sentence refer to people who swim often? Or does the sentence mean that improvement occurs frequently? That word *frequently* is called a **squinting modifier**—it looks in two directions. Because of its placement in the sentence, it could modify two separate things. The reader has no way of knowing which meaning was intended.

Revising sentences with squinting modifiers is easy if you are the writer. The revision involves repositioning the squinting modifier, as in the following sentences:

People who frequently swim will improve their physical condition.

People who swim will frequently improve their physical condition.

Squinting modifiers may also be phrases. Here is an example:

SQUINTING MODIFIER	The commission promised *at its final meeting* to make its recommendations public.
REVISIONS	*At its final meeting,* the commission promised to make its recommendations public.
	The commission promised to make its recommendations public *at its final meeting.*

Disruptive modifiers (40b)

Disruptive modifiers interrupt, disrupt, or obscure the usual connections between parts of a sentence. Disruptive placement causes readers to lose their grasp of the purpose of a sentence; often they have to reread the sentence many times to understand its meaning. Here is an example:

Rico felt *after eating two chicken breasts, a baked potato, a tossed salad, and strawberry shortcake* full. [*The phrase confusingly isolates the subject complement* full.]

Revise such a sentence by repositioning the modifiers:

After eating two chicken breasts, a baked potato, a tossed salad, and strawberry shortcake, Rico felt full.

Here are several other examples:

DISRUPTIVE PLACEMENT	In the next several months, Lynn hopes to *despite her busy schedule of entertaining* maintain her diet and actually lose weight. [*The phrase splits the infinitive* to maintain.]
REVISION	In the next several months, Lynn hopes to maintain her diet and actually lose weight *despite her busy schedule of entertaining.*
DISRUPTIVE PLACEMENT	A red-tailed hawk will, *if it has nothing else to do and if the weather is right*, spend most of an afternoon soaring high over the landscape. [*The clause interrupts a verb phrase.*]
REVISION	A red-tailed hawk will spend most of an afternoon soaring high over the landscape *if it has nothing else to do and if the weather is right.*
DISRUPTIVE PLACEMENT	The faculty grievance board, *although it had not done so in over three years*, ruled in favor of several students who claimed they had been graded unfairly. [*The clause separates subject from verb.*]
REVISION	*Although it had not done so in over three years*, the faculty grievance board ruled in favor of several students who claimed they had been graded unfairly.
DISRUPTIVE PLACEMENT	She sang *in her first public concert* a selection of traditional folk songs and ballads. [*The phrase separates the verb and its direct object.*]
REVISION	*In her first public concert*, she sang a selection of traditional folk songs and ballads.

Note that all the disruptive modifiers in those examples are relatively long phrases or clauses. In some cases, a single-word modifier may effectively be inserted within a verb phrase, as in this example:

Employers who ask their personnel to move will *often* pay for the cost of the move.

Try shifting the word *often* to a position outside the verb phrase. In a sentence such as this one, shifting the modifier results in a new meaning.

Employers who *often* ask their personnel to move will pay for the cost of the move.

Inserting a single-word modifier between *to* and the verb in an infinitive phrase may also be acceptable in some writing situations:

To *almost* succeed is better than to *utterly* fail.

However, some academic readers object to such split-infinitive constructions. In such cases, revise the sentence to eliminate the infinitives:

Near success is better than utter failure.

Dangling modifiers (40c)

When writers use modifiers without giving them anything to modify, those modifiers just "dangle"; they are not attached to anything. Consider the sentence *After swimming for an hour, lunch was delayed*. That sentence literally says that lunch swam for an hour and was delayed. Lunches can be delayed, but they cannot swim. So the initial phrase *After swimming for an hour* is a dangling modifier. The only solution is a revision that gives the phrase something or someone to modify. That something or someone must follow the comma after the modifying phrase itself: *After swimming for an hour, the team found that lunch was delayed.*

DANGLING PHRASE	*Singing in the shower*, the water suddenly turned cold.
REVISION	Singing in the shower, he felt the water suddenly turn cold.
DANGLING PHRASE	*Dressed and ready for the dance*, her car would not start.
REVISION	Dressed and ready for the dance, she found that her car would not start.

EXERCISE 25.1   MISPLACED MODIFIERS

NAME _____ **DATE** _____

Underline the misplaced modifiers in each of the following sentences. Then use an arrow to indicate the proper placement of the modifier within the sentence.

    EXAMPLE   <u>Only</u> Smith and Co. sells yarn and related knitting supplies.

1. Our advanced fabric wicks dampness away from skin better than ordinary fabrics, keeping you dry.

2. Jan only works eighty hours a week because she needs the money.

3. Even the excessively loud music irritated the teenagers.

4. Campers may play various games if it rains indoors.

5. Whistling loudly, she turned off the burner under the teakettle.

6. The professor gave a lecture about cannibalism at Harvard.

7. Ethan imagined the audience as he stood at the podium in their underwear.

8. We almost waited an hour for the crosstown bus, which was behind schedule.

9. Hand carved with remarkable skill, she admired the wooden figurine.

10. Carrying blankets and wearing warm coats, the stadium was filled with fans.

EXERCISE 25.2 SQUINTING MODIFIERS

NAME _____ **DATE** _____

A. **Read each of the following sentences carefully. In each, underline the squinting modifier, if any. Then, on a separate sheet of paper, rewrite the sentence in two ways to show two possible meanings that the writer may have intended. If a sentence is clear as written, write C on the line.**

EXAMPLE   Rita thought <u>after the meeting</u> she would like to go home.

REVISION   After the meeting, Rita thought she would like to go home. [*The meeting was already over when Rita thought about going home.*]

Rita thought she would like to go home after the meeting. [*Rita is thinking beforehand that she will want to go home when the meeting has finished.*]

1. Students working in this laboratory routinely are required to wear safety gear. _____

2. She promised frequently to put money aside for the future. _____

3. They planned finally to take a honeymoon trip. _____

4. Teenagers seldom consider the long-term effects of everyday decisions. _____

5. I knew by the end of the evening I would ask her to marry me. _____

6. Many people said within the year they hoped the war would end. _____

7. My plan to win the heart of my darling eventually drove her away. _____

8. His efforts to change his work habits completely surprised his boss. _____

9. Her excuses for being late constantly irritate me. _____

10. Outside the testing site, students paced nervously thinking about the high-stakes test ahead. _____

EXERCISE 25.3   DANGLING MODIFIERS

NAME _____ **DATE** _____

As you read the following passage, underline any dangling modifiers. Then make a list of all the modifiers you underlined, and explain briefly why they are inappropriately placed. Finally, rewrite the passage to clarify its content. Use the space below and on the back of this page. (The sentences have been numbered to make class discussion easier.)

(1) Brought on by the first hints of spring, the condition called spring fever shows up with at least two symptoms: a lack of desire to work and an almost irresistible longing to be outdoors. (2) When stricken by spring fever, the results may be disastrous. (3) Although not fatal, this disease can lead to a loss of productivity for individuals and for organizations. (4) Enduring hard winters, spring fever is a particular problem. (5) Warmed by the sun year-round, people in Hawaii and in southern California are not as susceptible to bouts of spring fever as are people in Boston. (6) Calling in sick, workplaces are deserted when the first beautiful weather hits the North. (7) Happy at the return of good weather and hoping for good luck, "Gone Fishing" signs appear in midwestern shop windows. (8) Sprawled on the grass at campuses everywhere, professors face half-empty lecture halls. (9) Going bare-legged for the first time in months, people of all ages bid cold weather and short days adieu.

EXERCISE 25.4   DISRUPTIVE AND DANGLING MODIFIERS

NAME _____ **DATE** _____

Underline the disruptive or dangling modifiers that you find in each of the following sentences. Then revise each sentence so that it reads smoothly and clearly. If a sentence is fine as written, write C on the line below the sentence.

EXAMPLE	She sang <u>in her first public concert</u> a selection of traditional folk songs and ballads.
REVISION	<u>In her first public concert, she sang a selection of traditional folk songs and ballads.</u>
EXAMPLE	<u>Winded and tired</u>, the race seemed endless.
REVISION	<u>Winded and tired, he felt the race would never end.</u>

1. Comics, though published separately in comic books and collections, are most often read in the daily newspaper.

   _____

   _____

2. After reading comics for years, the conventions used are understood by most readers.

   _____

   _____

3. These conventions include, as most comic strips illustrate, the way the dialogue is presented in a balloon or above a character's head.

   _____

   _____

4. Not all, it must be remembered, comic strips require dialogue.

   _____

   _____

5. Taken seriously by book reviewers, graphic novels use a comic-book format to tell a significant story.

   _____

   _____

6. Writing and illustrating graphic novels for a cult audience, this format rarely results in fame and fortune.

_____

_____

7. Young artists who, while working at day jobs they dislike, try to create funny and well-drawn comic strips are likely to find achieving success a struggle.

_____

_____

8. But planning to hit it big with comics is no more realistic than, as most would-be cartoonists are doomed to discover, expecting to make millions by playing in a rock band.

_____

_____

9. Even after writing an acclaimed graphic novel, making a living as a freelance illustrator is more common than making a living as a cartoonist.

_____

_____

10. Finding satisfying work every generation of artists must discover for itself is more important — and more likely — than finding financially rewarding work.

_____

_____

Consistent and Complete Structures

26

A sophisticated sentence often packs quite a bit of information between its initial capital letter and its ending period. Such sentences depend on a variety of phrases and clauses to carry all that meaning. Given the wide variety of possible sentence structures, it is no wonder that occasionally a writer begins a sentence in one way and ends it in quite another way. Read the following sentence aloud:

> White House officials said that in most deportation cases require a more thorough investigation than many illegal aliens can afford.

The sentence begins clearly enough: "White House officials said that . . ." The word *that* signals a dependent clause, and as readers we expect to find a subject and verb for that clause. Instead, we find a prepositional phrase beginning with *in*. Since all prepositions take nouns or pronouns as their objects, we look for the object—*in* what? "Deportation cases" looks as though it could be the object of *in*, but this same noun phrase acts as the subject of the verb *require*. We know that the same noun cannot act as both the object of a preposition and the subject of a verb. Clearly the grammatical pattern of this sentence is garbled. Here are three possible revisions:

> White House officials said that most deportation cases require a more thorough investigation than many illegal aliens can afford.

> White House officials said that most deportation cases require a thorough investigation, which many illegal aliens cannot afford.

> White House officials said that in most deportation cases, a thorough investigation is required—something many illegal aliens cannot afford.

Here is another example of a sentence that mixes grammatical patterns:

> As compact discs rapidly replace records are going to become obsolete.

Here, the word *records* tries to do two things at once: to act as the object of the verb *replace* and as the subject of the verb *are going*. The result is a confusing sentence. Once the grammatical problem is isolated, the revision is relatively easy:

As compact discs rapidly replace records, the latter are going to become obsolete.

Sometimes straightening out a garbled sentence requires a substantial amount of rewording but results in a much simpler sentence:

The increasing popularity of compact discs will make records obsolete.

COMPLETE STRUCTURES IN EVERYDAY USE

If you listen carefully to the conversations around you, you will hear inconsistent and incomplete grammatical structures, particularly in lively or heated discussion. For instance:

"The Bulls are . . . They must be the best team in . . . not in the league even . . . in the country."

"Wait till the Lakers take them. Because you know the Magic Men, they make magic happen, in a sweep."

In the flow of informal conversation, such structures pose few problems for speakers and listeners. To verify this statement, listen carefully for inconsistent and incomplete structures in conversations, and write down an example or two. Consider what helps you understand them with ease.

Consistent subjects and predicates (41b)

Writers need to make sure that subjects and predicates are carefully and accurately matched. If they are not, the result is **faulty predication**. Faulty predication occurs most frequently in sentences with the verb *be*.

FAULTY   The most important *qualification* is *applicants* with experience. [*This sentence literally says that a qualification is applicants.*]

REVISED   The most important *qualification* for applicants is *experience*.

Faulty predication can also occur when writers allow themselves to be confused by words coming between the subject and the verb.

FAULTY   The clock with the black hands circled regularly.

REVISED   The clock's black hands circled regularly.

The clock had black hands, which circled regularly.

Sometimes faulty predication is really the result of incomplete thinking. Consider this sentence: *The elevation of Mount Hood claimed several lives last summer*. Is this faulty?

Yes, it is faulty because a mountain's *elevation* cannot *do* anything. We can arrive at a grammatically correct revision by simply dropping any mention of elevation: *Mount Hood claimed several lives last summer*. However, this revision sacrifices some of what the writer wanted to say. The real question is this: what is it about the mountain's elevation that is important? Posing that question may lead to this revision: *Blizzard conditions at the ten-thousand-foot level of Mount Hood caused the death of several climbers last summer*.

Finally, writers need to be careful of *is when, is where*, and *the reason is because* constructions. A sentence such as *Your watch is where you left it* makes perfect sense. However, a sentence such as *Recess is where all the children play kickball* incorrectly turns recess into a place. Possible revisions include *At recess, all the children play kickball* or *Recess is the time when all the children play kickball*. A definition must have a noun or noun phrase on both sides of the verb *be*. Neither *when* nor *where* is a noun.

Sentences structured around *the reason is because* are redundant. The word *because* simply repeats the meaning of the phrase *the reason is*. Chances are, either *because* or *the reason is* can be eliminated.

REPETITIVE	The reason I ate the potato chips is because I was hungry.
REVISED	I ate the potato chips because I was hungry.
	The reason I ate the potato chips is that I was hungry.

Elliptical constructions (41c)

When a sentence repeats a structure, it is often acceptable to omit repeated words *as long as the repeated words are identical to those found earlier in the sentence*. If correctly done, this type of sentence structure, an **elliptical structure**, readily makes sense to readers. In the examples that follow, the italicized word or words are identical and the words in parentheses can be omitted.

Beth *owns* quite a few books, and Jane (*owns*) just as many.

Canon manufactures copiers *for the* home and (*for the*) office.

Remember, the omitted words must be identical, not just similar. Here is an example of an inappropriate omission:

Phil's native talents are obvious, and his paper wonderful.

To be accurate and grammatical, the sentence must be revised to read this way:

Phil's native talents are obvious, and his paper *is* wonderful.

Even if the verbs are identical, they should be retained whenever the sentence substantially changes its meaning as it goes along. In the next example, the italicized words are identical, but none of them should be omitted.

Will *wanted* to see a science fiction movie, Melanie *wanted* to see a romance, and Brian *wanted* to stay home.

Missing words (41d)

You and nearly every other writer working on a rough draft are likely to leave out a word or phrase from time to time. Usually you are able to correct these errors once they are identified. How do you identify such errors? You can ask someone to check a final draft for you; another pair of eyes can often see omissions that you have missed. (Ask for help in identifying your errors, but do not let others correct them. Instead, learn from your errors: keep a personal editing checklist. For more on the personal editing checklist, see Chapter 6.)

Read your draft aloud to yourself or to someone else. Read it backward, one sentence at a time, starting at the end. Concentrate on each word, and consciously keep your eyes from going too far ahead. Learning to read this way takes practice, but it can help you catch omissions and may also help you detect spelling errors.

Complete comparisons (41e)

Writers can also get into trouble with incomplete or carelessly phrased comparisons. Above all, comparisons must grammatically and logically compare items, qualities, or things that are comparable. As Chapter 20 discusses, the informality of speech and shared experience often allow people to make careless or incomplete comparisons with little confusion or loss of meaning. However, in formal or academic writing, readers expect both logic and completeness. Look carefully at the following examples.

INCOMPLETE	Fast food tastes better. [*better than what?*]
ILLOGICAL	Fast food tastes better than cooking. [*compares a thing* (fast food) *with an action* (cooking)]
REVISED	Fast food tastes better than what I cook.
ILLOGICAL / INCOMPLETE	This clam chowder is thicker and creamier than last week.
REVISED	This clam chowder is thicker and creamier than the one we had last week.
ILLOGICAL / INCOMPLETE	Bobbie Ann Mason's writing differs from Tim O'Brien.
REVISED	Bobbie Ann Mason's writing differs from Tim O'Brien's.
	Bobbie Ann Mason writes differently than Tim O'Brien.
INCOMPLETE	Tsunamis are a greater threat to some islands.
REVISED	Tsunamis are a great threat to some islands.

EXERCISE 26.1 RECOGNIZING AND REVISING INCONSISTENT OR INCOMPLETE STRUCTURES

NAME _____ **DATE** _____

Look for omissions, garbled structures, and inconsistent subjects and predicates in the following passage. In the space below, revise the passage to clarify its content. (To make classroom discussion easier, the sentences have been numbered.)

(1) A new flower bed can be a backbreaking chore. (2) Not only does the gardener need to dig out the old plants or lawn already in place, but he or she also has to prepare the soil for new plantings. (3) However, garden researchers have discovered that in just six or seven weeks are sufficient to let a new flower bed prepare itself — that is, do the bulk of the work while the gardener stands by and observes. (4) The trick is to spread a thick layer of newspaper and several inches of hardwood mulch over the plants already on the site will then die. (5) After about forty-five days is a long enough period to kill off the old plants. (6) Meanwhile, the old plants, newspaper, and mulch that will have decomposed to form a layer of fertile compost, which you can then plant new flowers with no further preparation or additional topsoil.

NAME _____ **DATE** _____

Read the following sentences aloud. If a sentence reads clearly and correctly, write C on the line below the sentence. If a sentence sounds garbled and confusing, revise the sentence, and write your revision on the lines provided.

> **EXAMPLE**   Allergies on an average spring day you will find many people suffering.
>
> **REVISION**   On an average spring day, you will find many people suffering from allergies.

1. On average, the rain here falls at a rate of 50 percent higher than east of the mountains.

   _____

   _____

2. The holiday bazaar that is held every year at the library featuring crafts made by local artisans.

   _____

   _____

3. I was stretched out on the grass, and the clouds looked like animals.

   _____

   _____

4. The creator of this Web site is either a sadist and probably also a puzzle master.

   _____

   _____

5. The appraiser said the ring looked as though it was more than two hundred dollars.

   _____

   _____

6. I can't believe we bought that video was a bootleg copy with terrible sound.

_____

_____

7. Although the most important thing was preparing the meal, but we wanted to clean the apartment, too.

_____

_____

8. The photographer explained that in most of his classes have already switched to digital photography.

_____

_____

9. Reading this blog every day is a great way to kill time.

_____

_____

10. The restaurant's advertisement said that the Mother's Day breakfast buffet would open its doors at 8:00 AM.

_____

_____

EXERCISE 26.3   MATCHING SUBJECTS AND PREDICATES

NAME _____ **DATE** _____

Read the following passage. Underline any sentences with faulty or unnecessarily wordy predication. Then revise each weak sentence to make it clearer. Add or clarify content if needed. Use the space below for your revision. (To make classroom discussion easier, the sentences have been numbered.)

(1) The reason most people can recognize a collie is because of television shows and movies featuring the collie Lassie. (2) Lassie, whose long fur always looked naturally impeccable, but the coats of long-haired (or "rough") collies such as Lassie require regular grooming. (3) A variation of the breed is the smooth collie, which is the same general build and long nose as the rough collie but has short hair. (4) One thing that contributes to the popularity of collies is when people have fond memories of Lassie, who was usually smarter and more aware than the human characters. (5) Even collies that are not film stars have great dispositions. (6) The nature of collies will accept abuse that other dogs would snarl or even bite. (7) But collies are too lovable to hurt or tease them is mean. (8) A collie's intelligence is easy to train, and its loyalty is where it resembles the heroic Lassie.

EXERCISE 26.4 USING ELLIPTICAL STRUCTURES

NAME _____ **DATE** _____

Read the following sentences. If a sentence omits words that should be included or if it repeats words that could be omitted, revise the sentence on the lines provided.

EXAMPLE	Will wanted to see a science fiction movie, Sabina wanted to see a romance movie, and Brian to stay home.
REVISION	Will wanted to see a science fiction movie, Sabina wanted to see a romance, and Brian wanted to stay home.
EXAMPLE	Cathy arrived first, and Lucy arrived ten minutes later.
REVISION	Cathy arrived first, and Lucy ten minutes later.

1. At the end of every day, the toys were put away and the mess cleaned up.

_____

_____

2. Let's stay home because I am sick and you exhausted.

_____

_____

3. Ari decided to take a nap, Michael decided to study for his chemistry test, and Susan to take a book back to the library.

_____

_____

4. The car's exterior is blue, but the vinyl seats black.

_____

_____

5. The candidate was jovial, he was glib, but not very smart.

_____

_____

6. His parents were clearly not poor and worried about money.

_____

_____

7. Caitlin plays on the school's field hockey team, she plays on the school's soccer team, and she plays on the school's tennis team.

_____

_____

8. My adviser suggested that I should plan my class schedule ahead of time, I should balance difficult and easy classes, and I should take the study-skills workshop.

_____

_____

_____

9. My mother redecorated the living room, the kitchen, but not my bedroom.

_____

_____

10. The house is Victorian, its windows enormous.

_____

_____

11. Hakim loved aerobic exercise, Josef loved yoga and meditation, and Harry sleeping all day.

_____

_____

12. Money buys power, and money buys influence, but not happiness.

_____

_____

EXERCISE 26.5   REVISING INADVERTENT OMISSIONS AND INCOMPLETE
COMPARISONS

NAME _____ DATE _____

Read the following sentences, and check carefully for omissions and faulty comparisons. If
a sentence needs revising, write your new version on the lines provided. Add new content as
necessary. If a sentence is accurate and acceptable as written, write C on the line below the
sentence.

EXAMPLE   The small-screen plasma television is more expensive.

REVISION   The small-screen plasma television is more expensive than the larger cathode-ray tube
model.

1. Antibiotics are derived from bacteria and fungi, which occur nature.

_____

_____

2. Once Louis Pasteur showed that bacteria do cause disease, scientists could look for better
ways to fight these microorganisms.

_____

_____

3. When Alexander Fleming found that penicillin kills bacteria, he realized that it could more
effectively fight infection.

_____

_____

4. Streptomycin was the next antibiotic discovered, giving doctors more than one treatment
option.

_____

_____

5. Antibiotics have been called "wonder drugs" because they have saved more people from illnesses that used to be fatal.

_____

_____

6. Initially, doctors were more careful to prescribe antibiotics only for bacterial infections because antibiotics were useless against viral illnesses.

_____

_____

7. Then people became more accustomed to getting a prescription every time they felt sick, so some doctors began prescribing antibiotics even when an illness was not due to bacteria.

_____

_____

8. Effectively fighting common bacteria now requires higher levels of antibiotics than fifty years ago because many bacterial strains have not only survived but adapted.

_____

_____

9. Indeed, new strains of bacteria are stronger than the past.

_____

_____

10. These antibiotic-resistant bacteria pose a greater threat to public health.

_____

_____

SENTENCE STYLE

"A university student asked [a
well-known writer], 'Do you think
I could be a writer?' 'Well,' the writer
said, 'do you like sentences?'"
— ANNIE DILLARD

PART 6

PREVIEW QUESTIONS

These questions are designed to help you decide what you need to study. (Answers to preview questions are at the back of the book.)

1. Can these two sentences be revised to be more concise? Answer *yes* or *no*.

   a. For more than thirty years, researchers have studied the effects of viewing media violence. _____

   b. At that point in time, the police apprehended and arrested the pair of two suspects. _____

2. Underline the coordinating conjunctions in these two sentences.

   a. The ancient carvings had suffered some damage from vandals, so the trails leading past the site were closed to the public.

   b. Usually Carolyn is never late, but this time she missed her train.

3. Can a dependent clause ever stand on its own? Answer *yes* or *no*. _____

4. Underline the dependent clauses in these three sentences.

   a. Young people who listen to loud music through ear jacks risk doing permanent damage to their ears.

   b. Some nutritionists recommend drinking pomegranate juice because it has antioxidant properties.

   c. Although some doctors endorse this new treatment for melanoma, others are waiting for more research.

5. Identify each of these three sentences as simple, compound, or complex.

   a. The building was in violation of zoning ordinances, but the owners had secured a waiver. _____

   b. The violent wind and roiling, churning surf tossed the boats violently to and fro in the inlet. _____

   c. The candidate we supported wasn't elected because some voters had doubts about her. _____

6. In the next five sentences, identify any of these stylistic weaknesses: passive verbs, wordiness, and weak verbs. If none of these weaknesses is present, write C next to the sentence.

   a. It is necessary that everyone arrive at the ticket booth at the same time. _____

   b. Pianists often wrestle with the technically treacherous passages of Bach's *Goldberg Variations*. _____

   c. Although the bronze and the silver medals were won by the other team, the gold was won by us. _____

   d. There were hard questions on that test. _____

   e. The office was a mess. _____

Effective Sentences

27

As you write sentences for a rough draft, you are thinking hard about what you want to say; you are struggling with ideas and words. A rough draft about capital punishment might contain this sentence: *It is true that the question of capital punishment is a complicated one because it involves a moral decision.* Getting this idea down on paper for the first time is itself an accomplishment. If you had written that sentence, you would have begun to understand your thoughts and feelings on the issue of capital punishment. You write rough drafts in large part to come to such realizations.

Rough drafts, however, need revising to clarify their content and their expression. Clarifying expression means rewriting sentences to make your meaning as clear and as straightforward as it can be. Part of revision involves examining the wording of each sentence, making it as emphatic and concise as possible.

Revision of the rough-draft sentence on capital punishment could begin with cutting *It is true that.* This kind of opening helps a writer get something on paper, but those four words add nothing to the meaning of the sentence and cause the writer to bury the main points in a relative clause beginning with *that.* Cutting the opening leaves *The question of capital punishment is a complicated one because it involves a moral decision.* Can the sentence be tightened further? *Capital punishment is a complicated question because it involves a moral decision.* Now the sentence consists of two parts connected with *because.* If we could figure out a way to combine those two parts, we would have an even more emphatic and concise sentence. Notice that the idea of a question is echoed in the word *decision.* Noticing that gives us the final revision: *Capital punishment is a complicated moral question.*

EFFECTIVE SENTENCES IN EVERYDAY USE

You can see the importance of emphasis and conciseness when you read directions. Directions for taking a prescription aim to state their message emphatically (to relay important information) and concisely (to fit on a small label). In the same way, a good cookbook's explanation of how to bake a loaf of bread is clear and brief, and it lists steps in a logical sequential order. Look around for other effective directions, such as product instructions, traffic signs, and safety warnings. Jot down the sentences you find, and see if you can draw any conclusions about what makes language concise and emphatic.

Emphasis (42a)

Using closing and opening positions for emphasis

Effective writing takes advantage of all you know about how readers read and remember what they read. Readers tend to remember what they read last, whether in an essay or in individual sentences. In the following set of sample sentences, notice that the closing position is held by a different idea, resulting in a different emphasis each time.

> David lost two pounds following his diet this week.
>
> This week, David lost two pounds following his diet.
>
> Following his diet this week, David lost two pounds.

The first sentence stresses time; it comes from a paragraph discussing the time David needed to lose weight. The second sentence stresses David's diet; it comes from a paragraph focusing on the diet itself. The third sentence stresses the number of pounds lost; it comes from a paragraph emphasizing David's achievement.

As a writer, you can use positioning to achieve emphasis. The results may not seem to make much difference in a single sentence, but used over the course of an entire essay, careful ordering of ideas within sentences can make the difference between merely competent writing and truly effective writing.

Using climactic order

Sentences using **climactic order** present their ideas — usually three or more — in a sequence of increasing importance, power, or drama. Sometimes this sequence also corresponds to a normal time sequence:

> As soon as you pass the courthouse, turn right onto Baxter Street, go six blocks straight ahead to Canal Street, and look for the blue-and-white sign that says *Library*.

Violating this normal time sequence lessens impact and may lead to confusion:

> Go six blocks down Baxter Street, onto which you turn right as soon as you pass the courthouse, and look for the blue-and-white sign that says *Library* when you get to Canal Street.

Sometimes climactic order has nothing to do with time and everything to do with intensity:

> Prison inmates face routine boredom, long separations from family and friends, and the risk of violence at the hands of other prisoners.

To revise sentences to achieve climactic order, first look for any sentences that present a series of ideas or actions. Look closely at the series to determine the most important idea or action; this one should come last. Position the remaining ideas or actions so that they proceed from lesser importance to greater importance, leading up to the most important (or dramatic or powerful) idea or action.

Three ideas about prison life are presented in our last sample sentence. Arranging them from least terrible to most terrible yields the most dramatic sentence. Try arranging the sequence of ideas differently, and you will see how much less dramatic the sentence becomes.

Conciseness (42b)

Whenever you are trying to make a sentence concise, eliminate **redundant** wording, language that unnecessarily repeats ideas. Certain common expressions are always redundant: *few in number, large in size, combine together, continue on, continue to remain, repeat again, red in color,* and *free gift.* You can identify redundant material by carefully rereading your draft, looking for sentences that say the same thing twice. Here are some additional examples:

REDUNDANT	Contemporary poets writing now use rhyme more sparingly than did the poets of the forties and fifties. [*By definition, contemporary poets* must *be writing now.*]
REVISED	Contemporary poets use rhyme more sparingly than did the poets of the forties and fifties.
REDUNDANT	A synthetic and artificially produced material made from oil, polyester now shows up in everything from clothing to ropes to seat cushions. [*If the material is produced from oil, it must be both synthetic and artificial.*]
REVISED	Produced from oil, polyester now shows up in everything from clothing to ropes to seat cushions.

A number of official-sounding phrases are simply wordy. In almost every case, these phrases can be replaced with more concise language, resulting in less pompous prose.

WORDY	CONCISE
at that point in time	then
at the present time	now, today
in the event that	if
general consensus of opinion	consensus
exhibits a tendency to	tends

Finally, be careful in your use of all-purpose modifiers such as *absolutely, awfully, central, definitely, fine, great, important, literally, major, quite, very,* and *weird*. Without specific details, such modifiers mean almost nothing:

We definitely had an absolutely and quite literally unbelievable time at the beach.

Although that sentence sounds emphatic, it does not give readers much real information. Only the writer has any idea as to what really happened at the beach to make the experience so wonderful.

EXERCISE 27.1 CLIMACTIC ORDER

NAME _____ **DATE** _____

Revise the following sentences so that they use climactic order.

EXAMPLE   Coast Guard personnel conduct boating safety classes, sometimes must risk their own lives to save others, and monitor emergency radio channels.

REVISION   Coast Guard personnel conduct boating safety classes, monitor emergency radio channels, and sometimes must risk their own lives to save others.

1. Depending on the institution, plagiarism can result in expulsion from school, failure of the course, or a semester's suspension.

2. Andrew led the cello section in the high school orchestra, played a solo with the city's youth symphony, and conscientiously practiced the cello.

3. Some drivers angrily claim that sport-utility vehicles use energy inefficiently, destroy smaller vehicles in collisions, and limit the visibility of people in cars alongside them on the road.

4. Swallow the tablet every morning with a large glass of water, and be sure to eat a light meal before taking the medicine.

5. For my literature class, I read the poems and wrote the required response paper after I had studied the assignment carefully.

_____

_____

6. The students' parents were upset because the school's music program had been cut, tests at the school revealed dangerous levels of radon gas, and its popular principal was being transferred.

_____

_____

7. Most agree that Martin Luther King Jr.'s career as a civil rights leader reached its high point when King addressed more than 200,000 protesters at the Washington Monument in August 1963; King helped establish the Southern Christian Leadership Conference in 1957 and became its first president that same year.

_____

_____

_____

_____

_____

8. The case baffled inspectors — even though they found the killer eventually — because of the bizarre nature of the clues and the fact that no one ever heard a thing.

_____

_____

_____

9. Actress Anne Bancroft, who died in 2005, won an Academy Award for *The Miracle Worker* in 1962 and married writer-director Mel Brooks two years later.

_____

_____

_____

10. The marching band won a state competition before participating in the Rose Bowl parade after practicing hard all semester.

_____

_____

EXERCISE 27.2 CONCISENESS

NAME _____ **DATE** _____

The following sentences are wordy, redundant, or plagued by all-purpose modifiers. Rewrite each sentence so that it is concise.

> **EXAMPLE** It is believed by many computer owners that a Mac has definite advantages that make it superior to a PC.
>
> **REVISION** Many computer owners believe that a Mac has advantages over a PC.

1. It is definitely important that Americans in contemporary society should fully and completely understand the complex intricate workings of their form of government known as democracy.

   _____

   _____

   _____

2. At the present time under current conditions, it truly continues to remain the case that health care reform is a really big, major, and crucial issue for the people of this great nation.

   _____

   _____

   _____

3. The occasion of an accidental and totally unexpected lighting of a house fire can lead to and result in much significant damage in terms of the home owners' personal property.

   _____

   _____

4. The absolutely worst thing a person who is suffering from a common cold can ever possibly do is to go to her or his place of work and spread it to her or his various co-workers.

   _____

   _____

5. It is believed by many experts who have studied this problem that workers who labor on graveyard shifts exhibit a tendency to commit more errors than workers commit during the shift during the day.

_____

_____

_____

6. By that point in time, the three triplets exhibited a tendency to pursue their own unique and separate interests, while earlier on they had really enjoyed doing things together as a group.

_____

_____

7. She is of the opinion that the supposed liberal bias in radio, television, and print news media is a fabricated myth.

_____

_____

_____

8. Very many customers who did their shopping at this clothing and menswear store continued to remain completely loyal customers up to the time of its final closing.

_____

_____

_____

9. It should be noted that Supreme Court justices wield a great deal of power given the fact that they are appointed to serve on the bench of the Supreme Court for their entire lives or until they retire from the bench or they die.

_____

_____

_____

10. Many dentists assert an argument about the use of anticavity mouthwash. They hold the position that the continued use of these oral rinses does not in fact reduce or lessen the chances of a user developing cavities.

_____

_____

_____

EXERCISE 27.3 WORDINESS

Read the following passage, and pay particular attention to any sentences that seem wordy. Work on a revision of the passage, and copy your best version onto a separate sheet of paper to hand in to your instructor. By way of example, a revision of the first sentence follows the passage.

Modern-day experts in matters of nutrition and nutritional eating now want school cafeterias to serve healthier and more nutritious noontime lunches to children. Although it is true that the lunches at the present time are filling and serve ample amounts to children, they are not literally the most healthful. Most of the lunches served in our nation's educational institutions have an amount of fat that is too great, quite definitely well above the established guideline set at 30 percent. They also contain amounts of salt that are large in size and that may be a causal agent for later problems in being and remaining healthy. In addition to having too much of these two food components, the noontime meals also have too small an amount of more healthful vegetables and fruits. Young people, students, and school-age children really need to partake of these healthful options and choices of foods, which are especially rich in vitamins and very good sources of fiber. Even if the institutional eateries improve the healthfulness of the meals that they provide and serve, some people are concerned that children will decide not to partake of the healthier foods. Other of the involved citizenry combine together in continuing to believe that children can learn to understand the importance of making their food choices better. The general consensus of opinion is that if children are taught and educated about nutritional information and if they are given wholesome and healthful options and alternatives, they will assuredly be able to learn about how to select foods effectively for themselves.

REVISED FIRST SENTENCE   Nutrition experts want school cafeterias to serve healthier lunches to children.

Coordination and Subordination

28

Consider these two sentences:

> The sun shone.
>
> The sky was a clear, deep blue.

Each sentence is a short independent clause: each has a subject and a verb, and each can stand alone. If you wished to combine these two sentences, you could use **coordination**, linking the two clauses with *and, or, but, nor, yet, for,* or *so.* These words are called **coordinating conjunctions** (for more on conjunctions, see Chapter 16). The most appropriate coordinating conjunction for linking the two clauses listed above is *and.*

> The sun shone, and the sky was a clear, deep blue.

The key to understanding sentence coordination is this: both halves of the sentence are grammatically equal; both are independent clauses.

The two simple sentences *The sun shone* and *The sky was a clear, deep blue* can also be combined by using **subordination**, making one sentence a dependent clause.

> *While the sun shone,* the sky was a clear, deep blue.

The italicized **dependent clause** contains a subject and a verb but cannot stand alone as a sentence because it begins with a subordinating conjunction. Reading that dependent clause, readers expect an independent clause to follow it. The independent clause almost always expresses the main idea of the sentence. Here, the dependent clause limits the independent clause, suggesting that only while the sun shone was the sky a clear, deep blue.

Coordination to relate equal ideas (43a)

The parts of a coordinate structure are of equal importance, and the coordinating conjunction indicates the nature of their relationship.

COORDINATION AND SUBORDINATION IN EVERYDAY USE

Small children tend to use the coordinating conjunctions *and, but,* and *so.* If you spend any time around small children, you have probably heard a sentence such as this one: "I went to the playground, and I wanted to swing on the swings, but Jason was there, and he wouldn't share the swing, so I pushed him, but he still wouldn't give me a turn." Excited adults may speak in a similar way, using more coordinate structures than most people would choose in writing. Make a note of sentences using coordinating conjunctions that you use (or that you hear someone else use) in speech.

Coordination can be used to convey accumulation (using *and, or,* or *nor*), contrast (using *but* or *yet*), and cause and effect (using *for* or *so*). Examples of each follow; the coordinating conjunctions joining the clauses are italicized.

ACCUMULATION	We were caught in the rain without an umbrella, *and* not one bus or taxi was in sight.
CONTRAST	Yesterday was hot and steamy, *but* today a cool wind has made the apartment more comfortable.
CAUSE AND EFFECT	The geography test had me worried, *so* I studied in the library for two hours after lunch.

When two clauses are joined by a coordinating conjunction, a comma usually precedes the conjunction. Notice that in each example above, the italicized coordinating conjunction is preceded by a comma.

Coordinating conjunctions can also join phrases or nouns or verbs or other parts of speech.

I've packed my dress shoes *and* clean shirts. [And *joins two nouns and their modifiers.*]

That order should be ready in the morning *or* in the early afternoon. [Or *joins two prepositional phrases.*]

Subordination to distinguish main ideas (43b)

Consider the following pair of sentences, one using coordination and the other using subordination. Note that the coordinate structure produces two sentence parts of roughly equal importance. The subordinate structure, by contrast, clearly emphasizes the meaning of the independent clause.

COORDINATION	The sprinkler has been running for forty-five minutes, yet the water has penetrated only an inch. [*roughly equal emphasis, making the terms of the contrast separate and clear*]

SUBORDINATION Although the sprinkler has been running for forty-five minutes, the water has penetrated only an inch. [*emphasizes the minimal water penetration*]

Most dependent clauses begin with **subordinating conjunctions** such as *when, since, because, if, although, unless, whenever, often, before, while, after, as,* and *until* (see also Chapter 16). Dependent clauses can also be introduced by the **relative pronouns** *who, which,* and *that* (occasionally these words are omitted).

Unless we decide otherwise, we'll meet you at Silver Creek State Park at noon.

The woman *who sold me this sweater* seemed to be about Debbie's size.

The pizza *that you ordered* tasted delicious.

The pizza *you ordered* tasted delicious. [*That is omitted.*]

Subordination and coordination may occur in the same sentence:

Although clouds gathered and darkened in the west, we decided to go ahead with the family picnic, so Dad packed the sandwiches. [*A dependent clause opens this sentence; it is followed by two independent clauses joined by* so. *Note that the subordinate structure gives emphasis to the picnic.*]

Notice how different the emphasis becomes when the other half of that sentence is subordinated:

As we prepared to go ahead with the picnic and Dad packed the sandwiches, clouds gathered and darkened in the west. [*The emphasis here is on the weather.*]

For more on the use of these structures, see Chapter 16.

Coordination and subordination for special effect (43a, 43b)

Imagine overhearing this complaint from the eleven-year-old in the apartment below you: *I've cleaned my room, and I've put away my laundry and Callie's, and I cooked breakfast this morning, and I cleaned the dishes, and I just finished fixing Tory's bicycle, and now you want me to go to the store?* That eleven-year-old speaker is using coordination for a very particular effect. The accumulation of independent clauses makes the final question (*and now you want me to go to the store?*) seem like an injustice. Writers can use the same technique, though sparingly. Whenever you pile independent clause on independent clause, the result will be emphatic.

Writers can also use repeated subordination to achieve special effects. Consider this sentence: *When you're a chemistry major who hates chemistry, when you're just barely scoring well enough to pass your chemistry classes, when you'd rather spend more time on your psychology class than on any chemistry class, maybe it's time to think hard about changing majors.* In this sentence, the accumulation of conditions makes the sentence's conclusion seem true and undeniable. That repetition also adds a note of sarcasm to the word *maybe.*

The kind of repetition discussed here is a matter of style. Such repetition adds emphasis whenever it is used, but if it is used too often, its effectiveness diminishes.

EXERCISE 28.1   COORDINATION

NAME _____ **DATE** _____

Use coordination to combine each pair of simple sentences. Make sure the resulting sentence is properly punctuated.

EXAMPLE   The geography test had me worried. I studied in the library for two hours after lunch.

REVISION   The geography test had me worried, so I studied in the library for two hours after lunch.

1. Movie prices have risen. The quality of films has declined.

   _____

   _____

2. It is difficult to predict whether a film will be a success. Audiences can be fickle.

   _____

   _____

3. A big-budget movie might rake in lots of money. It might tank at the box office.

   _____

   _____

4. Hollywood studios have a major interest in making successful films. Movie executives research audience preferences.

   _____

   _____

5. Films are prescreened for selected audiences. Surveys are conducted.

   _____

   _____

6. Few films become megahits. Even flops can take in millions at the box office.

_____

_____

7. Many films are modest successes. They may or may not recoup their costs.

_____

_____

8. The movie business attempts primarily to attract young males. Older audiences sometimes feel left out.

_____

_____

9. It is difficult to predict the future of Hollywood. Two things are certain.

_____

_____

10. Computer technology will continue to change the face of film. Big stars will continue to command huge salaries.

_____

_____

EXERCISE 28.2   SUBORDINATION

NAME _____ **DATE** _____

All together the following items make up a paragraph. Combine the simple sentences by making one sentence in each item a subordinate clause (more than one correct answer is possible). Try to use subordination to emphasize the main ideas of the whole passage.

> **EXAMPLE**   The woman sold me this sweater. She seemed to be about Debbie's size.
>
> **REVISION**   The woman who sold me this sweater seemed to be about Debbie's size.

1. Some people enjoy learning about their families. They are willing to spend hours doing research on the subject.

   _____

   _____

2. Their interest is both a hobby and a passion. Their interest is called *genealogy*.

   _____

   _____

3. Some people's interest in family history is sparked by discovering an old photo album. Others stumble across family papers.

   _____

   _____

4. Many people begin by talking to family members. These family members may have helpful information to share.

   _____

   _____

5. The search can even turn into a joint project. Other family members may also become interested in pursuing genealogy.

   _____

   _____

6. Other members of the family become interested in the project. Learning about long-gone relatives is likely to be an easier job.

_____

_____

7. Each relative is identified and placed on the tree. The avid genealogist wants to know the dates and places of birth and death, dates of weddings, names of spouses and children, and other such details.

_____

_____

8. The dates and locations for these significant events can be discovered. The genealogist may need to search diligently for church and government records.

_____

_____

9. The certificates of birth, marriage, and death can supply additional information. Family letters and diaries may add personal details.

_____

_____

10. Genealogical researchers may discover that they are related to someone famous. More often family history is fascinating just for the many characters that turn up.

_____

_____

COORDINATION AND SUBORDINATION FOR SPECIAL EFFECT

NAME _____ **DATE** _____

The following paragraph uses coordination and subordination in some sentences, but other sentences could be combined by using one of these techniques. Rewrite any sentences you feel would benefit from coordination or subordination.

    Americans associate Halloween with trick-or-treating children and costumes. Some Halloween customs are old. Most of the traditions that remind people of Halloween began no earlier than the 1920s. That was a time when young people celebrated the holiday by looking for mischief. People sometimes went door-to-door dressed in ragged costumes and asked for charity in the nineteenth century. This was a Christian custom. Halloween trick-or-treating probably had its origin during the Depression. Wealthy people of the time sponsored Halloween open houses to discourage vandalism. The phrase "trick or treat" first appeared in a national magazine in 1939. Soon, children across the country dressed up as goblins. Houses everywhere planned for trick-or-treaters. Later, Halloween became more frightening for many people. Stories about strangers giving poisoned treats appeared in the 1970s. However, tales about apples filled with razor blades seem to be urban legends. No one knows where the stories come from. No one has ever reported an injury from a Halloween treat received from a stranger. The worst problems from Halloween candy tend to be weight gain and tooth decay. Chocolate-loving ghouls should be on guard.

Sentence Variety 29

The length of a sentence has a strong effect on its message and its impact. Short sentences express simple assertions: *I want ice cream* or *This blanket's mine.* Short sentences can be blunt and forceful. Sometimes they crystallize complex thought or emotion: *Question authority* or *The buck stops here.*

In contrast, longer sentences can depict more fully the complications and complexities of experience. Notice how this sentence accommodates two conflicting possibilities and then resolves them: *On the one hand, I would love to make a living playing music; on the other hand, my parents want me to study something practical: I'm going to compromise and major in music education.*

Sometimes alternating long and short sentences capitalizes on the advantages of each—and adds variety to prose as well. *On the one hand, I would love to make a living playing music; on the other hand, my parents want me to study something practical. Can I compromise? I'll major in music education.*

SENTENCE VARIETY IN EVERYDAY USE

Very short capsule reviews usually contain varied sentence structures, perhaps to hold readers' attention with a snappy, fast-paced description. This brief review appeared on the Web site *Television without Pity*:

> So long, stern-looking tikis! Farewell, hungry little No-Nos! Adieu, horrible clue writers! Yes, another season of *Survivor* comes to an end, and another American moron gets handed a million dollars for no good reason at all except the entertainment of the home viewing audience.

The writer of this review varies sentence length by starting with three short sentences and ending with a long one. The short sentences are all good-byes; the long compound sentence sums up the season-ending episode. The variety makes the brief synopsis readable and entertaining.

Study some capsule reviews in a magazine or newspaper (or on television or a Web site), noticing the variety of sentences used. Write down an example or two. Can you draw any conclusions about the effect of sentence variety on readers?

Sentence length (44a)

When should you use short sentences? When should you use long sentences? You learn to make such choices for yourself, but you begin by noting what happens when different stylistic choices are made.

SHORT-SENTENCE VERSION	Live free or die.
LONG-SENTENCE VERSION	If we do not live under a government that guarantees our freedom, then we ought to fight for freedom, just as we would fight for life itself; we ought to fight for freedom even if it means giving our lives.

The short example is a fine rallying cry. It is easy to remember. The long-sentence version is far more complicated; it cannot be easily remembered. But it does carry its own kind of careful persuasion.

SHORT-SENTENCE VERSION	I'm fond of roast beef. It reminds me of Saturday dinners. I was a kid then. I went to the doctor not long ago. She did some tests. She says I should change my diet by avoiding red meat. So I'll order fish.
LONG-SENTENCE VERSION	On the one hand, I'm fond of roast beef because it reminds me of Saturday dinners when I was a kid; on the other hand, my doctor encourages me to avoid red meat: I'll order the fish.

The short-sentence version is grammatically correct, but it is also choppy and sounds scattered and confusing. The long one-sentence version is clearer because its structure and punctuation indicate the relationships among all of those clauses. As a result, readers have an easier time following the writer's thought. The long-sentence version unites content and form; it is a much better choice.

Choosing the length you feel is most appropriate for each sentence you write is a good way to begin thinking about varying your sentences. Even after thinking about it, however, you may find that all your sentences are about the same length. If this happens to you, select some of your sentences and revise them to be of a noticeably different length, even if you think this will not make them better. Many times, we stick with one version of a sentence or paragraph simply because we have not fully explored the alternatives and therefore do not realize how they might improve what we have written. This sort of experimentation will usually lead you to a more effective version than you had thought was possible.

Sentence openings (44b)

If you are writing to hold readers' attention, you will probably want to vary your sentence openings, as well as your sentence lengths. Such variety will add interest and pizzazz to your writing. Read this passage:

The first afternoon and evening was sunny and hot. We ate dinner in a meadow overlooking the Pacific, and we watched the sun set. It was almost every shade of orange, red, and purple going down. We went to bed expecting good weather. It rained that night. We woke up in the morning and tried to make pancakes while staying warm in our sleeping bags. Some of the batter spilled onto the sleeping bags. The spill made an unpleasant mess.

What you have just read is part of a narrative of a camping trip. Every sentence starts with a simple subject and is immediately followed by a verb. The passage carries some interest because of its details, but it conveys a rather boring trip overall. Why? Its sentences all begin the same way.

Here are three ways to vary sentence openings:

- Begin with single-word transitions. (For more information about transitions, see Chapter 7.)

  Afterward, we discussed the difficulties of being a single parent.

  Hence, the board has approved your design.

- Begin with prepositional, verbal, or absolute phrases. (See Chapter 16.)

  Before dawn, the mountain etches its silhouette against the sky.

  Talking around the clock, negotiators finally reached a settlement.

  Our business concluded, we decided to go out to lunch.

- Begin with a dependent clause. (See Chapter 28.)

  While we were frantically trying to finish the proposal, our boss was calmly preparing to take credit for it.

  Once Valerie had become a vegetarian, the thought of a medium-rare steak no longer tempted her.

Sentence types (44c)

Are there other ways to vary your prose, making it more vibrant and lively? Certainly. Although most of the sentences you write in formal or academic situations will be declarative, you may also be able to use an occasional question, command, or exclamation. Using different functional types of sentences varies the routine for readers and keeps them interested. Beginning a paragraph with a question is but one way to add such variety.

This chapter has already discussed variety in sentence lengths and openings; it is only a small step from that discussion to a larger discussion of grammatical sentence types. Here is a brief review of grammatical types, introduced in Chapter 16. You ought to be able to use all of them in your writing.

- **Simple sentence** (one independent clause)

  Some people go to college to obtain a good job.

- **Compound sentence** (two or more independent clauses)

  Some people go to college to obtain a good job, but others go to gain an understanding of their values and beliefs.

- **Complex sentence** (one or more dependent clauses and an independent clause)

  While some people go to college to obtain a good job, others go to gain an understanding of their values and beliefs.

- **Compound-complex sentence** (two or more independent clauses and one or more dependent clauses)

  While some people go to college to obtain a good job, a significant number go to meet people with similar interests, and others go to gain an understanding of their values and beliefs.

Two other rhetorical types of sentences provide variety: periodic and cumulative sentences. A **periodic sentence** expresses its main idea (usually in an independent clause) at the end of the sentence. Often, several phrases or dependent clauses build up to the independent clause.

For job training, for fostering an understanding of values and beliefs, for meeting other people with similar interests, for drama or forestry or philosophy, for waking yourself up—a college campus is the place.

In contrast, a **cumulative sentence** begins with the main idea (usually in an independent clause), which is followed by several phrases or dependent clauses.

A college campus is a place for job training, for fostering an understanding of values and beliefs, for meeting other people with similar interests, for drama or forestry or philosophy, for waking yourself up.

EXERCISE 29.1   SENTENCE LENGTH

NAME _____ **DATE** _____

Revise each of the following items as specified. Be ready to discuss differences in meaning and emphasis between the original version and your revision.

EXAMPLE   Since we've lost two games already and since this week's opponent has lost only one game, you can see that it's really important that we come out on top. (Summarize in a short sentence.)

REVISION   We need to win!

EXAMPLE   It was Sunday afternoon. The sun was shining. The hammock was in the backyard. It was a perfect day for resting in the hammock. (Combine into one long sentence.)

REVISION   That sunny Sunday afternoon was perfect for resting in the hammock in the backyard.

1. First cook the noodles according to package directions, then drain and return to the pot, then mix in butter and cream, and then toss lightly with grated cheese. (Break into several short sentences.)

_____

_____

_____

2. Do the right thing. (Write a longer single-sentence version that emphasizes the importance of doing what is right.)

_____

_____

_____

3. The elephant Tika was transferred to the Delray Park Zoo two years ago. Tika didn't adapt well to the new environment. She shunned the other elephants. Now she seems depressed. She is being transferred back to the local zoo. Supporters had hoped she would be sent to a preserve. They are outraged. (Combine into two or three smooth sentences.)

_____

_____

449

_____

_____

4. You should approach your life in such a way that you take every opportunity possible to experience as much as you can as fully and completely as you can every single day. (Summarize in a short sentence.)

_____

_____

_____

5. Love hurts. (Write a longer single-sentence version that emphasizes the pain involved in a romantic relationship.)

_____

_____

_____

6. A good dictionary tells you how to pronounce words. It does a lot more. It can help you spell words correctly. It can teach you how to use words and phrases properly. It can alert you to words that are offensive or old-fashioned. (Combine into one or two smooth sentences.)

_____

_____

_____

_____

7. The no-smoking initiative had a number of vocal opponents. Voters approved it in November. The smoking ban went into effect in January. It prevents smoking in any restaurant or bar. (Combine into one smooth sentence.)

_____

_____

_____

_____

8. As people grow older, they have many important experiences encountering different kinds of problems and facing different life situations, so they are better able to understand what they face and act more wisely. (Summarize in a short sentence.)

_____

_____

_____

_____

9. The benefits of working from home are having flexibility in terms of choosing when you work and where you work, not having to dress up for work or even dress at all, and even being able to do your laundry as you are working. (Break into short sentences.)

_____

_____

_____

_____

10. There are three important things to do in finding a good job. You need to follow up on contacts. You need to vary your application letter and résumé to suit the position you are applying for. You also need to remain optimistic, even though the process may consume a lot of time and energy. (Combine into one smooth sentence.)

_____

_____

_____

_____

EXERCISE 29.2   SENTENCE OPENINGS

NAME _____ **DATE** _____

In the sentences below, underline the opening of any sentence that begins with a single-word transition; a prepositional, a verbal, or an absolute phrase; or a subordinate clause. Then identify the type of sentence opening by writing "transition," "phrase," or "clause" on the line following the sentence. If a sentence does not open with one of these, write "none" on the line.

> **EXAMPLE**   With his appointment to the Supreme Court in 1967, Thurgood Marshall became the first African American justice. _phrase_ _____

1. In 1933, Thurgood Marshall received a law degree from Howard University, a historically black college. _____

2. Afterward, he worked for the National Association for the Advancement of Colored People. _____

3. As a practicing attorney, he became the head of the Legal Defense and Education Fund of the NAACP. _____

4. While he represented the NAACP, Marshall argued *Brown v. Board of Education of Topeka, Kansas* in front of the Supreme Court. _____

5. Although the case was decided in 1954, it remains influential. _____

6. Marshall helped to create the NAACP's strategy to end racial segregation in voting, housing, and education. _____

7. After President John F. Kennedy appointed him to the U.S. Court of Appeals, Marshall became a well-known jurist. _____

8. Later, Marshall ascended to the Supreme Court of the United States when President Lyndon Johnson appointed him to fill a vacancy. _____

9. Noted for his liberal views on civil rights and individual liberties, Marshall served on the nation's highest court for more than two decades. _____

10. Marshall left the court in 1991 and died in 1993, but his contributions to the U.S. legal system survive. _____

EXERCISE 29.3   SENTENCE LENGTHS AND SENTENCE OPENINGS

Revise the following passage by varying sentence lengths and sentence openings. You may combine or recombine sentences; you may add new content. Make sure that your final version is smoother than the original version. Copy your final version onto a separate sheet of paper.

A recent survey was conducted of car owners. It found that over half of all Americans choose a car they think is a reflection of their personality. Many psychologists agree. People may think that they purchase a car based on practical issues. The decision is more likely made based on the buyer's individual psychology. One example is a buyer's desire to feel powerful. Such a person is likely to opt for an automobile along the lines of a Hummer. A buyer might also seek a sense of independence. This desire might lead to the purchase of a sport-utility or all-terrain vehicle. It is even possible that one would wish to seem like everyone else. This buyer would probably go for a conservative sedan in a neutral color. Cars can additionally be a status symbol for some. Such expensive automobiles are meant to show off their owners' financial success. Convertibles suggest a certain carefree approach to life. Fuel-efficient cars suggest a sense of frugality and concern for the environment. Many options exist today for expressing oneself through one's automobile.

EXERCISE 29.4   SENTENCE VARIETY

For each item below, create the kind of sentence named, and then connect the sentences to form a paragraph. Read the paragraph back to yourself; as you read, think about how effective the sentence variation is. Would you change any of the sentence types to create a better flow?

EXAMPLE   cat, feline (Write a simple sentence.)

A cat is also called a feline.
_____

1. what happened to me last night (Write an imperative sentence.)

_____

_____

2. waiting for a bus, saw my old friend Marcus for the first time in three years (Write a complex sentence.)

_____

_____

3. told me he was a record producer (Write a simple sentence.)

_____

_____

4. what he invited me to do (Write an interrogative sentence.)

_____

_____

5. asked to attend a business party at his apartment, well-known musicians there (Write a compound sentence.)

_____

_____

6. couldn't believe it (Write an exclamatory sentence.)

   _____

7. talked to Marcus, had interesting conversations with other people interested in music, heard about a possible job opportunity at a recording studio, suddenly saw my idol, Patti Smith (Write a periodic sentence.)

   _____

   _____

   _____

8. huge influence on my music and writing, almost afraid to speak to her, made me feel at ease (Write a compound-complex sentence.)

   _____

   _____

9. changed my life, found an old friend again, realized I might be able to work in music after all, met some exciting people, even got my idol's email address (Write a cumulative sentence.)

   _____

   _____

   _____

10. only lasted a few hours, remember the experience forever (Write a complex sentence.)

   _____

   _____

Memorable Prose

30

The best prose accomplishes two difficult tasks: it expresses what the writer wishes to say, and it moves readers to feelings, action, or agreement exactly as the writer intended. Such prose depends on a writer's sincerity and commitment, but it just as surely depends on stylistic principles that all writers can learn. For example, notice the use of parallelism and rhythm in the following sentence from President John F. Kennedy's Inaugural Address:

MEMORABLE PROSE IN EVERYDAY USE

Language can be so memorable that it is quoted and referred to over and over again, sometimes for many years. Screenwriters, for example, struggle to create prose that will strike a chord with movie viewers, and sometimes they succeed admirably. Here is a selection of dialogue from one of the most famous—and most quoted—scenes in film, the end of the 1942 classic *Casablanca*, when Rick (Humphrey Bogart) sends his old flame Ilsa (Ingrid Bergman) away with her husband, Victor, a resistance fighter.

ILSA: But what about us?

RICK: We'll always have Paris. We didn't have it, we'd lost it, until you came to Casablanca. We got it back last night.

ILSA: And I said I would never leave you!

RICK: And you never will. But I've got a job to do, too. Where I'm going you can't follow. What I've got to do, you can't be any part of. Ilsa, I'm no good at being noble, but it doesn't take much to see that the problems of three little people don't amount to a hill of beans in this crazy world. Someday you'll understand that. Not now. Here's looking at you, kid.

Look at the structures that help to make dialogue memorable. You may notice the powerful use of repetition (*We'll always have Paris; We didn't have it, we'd lost it*) and inverted word order (*Where I'm going you can't follow*). Each of these structures is used more than once in just this short passage. Notice the way Ilsa's questions (*But what about us?*) and exclamations (*And I said I would never leave you!*) add to the urgent feeling of the conversation. Consider what you find striking about this dialogue.

Now think of some other movie dialogue that you find unforgettable. Watch the film again, and note the exact words. What makes the dialogue memorable?

And so, my fellow Americans, ask not what your country can do for you; ask what you can do for your country.

Or note the variation in sentence length and the power of these words from Sitting Bull's *Touch the Earth*:

What treaty that the whites have kept has the red man broken? Not one. What treaty that the white man ever made with us have they kept? Not one.

Strong verbs (45a)

Strong verbs convey their meaning in precise and unmistakable terms. Consider these three ways of saying basically the same thing:

The gulls *were flying* into the wind.

The gulls *flew* into the wind.

The gulls *soared* into the wind.

The last example is the strongest; the verb *soared* conveys most precisely and vividly the actual motion of the gulls. All three examples are grammatically correct, but only the final one conveys any real sense of motion or grace.

Unlike the action verb *soar*, verbs formed from *be*, *do*, and *have* carry no sense of specific movement. Because these verbs can work in almost any sentence, they frequently crop up in rough drafts. Notice how sentences with these weak verbs can be revised to produce more vibrant prose:

WEAK	The traffic downtown today was bad.
REVISED	Heavy traffic clogged downtown streets today.
WEAK	We had a two-mile run this morning in P.E.
REVISED	We sweated through a two-mile run this morning in P.E.

Sentences beginning with *It is* or *There are* also tend to clutter rough drafts. These constructions do have their uses, but when they begin a sentence, they guarantee that the sentence's main verb will be *is* or *are*—forms of *be*. Combing through your rough draft to revise such sentences will almost always result in stronger prose. See how the following examples are strengthened by revision:

WEAK	There are many comedians who perform to conquer their shyness.
REVISED	Many comedians perform to conquer their shyness.
WEAK	It was the fog that obscured our view of Seal Rock.
REVISED	The fog obscured our view of Seal Rock.

Changing nouns to verbs

Much contemporary writing depends unnecessarily on noun-heavy prose, which sounds pompous and self-important. Consider this sentence:

> Our research department has a consistent involvement in the development of new products.

What is wrong here? The sentence is grammatically correct but is crammed full of weighty nouns around the bland verb *has*. If you find yourself writing such stuffy sentences, revise them by changing nouns and noun phrases into verbs. For example, the entire concept expressed by *has a consistent involvement in the development of* can be conveyed by the single vivid verb *develops*:

> Our research department develops new products.

Here is another example:

WORDY AND STUFFY	For this job, *the requirement* of the Occupational Safety and Health Administration *is* that men be clean shaven.
REVISED	For this job, the Occupational Safety and Health Administration *requires* that men be clean shaven.

Active and passive voice (45b)

Consider these two ways of describing the same event:

ACTIVE VOICE	On the deck of the USS *Missouri*, General Douglas MacArthur signed the peace treaty ending World War II in the Pacific.
PASSIVE VOICE	The peace treaty ending World War II in the Pacific was signed by General Douglas MacArthur on the deck of the USS *Missouri*.

As you can see, the active voice focuses readers' attention on somebody or something performing an action: subject (*General Douglas MacArthur*) and action verb (*signed*). In contrast, the passive voice focuses attention on whatever receives the action (*the peace treaty*). Recognizing these different emphases is another key to writing memorable prose.

Weak prose overuses the passive voice, choosing it when there is no good reason to do so. In practice, most academic prose uses the active voice, and much scientific reporting uses the passive voice.

ACTIVE	Maxine Kumin's poems often illuminate New England life. [*Here, the subject*, poems, *performs the action*, illuminate.]
PASSIVE	Temperatures were recorded for a thirty-minute period. [*Here, the action*, were recorded, *is performed by an unnamed agent*.]

Notice that in the passive voice, the performer of the action might not be named at all.

Here is one way to help you choose between the active and the passive voice. First, write the sentence or clause with the verb in the active voice: *The committee reviewed all proposals.* Then determine the subject (the performer of the action), the verb, and the direct object of the verb:

> | SUBJECT | VERB | DIRECT OBJECT |
> The committee reviewed all proposals.

If you wish to emphasize the subject and the action performed, keep the verb in the active voice. If you wish to emphasize the direct object (the receiver of the action), use the passive. Notice that in the passive voice, the direct object (*all proposals*) becomes the subject: *All proposals were reviewed by the committee.* The active voice emphasizes the committee and what it did; the passive voice emphasizes the proposals and what was done to them.

Finally, if you have no good reason to use the passive voice, it is probably better to choose the active voice.

Special effects (45c)

Repetition—repeating particular sounds, words, phrases, or grammatical structures—can result in memorable prose. Here is an exasperated parent using repetition to underscore the urgency of a required action:

> Before you turn on the television, before you leave to play baseball or ride your skateboard, before you call anyone on the telephone, before you so much as think of what you are going to do next, you must clean your room.

That sentence repeats similar structures to achieve its emphasis.

Another special effect is **antithesis**, which uses parallel structures to highlight contrast or opposition.

> When I was a youngster, I ate everything in sight and never gained weight; now, everything I eat goes straight to my thighs.

The emphasis in this sentence is the difference between the past and the present. The tension in such contrast sentences makes them interesting.

Writers can also achieve special emphasis by changing the normal word order in a sentence. Most English sentences follow the subject→verb→object word order. Changing that order calls attention to the sentence.

NORMAL ORDER	A deer stood less than ten feet away.
INVERTED ORDER	Less than ten feet away stood a deer.

NORMAL ORDER	A new era in American foreign policy came with the war's end.
INVERTED ORDER	With the war's end came a new era in American foreign policy.

Notice that in each case, the normal word order seems matter-of-fact, whereas the reversed or **inverted order** tends to convey a dramatic overtone.

Use inverted word order, antithesis, and repetition sparingly and judiciously. Such techniques work only because their rarity makes them stand out.

EXERCISE 30.1   STRONGER VERBS

NAME _____ **DATE** _____

Weak verbs and unnecessarily wordy constructions plague the following sentences. Revise the sentences by substituting stronger verbs.

EXAMPLE	It is necessary that the cast arrive for rehearsal at 6:00 PM.
REVISION	The cast must arrive for rehearsal at 6:00 PM.

EXAMPLE	A large amount of electrical energy is a requirement for aluminum production.
REVISION	Aluminum production requires a large amount of electrical energy.

1. Various urban problems exist that can make life difficult for city dwellers.

_____

_____

2. There are high crime rates in many cities that are worrisome to their residents.

_____

_____

3. It is this fear of crime that can be a special problem for children and elderly people.

_____

_____

4. Another difficulty that city dwellers face is the problem of high rents.

_____

_____

5. A necessity of most people is a decent place to live that they can afford, but this may be impossible for working-class people in cities.

_____

_____

6. Another problem for city residents is public schools that are understaffed and not well equipped.

_____

_____

7. Although many urban schools have tried to participate in the development of strong educational programs, their high failure rates have not always lessened.

_____

_____

8. Still, there are many things that cities offer that are attractive to educated people with an interest in cultural events.

_____

_____

9. Important museums, fine theater, and diverse musical events are available for residents to take advantage of.

_____

_____

10. Therefore, cities are places that often draw people who are looking for an exciting place to live.

_____

_____

EXERCISE 30.2   ACTIVE AND PASSIVE VOICE

NAME _____ **DATE** _____

Identify the main verbs in the following sentences as either active or passive. Then note the intended emphasis of each sentence. If the original version accomplishes that emphasis, write *OK*. If the original version does not accomplish that emphasis, rewrite the sentence by changing the voice of its main verb.

EXAMPLES   My supervisor approved your memo.

Main verb is _____active_____. Intended emphasis: your memo

Your memo was approved by my supervisor.

The weather forecast was given as the last news item.

Main verb is _____passive_____. Intended emphasis: the weekend news anchor

The weekend news anchor gave the weather forecast as her last news item.

Kenyan coffee is grown in Africa.

Main verb is _____passive_____. Intended emphasis: the coffee

OK

1. The bill was passed by both houses of Congress in 2005.

Main verb is _____. Intended emphasis: both houses of Congress

_____

2. The newly acquired painting was contributed by an anonymous donor.

Main verb is _____. Intended emphasis: the newly acquired painting

_____

3. Unscrupulous scam artists often target unsuspecting elderly people.

Main verb is _____. Intended emphasis: unsuspecting elderly people

_____

4. The prosecution's request for a delay in the proceedings was denied by the judge.

Main verb is _____. Intended emphasis: the judge

_____

5. The cards were thrown down on the table by José as the game ended.

Main verb is _____ . Intended emphasis: José

_____

6. A mandate for social change was given by the citizens in the last election.

Main verb is _____ . Intended emphasis: the citizens

_____

7. Pottery is a wonderfully tactile art that uses natural substances to create beauty.

Main verb is _____ . Intended emphasis: pottery

_____

8. You are invited by Mr. Mark Brown and Ms. Janet Solomon to attend the wedding of their daughter, Silvia Brown-Solomon, to Jaime Quiñones.

Main verb is _____ . Intended emphasis: Mr. Mark Brown and Ms. Janet Solomon

_____

_____

9. I was bitten by my son's pet rabbit.

Main verb is _____ . Intended emphasis: my son's pet rabbit

_____

10. A falling branch knocked down the tent.

Main verb is _____ . Intended emphasis: the tent

_____

EXERCISE 30.3   SPECIAL EFFECTS

NAME _____ **DATE** _____

The chapter identifies three special effects that writers can use: repetition, antithesis, and inverted word order. For this exercise, compose a sentence using each kind. An example of each is provided.

EXAMPLE OF REPETITION   When I wanted to make a good living, I went to law school; when I wanted to make a name for myself, I took a job in the district attorney's office; but when I wanted to make a difference, I decided to start a campaign to reform the legal system.

YOUR EXAMPLE OF REPETITION

1. _____

_____

_____

_____

EXAMPLE OF ANTITHESIS   We began the project full of energy and enthusiasm; we finished weary and relieved that it was over.

YOUR EXAMPLE OF ANTITHESIS

2. _____

_____

_____

_____

EXAMPLE OF INVERTED WORD ORDER   On the end of a limb high above the street sat a frightened kitten.

YOUR EXAMPLE OF INVERTED WORD ORDER

3. _____

_____

_____

_____

EXERCISE 30.4 SENTENCE STYLE

NAME _____ **DATE** _____

Using any of the structures and revision suggestions covered in Chapters 27 to 30, revise the following short passages to create what you feel is more varied, interesting, and effective prose. You may want to write partial revisions on the passages themselves before beginning work on the lines provided below.

1. Inventors think of possibilities that other people would not consider. They see the need for tools. People have done without those tools for years. Inventors solve problems. Some problems are those that others have never even been aware of. An inventor was responsible for the creation of nonstick coatings for frying pans. Another inventor was the developer of clumping cat litter. The concept of the remote control was come up with by yet another inventor. Many Americans use these inventions routinely. Everyday life would be hard for us to recognize without the contributions of thousands of inventors.

_____

_____

_____

_____

_____

_____

2. There are many different ways that violence can be encouraged among young and school-age children by the various and sundry media. One way is that they may see the kind of violent actions in cartoons that are unrealistic because no one really gets hurt, and then they may carry out those very same actions in real life, resulting in really serious injury to another child. Another way is that they may simply learn or come to believe that the huge amount of violence depicted in the images they find in the media is appropriate behavior. It is definitely true that children need to be limited by their parents in terms of the amount of violence in the media they are exposed to.

_____

_____

_____

3. Global warming is a very serious problem. A number of troubling factors cause it. First, it is caused by an increase in the carbon dioxide existing in the atmosphere. There has also been an increase in other very harmful gases that are destroying the ozone layer. These gases trap heat in the upper atmosphere, and global temperatures are raised by them. And another major reason for global warming is deforestation. The decrease in the number of trees that are presently existing on our great planet Earth is having a devastating and serious effect on the amount of oxygen produced on a global level.

PUNCTUATION

"You can show a lot with a look. . . .
It's punctuation."
— CLINT EASTWOOD

PREVIEW QUESTIONS

These questions are designed to help you decide what to study. Correct the punctuation in the following sentences. If the punctuation is already correct, write C next to the sentence. (Answers to preview questions are at the back of the book.)

1. After an enormous dinner at the long table in the banquet hall, the men retired to the library for cigars and brandy.

2. Sharon wandered around the mall for two hours, but she decided not to buy anything.

3. The china was totally ruined in the dishwasher.

4. My next-door neighbor Matt, who spends all his time using machines to keep his yard neat, irritates everyone on the block.

5. The restaurant advertised for all sorts of positions: short-order cook, busboys, waiters, and bartenders.

6. Whereas Raashid kept calling the library a "bookhouse," I referred to it as "the house of naps."

7. "When are we going to eat?" Marisa asked.

8. Yes, I would like another cup of coffee; however, give me decaf this time.

9. Did she really say, "I don't think I need another pair of shoes?"

10. Just as Richard passed through customs, a guard shouted, "Stop!"

11. When I read the judges' decision, I decided that they had not paid sufficient attention to the defense's arguments.

12. Mother does not care what the critics say; she just doesn't want to see that movie.

13. The director said that he wanted Samuel L. Jackson in the role of Dr. Martin Luther King Jr.

14. The class has its good moments, but in general, I don't find it very interesting.

15. I did not know that this bicycle was theirs.

16. "I did not know that Anne was coming with us this evening," Peter said.

17. "Sri said that her job was 'very taxing,'" Vincent reported.

18. She has two older brothers, and one of them repeatedly tells her that "she shouldn't be going out with me."

19. "The next time I say I want to visit the haunted house," Melanie whispered, "talk me out of it."

20. Raising children requires patience—Byron, stop that this instant—and the ability to focus on more than one thing at a time.

21. A very wise person once said that there are only two types of literature: good and bad.

22. I had wanted (or at least thought I wanted) to go to medical school, but I decided that I was too old to keep an intern's hours.

Commas

31

Commas allow writers to link sentence elements and to separate them. Since commas have such a dual function, their use can puzzle even the most accomplished writers. Part of the difficulty writers have with commas lies in the fact that sometimes commas are required, sometimes they might be "optional" (depending on the writer's intention), and sometimes they simply do not belong. And writers do have difficulty with commas: four of the top twenty errors result from inaccurate comma usage. This chapter begins by discussing sentence structures that regularly use commas. If you need to review the basics of sentence grammar, see Chapter 16.

COMMAS IN EVERYDAY USE

Commas play an important role in recipes. Study their use in the following recipe for sweet-potato pie:

$1^1/_4$ c. sweet potatoes, cooked and mashed   1 T. butter, melted
$^1/_2$ c. brown sugar, firmly packed   2 eggs, well beaten
$^1/_2$ t. salt $^3/_4$ c. milk
$^1/_4$ t. cinnamon

Prepare pastry for a one-crust pie, and line an 8-inch pie pan; chill. Preheat oven to 400° F. Combine sweet potatoes, brown sugar, salt, cinnamon, and butter. Mix together eggs and milk. Combine all ingredients. Pour into the pie shell, and bake for 45 minutes.

One function of the commas here is to separate ingredients (sweet potatoes) from what the cook is supposed to do (cook and mash them). How else are the commas used? Look at some directions you use — for installing a new piece of software, perhaps, or for knitting a sweater or for playing a board game — and take note of some of the ways commas are used.

➔ **COMMON ERROR: MISSING COMMA AFTER AN INTRODUCTORY ELEMENT**

Commas after introductory elements (46a)

A comma regularly follows an **introductory element** in a sentence, separating it from the main clause, which follows it. The introductory element may be a word, a phrase, or an adverb clause.

[Introductory element], [rest of sentence].

Do not be fooled by the length of an adverb clause compared with the length of the main clause: *Once we have the fire net positioned under the window, you jump!* Here are other examples:

> Moreover, we will refuse to pay. [*introductory word*]
>
> To prevent polio, children receive an oral vaccine. [*introductory phrase*]
>
> Their attic and closets full to the rafters, the couple planned a garage sale. [*introductory phrase*]
>
> Since Town and Country Realtors helped us sell our house, we have recommended them to other sellers. [*introductory adverb clause*]

EXCEPTIONS

If an introductory element is short and easily understood without a comma, the comma may be omitted: *While I was waiting I stirred the soup.* If the introductory element is followed by inverted word order (verb before subject), a comma is not used: *From the back of the car came a series of giggles.*

→ **COMMON ERROR: MISSING COMMA IN A COMPOUND SENTENCE**

Commas in compound sentences (46b)

Commas routinely appear before **coordinating conjunctions** (*and, but, or, for, nor, so, yet*) that link two independent clauses. (See Chapter 16 for a review of independent clauses.)

> [Independent clause], coordinating conjunction + [independent clause].

Be careful to use both the comma and the coordinating conjunction. Leaving out the conjunction will result in a comma splice (see Chapter 23).

> The garage light had been left on all weekend, *but* it burned out in one big flash this morning.

Writers may also choose to join independent clauses by using semicolons. These are the only correct ways to join two independent clauses:

1. [Independent clause], coordinating conjunction + [independent clause].
2. [Independent clause]; [independent clause].

Joining independent clauses only with commas is acceptable when there are three (or more) such clauses in a series and the last two are linked by a coordinating conjunction.

EXAMPLE   We walked the dog, Jane came home after her night at Rachel's, Beth and Will played in the tree house, and we spent the hot afternoon being lazy.

Note that in this kind of sentence, commas can effectively separate clauses only when they are not used in other ways. *I went home, he saw that I was calm, happy, and smiling, and he became calm and happy, too* is a confusing sentence. It is clearer when punctuated this way: *I went home; he saw that I was calm, happy, and smiling; and he became calm and happy, too.*

➡ **COMMON ERROR: MISSING COMMA WITH A NONRESTRICTIVE ELEMENT**

Commas to set off nonrestrictive elements (46c)

Suppose that you have been conducting a study of men and women who are substantially overweight. Some of your results indicate that a large percentage of these individuals also suffer from low self-esteem. In your report, do you write *Men and women, who are substantially overweight, tend to suffer from low self-esteem* or *Men and women who are substantially overweight tend to suffer from low self-esteem*? The only difference between the two sentences is a set of commas.

Here is the relevant guideline: if you mean *only* men and women who are substantially overweight, you want a **restrictive modifier**. In this case, use no commas. Leaving commas out restricts (or limits) the general category of men and women to a specific number within the group.

If you do use commas, you are saying that the information between the commas is of secondary importance; furthermore, the information between the commas does not restrict the original noun—it is a **nonrestrictive modifier**. Here are some examples:

All children who are taller than four feet may ride on the Scrambler. [*Restrictive, hence no commas; the sentence means* only *children taller than four feet.*]

The Deschutes, which is a popular rafting river, winds its way north through central Oregon. [*Nonrestrictive, hence commas used; the information between the commas is secondary information. Note that the sentence keeps its main meaning even if the information between the commas is dropped.*]

The candidate who seems most genuine and trustworthy will get my vote.

Employees, whether they be male or female, must conform to company safety regulations regarding hair length.

The inventor of the diesel engine, Rudolph Diesel, anticipated fueling the engine with vegetable oil.

An adjective clause that begins with *that* is always restrictive and is not set off by commas. An adjective clause beginning with *which* may be either restrictive or nonrestrictive; however, some writers prefer to use *which* only for nonrestrictive clauses.

The sculpture that she entered in the competition won first place. [*restrictive clause introduced by* that; *hence no commas used*]

The movie *This is Spinal Tap*, which follows a fictional heavy-metal band on tour, makes me laugh every time I watch it. [*nonrestrictive clause introduced by* which; *hence commas used*]

To summarize: Use commas to set off secondary information. Omit commas to restrict or limit.

Commas to separate items in a series (46d)

Commas are routinely used to separate three or more words, phrases, or clauses in a series. Here are some examples:

Our office ordered three boxes of computer paper, two boxes of ink cartridges, a stapler, and four rolls of tape. [*four items in a series*]

During the heat wave, some people bought air conditioners, others settled for fans, and some just drank glass after glass of iced tea. [*introductory element set off by a comma, then three independent clauses in a series*]

When the items in a series are long and complex or when they contain commas of their own, use semicolons rather than commas to separate them. For examples, see Chapter 32.

Coordinate adjectives are also separated by commas. Coordinate adjectives are adjectives that can be placed in any order in front of the noun they modify. In *Her straight, long drive took a large bounce and rolled another five yards*, the words *straight* and *long* are coordinate adjectives; their order can be switched without changing the meaning of the sentence: *Her long, straight drive took a large bounce and rolled another five yards.*

If two adjectives are not coordinate, they should be left unpunctuated: *Ellen is an accomplished freelance ad writer*. In that sentence, *accomplished, freelance,* and *ad* are all adjectives modifying the noun *writer*. However, changing the order of these adjectives plays havoc with the sentence's meaning: *Ellen is an ad accomplished freelance writer.* Since these adjectives are not coordinate, no commas are used.

Commas to set off parenthetical and transitional expressions, interjections, direct address, contrasting elements, and tag questions (46e, 46f)

Parenthetical expressions are defined as relatively unimportant supplementary information or comments by the writer. **Transitional expressions** are words and phrases used to connect parts of sentences, including conjunctive adverbs such as *however* and *furthermore*. Parenthetical and transitional expressions are always set off by commas.

PARENTHETICAL AND TRANSITIONAL EXPRESSIONS	His Web site is, in my opinion, a little short on content.
	The graphics, however, are stunning.

Interjections and words used in direct address are routinely set off by commas.

INTERJECTIONS	Well, this is an interesting turn of events.
	Oh my, it is hot today!
DIRECT ADDRESS	Beth, go give your dog some exercise.
	Now, ladies and gentlemen, let us bow our heads.

Writers may use commas to set off contrasting elements in a sentence.

CONTRASTING ELEMENTS	Her days were numbered, but not her hopes.
	Available credit, not ready cash, determines a consumer's purchasing power.

A question that follows a statement and calls that statement into doubt is called a **tag question**. Use a comma to separate such a question from the rest of the sentence.

TAG QUESTION	You ordered your hot dog with chili and onions, didn't you?

Commas with dates, addresses, titles, and numbers (46g)

Commas routinely separate parts of dates, addresses and place-names, titles, and numbers.

DATES	She was born on Tuesday, July 31, 1952, in Alabama.

When only a month and year are given, the comma is omitted, as in *August 1999 was an unusually warm month*. Commas are also omitted when dates appear in inverted order: *31 July 2003*.

ADDRESSES AND PLACE-NAMES	Her address is Azalea House, 12856 S.W. Jackson Street, Cairo, Texas 66731. [*Note that no comma is used in street numbers or between state and ZIP code.*]
	He lived in Malta, Montana, in the 1970s.
TITLES AND NUMBERS	Danielle Smith, M.D., performed the surgery.
	Martin Luther King Jr. was one of the twentieth century's greatest orators. [*Note that the titles* Jr. *and* Sr. *are not set off by commas.*]
	She thinks Philomath's population is about 7,500. [*Note that the comma is used in numbers of five digits or more but is optional in numbers of four digits. Do not use a comma in years or page numbers.*]
	The Scholarship Committee reviewed 12,000 applications in 1997.

Commas with quotations (46h)

Use commas to set off quotations from words that introduce or explain those quotations. A comma following a quotation always goes inside the quotation marks.

> "Autobiography," said Claude Simon, "is the most fictional of forms."

EXCEPTIONS

- Do not use a comma after a question mark or an exclamation point.

  "Are you planning to take the 6:05 train?" he asked.

- Do not use a comma when a quotation is introduced by *that*.

  The writer of Ecclesiastes concludes that "all is vanity."

- Do not use a comma when quoted material in a sentence is both preceded and followed by other material.

  His repetitions of "Please don't panic" failed to calm the crowd.

- Do not use a comma before a paraphrase.

  Mary Louise said that she would read the report this week.

Commas for understanding (46i)

Sometimes commas make difficult sentences easier to read, as in these examples:

The band members strutted in in matching uniforms and hats.

The band members strutted in, in matching uniforms and hats.

Shortly after the rock concert began in earnest.

Shortly after, the rock concert began in earnest.

Sometimes the way to cure punctuation problems is to rewrite the sentence. The awkwardness of *The band members strutted in, in matching uniforms and hats* can be relieved by revising the sentence to read *The band members strutted in wearing matching uniforms and hats.* The fact that a sentence is accurately punctuated does not necessarily mean that it is well written.

→ **COMMON ERROR: UNNECESSARY COMMA**

Unnecessary commas (46j)

Around restrictive elements

Sometimes using too many commas causes readers confusion. Nowhere is correct usage more important than in sentences with **restrictive** elements that limit the meaning of the words to which they refer. Commas incorrectly used in such situations radically alter sentence meaning. Consider this sentence, and ask yourself whether its punctuation is accurate:

Candidates, who were selected as the five finalists, were to be interviewed beginning Monday of next week.

Now examine this grammatically identical sentence:

Candidates, who ranged in age from twenty-two to sixty, were to be interviewed beginning Monday of next week.

Only one of these two sentences is accurately punctuated. Which one? Remember the guidelines:

1. Omit commas when your intent is to restrict or limit.
2. Use commas to set off secondary, nonessential information.

Clearly the sentence specifying the five finalists means *only* those five candidates. Thus that first sentence should not have any commas: *Candidates who were selected as the five finalists were to be interviewed beginning Monday of next week.*

Between subjects and verbs and between verbs and objects

Misused commas confuse readers by failing to follow predictable patterns. Look at these sentences with misplaced commas:

The Avery Square shopping mall, will be advertising heavily during November.

Dolphins, are a joy to watch.

The Forest Service representative said, that fire crews were being flown in from Nevada and Arizona.

Satellite photographs now form, the basis for most weather forecasts.

In the first two sentences, commas unnecessarily and incorrectly separate subjects and verbs. In the last two, commas unnecessarily and incorrectly separate verbs and objects. These commas distract readers from content; they also identify the writer as either careless or ignorant of the rules. The rule of grammar is simple: never use a single comma to separate a subject and its verb or a verb and its object. A *pair* of commas may be used to enclose appropriate words, phrases, or clauses.

INCORRECT	Running two miles every other day, helps keep me fit. [*no comma needed between subject and verb*]
CORRECT	Running two miles every other day helps keep me fit. [*gerund phrase as subject; no comma between subject and verb*]
CORRECT	Running two miles every other day, which is what Mavis does, helps keep her fit. [*pair of commas correctly used to set off nonrestrictive information*]
INCORRECT	Alan decided, his father loved him. [*no comma needed between verb and object*]
CORRECT	Alan decided his father loved him.
CORRECT	Alan decided, however, that his father did love him. [*pair of commas sets off however*]

Other unnecessary commas

- Do not use commas before or after **coordinating conjunctions** used in compound constructions with two elements. (The coordinating conjunctions are *and, or, but, nor, for, so,* and *yet.*)

INCORRECT	Jack, and Jill went up the hill.
CORRECT	Jack and Jill went up the hill. [*compound subject*]
INCORRECT	Jack fell down, and broke his crown.

CORRECT	Jack fell down and broke his crown. [*compound verb*]
CORRECT	Jack fell down and broke his crown, and Jill came tumbling after. [*comma +* and *joining two independent clauses*]

- Do not use commas after the last item in a series or before the first.

INCORRECT	Tonight at Papa's we ordered a pizza with, mushrooms, sausage, and green pepper, for dinner.
INCORRECT	Tonight at Papa's we ordered a pizza with mushrooms, sausage, and green pepper, for dinner.
CORRECT	Tonight at Papa's we ordered a pizza with mushrooms, sausage, and green pepper for dinner.

- Do not use a comma before an opening or a closing parenthesis.

INCORRECT	Portland's Pacific Coast League, (PCL) baseball team is the Beavers.
CORRECT	Portland's Pacific Coast League (PCL) baseball team is the Beavers.

If a phrase or clause set off by commas ends with parenthetical material, the second comma comes after the closing parenthesis, as in *If you live in Athens (the one in Georgia), chances are that you know the University of Georgia.*

EXERCISE 31.1   USING COMMAS AFTER INTRODUCTORY ELEMENTS

NAME _____ **DATE** _____

Some of the sentences in the following paragraph lack commas after introductory elements. Insert commas where necessary, and circle the commas you add. The first comma has been added and circled for you. For each comma you add (or decide not to add), be ready to discuss your decision.

Since its introduction by Parker Brothers in 1935, Monopoly has taught several generations its unique version of American capitalism. In this game of wish fulfillment everyone starts with ready cash. Decision making is reduced to a roll of the dice. And wonder of wonders nobody works. Instead game players simply wait to arrive again at Go in order to collect another $200. Besides a life of leisure Monopoly players come to expect remarkably depressed real estate prices. For instance the Mediterranean Avenue property still sells for only $60. Even though the prices are a bit out-of-date Monopoly can still teach many a budding entrepreneur about business. For those who are already successful adults the game offers a chance to use strategies that are hard to implement in reality. Of course the game also reinforces some questionable values. For instance those with enough money can buy themselves out of jail. And don't forget monopolies themselves are illegal in the real world too. That break with reality is part of the fun it seems.

NAME _____ **DATE** _____

If commas are needed for accurate punctuation in any of the following sentences, insert them. Circle any comma you add. On the lines provided, indicate the grammatical pattern of each sentence.

EXAMPLE   Before we leave for home(,)Alison needs to make sure the windows are tightly latched, and Jed needs to empty the refrigerator.

[Introductory element], [independent clause], [coordinating conjunction] [independent clause]. _____

1. My paper is due next week and I need to spend an afternoon in the library yet I'm still confident that I'll finish on time.

_____

_____

2. My father likes to talk about the soda fountain in his hometown so I decided to make him an egg cream.

_____

_____

3. The field behind the house held an old Studebaker pickup and a rusted combine in addition to a herd of Holstein cows and a donkey.

_____

_____

4. New housing starts have not increased again this year and the local economy is stagnant.

_____

_____

5. Although we are not finished discussing this material the bell will ring soon so let me give you the assignment for tomorrow.

_____

_____

6. New York's subway station mosaics are true works of art and we feel strongly about preserving them.

_____

_____

7. The Boundary Waters area of Minnesota boasts many miles of hiking trails and quiet water.

_____

_____

8. Our instructor has not returned our midterm exams nor has she given us any grades so far this semester.

_____

_____

9. In addition to the ducks in the front yard there were geese in the backyard.

_____

_____

10. In the so-called spaghetti westerns made in Italy in the 1960s an American television actor named Clint Eastwood became a movie star and a box-office favorite.

_____

_____

EXERCISE 31.3   USING COMMAS TO SET OFF NONRESTRICTIVE (SECONDARY) INFORMATION

NAME _____ **DATE** _____

The following sentences contain information that is either nonrestrictive (secondary) or restrictive. Read each sentence carefully, and add commas as needed. Underline the nonrestrictive or restrictive element in each sentence. On the line provided, indicate whether the information you underlined is nonrestrictive or restrictive, and indicate whether you added commas.

EXAMPLES   The candidate <u>who seems most genuine and trustworthy</u> will get my vote.
restrictive; no commas added _____

Our firewood, <u>maple and fir</u>, should last us through the winter.
nonrestrictive; commas added _____

1. Most residents consider Terry Thornton a good mayor one who promotes the town and helps protect its economic base.

   _____

2. The beach that I loved last summer eroded terribly over the winter.

   _____

3. Grandma's old rocker which traveled across the country in a wagon train remains a family treasure.

   _____

4. The horse standing at the end of the field is Comet.

   _____

5. We were asked to bring fruit preferably some kind of melon to the picnic.

   _____

6. Harnly Hall which had given the campus beauty and character for more than a century was demolished by order of the previous college president.

   _____

7. All of the spices that I buy at the Indian grocery store are fresh and inexpensive.

   _____

8. Bicycles which have provided transportation for millions of Chinese for decades are now banned in parts of downtown Beijing.

_____

9. The dean with whom you spoke resigned.

_____

10. Most people here view the woman who wrote that letter to the local paper as a notorious crackpot.

_____

EXERCISE 31.4   USING COMMAS TO SEPARATE COORDINATE ADJECTIVES AND ITEMS IN A SERIES

NAME _____ **DATE** _____

A. The sentences listed below contain coordinate adjectives, noncoordinate adjectives, and items in a series. Add commas where needed, and circle any commas you add. Indicate whether a sentence contains coordinate adjectives or items in a series. If a sentence contains any noncoordinate adjectives, copy them on the lines provided.

EXAMPLE   Marta arrived carrying a doll, a lollipop, and a large crayon picture she had drawn.

items in a series; noncoordinate adjectives: large, crayon

1. We're confronted with continuing drought a possible labor strike and the highest rate of bankruptcies in two decades.

_____

_____

2. The Vietnam Veterans Memorial is a dramatic example of a monument to the fallen.

_____

_____

3. The moon circles the earth the earth revolves around the sun and out in space the sun is just one star among many in the Milky Way galaxy.

_____

_____

4. Some cars run on gasoline some run on diesel fuel some run on alternative fuels and some don't run at all.

_____

_____

5. Mira bought a beautiful handmade quilt from the Amish woman at the market.

_____

_____

B. Compose your own sentences as directed below. For subject matter, think of the room in which you normally eat your meals. Make sure each sentence you write is punctuated correctly.

EXAMPLE   Write a sentence with coordinate adjectives and noncoordinate adjectives. Underline the noncoordinate adjectives.

The table is covered by a <u>pale blue</u> cloth fringed with long, silky threads.

1. Write a sentence with noncoordinate adjectives. Underline them.

_____

_____

2. Write a sentence with three parallel clauses. Circle any commas in the sentence.

_____

_____

3. Write a sentence with coordinate adjectives. Circle any commas in the sentence.

_____

_____

4. Write a sentence with only two items in a series. Circle any commas in the sentence.

_____

_____

5. Write a sentence with coordinate adjectives and noncoordinate adjectives. Underline the noncoordinate adjectives.

_____

_____

EXERCISE 31.5 USING COMMAS WITH PARENTHETICAL AND TRANSITIONAL EXPRESSIONS, INTERJECTIONS, DIRECT ADDRESS, CONTRASTING ELEMENTS, TAG QUESTIONS, DATES, ADDRESSES, TITLES, AND NUMBERS

NAME _____ **DATE** _____

A. Write sentences incorporating the elements specified in each numbered item. Make sure that your sentences use commas correctly for the specified elements and anywhere else that commas may be necessary. In each case, be ready to discuss your comma usage.

> **EXAMPLE**   Write a sentence that includes a city and a state.
>
> The Nike headquarters are in Portland, Oregon. _____

1. Write a sentence that includes contrasting elements.

   _____

   _____

2. Write a sentence that includes a number greater than ten thousand.

   _____

   _____

3. Write a sentence that includes a month and year only.

   _____

   _____

4. Write a sentence that includes a mailing address and ZIP code.

   _____

   _____

5. Write a sentence that includes an interjection.

   _____

   _____

B. **Add needed commas to the sentences below, and circle the commas you add.**

> **EXAMPLE** Both wanted a Halloween wedding, so they were married on October 31, 2000.

1. Easter falls on Sunday April 16.

2. Angie would you pick up the supplies for our project on your way home tonight?

3. Lon Chaney Jr. did in fact star in some creepy horror films.

4. Could I see this sweater in a size eight please?

5. In the 1980s I am sorry to say many elms had to be destroyed because of Dutch elm disease.

EXERCISE 31.6   USING COMMAS WITH QUOTATIONS

NAME _____   **DATE** _____

Add any needed commas to the following sentences. Circle the commas you add. Cross out any unnecessary commas.

EXAMPLE   "Showers tomorrow, with a high near 50," said the forecaster.

1. "Few Americans" she said "are able to understand the history of conflict in Northern Ireland."

2. "Yesterday" he said, "I disagreed with you. But after my experience today, I have changed my mind."

3. "Why do I watch this show week after week?", I wondered.

4. The candidate's campaign manager observed that, "turnout will decide this election."

5. Mandel, after defining the importance of cultural differences, says "In Western society, these trends can be traced back as far as the 1860s."

6. "Marriage is a great institution," said Mae West "but I'm not ready for an institution yet."

7. Juliet asks, "Wherefore art thou Romeo?"

8. Bank tellers who take my check and say, "I'll be right back" make me worry that my account is overdrawn.

9. The menu said that the restaurant specialized in, "fresh local produce."

10. The Supreme Court in 2004 decided against hearing a case about the words, "under God," in the Pledge of Allegiance.

NAME _____ **DATE** _____

Underline the restrictive or nonrestrictive elements in each sentence. Indicate whether the material you underlined is restrictive or nonrestrictive. Punctuate the sentences correctly, and circle any commas you add.

EXAMPLES   The lab technician reports that the blood tests(,)which were performed yesterday(,) were negative. nonrestrictive_____

The lab technician reports that the blood tests that were performed yesterday were negative. restrictive_____

1. The uncle whom you have visited every summer needs your help now. _____

2. In the field of popular music, even a performer who makes millions on his or her first recording will probably have only a brief career. _____

3. The cars recalled by the dealer need only one replacement part. _____

4. Dogs that are trained to assist people with hearing impairments learn how to alert their owners to ringing doorbells and telephones. _____

5. The evacuees some with only the clothes on their backs prepared to spend the night inside the high school gym. _____

6. Chris's beat-up old red Chevy which she bought in high school for $50 still runs.

   _____

7. My ears which stick out prominently look just like my grandfather's ears.

   _____

8. The city evicted people who lived in a New York park from their tents and shacks.

   _____

9. The roast turkey that my brother-in-law serves at his annual Thanksgiving dinner is always dry and tasteless. _____

10. Do Internet addicts those spending more than three hours a day online lack face-to-face social skills? _____

EXERCISE 31.8   OMITTING COMMAS BETWEEN SUBJECTS AND VERBS AND BETWEEN VERBS AND OBJECTS

NAME _____ **DATE** _____

Some sentences in this passage are punctuated correctly, and some are not. Read each sentence carefully, paying close attention to the use of commas. Put an X through any misplaced commas. Be ready to explain your decisions.

For centuries, people in the business of making other people laugh, have tried to understand humor. Humorists have developed, theories to explain why jokes are funny. One problem with most such theories, is that different people laugh at different things. For example, people from one culture, may find a joke hysterically funny, while people from another simply scratch their heads. Scientists cannot shed much light on the biological reasons for human laughter, either, although they have discovered, that puns and wordplay are processed by a different part of the brain than are other kinds of jokes. It may not be possible to analyze jokes scientifically, but comedians have made observations about what makes Americans laugh. One conclusion, is that Americans consider ducks to be the funniest animal. Another is that to Americans words containing a *k* sound, are funnier than other words. (Perhaps this *k* business explains, the duck phenomenon.) The sounds of some words, such as *goulash* and *phlegm*, strike many people as simply funny. And sometimes, when words are put together just right, people split their sides laughing for reasons no one really understands.

NAME _____ **DATE** _____

Cross out any unnecessary commas in the following sentences. If a sentence is correct as shown, write C next to its number.

> **EXAMPLE**   For twenty-six straight days, the high temperature in Salt Lake City/reached over ninety degrees.

1. Jun goes to soccer practice, a trumpet lesson, and a tutoring session, after school on Tuesdays.

2. Jim runs ten miles every other day, and he says he feels strong, healthy, and fit.

3. Two lanes (usually those on the far left side of the pool), are routinely reserved for lap swimming.

4. The sentences in this essay sound beautiful, but, do they mean anything?

5. Cats like heat better than cold, and will actively avoid air conditioning if they can help it.

6. On September, 1, 1939, Adolf Hitler invaded Poland, and defied the rest of the world to stop him.

7. The account covered all overdrafts, up to $2,000, but we still managed to bounce a check.

8. Once you are prepared for your clinic tour, call the office to schedule a date, return this form to your adviser, and follow the directions for writing out your goals for the visit.

9. Deborah is nicer, than you would expect her to be at first sight.

10. The campus cinema series makes, for good entertainment, and, surprisingly energetic discussions about the strengths and weaknesses of the films.

EXERCISE 31.10 USING COMMAS CORRECTLY

NAME _____ **DATE** _____

A. The following sentences are punctuated correctly. Revise each item or combine sentences, according to the specific directions. Make sure your new version is punctuated accurately.

> **EXAMPLE** My father graduated from Portland's Washington High School in 1963. (Revise so that the sentence begins *In 1963 . . .*)
> <u>In 1963, my father graduated from Portland's Washington High School.</u>

1. Some writers like to read a bit before writing. Some writers make notes to themselves. Some writers are too terrified to do anything. Some writers just sit down and start writing effortlessly. (Combine into one sentence with multiple independent clauses.)

    _____

    _____

    _____

2. You wake up in Los Angeles. You look out the window. It's smogless. You understand why everyone moved here. This happens on those rare April mornings after a heavy rain. (Combine into one sentence with an introductory element followed by several independent clauses.)

    _____

    _____

    _____

3. Carmine's serves enormous portions. Carmine's offers doggie bags to every diner. (Combine into a single sentence containing nonrestrictive information.)

    _____

    _____

4. The dog followed me home. It was hoping for a good meal before continuing on its way. (Combine into a single sentence containing restrictive information.)

    _____

    _____

5. It's snowing. (Revise so that the sentence begins with an interjection and ends with the name of the person being addressed.)

_____

B. On the lines provided, combine each of the following groups of sentences into one sentence of connected independent clauses. Join the independent clauses by using commas and appropriate coordinating conjunctions. Use pronouns as necessary.

EXAMPLE   Hay fever season has arrived. We had better buy more tissues.

Hay fever season has arrived, so we had better buy more tissues.

1. The center was elbowed repeatedly by the opposing team. He maintained the fast pace of the game.

_____

_____

2. You may want to stay on the East Coast for graduate school. You may already be missing the West Coast too much.

_____

_____

3. Studying a foreign language was difficult. I did not get very good grades. I learned something about communicating with people in other cultures.

_____

_____

4. The laser printer is fast. The laser printer produces professional-looking documents. I still prefer to handwrite my thank-you notes.

_____

_____

5. The muffler has fallen off. The odometer has 200,000 miles. The engine leaks oil. Maybe it's time to get a different car.

_____

_____

Semicolons

32

Powerful effects can sometimes be achieved by joining two or more ideas inside a single sentence. Semicolons can be used for such juxtaposition by linking independent clauses and by separating items in a complicated series. In the following example, the semicolon helps to emphasize how closely the two ideas are related.

> The brilliant rainbow glowed in the sky above the garden; the fragrance of moist earth mingled with the deep scent of the roses.

SEMICOLONS IN EVERYDAY USE

Although semicolons are among the more formal punctuation marks, you can sometimes spot them working quite well in informal settings — as these two bumper stickers illustrate.

> Careful! Baby on board; driver on edge.

> Vote for Espy; he means business!

Try replacing these semicolons with commas and conjunctions, with periods, or with exclamation points, and you'll see how useful the semicolon is. Watch for everyday uses of semicolons — in ads, on billboards, wherever — and jot down the examples you find.

Semicolons with independent clauses (47a)

Chapter 31 discusses the use of a comma plus a coordinating conjunction to link two independent clauses. Using coordinating conjunctions allows you to indicate the relationship between the two independent clauses. Semicolons can also be used to link independent clauses and to make your prose concise, even blunt. (For more on this topic, see Chapter 23.) Here are two correct examples:

> Karen votes for a movie, so we are going to a movie. [*comma + coordinating conjunction* so *indicating cause and effect*]

Karen votes for a movie; we are going to a movie. [*semicolon linking the two independent clauses and resulting in a blunt, direct statement*]

When joining two independent clauses, remember that a comma *cannot* substitute for a semicolon; if a comma is used, it must be followed by a coordinating conjunction.

Semicolons are also used to link independent clauses when the second clause contains a conjunctive adverb or a transitional phrase.

I know starting early means I will accomplish more; however, 5:30 in the morning is just too early.

We can expect afternoon temperatures to be cooler today; it is midmorning, after all, and the sun has yet to burn off the fog.

REVIEW

Common **conjunctive adverbs** include *also, anyway, besides, finally, furthermore, hence, however, indeed, instead, meanwhile, moreover, nevertheless, otherwise, still, then, therefore,* and *thus.* Common **transitional phrases** include *after all, as a result, at any rate, even so, for example, in addition, in fact, in other words, on the contrary,* and *on the other hand.*

Remember that semicolons separate *sentences.* The last example given can also be accurately punctuated as follows: *We can expect afternoon temperatures to be cooler today. It is midmorning, after all, and the sun has yet to burn off the fog.*

Do not use a semicolon to separate a dependent clause from an independent clause.

INCORRECT   While we were walking the dog after dinner; the moon rose.

We were up until after two last night; because our group project is due this afternoon.

REVISED   While we were walking the dog after dinner, the moon rose.

We were up until after two last night because our group project is due this afternoon.

or

We were up until after two last night; our group project is due this afternoon.

Semicolons to separate items in a series (47b)

Besides joining what would otherwise be complete sentences, semicolons have only one other use: to separate complex items in a series. Recall from Chapter 31 that commas are used in this way, too. Use semicolons whenever one or more of the items you are listing includes commas already.

Pitcher, catcher, short stop; goalie, center, right wing; tackle, quarterback, end—positions in baseball, hockey, and football have vivid, descriptive names. [*Here commas separate the individual positions, with semicolons separating the different sports.*]

In the attic of one rental house, we discovered a yellowed, still readable newspaper from 1945; a wicker, two-wheeled baby carriage; and fifty-five cents' worth of buffalo nickels. [*Here commas are used as part of the identification of items, and semicolons are used to separate the items themselves.*]

As you can see, the semicolons in the preceding sentences serve the useful function of separating items. Those sentences require semicolons; commas used in place of the semicolons would be confusing to readers.

Remember to use a colon, not a semicolon, to *introduce* a series, as in this example: *The buffet featured several kinds of fruit: apples, pears, kiwis, mangoes, and persimmons.* For more on colon usage, see Chapter 36.

Overused semicolons (47c)

Knowing the rules of semicolon usage presents writers with new choices: should I join two independent clauses, or should I punctuate them as separate sentences? One thing is certain: the use of too many sentences joined with semicolons results in dull, formally repetitious prose. Using too many semicolons also deprives the writer of the clarity that dependent clauses can afford. *I see it has begun to rain; I'll turn off the sprinklers* is grammatically accurate, but its full meaning depends on readers' willingness and ability to see the connection between the two independent clauses. Subordinating one clause to the other spells out the cause-and-effect relationship between the observation and the action: *Since it is raining, I'll turn off the sprinklers.* In general, joining sentences with semicolons should produce some obvious and positive benefit. If you join two or more sentences with semicolons, you ought to be able to point to the resulting benefit.

Semicolons with other punctuation (47d)

Occasionally, you may want to use semicolons with quotation marks, parentheses, or abbreviations. The following examples show you how to handle these situations.

- *Semicolons and quotation marks.* Semicolons are normally placed outside any quotation marks.

  Sometimes the British hesitate to speak in the first person, saying "one" rather than "I"; most Americans say "I" without giving it a thought.

- *Semicolons and parentheses.* Semicolons are placed after and outside parentheses. Semicolons never precede parentheses.

The actress was nominated for an Academy Award (her third nomination in three years); this year she may win.

- *Semicolons and abbreviations.* When a semicolon follows an abbreviation using a period, use both the period and the semicolon.

The unwanted package arrived C.O.D.; I politely refused to pay the charges.

NAME _____   **DATE** _____

A. Carefully check the punctuation in the following sentences. If the punctuation is accurate, write C on the lines provided. If it is inaccurate, write a corrected version with or without a semicolon, as appropriate.

> **EXAMPLE**   The unwanted package arrived C.O.D., I politely refused to pay the charges.
>
> **REVISION**   The unwanted package arrived C.O.D.; I politely refused to pay the charges.

1. When I returned to the Web site; the items were no longer on sale.

   _____

   _____

2. Two games were rained out this season, however, the makeup games have been scheduled for next week.

   _____

   _____

3. Telecommuting to a job has advantages; such as allowing the employee more time in the morning before starting work, but it also has disadvantages; such as making a worker feel isolated from daily life at the office.

   _____

   _____

   _____

4. During much of the summer; I will be working as a lifeguard at my neighborhood pool.

   _____

   _____

5. The memo that Josh sent to everyone in the office this morning is marked urgent; it asks us all to sign up to contribute food for the December holiday party, but I don't find that especially urgent since it's only August.

_____

_____

_____

6. My current work-study job ends in two weeks. I'll need to find a new position; starting next term.

_____

_____

7. Female lions do all of the hunting for the whole family group, nevertheless, the male lions get to eat first.

_____

_____

8. Oak burns slowly and makes a hot fire; fir splits easily and makes superior kindling.

_____

_____

9. Spring and fall are my favorite seasons, perhaps because they seem so brief fall, for instance, seems to start in mid-September in this part of the country, but by the beginning of November, the weather already feels like winter.

_____

_____

_____

10. Carla complained that she hated country music, we put on a Johnny Cash album.

_____

_____

B. Use a semicolon, a conjunctive adverb or transitional phrase, and whatever other punctuation is required to combine each of the following sets of brief sentences into one longer sentence. You may revise the sentences slightly as needed. Make sure that your new sentence is punctuated correctly.

> **EXAMPLE** We walked the dog after dinner. The moon rose. The moon shone round and white as a bone china saucer.
>
> **REVISION** <u>While we were walking the dog after dinner, the moon rose; it shone round and white</u> <u>as a bone china saucer.</u>

1. The dishwater went down the drain in the kitchen sink. The dishwater came back up the drain in the bathtub. I think a pipe is clogged somewhere.

   _____

   _____

2. There are fewer drive-in theaters than there once were. The Canyon Drive-In, for example, has been demolished for a shopping mall.

   _____

   _____

3. An anemic patient may feel tired or worn out. The patient may complain of dizziness, shortness of breath, or a headache.

   _____

   _____

4. She left her bicycle chained to a bike rack outside the science building. She came back out after her biology class. The bicycle had been stolen.

   _____

   _____

5. Drivers sometimes decide not to wear seat belts for short trips in the car. They feel reasonably safe. Most accidents occur within twenty-five miles of home.

   _____

   _____

6. Many people do not get enough daylight during the winter. They become depressed.

_____

_____

7. I learned as a child that Pluto was the ninth planet in our solar system. Scientists now believe it is not really a planet. The redefinition makes me a little sad.

_____

_____

8. Kodiak Island is a beautiful part of Alaska. It has scenic peaks and broad valleys. They were carved by glaciers.

_____

_____

9. New York has welcomed millions of immigrants. Many have been fleeing famine, poverty, and persecution in Europe. California, however, has been a gateway for those coming from Asia.

_____

_____

10. I use computers incessantly for schoolwork and for shopping. I see no reduction in the amount of paper or the number of catalogs in my apartment.

_____

_____

EXERCISE 32.2   USING SEMICOLONS TO SEPARATE ITEMS IN A SERIES

NAME _____ **DATE** _____

Carefully check the punctuation, especially the use of semicolons, in the following passage. Cross out unnecessary punctuation, and add any missing marks. Circle your additions.

In the years since his death in 1882, Jesse James has appeared in folklore; stories; and songs; usually as a kind of Robin Hood who stole from rich railroads and banks to support the everyday people around him. However, the truth about the famous outlaw from Missouri may not be very pretty. During the Civil War, when Jesse James was a teenager, he supported the Confederacy and the pro-slavery fighting in Missouri and Kansas, joined his brother, Frank, in a band of anti-abolitionist guerrillas, helped the guerrillas loot and burn the town of Lawrence, Kansas, and slaughtered twenty-three unarmed Union soldiers during a train robbery. He never joined the Confederate army, preferring instead to work outside the law to terrorize abolitionists and suspected abolitionists. When the war ended in 1865, Jesse was an eighteen-year-old, he and his brother, along with other members of their gang, feared that they would be tried as criminals in Missouri since they had not officially been part of the military. Remaining an outlaw; robbing banks and trains in increasingly daring daylight raids; and killing anyone who got in the way seemed to Jesse to be the best way to go on with his life. For the next ten years, some newspaper reports described Jesse James as a patriotic Southerner defending his ideals, Jesse played along, enjoying the publicity, the stories, and the fame, and some people, especially those who still regretted the end of the Confederacy, regarded him as a hero.

EXERCISE 32.3　REVISING USING SEMICOLONS

NAME _____ **DATE** _____

Some sentences in the passage that follows are punctuated inaccurately. Others may be accurate in their punctuation, but you may not think the current version is the most effective one. Edit the passage, making whatever minor revisions you feel are necessary. Copy your best version on your own paper, and make sure that your version is punctuated accurately. Also make sure that your revised version uses semicolons in at least three instances. Finally, underline your changes.

Recovering alcoholics are some of the nicest people you'd ever want to meet, unfortunately, they also tell some of the saddest, most distressing stories. Many of them come from alcoholic families maybe the father was a functional, low-profile drinker for years; maybe the mother drank during the day and locked her own kids out of the house because she couldn't stand their noise; maybe the kids suffered from sexual abuse or other physical violence; when these kids reached adulthood, they hid their hurt in a bottle. Some of them didn't wait for adulthood. Some drank right along with their parents.

Untreated alcoholics believe they have every reason to drink. Through treatment, however, they come to learn that there is no such thing as a good enough reason for them to drink. For the alcoholic, that beer or wine or gin makes every problem worse, without fail, excessive, compulsive drinking creates new problems. Staying clean and sober doesn't do away with the alcoholic's problems; it does eliminate one pressing, overpowering difficulty, the sober alcoholic then has at least the opportunity to deal with other problems. Recovery isn't easy. Recovery is never complete. But with family support and the help of organizations such as Alcoholics Anonymous, people do dry out, families do get better.

End Punctuation

33

Periods, question marks, and exclamation points are called **end punctuation** because they end sentences. As they do so, they indicate whether a sentence is a statement, a question, or an emphatic exclamation.

END PUNCTUATION IN EVERYDAY USE

You don't use punctuation when you speak, but you do provide vocal cues that tell a listener — even someone who does not understand the words you say — whether you mean to ask a question, make a statement, or give an exclamation. Think about the way your vocal tone would differentiate the following sentences:

Where is my bus pass

Get that spider off my leg

I am going to the store

Make note of a few sentences you hear or speak that give a listener cues about the kind of end punctuation you would use if you wrote the sentence down. What kinds of vocal cues do you give for periods, question marks, and exclamation points? Do you use these vocal "punctuation marks" the same way you use punctuation marks when you write? Explain.

Periods (48a)

Using periods correctly makes life easier on your readers. It is not a complex skill to master. A period should end any sentence that is not a question or an exclamation.

> I expect your essays on Tuesday. [*statement*]

> Turn in your essays on Tuesday. [*mild command*]

Periods are often used in sentences containing direct quotations, even if the quoted material is a question: *"Are you going home now?" she asked.* However, if the sentence is turned around, the question mark alone is sufficient; no period is necessary: *She asked me, "Are you going home now?"*

Some abbreviations also use periods:

Ms.	a.m.*	etc.	Dr.
Mr.	p.m.*	et al.	C.O.D.
Jr.	Mrs.	ibid.	Sen.

See Chapter 38 for more on abbreviations.

Question marks (48b)

Sentences that ask direct questions end with question marks. Sentences that report questions (that is, sentences that contain indirect questions) end with periods. Note the difference.

DIRECT QUESTION   Did you air out the house after the exterminators were finished?

INDIRECT QUESTION   I was wondering if you aired out the house after the exterminators were finished.

When quotation marks are used with direct questions, the order in which sentence elements are presented makes a difference.

I said, "What time will the exterminators leave?" [*Here the quoted question ends the sentence. In this case, the question mark is the sentence's end punctuation.*]

Did I just say, "Be there or be square"? [*Here the question mark applies to the whole sentence and so goes outside the quoted material.*]

Did I just say, "Can I have your telephone number?" [*Here both the sentence itself and the quoted material are questions. A second question mark does* not *follow the quotation marks.*]

Writers also use question marks between questions in a series, even when the questions do not form separate sentences.

Is that dog a collie? a Labrador retriever? or what?

Exclamation points (48c)

Exclamation points close emphatic and emotional statements. Using too many exclamation points is like being the boy who cried wolf; after a while, nobody listens. Sparingly used, however, exclamation points can indicate subtle differences in tone or meaning. Suppose that you have just given someone an expensive present in a small box. This someone opens the wrappings, looks at what is inside, and says only

---

* The abbreviations *a.m.* and *p.m.* are frequently written without periods and in small capital letters — AM and PM — as has been done throughout this book.

one word. This word could be punctuated three ways: "*Oh.*" or "*Oh?*" or "*Oh!*" Which punctuation would indicate the most positive response?

Exclamation points are not followed by commas or periods. When part of a direct quotation, the exclamation point goes inside the quotation marks, as in "*Oh!*"

> When informed that she had won the lottery, all Erin Johannsen could do was scream over and over, "I can't believe it! I can't believe it!"

> The border guard yelled, "Halt!"

> "Halt!" yelled the border guard.

EXERCISE 33.1   USING PERIODS TO SIGNAL THE ENDS OF SENTENCES

NAME _____ **DATE** _____

A. Read this paragraph:

Without periods and the spaces that conventionally follow them, readers would have no easy way of recognizing the end of a sentence instead of being able to read quickly and effortlessly, we would all be required to slow down and continually ask ourselves whether or not the words we have just read make a complete sentence in short, we would be analyzing the form of the writing as well as trying to grasp its content; we would be doing two things at once chances are we would not be entirely successful with either task the end result would be frustration and an unwillingness to read

Now go back and reread the paragraph, putting in a period every time you think you have come to the end of a sentence. Does reading the paragraph feel easier and more comfortable now?

B. Now read this paragraph:

Sometimes there can be. More punctuation than is really needed, and it can. Often be in the wrong places. What's more. Without periods and other proper punctuation. Your readers will be totally confused. By what you have written. The inappropriate periods will make your audience stop reading. Even though you want them to finish a thought. And the lack of periods where you should have them will cause your readers to go on indefinitely they will lose the ideas you are trying to convey to avoid confusion periods are essential they stop and start your readers. At the places you feel are most effective.

Now go back and punctuate this paragraph properly by putting an *X* through unnecessary periods and adding appropriate punctuation where necessary. Can you see where the periods are needed and where they are not?

EXERCISE 33.2   IDENTIFYING AND CORRECTING END-PUNCTUATION ERRORS

NAME _____ **DATE** _____

Some of the following sentences use question marks and exclamation points correctly, but many do not. Proofread each sentence. **If the printed version is accurate, write C on the line below the sentence. If the printed version needs correction, copy the sentence with corrected punctuation on the lines.**

> **EXAMPLE**   Will you clean your room before I lose my temper.
>
> **REVISION**   Will you clean your room before I lose my temper?

1. Didn't I say? "Either clean up your room, or there'll be no dessert after dinner?"

   _____

   _____

2. If you're not sure which bus to ride, just ask the driver if the bus is going to the Raleigh Hills area?

   _____

   _____

3. I don't know why people move here if they don't like snow?

   _____

   _____

4. "You did this to me," she shrieked at her husband during every contraction.

   _____

   _____

5. My opponent has posed an interesting question: "Should the United States *ever* engage in the covert overthrow of a foreign government."?

   _____

   _____

6. Behaving rudely as usual, she yelled, "Why is the service here so slow?"

_____

_____

7. How on earth are you going to submit your paper before the deadline!

_____

_____

8. What do you mean coming in here and telling me to leave the room.

_____

_____

9. When you went to the animal shelter, were you looking for a cat or a dog?

_____

_____

10. Do you know how it makes me feel when you say, "Why don't you lose some weight?"?

_____

_____

11. "Are we there yet," the children in the back seat asked again and again?

_____

_____

12. The police officer asked the crowd to get out of his way?

_____

_____

NAME _____ **DATE** _____

Proofread the following passage for errors with end punctuation (periods, question marks, and exclamation points). Add needed end punctuation, and cross out any punctuation that should not be there. If you are not sure whether to use periods in particular abbreviations, consult your dictionary.

People have answered "yes" to the question of whether W. E. B. Du Bois (1868–1963) — the historian, educator, and civil rights leader — is a controversial figure? Some have responded to the question with a question of their own! They ask, "How can a leader lead without being controversial"? The dispute about whether to honor Dr Du Bois in his hometown and elsewhere stems from actions he took toward the end of his life. He had communist leanings and went so far as to renounce his American citizenship and take up residence in Ghana! Many Americans in general and veterans in particular criticized him for those actions. Even with the passage of time, people who live today in Great Barrington, Massachusetts, where Dr Du Bois was born and spent his childhood, have asked, "Should we put up signs in his honor name a school after him make his onetime home into a memorial." What would the man who once exclaimed, "Believe in life" make of the fact that as we approach the fiftieth anniversary of his death, his reputation is still questioned.

Apostrophes

34

The apostrophe can signal possession (*the cat's dinner*), form a contraction (*It's warm today*), indicate the omission of words or letters (*The class of '62 danced to early rock 'n' roll*), and form certain plurals (*r's* and *4's*).

APOSTROPHES IN EVERYDAY USE

Because the apostrophe is a small mark and its exact placement may determine its meaning, apostrophe errors are common. Sometimes an apostrophe is omitted, mistakenly added to a plural form, or incorrectly placed before or after an *s* (forming a singular form rather than a plural or vice versa). Look carefully at ads printed in the newspaper or the telephone book, distributed as flyers, mailed to prospective customers, or posted in public places. Keep a list of these ads, and note examples that use apostrophes. Do any of these seem to use apostrophes incorrectly?

→ **COMMON ERROR: UNNECESSARY OR MISSING APOSTROPHE (INCLUDING *ITS/IT'S*)**

Apostrophes to signal possessive case (49a)

An apostrophe plus -*s* at the end of a singular noun shows **possession**, saying that whatever follows the *'s* either belongs to the noun, is part of the noun, was made by the noun, or is directly connected to the noun in some other way.

> Raymond's bicycle [*the bicycle belonging to Raymond*]
>
> the album's first song [*the song that is part of the album*]
>
> Keats's poems [*the poems written by Keats*]
>
> a day's journey [*a journey lasting a day*]

As you can see, the possessive of a singular noun is formed by adding *'s*. This rule also holds true for acronyms (words formed by several first initials) and for indefinite pronouns. In job titles and compound (multiword) nouns, the *'s* follows the last word. Note that the rule applies even if the noun ends in -*s* (as in *Keats's*).

ACRONYM	NASA's performance record [*the record belonging to NASA*]
INDEFINITE PRONOUN	everyone's choice [*the choice made by everyone*]
TITLE	the transportation secretary's speech [*the speech made by the transportation secretary*]
MULTIWORD NOUN	her father-in-law's car [*the car belonging to her father-in-law*]

What about plural nouns? Many plural nouns end in *-s* or *-es*. To form the possessive of plural nouns ending in *-s* or *-es*, add only an apostrophe. To form the possessive of plural nouns that do not end in *-s* or *-es*, such as *children*, add *'s* as you would to form the possessive of any singular noun.

Walking along the rocky shoreline, we could see the *seals'* faces. [*the faces of more than one seal*]

The *children's* room is here at the end of the hall. [*the room belonging to the children*]

Suppose that you wish to indicate joint ownership. The boat belonging to Mo and Ann would be referred to as *Mo and Ann's boat.* To indicate joint ownership, add *'s* only to the last noun. Suppose both Mo and Ann own their own boats. Then both of their names would carry apostrophes, as in *Mo's and Ann's boats are entered in the race on Saturday.*

Since missing or misused possessive apostrophes occur frequently, rereading your draft to look for such errors is a good idea. As you reread, watch for any nouns ending in *-s.* Is the noun meant to show ownership or possession? If so, it needs an apostrophe.

Finally, remember that possessive pronouns — *my, your, his, her, its, our(s), your(s), their(s),* and *whose* — are already possessive; they do not need apostrophes. *The stolen bicycles were ours* (not *our's*).

Remember, *its* is a possessive pronoun, as in *The bird watched its nest fall to the ground. It's* is a contraction for *it is*, as in *It's nearly time for lunch.* To check for this error in your own writing, reread your draft, paying particular attention to every use of *its* or *it's.* Use *it's* to indicate *it is*; use *its* to show possession. (In academic writing, it is best not to use contractions at all.)

Apostrophes to signal contractions and other omissions (49b)

Apostrophes are used in **contractions**, which are usually two words shortened to one. Here is a list of some common contractions:

FULL FORM	CONTRACTION	FULL FORM	CONTRACTION
are not	aren't	did not	didn't
cannot	can't	do not	don't
could not	couldn't	does not	doesn't

he had, he would	he'd	she has, she is	she's
he has, he is	he's	she will	she'll
he will	he'll	there has, there is	there's
I am	I'm	was not	wasn't
I had, I would	I'd	were not	weren't
I have	I've	who has, who is	who's
I will	I'll	will not	won't
is not	isn't	would not	wouldn't
it has, it is	it's	you are	you're
let us	let's	you have	you've
she had, she would	she'd	you will	you'll

Note that certain contractions sound identical to other words — *whose/who's, theirs/ there's, lets/let's, its/it's* — though they have quite separate meanings. Using the wrong spelling in a particular sentence is a common error; recall that confusing *its* and *it's* is one of the top twenty errors in student writing. The only sure cure is careful proofreading.

Apostrophes are also used in some common phrases to signal that letters or numbers have been left out. Thus *of the clock* becomes *o'clock* and *class of 1989* becomes *class of '89*. Occasionally writers trying to convey the sound of spoken dialects use apostrophes to signal omitted letters. Thus *suppose* might become *s'pose*, or *probably* might be written *prob'ly*.

Contractions result in more informal prose; full forms make prose somewhat more formal and precise. Using contractions in formal situations sometimes creates an inappropriate tone. Here is an example:

> Let's assume the awesome responsibility of forging a peaceful world for our children to inherit.

Here the informality of the contraction seems at odds with the seriousness of the responsibility discussed; the full form would be more appropriate. Some contractions, such as *ain't*, are so informal (or incorrect) that they should not appear in college writing. (For a fuller discussion of formal and informal tone, see Chapter 14.)

Apostrophes to form certain plurals (49c)

An apostrophe plus *-s* is used to form the plural of numbers, lowercase letters, symbols, and words used as words. The plural of capital letters do not require an apostrophe.

PLURAL NUMBERS	All my psychology test scores have been in the 90's.
PLURAL LETTERS	Young children sometimes confuse *b*'s and *d*'s. [*Note that letters of the alphabet referred to as letters are either set in italics or underlined.*]

PLURAL SYMBOLS   When I looked at the page I was typing, all the $'s were 4's.

PLURAL WORDS   Every one of her *separate*'s was spelled incorrectly. [*Note that*
REFERRED TO AS   *words referred to as words are either set in italics or underlined.*]
WORDS

Decades are usually written without an apostrophe.

EXAMPLE   The 1990s saw a rise in the number of high school students.

EXERCISE 34.1   USING APOSTROPHES TO SIGNAL POSSESSION

NAME _____ **DATE** _____

Use the cues in parentheses to create possessive forms to fill in the blanks. Be sure to use any apostrophes correctly.

> **EXAMPLE**   Several of _____ buildings (designed by Frank Lloyd Wright) are still used as private residences.
>
> **REVISION**   Several of <u>Frank Lloyd Wright's</u> buildings are still used as private residences.

1. The _____ (of the university) night classes are a relatively painless way to return

    to school.

2. I've been able to arrange my classes around my _____ (required by my company)

    schedule.

3. One problem I have faced is trying to meet the _____ (of the department)

    requirements for completing a degree.

4. Fortunately, most of my professors have realized that the _____ (of the university)

    night students take _____ (belonging to them) courses seriously, so the instruc-

    tors tend to meet me halfway.

5. A _____ (of a night student) life is not easy, and I have bonded with other stu-

    dents over this crazy life of _____ (belonging to us).

6. _____ (of these women) time is valuable, so it is important for each _____

    (of each class) pace to be efficient and _____ (of it) objectives to be clear.

7. My _____ (of my family) patience has been wearing thin as I have had to spend most evenings at school or in the library keeping up with my _____ (of my classes) assignments and homework.

8. Despite my being so busy, I feel that I am accomplishing my _____ (of my parents) dream in finally finishing college.

9. My _____ (of my children) complaints about my absence are offset by _____ (belonging to them) pride in me.

10. I hope that my _____ (of my son and daughters) lives will be easier when I finish this degree.

11. Having a college degree is a dream of _____ (belonging to me) so that I can earn a promotion to _____ (of a manager) position.

12. When I'm finished, I will be ready for new responsibilities, and I will accept _____ (of everyone) congratulations.

EXERCISE 34.2 USING APOSTROPHES TO SIGNAL CONTRACTIONS AND OMISSIONS AND TO FORM PLURALS

NAME _____ **DATE** _____

Read each sentence below. Correct any errors in the use of apostrophes to signal contractions or omissions or in the use of apostrophes to form certain plurals. If a sentence contains no errors, write *C* next to its number.

> **EXAMPLE**   I hope you're planning to mind your *p*'s and *q*'s while you visit your grandparents.

1. The soup theyre making is full of vegetables but wo'nt include spinach.

2. Shouldnt we have stopped at Al's and Lucy's Market for more milk?

3. That guy whose been giving you a ride to and from work called about nine oclock.

4. I could'nt post the title of the sermon on the message board outside the church because I ran out of *g*'s.

5. The distributor informs me that you're order has not received it's required approval from the business office.

6. Until the late 90s, I never had to write @s, but now my notes are full of them.

7. Anyone whose responsible for an accident has a legal obligation to compensate injured parties.

8. They're coming over on October 30 to carve jack-o'-lanterns.

9. The .'s in a Web address are called *dots*, as in *dot-com*, and youve got to remember that they aren't decimals.

10. Im afraid that they've figured out what were doing.

NAME _____ **DATE** _____

The following passage contains numerous errors involving apostrophes. Circle any errors you find, and pencil in your corrections.

The beginning of each fall term is much the same. The same questions emerge: Whose had whom in which classes? Hows so-and-so in history? How many Cs did so-and-so give in psychology last term? Anyone heard how many sections of French there'll be? Hallways buzz, and the tables in the student union fill up once more. All over campus, department secretaries patience wears thin even as they politely answer question's about adding or dropping classes, changing majors, and so forth. Faculty members offices echo with the sound of typing and computers printing. Meanwhile, the bookstores lines stretch back from the cash registers all the way to the next years calendars, which are already on sale. Returning student's sometimes find its not possible to walk across campus without running into old acquaintances. They keep "Hows it going?" and "What's up?" at the ready.

By late November, the elms dont rustle; theyre bare. Maybe its even snowed already. Snow or not, much of the terms earlier anticipation has been replaced by specific challenges: the paper due tomorrow, the necessary A on the next test (after two Cs and a C–), the P.E. class' required twenty laps. But at the beginning of the semester, all thats in the future. The sun shines, the summers moneys in the bank, and everyone secretly believes that again this term the registrars computer will be friendly.

Quotation Marks

35

Quotation marks indicate when people are speaking for themselves; they identify speakers' exact words. Notice in the following sentences how moving one of the quotation marks (and rewording accordingly) changes the meaning.

"Stop!" the guard shouted.

"Stop the guard!" shouted the museum director.

Quotation marks are also used to identify titles, definitions, and ironic or other special uses of words.

QUOTATION MARKS IN EVERYDAY USE

It's often useful to repeat someone's exact words — to make sure that classmates understand what a teacher said, to gossip in detail about an argument you overheard, or to tell a child whom you are baby-sitting what his parents told you about bedtime, for example. Sometimes people even emphasize that they are reporting a direct quotation by using the words "quote-unquote" or a hand motion meant to suggest quotation marks.

What kinds of everyday situations do you notice in which people quote exactly what someone else said? Make note of a few such instances. What reasons do people have for using someone else's exact words? Do you think the use of quotations makes a difference in how you respond to the information being reported? Would any of the conversations you noted have been different if the direct quotation had been paraphrased instead?

Quotation marks to signal direct quotations (50a)

In the United States, words have a status similar to that of personal property; thus, we use double quotation marks to signal **quotation** — the reproduction of someone else's exact words. Doing so also helps ensure that readers understand accurately who said what.

"I vote for eating breakfast out this morning," she said.

Use single quotation marks to enclose a quotation within a quotation:

> "When you say 'Speak now or forever hold your peace,'" Jeremy asked, "do you mean it?"

Remember that quotation marks, whether single or double, identify someone else's *exact words*. When **paraphrasing**, expressing someone else's words in words of your own, do not use quotation marks.

PARAPHRASE	Lisa said that she thought it would be a good idea for me to speak to the accountants' organization. [*no quotation marks*]
DIRECT QUOTATION	Lisa said, "You know, I think it would be good for you to speak to the accountants' organization." [*quotation marks required*]

If the quoted material itself includes a quotation, use the usual double quotation marks to open and close your quotation and single quotation marks for the quotation within the quotation.

> Hoffman remembers trying to explain his equations to Albert Einstein. "Then came the staggering—and altogether endearing—request: 'Please go slowly. I do not understand things quickly.' This from Einstein!"

Quoting longer passages

If you use quoted material in an essay or an argument and that quoted material runs only four lines or less, use quotation marks and incorporate the quoted material as part of your paragraph. Quoted material that runs longer than four lines should be indented ten spaces from the left margin, without quotation marks. (Indented quotations are also known as **block quotations**.) When material from another speaker or source appears inside a block quotation, use double quotation marks. When quoted material runs to two or more paragraphs, indent the first line of each paragraph an additional three spaces. When typing block quotations, double-space them just like you do the rest of your paper. (Note: These guidelines follow the style set by the Modern Language Association. There are other styles, some of them specific to disciplines other than English. Ask your instructors in all classes whether they require specific styles of quotation.)

EXAMPLE

Lacking visitors because of the heavy storms and unable to journey to town for the same reason, Thoreau says he was forced to imagine his company. That is precisely what he does:

> For human society I was obliged to conjure up the former occupants of these woods. Within the memory of many of my townsmen the road near which my house stands resounded with the laughter and gossip of inhabitants, and the woods which border it were notched and dotted here and there with their little gardens and dwellings. ("Civil Disobedience" 172)

Quoting poetry

The guidelines for indentation of quoted prose generally hold true for poetry. Three lines or less may be incorporated into the body of your essay (using appropriate quotation marks); more than three lines should be indented without using quotation marks. When lines of poetry are quoted within quotation marks, a slash mark (with a space on either side of it) is used to indicate the end of each line. Here, for example, are the opening two lines of Anne Bradstreet's early poem "In Memory of My Dear Grandchild Anne Bradstreet Who Deceased June 20, 1669, Being Three Years and Seven Months Old": "With troubled heart and trembling hand I write, / The heavens have changed to sorrow my delight." Because line breaks in a poem are often as important as the punctuation and the actual words, you must not omit the slash marks.

When quoting four or more lines in a block quotation, make sure that you accurately reproduce the line breaks, indentations, capitalizations, and stanza breaks of the original.

Signaling dialogue

When writing dialogue, start a new paragraph to indicate every change of speaker. Sometimes these paragraph shifts are the only indication readers need.

> "You're going," he said, as though it were a fact.
> "Yes." Her voice was quiet but firm.
> "And you believe you ought to have the Ferrari and the Picasso?"
> "It was my money that bought them."
> "So it was," he said. "So it was."

To signal that a single speech extends over several paragraphs, use quotation marks at the beginning of the speech, at the beginning of every new paragraph continuing the speech, and at the end of the speech. The omission of quotation marks at the end of a paragraph signals to readers that the same speaker continues speaking in the new paragraph.

Quotation marks to signal titles and definitions (50b)

Identifying titles

Use quotation marks to identify titles of works that are part of larger works, such as titles of individual poems, short stories, articles, chapters, and essays. In contrast, full collections of poems, short stories, articles, and essays should be either italicized or underlined (for more on the use of italics and underlining, see Chapter 39). Songs and individual episodes of television or radio shows are also identified by quotation marks.

SONG   Bing Crosby's "White Christmas" gets radio airplay every December.

TELEVISION EPISODE	"Watching Too Much Television" was the best episode of *The Sopranos* last year. [*Note that the television series title is italicized or underlined.*]
SHORT STORY	Tim O'Brien's "Quantum Jumps" later became part of his third novel.
ESSAY	Joan Didion's "God's Country" analyzes the history of the "compassionate conservative."
POEM	In Elizabeth Bishop's poem "The Waiting Room," the speaker is an adult remembering herself as a young girl.
CHAPTER	This chapter is titled "Quotation Marks."

When titles normally set off by quotation marks appear inside other quoted material, use single quotation marks to indicate the title:

Shane sighed, "When the deejay played 'Smells Like Teen Spirit' on his oldies show, I realized I was middle-aged."

Identifying definitions

Writers use quotation marks to indicate definitions.

The word *radical* originally meant "root."

Forte comes from French and originally meant "strong" or "brave."

Note that words used as words are italicized.

Quotation marks to signal irony and invented words (50c)

Writers may use quotation marks sparingly to indicate irony or skepticism. Such punctuation works only when used prudently.

Our "dinner date" turned out to be a fifteen-minute stop at a hamburger drive-in.

Used carelessly, quotation marks may communicate a meaning directly opposed to that of the words alone. For example, most readers will interpret the following example as ironic rather than emphatically sincere: I *"love"* your mother's creamed broccoli. For emphasis, use italics or underline:

I *love* your mother's creamed broccoli.

Quotation marks are also used to signal the invention of a new word or the use of an old word in a new context. Here is an example:

Computer companies occasionally announce new software only to discontinue its development later; some people call such software "vaporware."

Quotation marks with other punctuation (50e)

Quotation marks are almost always used with other punctuation marks. Commas and colons are often (but not always) used to introduce quoted material. In general, a comma or a colon is used whenever there is a perceptible pause or interruption separating the writer's words from the quoted words. Verbs describing speech are frequently set off by commas, especially if the quoted material is a complete sentence.

- *Quotation marks with periods and commas.* Periods or commas always go before the closing quotation marks.

  The Coast Guard officer called the rescue "routine."

  "For Eastern Oregon, it should be fair but quite cold tonight," said the radio announcer. [*comma used to set off quotation from the verb* said]

  Martha said that she "wouldn't be caught dead in that place." [*no comma because quote is only part of a sentence*]

  "If you go in there," he threatened, "I'll walk away, and you'll never see me again." [*commas used to set off material that interrupts the quoted material*]

  Exception: When you follow MLA style for documenting a short quotation, place the period after the parenthesis that ends the source information.

  She refers to California as "the Golden Land" (Didion 3).

- *Quotation marks with colons and semicolons.* Colons and semicolons go outside the quotation marks.

  Mr. Ono smiled and said, "I have brought you one example": there before us was a watermelon almost the size of an oil drum.

  The cowboy said, "Smile when you say that"; he reached for his gun as he spoke.

- *Quotation marks with exclamation points, question marks, and dashes.* These punctuation marks go inside when they are part of the quotation; they go outside when they are not part of the quotation.

  "Jack! Wait!" [*Exclamation is part of the meaning of the quoted material; thus the exclamation point goes inside the quotation marks.*]

Who said, "There's a sucker born every minute"? [*The quotation itself is a statement. However, the entire sentence is a question. Hence, the question mark punctuates the sentence and is placed outside the quotation marks.*]

Frankie called after her, "Wait! I need — " but she was already gone. [*The dash here indicates that Frankie stopped speaking abruptly.*]

- *Quotation marks with apostrophes.* The quotation marks follow the 's.

I distinctly recall Luigi saying, "We'll meet after work at Pizza Bill's."

EXERCISE 35.1   USING QUOTATION MARKS TO SIGNAL DIRECT QUOTATION

NAME _____ **DATE** _____

A. In the following sentences, add quotation marks as needed to identify someone else's exact words, and cross out any unnecessary quotation marks. Make sure that you use quotation marks with other punctuation marks correctly.

>   **EXAMPLE**   Your phone's ringing! yelled Phil from the end of the hall.
>
>   **REVISION**   "Your phone's ringing!" yelled Phil from the end of the hall. _____

1. "The tests look normal," but you should still watch your cholesterol, the doctor told me.

   _____

   _____

2. Did you hear that Principal McKee warned Henry, Go back to class or you'll be expelled?

   _____

   _____

3. Emerson didn't say Consistency is the hobgoblin of little minds; he said, A foolish consistency is the hobgoblin of little minds.

   _____

   _____

4. I learned more about economy from one South Dakota dust storm, said Hubert Humphrey, than I did in all my years at college.

   _____

   _____

5. In a letter to an editor, Mark Twain wrote that "reports of his death had been greatly exaggerated."

   _____

   _____

B. On the line after each sentence below, identify the quotation as either direct or indirect. Add quotation marks as needed.

> **EXAMPLE**   It was the American revolutionary Patrick Henry who said, "Give me liberty or give me death."   <u>direct</u>

1. Call me Ishmael is the first sentence of Herman Melville's *Moby-Dick*. _____

2. Most people like to characterize themselves as open minded and flexible enough to change when the circumstances demand. _____

3. The Internal Revenue Service reported that it did not have enough funding to go after wealthy tax cheats. _____

4. Appealing to the public to help find her lost child, the little girl's mother said, One minute, she was walking right in front of us. The next, she had vanished into the trees. _____

5. Give me a one-handed economist! cried Harry S Truman. He explained, All my economists say, "on the one hand . . . on the other." _____

EXERCISE 35.2   USING QUOTATION MARKS TO SIGNAL DIALOGUE

The following excerpt is from the play *Waiting for Lefty* by American playwright Clifford Odets. Read the exchange between the two characters; then, on your own paper, rewrite it in paragraphs, using quotation marks correctly.

A tired but attractive woman of thirty comes into the room, drying her hands on an apron. She stands there sullenly as JOE *comes in from the other side, home from work. For a moment they stand and look at each other in silence.*

JOE: Where's all the furniture, honey?

EDNA: They took it away. No installments paid.

JOE: When?

EDNA: Three o'clock.

JOE: They can't do that.

EDNA: Can't? They did it.

JOE: Why, the palookas, we paid three-quarters.

EDNA: The man said read the contract.

JOE: We must have signed a phoney. . . .

EDNA: It's a regular contract and you signed it.

JOE: Don't be so sour, Edna. . . . *(Tries to embrace her.)*

EDNA: Do it in the movies, Joe — they pay Clark Gable big money for it.

JOE: This is a helluva house to come home to. Take my word!

EDNA: Take MY word! Whose fault is it?

JOE: Must you start that stuff again?

EDNA: Maybe you'd like to talk about books?

JOE: I'd like to slap you in the mouth!

EDNA: No you won't.

JOE: *(sheepishly)* Jeez, Edna, you get me sore some time. . . .

EDNA: But just look at me — I'm laughing all over!

JOE: Don't insult me. Can I help it if times are bad? What the hell do you want me to do, jump off a bridge or something?

EXERCISE 35.3   USING QUOTATION MARKS CORRECTLY

NAME _____ **DATE** _____

Proofread the following sentences for correct use of quotation marks. If a sentence is correct, write *C* on the line below the sentence. If a sentence needs to be repunctuated, copy the sentence and punctuate it accurately.

    EXAMPLE   "Under Stars and The Ritual of Memories" remain two of my favorite Tess Gallagher poems.

    REVISION   "Under Stars" and "The Ritual of Memories" remain two of my favorite Tess Gallagher poems.

1. After I finished the chapter about the transition from Middle to Modern English, I started reading Language Variations in Chaucer's *Tales*, an essay on reserve in the library.

   _____

   _____

2. Although I did not understand it for a long time, I am glad I studied T. S. Eliot's poem The Love Song of J. Alfred Prufrock.

   _____

   _____

3. An article in the business section of the newspaper enumerates the certifications held by geriatric care managers.

   _____

   _____

4. If you want me again look for me under your boot-soles, advises Walt Whitman at the end of his masterpiece, *Song of Myself.*

   _____

   _____

5. As he stepped onto the elevator, Houlihan heard an instrumental version of Good Vibrations playing through tinny little speakers.

   _____

   _____

6. "As I was telling you, he sat there in his library, sipped his drink, and said, I find it delightfully reassuring to live among all these words."

_____

_____

7. "Who but the British," the guide remarked, "would knit 'sweaters' for their teapots?"

_____

_____

8. The minister began the eulogy by saying, "Ralph had always known that he wanted to live "la vida loca."

_____

_____

9. When I finished the short story called An Ornithologist's Guide to Life, I was afraid I would have to stay up all night to finish the ten other stories in Ann Hood's collection.

_____

_____

_____

10. Regarding the second edition of its book on managing diabetes, the Mayo Clinic states: "Forget about trying to stick to a 'diabetic diet.' You really don't need to do much more than follow the same sensible eating plan that everyone else should."

_____

_____

_____

EXERCISE 35.4   IDENTIFYING AND CORRECTING ERRORS WITH QUOTATION MARKS

NAME _____ **DATE** _____

Read each of the following passages, and then proofread for errors involving quotation marks. Cross out whatever should not be present, and add anything that you feel should be included. Reposition quotations if they need to be moved. If a passage does not contain any errors involving quotation marks, write _C_ next to the item number.

1. The opening stanza of Dylan Thomas's Fern Hill contains some of the most gorgeous sounds in English: "Now as I was young and easy under the apple bough / About the lilting house and happy as the grass was green. / The night above the dingle starry, / Time let me hail and climb / Golden in the heydays of his eyes, / And honoured among wagons I was prince of the apple towns / And once below a time I lordly had the trees and leaves / Trail with daisies and barley / Down the rivers of the windfall light."

2. On March 5, 1861, Mary Chesnut, the wife of an aide to President Jefferson Davis of the Confederacy, wrote: "We stood on the balcony to see our Confederate flag go up. Roars of cannon, etc., etc. Miss Sanders complained (so said Captain Ingraham) of the deadness of the mob. 'It was utterly spiritless,' she said; 'no cheering, or so little, and no enthusiasm.' Captain Ingraham suggested that gentlemen 'are apt to be quiet,' and this was 'a thoughtful crowd — the true mob element with us just now is hoeing corn.' And yet! It is uncomfortable that the idea has gone abroad that we have no joy, no pride in this thing. The band was playing 'Massa in the cold, cold ground.' Miss Tyler, daughter of the former President of the United States, ran up the flag."

3. Sara sighed. "You think it's enough that you come home every night and kiss the baby before she goes to sleep. You think it's enough that you bring home a paycheck, that you have a steady job, that you take good care of us. You think it's enough to be an old-fashioned father and husband. You think it's enough that you love us.

    "Well, I have news for you. It isn't enough."

4. Abraham Lincoln was quoting from the Bible when he said, "'A house divided against itself cannot stand.'"

5. Harriet Jacobs (1813–1897) describes, as follows, the space in which she hid from her slave master:

> "A small shed had been added to my grandmother's house years ago. Some boards were laid across the joists at the top, and between these boards and the roof was a very small garret, never occupied by any thing but rats and mice. It was a pent roof, covered with nothing but shingles, according to the southern custom for such buildings. The garret was only nine feet long and seven wide. The highest part was three feet high, and sloped down abruptly to the loose board floor. There was no admission for either light or air. My uncle Phillip, who was a carpenter, had very skilfully made a concealed trap-door, which communicated with the storeroom. He had been doing this while I was waiting in the swamp. The storeroom opened upon a piazza. To this hole I was conveyed as soon as I entered the house. The air was stifling; the darkness total. A bed had been spread on the floor. I could sleep quite comfortably on one side; but the slope was so sudden that I could not turn on the other without hitting the roof." (12)

Other Punctuation Marks

36

Parentheses, brackets, dashes, colons, slashes, and ellipses are all around us, setting off, inserting, or marking the absence of information.

According to the student guide to the library, "The new books (shelved near the entrance to the library [the main building]) reflect campus reading tastes . . . rather than the best-seller lists." Some of the current books include scholarly works such as *Perspectives on the California Gold Rush: Journals and Diaries of the Forty-Niners*, volumes of poetry such as *Him/Her: Golden Reflections*, and suspense novels—including the latest from Mary Higgins Clark.

OTHER PUNCTUATION MARKS IN EVERYDAY USE

Notice how *TV Guide,* for instance, freely uses punctuation marks such as parentheses, brackets, dashes, colons, slashes, and ellipses in its program previews. These marks help present information for viewers clearly and efficiently, as this example illustrates.

9 PM Movie (CC)—Drama: 120 min. *Escape from Alcatraz* (1979). An inmate (Clint Eastwood) at a high-security prison plans a breakout. (PG—Adult content/violence/adult language. [Time approximate after baseball.])

Check the newspaper, a magazine, or other reading material to see where you find these marks. Which marks do you see most often? Which ones less often?

Parentheses (51a)

Writers use parentheses to set off supplementary information. Such information may be only a word or two or may form an entire sentence. Whatever this information may be, readers will view it as less important than the rest of the sentence. Any sentence containing parenthetical information should be grammatically complete and clear without the material in parentheses. Here are some examples of sentences containing parenthetical information:

Walt Disney's movie *Alice in Wonderland* (1951) remains a bright, weird tale even on television's small screen.

Nadine works for the American Association of University Women (AAUW).

Just as I rounded the corner (and I could tell something smelled funny), I saw flames licking at the Whittleseys' garage.

Occasionally, writers place important information in parentheses. These writers count on the surprise value such information yields. Here is an example:

The taxi driver was finally persuaded (by means of $600) that the damage to his back seat could be repaired after all.

Like exclamation points and quotation marks used for irony, parenthetical explanations or additions should be used carefully. The following sentence makes two tactical errors. It contains too much parenthetical information, and that information is crucial, not supplementary:

Employees (by which is here meant all employed half-time or less) are not expected to resume work (that is, should not be physically present on company premises) until the last Monday of this month (when it is expected that line repairs will be complete).

Revising such a sentence may involve writing several short sentences. In this way, each important idea receives its due attention from readers:

Part-time employees (half-time or less) should plan to return to work on the last Monday of this month. Line repairs should be completed by that time. Until then, we ask these employees to remain off company premises in order to allow repairs to proceed.

The second version is a little bit longer but quite a bit clearer.

Writers also use parentheses to set off numbered or lettered items.

Once you have finished dinner, I want you to (1) clear your place, (2) load the dishwasher, and (3) give your old dog a walk before it gets too dark.

End punctuation goes outside the parentheses unless the parenthetical material is a separate and complete sentence.

Geri says she is smart because she has ESP (whatever that is).

We will meet at the lodge at noon. (Remember your lunch.)

When needed, commas follow closing parentheses; commas are never used before a parenthesis.

If we decide to climb Mount Rainier (or any of the Alaskan peaks), we will do so only with an experienced guide.

Brackets (51b)

Writers use brackets in two specialized ways:

1. to set off a parenthetical element within an already parenthesized passage:

The Republican Party has not always been unsympathetic to feminist concerns (such as the Equal Rights Amendment [ERA], which the Nixon administration supported).

2. to insert explanatory words or comments into a quoted passage:

Then she turned and said, "Will you [meaning my father] be joining us for dinner?"

In sentences like the one just given, readers attribute the bracketed material to the author of the sentence, not to the person who is quoted. (If your keyboard lacks bracket keys, it is acceptable to write brackets in by hand.)

Dashes (51c)

Dashes may be used singly or in pairs. A single dash indicates a sudden change or contrast; occasionally, a single dash can be used repeatedly to mimic the breathlessness or fragmentary quality of thought or speech. (To type a dash, you can always hit the hyphen key twice, leaving no spaces between the ends of the dash and the words on either side of it. Some word-processing programs enable you to type dashes like the ones in this book.)

We'll meet you at nine at Woodstock's for pizza—if Rob's aging Buick can get us there. [*single dash used to signal sudden change or contrast*]

"I—wait—no—don't shoot—I'll tell you—I'll tell you what you want to know." [*single dash used repeatedly to mimic the breathlessness or fragmentary quality of thought or speech*]

Writers use dashes in pairs to set off material from the rest of the sentence. You may recall that commas and parentheses also set off material from the rest of the sentence. What are the differences here? The contrast with parentheses is one of emphasis. Parenthetical information is almost always considered to be of lesser importance than the information contained in the rest of the sentence. Dashes, by contrast, tend to emphasize the material they enclose. In the first of the following sentences, the writer is trying to downplay John Glenn's fame; in the second, the intent is to make that fame an integral part of the sentence's meaning.

> As a boy, I lived next door to John Glenn (the former astronaut who was later a U.S. senator) and mowed his lawn every Saturday. [*parentheses used to minimize*]

> As a boy, I lived next door to John Glenn — the former astronaut who was later a U.S. senator—and mowed his lawn every Saturday. [*dashes used to emphasize*]

The difference may be lost on casual readers. However, as a writer, you ought to be able to see that these two sentences do not communicate quite the same thing.

Could commas be substituted for either the dashes or the parentheses in the two sentences just discussed? Yes. A writer using commas would be neither emphasizing nor minimizing. (For more on comma usage, see Chapter 31.)

Writers may also use dashes to set off a list from the rest of the sentence. When commas separate items in a list, dashes may be used to set off the entire list.

> Stunned, sad, and finally bitter — I felt miserable in several different ways when she broke up with me.

> While Nancy was in the hospital, her friends took care of everything — feeding her cat, watering her plants, cleaning her apartment, even paying her rent and telephone bill — and showed her how glad they were to have her in their lives.

Finally, if the material inside the dashes is a question or an exclamation, the appropriate punctuation mark precedes the final dash.

> Swift's argument is — who can dispute this? — both cunning and abhorrent.

Colons (51d)

A colon says that whatever follows is an example or an explanation of what was just said.

> The registrar's computer has given me four classes: Introduction to Biology, Composition, History of American Thought, and Fitness Aerobics.

> The district attorney's announcement was entirely unexpected: two highly regarded local doctors had been indicted on fraud charges.

A colon that is used to introduce an example or an explanation should follow a grammatically complete independent clause. The colon should *not* separate a verb or preposition from its object, nor should a colon follow *especially, including,* or *such as.*

INCORRECT	The recipes in this cookbook are: delicious, simple, and inexpensive. [*colon incorrectly separates verb and subject complement*]
CORRECT	The recipes in this cookbook are delicious, simple, and inexpensive. [*no colon needed*]
	The recipes in this cookbook are perfect for young adults: delicious, simple, and inexpensive. [*colon follows grammatically complete independent clause*]
INCORRECT	Curtis Hanson has directed several films, including: *L.A. Confidential* and *8 Mile.*
CORRECT	Curtis Hanson has directed several films, including *L.A. Confidential* and *8 Mile.*

Colons are also frequently used in the following ways:

- following parts of memos

  To: Dean Wilkins

  From: Robert Frank

- after salutations

  Dear Scholarship Committee:

- to separate hours, minutes, and seconds

  Class begins promptly at 8:30.

  The seismograph indicates that the earthquake began at 2:15:36 AM.

- to separate biblical chapters and verses

  We learned about Noah in Genesis 5:28.

- to separate titles and subtitles

  In *Water Wars: Drought, Flood, Folly, and the Politics of Thirst,* Diane Raines Ward discusses the need for cooperative government action to prevent conflicts over scarce water resources.

- to separate volumes and page numbers

  Check the *Encyclopaedia Britannica* 3:187. [*volume 3, page 187*]

- to separate items in bibliographic entries

  Simpson, Eileen. *Poets in Their Youth: A Memoir.* New York: Random, 1982. [*colon separates title from subtitle and place of publication from publisher*]

  Surowiecki, James. "The Goldilocks Effect." *The New Yorker* 27 May 2002: 50. [*colon separates the year from the page number*]

Slashes (51e)

Use slashes in any of these three ways:

1. to indicate line divisions in quotations of poetry or song lyrics that run four lines or less

    Dylan Thomas writes: "Old age should burn and rave at close of day; / Rage, rage against the dying of the light." [*Leave a space before and after the slash. Use two slashes to show a stanza break.*]

2. to separate equally applicable terms

    This form must be signed by the applicant's parent/legal guardian. [*no space before or after the slash*]

3. to indicate numeric fractions

    The baby measured 20 3/4 inches. [*no space before or after the slash*]

Ellipses (51f)

Writers use ellipses—three dots, equally spaced—to let readers know that something has been left out. Ellipses show omissions from a sentence. Use ellipses plus a period (four dots in all) when, in the middle of a quoted passage, you omit the end of a sentence, the beginning of a succeeding sentence, or one or more complete sentences. Be sure a complete sentence comes before and after the four dots.

EXAMPLES   Ellen wrote, ". . . I really do love him." [*Ellen's full sentence read,* "Even though I've only known him for three weeks, I really do love him."]

Reynaldo wrote, "I love her very much. . . ." [*Reynaldo's full sentence read,* "I love her very much, even though I've only known her for three weeks." *Four ellipsis points are used in the quoted sentence: the first is the sentence's period, and the next three indicate ellipsis. Note that the quotation marks follow the final point without any intervening space.*]

"Before we leave for the beach, . . . make sure the downstairs door is locked." [*The entire sentence read,* "Before we leave for the beach, I'll make sure the windows are closed, and you make sure the downstairs door is locked."]

"This Sunday we'll cut the wood. . . . And next Sunday, we'll be able to have a fire in the fireplace." [*The original passage read,* "This Sunday we'll cut the wood. We'll have the chimney cleaned during the week. And next Sunday, we'll be able to have a fire in the fireplace." *The first point is the first sentence's period. The three ellipsis points then follow.*]

As a writer, you are obliged to preserve the tone and meaning of your sources. When you use ellipses, make sure that your shortened version does not distort the original in spirit or content.

Ellipses may also be used to signal a pause or hesitation. This usage occurs most often in dialogue, but it may also appear in unquoted prose.

EXAMPLES   *Fidelity* . . . She was saying the word over and over to herself, as though it might have a taste, as though by saying it over and over she could determine what it meant to her.

"Billy . . . Billy . . . Billy . . ." Someone was calling him. Someone far away was looking for him and calling his name.

EXERCISE 36.1 USING PARENTHESES AND BRACKETS

NAME _____ **DATE** _____

Parentheses and brackets are used incorrectly in some of the following sentences. If a sentence uses these punctuation marks correctly, write *C* in the margin next to it. If a sentence uses these punctuation marks incorrectly, write in the necessary corrections.

EXAMPLE   "I think he [Robinson Jeffers] thought of people as wild, passionate, and usually not very rational or altruistic," Alfred said. (Assume that the name did not form part of the quotation and was inserted by the writer reporting this opinion.)

1. "The Security and Exchange Commission proposed that companies clarify how much (and in what ways) they compensate their top executives." (Assume that the same speaker said all of these words.)

2. Cornell University (with its main campus in Ithaca, New York) offers a program in industrial and labor relations in New York City.

3. She said, "I have never seen the movie [*Black Narcissus*] that everyone else in the film class was talking about." (Assume that the title of the movie is not part of the quotation.)

4. Feeling *schadenfreude* [pleasure in the misfortunes of others] seems more socially acceptable if the people suffering are your enemies than it does if they are your friends.

5. The debate continued over whether the president had broken a law (the Federal Intelligence Security Act (FISA)).

6. We were expressly forbidden by the guards to scale the wall. [We went anyway.]

7. Mrs. Chu said firmly, "That man [pointing at the defendant] is the one who robbed my store."

8. In his campaign literature, Wharton said, "My opponent (French) has consistently supported tax benefits for developers despite overcrowding." (Assume that the opponent's name was not part of the campaign literature.)

9. I told her that I was sorry [although I really didn't regret anything I had said or done].

10. Instead of calling for teachers to develop academic standards collaboratively for each grade, this proposal outlines two extremes: (1) allowing individual teachers to develop their own standards and (2) imposing uniform standards on all schools.

EXERCISE 36.2 REVISING TO ENSURE CORRECT USE OF PARENTHESES

A. In the passage that follows, parentheses are overused or used inappropriately. Using your own paper, rewrite the passage so that parentheses are used sparingly and appropriately. Make sure that crucial information does not appear in parentheses.

> Our car was approaching the intersection from the west (we were arguing about which movie we were going to see, so maybe we weren't paying close attention) when somebody (maybe Judy, who was driving) yelled "No!" Just seconds after that (I think by then Judy had begun to swerve right to try to get out of the way), the station wagon hit our front end behind the wheel (the left one). As metal crunched and we spun around, it all seemed to be happening in slow motion.

B. Determine whether each of the following sentences uses parentheses appropriately and is punctuated correctly. Using your own paper, rewrite each sentence that contains errors. Make sure that crucial information does not appear in parentheses and that sentences containing parentheses have correct punctuation. If a sentence is correct, write C next to the sentence number.

1. My nieces Roberta and Nora, who are eighteen and fifteen, are deathly afraid of spiders, (as well as other kinds of crawling creatures.)

2. I have always heard that it is bad luck to kill a spider in the house (although I do not think of myself as superstitious.

3. I don't mind a few spiders around the house, for they make themselves useful by (for instance, catching flies).

4. (Now that I think about it), the usefulness of spiders probably explains why superstitions tell people not to kill them.

5. I wish that my nieces would not have fits every time they see a harmless little spider in my house (didn't they ever read *Charlotte's Web*?).

EXERCISE 36.3   USING DASHES

NAME _____ **DATE** _____

A. Read the sentences below, paying particular attention to the use of dashes. If a sentence is acceptable as written, write C on the line below the sentence. If a sentence needs revising, write your corrected version.

EXAMPLE   Hamburg today the largest city — and busiest port — in Germany — has twice risen from the ashes of fire and destruction.

REVISION   Hamburg — today the largest city and busiest port in Germany — has twice risen from the ashes of fire and destruction.

1. Your term papers will be returned promptly grades are due Tuesday morning to the student basket in the science office.

   _____

   _____

2. The pressure to carry on the family tradition — including attending Grandfather's alma mater — can limit the choices available to a teenager from a wealthy and influential family.

   _____

   _____

3. The play *Barefoot in the Park* — my mother and father saw it together on their first date! made its way back to Broadway recently.

   _____

   _____

4. Not that long ago, shortly before the Revolutionary War, in fact — English law made stealing a crime punishable by death.

   _____

   _____

5. Children's pictures can tell us much — about the children who drew them — their sophistication, their perceptual abilities, and their self-image.

   _____

   _____

B. Combine each group of short sentences, using dashes appropriately as needed.

EXAMPLE   That dog sits in the yard yapping all day and all night. It is a chihuahua with a particularly irritating bark.

REVISION   <u>That dog—a chihuahua with a particularly irritating bark—sits in the yard yapping</u>
<u>all day and all night.</u>

1. The chef claims the dessert was a mistake. The mistake was delicious, if you ask me.

_____

_____

_____

2. Pets should be treated like animals. They should not be treated like family members!

_____

_____

3. Paul Klee was a renowned graphic artist, painter, and art theorist. He died in 1940. He remains an influential presence for contemporary artists.

_____

_____

4. Delhi has a state college. I mean the one in New York, not the one in India.

_____

_____

5. Emily Dickinson used dashes in her poems. Some say she used too many.

_____

_____

EXERCISE 36.4   USING COLONS

NAME _____   **DATE** _____

A.   Use colons to combine the following sentences.

    EXAMPLE   Check the *Encyclopaedia Britannica.* The volume to check is volume 3. The page number is 187.

    REVISION   <u>Check the *Encyclopaedia Britannica* 3:187.</u>

1. Bill's decision was a difficult one, but he stuck to it. Bill quit smoking for good.

_____

_____

2. There is only one good way to give a cat medicine. Have the veterinarian do it.

_____

_____

3. The instructor was annoyed with his new student's behavior. Her tardiness and her constant talking in class struck him as rude.

_____

_____

4. Although the trip was only for a weekend in the mountains, the family stuffed supplies for a week into the car. They packed fishing poles, tackle boxes, a large cooler, food, swimsuits, towels, parkas, and even some deck chairs.

_____

_____

_____

5. The server displayed the dessert choices. The desserts included chocolate torte, cherry crepes, and blueberry cheesecake.

_____

_____

B. Read each of the sentences below, paying attention to the use of colons. If a sentence needs revising, write your revision on the lines provided. If a sentence is punctuated accurately, write C on the line below the sentence.

> **EXAMPLE**   Advertisers assume that we all want to be: beautiful, protected, stylish, and trendy.
>
> **REVISION**   Advertisers assume that we all want to be beautiful, protected, stylish, and trendy.

1. Take my advice, stay in school until you have other plans: for finding a career.

   _____

   _____

2. The horse was enormous his shoulder was even with the top of my head: and I had to stand on tiptoe to reach his ears.

   _____

   _____

3. Now, now, sweetie: what's the matter?

   _____

   _____

4. Leonid Telyatnikov has done something he hopes no one else will have to do he has: commanded a fire crew attempting to extinguish a nuclear reactor fire.

   _____

   _____

5. Recognized as perhaps the nation's best prison newspaper, the *Prison Mirror* of Stillwater, Minnesota, publishes articles on: stress management, smoking, education, and the alternatives to execution.

   _____

   _____

   _____

6. With all due respect to this committee: I will not tell you how I will decide an abortion-related case.

_____

_____

7. A nutritionist I know may hold the record for housing moves as an adult: she's only thirty but has just moved into her fortieth home.

_____

_____

8. Every town has restaurant ads proclaiming: "All You Can Eat" or "Home-Cooked Food."

_____

_____

9. J. R. R. Tolkien understood many languages, including: several medieval ones, but he gave up trying to learn one that he considered too difficult; Finnish.

_____

_____

10. The complete title of the third volume of Bruce Catton's classic trilogy is *The Army of the Potomac, A Stillness at Appomattox.*

_____

_____

EXERCISE 36.5   USING ELLIPSES

NAME _____ **DATE** _____

Read the following passage. Then copy it, leaving out the underlined portions. Make sure that you use ellipses correctly.

Not all states allow the public to remove elected officials from office by recalling them. <u>Even among</u> the fifteen states that do provide for recall, <u>requirements differ. States</u> have their own formulas for determining the required number of signatures to be collected. <u>If the formula is based on the number voting in the last election for the office involved, the number of signatures could vary considerably depending on the intensity of the contests that year or the other offices on the ballot.</u> Simply filing the required number of valid signatures might <u>in itself</u> be sufficient to require a recall election. On the other hand, the petitions might need to spell out specific grounds <u>that would justify a recall election.</u> Other differences might occur in registration procedures for petition carriers, signature requirements, <u>and so forth; similar variations might exist in</u> filing deadlines, petition formats, and other details.

PART 8

MECHANICS

"If writing must be a precise form of communication, it should be treated like a precision instrument. It should be sharpened, and it should not be used carelessly."
— THEODORE M. BERNSTEIN

PREVIEW QUESTIONS

These questions are to help you decide what to study. **Correct any mistakes in capitaliza-tion, abbreviations, use of numbers, use of italics, or hyphenation. If there are no mis-takes, write C next to the sentence. (Answers to preview questions are at the back of the book.)**

1. most tourists who visit New York city for the first time make a trip to the empire state building.
2. My father always says, "expect the worst, and you'll never be disappointed."
3. The eldest of the sisters — She was born in 1920 — performed internationally as a classical pianist.
4. Ms. Davis was granted a Ph.d in physics by the Univ. of Texas.
5. Marie & Pierre Curie were pioneers in research involving radium.
6. We were supposed to arrive at 7:30 p.m., but our flight was delayed until after midnight.
7. Rep. Barbara Lee serves in the House of Representatives.
8. The test begins at 8:15 am, so get up early enough to be on time.
9. Whenever you go to Jane's Bakery, you must take a #.
10. My parents live in Cal., but I now go to school in Ariz.
11. 6 people came to hear the lecture.
12. He has about 10,000 records.
13. Everyone on the trip found it difficult to bid adieu to Paris.
14. Malcolm Gladwell is a regular contributor to the New Yorker magazine and is the author of several books, including *The Tipping Point*.
15. I always enjoy listening to Morning Edition on the radio as I drive to work.
16. He told his lawyer he was not sure what *grievous* meant.
17. *Halloween* always falls on October 31, and *Christmas* always falls on December 25, but the dates of *Thanksgiving* and *Hanukkah* change from year to year.
18. The long poem "Beowulf" was written in Old English, Chaucer wrote in Middle English, and — to the surprise of everyone in my English class — the language in Shakespeare plays such as *Othello* is considered modern English.
19. Oprah Winfrey selected the novel The Corrections by Jonathan Franzen for her book club, but the author refused to appear on her television show.
20. Although Beethoven wrote many works for piano, his *Moonlight Sonata* is the best-known.
21. The company ended its season with the rarely-performed play *The Duchess of Malfi*.
22. Fully eighty-five percent of the respondents to the survey said they had a positive view of the mayor elect.
23. My family were all mind-ful that my home remodeling job would be a seat-of-the-pants kind of endeavor.
24. None of the television stations had better-coverage of the election.
25. Only one-third of the class showed up today.
26. The new development contains one and two-family homes.

Capital Letters

37

Capitalization depends almost entirely on convention—the customary habits writers follow and readers expect. Once you understand these conventions, you expect capital letters to mark the beginning of each new sentence, to help name Aunt Fran or Seattle, to distinguish a Xerox machine from any other copier, and to help you understand how you might drive south in order to reach the South.

CAPITAL LETTERS IN EVERYDAY USE

In print, writers may capitalize words or even whole passages for special emphasis (WOW! BAM!). The humor writer Dave Barry uses this technique: "Today I saw a chicken driving a car. (I AM NOT MAKING THIS UP.)" On the Internet, however, rules for capitalization are often different. There, writers who capitalize too many words are accused of "shouting" and seen as aggressive or unfriendly, and in many online situations—casual emails, instant messages—writers do not use capital letters at all.

Collect a few examples of how capital letters are used in print and how they are used or omitted in electronic media. What is the most effective use of capitals?

The first word of a sentence or a line of poetry (52a)

One of the oldest conventions regarding capital letters is the capitalization of the first letter of the first word in a sentence. Every sentence on this page provides you with an example of this capitalization convention, which holds true for quoted material as well as for your own words. Here is an example of a quoted sentence appearing inside another. The first word of the sentence is capitalized; so is the first word of the quoted sentence:

Mark yelled, "Will you be in early tomorrow?"

When a sentence follows a colon, capitalization is optional. Either version of the following sentence is acceptable:

Writers speculate that Lindbergh's aerial tour of the United States contributed to his interest in conservation: he [*or* He] saw firsthand the still unspoiled beauty of his country.

If your sentence contains a sentence set off by dashes or parentheses, the sentence inside the dashes or parentheses does *not* begin with a capital letter. Here is an example:

All requests — please keep them to one page — should be on Jennifer's desk by noon Friday.

When writing or typing a letter, capitalize the first word of the salutation (*My dear Angela*) and the first word of the closing (*Very truly yours*).

Finally, if you are quoting lines of poetry, follow the poet's example when it comes to capitalization. If the poet capitalizes the first letter of every line, follow suit. If the poet does not capitalize the first letter of every line, again follow suit.

Proper nouns and proper adjectives (52b)

The names of specific persons, places, or objects are **proper nouns** and should be capitalized. For example, in the sentence *Marilyn lives in New York*, it is accurate to capitalize the *M* in *Marilyn* and the *N* and *Y* in *New York* because both are proper nouns. **Proper adjectives** (made from proper nouns) are also capitalized. Thus the adjective *New Yorker* (made from the proper noun) is capitalized in the sentence *Marilyn is a New Yorker*.

When a title precedes a person's name, in effect becoming part of the name, both are capitalized, as in *Aunt Bernie, Grandma Berry, Senator Byrd*, and *Police Chief Harrington*. However, when a title follows a name or is used instead of the name, the title usually is not capitalized. The only exceptions are the titles of very high-ranking officials, such as *president* or *prime minister*; such titles are sometimes capitalized even when used alone.

EXAMPLES

Senator Byrd	Robert Byrd, senator from West Virginia
Police Chief Harrington	Penny Harrington, the police chief
Aunt Bernie	Bernardine Matusek, my aunt
Prime Minister Tony Blair	Tony Blair, Prime Minister [*or* prime minister] of Great Britain

The names of products, corporations, and businesses are also capitalized, as in *First Interstate Bank*; *American Express*; *Floating Point, Inc.*; *Wheaties*; and *Campbell's Soup*.

Specific geographic sites and formations are capitalized, as in *Patterson Falls Fifth Avenue, Europe, the Flatiron Building*, and *the Great Salt Lake*. Note that although the articles *the, an*, and *a* usually accompany proper nouns or proper adjectives, they are not normally capitalized.

Common nouns such as *road, brook*, and *avenue* are capitalized only when they form part of a proper noun or an address. The same is true of directional words such as *west* and *southeast*.

Southeast Missouri State University   the southeast corner

Ponderosa Road   the road to town

Fairhaven Brook   the rocky brook

Consider this sentence: *The Waterfall at Alsea falls forms the focus for a Picnic Ground and an overnight camping area.* Should all the underlined words be capitalized? Should other words be capitalized? *Waterfall* is not part of a proper noun; hence it should not be capitalized. *Alsea* is part of a proper noun, so its capitalization is correct. *Falls* is also part of the proper noun, so it should be capitalized. *Picnic Ground* is a common noun; hence it should not be capitalized. Thus the sentence should really look like this: *The waterfall at Alsea Falls forms the focus for a picnic ground and an overnight camping area.*

Many other names and titles are routinely capitalized. Here are some examples:

- days of the week, months, and holidays

  Monday   October   Columbus Day   Easter   Ramadan   Passover

- historical events, movements, and periods

  the Civil War   the Victorian Era   the Battle of Hastings

- government or public offices, institutions, and departments

  West Slope Water District   the U.S. Senate   the Commerce Department

- organizations, associations, and their members

  United Auto Workers   Rotarians   The Crazy 8's   the League of Women Voters

- races, nationalities, and languages

  Hispanic   Filipino   Dutch   Haitian   Arabic   Russian

  (Note: The terms *black* and *white* are not usually capitalized when used to refer to race.)

- religions and their adherents

  Judaism/Jews   Protestantism/Protestants   Hinduism/Hindus

  Islam/Muslims   Buddhism/Buddhists   Roman Catholicism/Catholics

- sacred persons, places, or things

Allah	Rama	the Koran	the Angel Moroni
God	Jesus	the Bible [*but* biblical]	Saint Peter's Basilica

- trade names

IBM   Pepsi   Lexus   Kleenex   Xerox   Charmin

Some trade names have become generic and hence are not usually capitalized; an example is *aspirin*. When in doubt about a trade name, consult a dictionary.

- academic units, colleges, departments, and courses

College of Mechanical Engineering   Department of Art   Writing 121

Do not capitalize the name of a subject area unless it is a language: *I was bumped from both psychology and French.* The name of a specific course is capitalized, as in *Writing 121.*

Titles of works (52c)

Important words in the titles of books, articles, essays, poems, songs, paintings, musical and dance compositions, films, plays, short stories, documents, and television series are capitalized.

The Seven Samurai	"How I Found My Runaway Husband"
"A Modest Proposal"	"Ode on a Grecian Urn"
"Two Turntables and a Microphone"	*The Peaceable Kingdom*
Great Mass in C Minor, K. 427	*Swan Lake*
Grey's Anatomy	*Hairspray*
The Wizard of Oz	Treaty of Versailles
"The Lottery"	*I Love Lucy*

As in the case of poetry, an author or artist occasionally decides not to capitalize the title of a work. The poet e. e. cummings made a stylistic statement by avoiding capitalization in most of his works, for instance. Always check to see how the title of a work is capitalized in its original form, and follow that styling when in doubt.

A, an, and *the* are not capitalized unless they are the first word of the title itself. *The* is not capitalized when it is the first word in a magazine's or newspapers name, even if it is part of the title itself (the *New York Times*). Prepositions and conjunctions are not capitalized unless they are the first or last words in the title. Remember to capitalize the titles of your own works as well as others'.

Unnecessary capitalization (52e)

Inexperienced writers sometimes punctuate sentences almost solely according to the thought process that produced them: any pause in the process produces a punctuation mark (usually a comma), and a long pause produces a period. These writers then capitalize the first word of the "new sentence." The results might look something like this:

> Any discussion of the death penalty, makes me uncomfortable. Because it goes against everything I believe. Namely, that life is sacred and no government has the right to kill.

In such instances, writers cannot correct their punctuation until they are able to distinguish between sentences and fragments (see Chapter 24). Accurately punctuated (and only slightly rewritten), the same passage looks like this:

> Any discussion of the death penalty makes me uncomfortable because it goes against everything I believe. In my opinion, life is sacred, and no government has the right to kill.

Overall, good writers recognize that capitalization is not a matter of style or emphasis. Capitalizing for emphasis, as in *The test subjects did NOT respond as we had predicted*, is not helpful to readers or appropriate in most writing. Capitalization is, rather, a matter of following generally accepted conventions. Some of the most common capitalization errors are detailed here.

- Seasons, academic terms, and academic years are not capitalized.

  spring   fall quarter   summer semester   junior year

- Compass directions are not capitalized unless they refer to the accepted name of a geographic region.

  The wind blew fitfully from the southeast.

  The West was hit by an unseasonably early frost.

- The names of family relationships are not capitalized unless they substitute for a proper name.

  My father took me to my first circus when I was six.

  I asked Father if he would buy me cotton candy.

The letter said my uncle had open-heart surgery.

The letter said Uncle Herman had open-heart surgery.

Worrying about capitalization too early in the writing process can distract you from concentrating on what you want to say. Try saving such concerns for proofreading — usually the last stage of the writing process. Here is a capitalization checklist you can use as you proofread.

- Did you remember to capitalize the following words?

    proper nouns and proper adjectives

    names of people, places, events, institutions, products, and businesses

    titles of works of art, music, and literature

- Did you correctly use capitals for any of these words?

    seasons

    compass directions

    family relations

EXERCISE 37.1   CAPITALIZING THE FIRST WORD OF A NEW SENTENCE

NAME _____ **DATE** _____

Look for errors in capitalization in the following passage. Capitalize any words that should be capitalized, and substitute lowercase letters where necessary. Make your revisions in the space above each line.

One day when I was about fifteen, My mother called to me in my room, "come downstairs, would you please?" Wondering what she could want, I complied. When I reached the kitchen, I found her sitting at the table with her hands folded. she looked so serious that I was afraid someone in the family had died — Or maybe something had happened to one of our dogs — but I just waited for her to speak. She looked at me a long time and then finally said, "you'd better sit down." even more worried now, I sat in a chair opposite her. Again, She waited a long time — It seemed an eternity — before speaking. Her voice was soft and a little hoarse; It cracked a bit, and she coughed to clear her throat.

"I had a phone call this afternoon from my mother," She said. "No, not Gran. it was my birth mother. She has been looking for me for a long time." I knew my mother had never known her birth mother — She was adopted as an infant — and I wasn't sure how she would respond to hearing from her now. I asked, "what are you going to do?" My mother smiled faintly; She seemed more composed than when I'd first come into the kitchen. "I've arranged to meet with her tomorrow afternoon," My mother answered. She did — And that is how a third loving grandmother came into my life.

EXERCISE 37.2   CAPITALIZING PROPER NOUNS AND PROPER ADJECTIVES

In each of the sentences that follow, analyze how each underlined word is used, and decide whether it should be capitalized. Then rewrite each sentence so that it uses capitalization accurately. Write your analyses and your revised sentences on a separate sheet of paper.

EXAMPLE   Dr. Lambert is Chair of the department of Political science at the University.

Dr. Lambert: title preceding name — capitalize

Chair: noun, not title — no capitalization

department of Political science: proper name — capitalize

University: noun, not title — no capitalization

REVISION   Dr. Lambert is chair of the Department of Political Science at the university.

1. The Head of the Florida department of transportation hopes to increase Driver's License fees by the end of november of this Year.

2. The Ford motor company produces a variety of models, including the focus and the navigator; the Company also owns Mazda and volvo.

3. The Health Insurance Plan for the Company is administered by Blue Cross, Blue Shield of pennsylvania.

4. Main street in my hometown, Cold spring, New York, runs uphill as you travel East from the Hudson river.

5. Former President Jimmy Carter was awarded the Nobel peace prize in december of 2002.

6. Government Officials announced that soldiers who had served in the korean war would be honored with a statue by local Artist Ruby Lime.

7. On tuesday, we'll go to the art institute of chicago and look at the Exhibits of picasso's works.

8. The chinese-born Director Ang Lee won many Awards, including an oscar, for the film *Brokeback mountain*.

9. We plan to spend the Month of June touring the south to visit monuments of the Civil War.

10. Chinatown in New York city is growing as chinese, vietnamese, laotian, and other asian immigrants arrive; it is expanding into the streets that were once part of little Italy, another Immigrant Neighborhood that was once the home of Martin Scorsese and other well-known italian Americans.

EXERCISE 37.3   MORE PRACTICE WITH CAPITALIZING PROPER NOUNS AND PROPER ADJECTIVES

NAME _____ **DATE** _____

In the following sentences, correct any errors in the capitalization of proper nouns and proper adjectives. If a sentence contains no errors, write *C* next to the sentence number.

> **EXAMPLE**   That Botany 201 class looks tough, but not as tough as french or physics.
>
> **REVISION**   That Botany 201 class looks tough, but not as tough as French or physics.

1. Over Memorial day weekend last may, mayor Barbara Abruzzo attended a Rally for city workers and their Families.

2. The United States postal service now attempts to compete with private Delivery Services such as UPS and FedEx.

3. The cable network Al-Jazeera has its main offices in Qatar, but it broadcasts throughout the middle east and reaches a large arabic-speaking audience.

4. The Division of Language and Literature is happy to announce that it is the recipient of a grant from the United States Department of education.

5. The *Washington post* reported that the new Ambassador to India would be named shortly.

6. The biblical injunction to honor one's parents is echoed in the koran and can also be found in various sayings attributed to Confucius.

7. The now famous works of Kate Chopin, such as the novel *The Awakening* and the short story "The Storm," were only rediscovered many years after her death.

8. My Mother told aunt Mary that she was going to get me a Dog for my birthday.

9. The Apollo theater has been a testing ground for many of this Country's greatest Musicians and Dancers.

10. I don't speak spanish, italian, or french, but I am fluent in "the Language of Love."

EXERCISE 37.4   REVISING FOR CORRECT CAPITALIZATION

NAME _____ **DATE** _____

In the following sentences, if capitalization is used correctly, write C on the line below the sentence. If a sentence needs revising, write your new version on the lines provided.

EXAMPLE   In 1987, philadelphia's Independence hall was the site of numerous festivities celebrating the American Form of Government.

REVISION   In 1987, Philadelphia's Independence Hall was the site of numerous festivities celebrating the American form of government.

1. Last year, I saw a History Channel documentary about our Nation's capital and decided that I wanted to visit Washington, d.c.

   _____

   _____

2. My uncle Tim, who is a flight attendant based at reagan international airport, lives in Chevy chase, Maryland, and he agreed to show me the sights over Spring break.

   _____

   _____

3. I wanted to see the Declaration of independence, which is displayed at the national archives building.

   _____

   _____

4. We went to the Building, which is at 700 Pennsylvania avenue, but we discovered that we had to enter from Constitution avenue to see the Documents on display.

   _____

   _____

5. Inside, we saw the United States constitution, perhaps the most important document in American History.

   _____

   _____

566

6. later, we went to the Lincoln Memorial, the Jefferson Memorial, and the Washington monument.

_____

_____

7. I was moved by the vietnam veterans memorial, where many people leave notes and mementos of their Loved Ones lost in that War.

_____

_____

8. Down the Mall is the Smithsonian Institution, founded decades ago to preserve national memorabilia of all varieties.

_____

_____

9. I wanted to visit the National Gallery of art, which was exhibiting Pablo Picasso's monumental painting _guernica_, but I ran out of time.

_____

_____

10. All in all, i loved the reminders of all of the people and ideas that made this country what it is, and I even got to see the cherry blossoms—a gift from japan—in bloom.

_____

_____

Abbreviations and Numbers

38

Like the use of capital letters, the use of abbreviations and numbers involves conventions — customary habits accepted by writers and expected by readers. For example, a reader might be able to puzzle out *One Hundred Eleven Est. Eighty-Eighth Anue.* but would find the more conventional form — 111 E. 88th Ave. — far easier to decode. In addition, the conventions for abbreviations and numbers are economical — briefly and efficiently conveying useful information.

ABBREVIATIONS AND NUMBERS IN EVERYDAY USE

Any time you use a telephone book, you see an abundance of abbreviations and numbers that are meant to help readers find the proper information quickly and efficiently. If you look up the American Automobile Association in Chicago, for example, here's what you find.

AAA — CHICAGO MOTOR CLUB
　Emergency 24 Hr. Road Service
　　Toll Free 800-262-6327
　Membership Services and Insurance
　　68 E. Wacker Pl 372-1818

Abbreviations and figures obviously allow the publisher to include a great deal of information in a small amount of space — imagine the phone book without them! Find some other uses of abbreviations and figures in the phone book, the classified ads, or other material where saving space is a high priority. Jot down examples of what you find.

ABBREVIATIONS

Abbreviating titles and academic degrees (53a)

In general, the more common a personal or professional title is, the more often it is abbreviated. Two titles, *Ms.* and *Mrs.*, are always abbreviated; no expanded or full forms of these titles are in use. *Mr.* is almost never spelled out, except perhaps as a way of addressing someone, as in "Listen, mister."

　　Abbreviate certain personal titles when used with specific names. Some titles appear before the name.

Ms. Barbara Hogg	Mr. Gregory Pfarr	Rev. John Dennis
Dr. Erret Hummel	St. Teresa of Avila	

Other titles follow the name.

Alan Palmer, D.D.S.	Suzanne Clark, Ph.D.	Hank Williams Jr.

Use *Ms.* as the common title for women, just as *Mr.* is the common title for men. In current usage, neither term relates to an individual's marital status. Substitute *Miss* or *Mrs.* only when you know that a particular woman prefers to be addressed that way.

Other religious, military, academic, and government titles may be abbreviated whenever they precede a full name; if they appear before only the last name, the title should be written in full.

Sen. Olympia Snowe *or* Senator Snowe

Rev. David Olivier *or* Reverend Olivier

Prof. Laura Rice-Sayre *or* Professor Rice-Sayre

Gen. Amos Halftrack *or* General Halftrack

Note, however, that *Dr.*, like *Mr.*, *Ms.*, or *Mrs.*, may precede a lone surname: *Dr. Spock* is as correct as *Dr. Richard Kimble.*

Do not abbreviate religious, military, academic, and government titles when used without any names.

INCORRECT	My Dr. said the lab results would be ready Wednesday.
	The Sen. took the floor.
CORRECT	My doctor said the lab results would be ready Wednesday.
	The senator took the floor.

Spell out *Reverend* and *Honorable* whenever they are used with *the* and precede an individual's name, as in *the Reverend John Dennis.*

The abbreviations for educational degrees are commonly used whether attached to the names of particular people or not.

BA (bachelor of arts)	BS (bachelor of science)
MA (master of arts)	MS (master of science)
PhD (doctor of philosophy)	

EXAMPLE	He is finishing his MA work this spring.

Abbreviations with years and hours (53b)

Some abbreviations—for example, *F* for *Fahrenheit* and AM for *ante meridiem* ("before noon")—should be used only when preceded by numbers, as in *75°F* or *6:45 AM*. In general, these abbreviations deal with units of measure—temperature, size, quantity, time, and the like.

ABBREVIATION	MEANING	EXAMPLE OF USE
BC or BCE	before Christ or before the common era	399 BC, 12 BCE
AD or CE	*anno Domini,* Latin for "year of our Lord," or common era	AD 49, 49 CE
AM *or* a.m.	*ante meridiem,* Latin for "before noon"	11:15 AM *or* a.m.
PM *or* p.m.	*post meridiem,* Latin for "after noon"	9:00 PM *or* p.m.
r.p.m. *or* rpm	revolutions per minute	2,000 r.p.m. *or* rpm
m.p.h. *or* mph	miles per hour	55 m.p.h. *or* mph
F	Fahrenheit scale	212°F
C	Celsius scale	100°C

Writers traditionally capitalize *BC, BCE, CE,* and *AD* but use lowercase letters for *a.m.* and *p.m.* (Printers and publishers often use small capitals for all six of these abbreviations; when small capitals are used for AM and PM, periods are not necessary.) Note that *BCE* and *CE* are becoming the preferred abbreviations with dates, and both are placed after the year.

The common symbols on the top line of your keyboard are also abbreviations. With the exception of the dollar sign ($), which is allowable in formal writing as long as it is followed by a number, none of the other symbols should be part of formal essay prose. (Graphs, charts, and other modes of visual presentation do sometimes employ some of these abbreviations in captions or identifications, but such charts or graphs are typically parts of memos or technical reports, not essays.)

Acronyms and initial abbreviations (53c)

Countries, companies, and a variety of other organizations regularly shorten their own names to initials. The National Broadcasting Company advertises and identifies itself as *NBC*; Mothers Against Drunk Driving regularly refers to itself as *MADD*. *MADD* is an example of an **acronym**—a set of initials that form a pronounceable word. *NBC*, by contrast, is simply a set of initials. Sets of initials and acronyms are typically written in capital letters and without periods separating them. An exception is *U.S.*, which is usually written with periods. (If you are unsure about the use of periods in a particular abbreviation, consult your dictionary.)

How can you know whether an organization's name can be shortened? Two factors should guide you. If the organization itself uses initials or an acronym, chances are that you may acceptably do so as well. Examples here include *IBM* and *AFL-CIO*. Be sure that your readers will recognize any initials or acronyms you use. For example, the initials *COLA* probably suggest a soft drink to most people. Only a very few readers (those involved in labor-management contracts) may recognize those initials as standing for *cost-of-living adjustment*. When in doubt, write the name or title in full and enclose the initials or the acronym in parentheses immediately following the title.

> In the 1950s and early 1960s, doctors commonly prescribed the drug diethylstilbestrol (DES) for pregnant women. Not until the late 1970s did researchers discover its dangers for female children. Since 1973, more than seventy thousand "DES babies" have been diagnosed with cervical cancer.

Here is a short list of common acronyms and sets of initials:

NATIONS

UK	United Kingdom
UAE	United Arab Emirates

CORPORATIONS

AT&T*	American Telephone and Telegraph
UPI	United Press International

ORGANIZATIONS

OAS	Organization of American States
UN	United Nations
NASA	National Aeronautics and Space Administration
ACLU	American Civil Liberties Union

SCIENTIFIC AND TECHNICAL TERMS

DNA	deoxyribonucleic acid
ROM	read-only memory
AIDS	acquired immune deficiency syndrome
ABM	antiballistic missile

Other kinds of abbreviations (53d, 53e, 53f, 53g)

In composing notes, rough drafts, informal letters, and the like, writers often abbreviate in order to write quickly. Abbreviations can be helpful, but they should generally not appear in the final draft of a college essay.

- Units of measure should be spelled out, not abbreviated.

---

*This example illustrates one of the few instances in which an ampersand (&) is acceptable in college writing.

Our smooth collie weighs ninety-two pounds. [*not* 92 lbs.]

Deke's Harley gets over fifty miles to the gallon. [*not* 50 m.p.g.]

- Names of days, months, and holidays should be spelled out.

Sunday turned out warm and cloudless. [*not* Sun.]

October 21 was our first day of heavy rain. [*not* Oct. 21]

- Geographic names should be spelled out.

New York boasts several major-league sports teams. [*not* N.Y.]

The Columbia River empties into the Pacific at Astoria, Oregon. [*not* Col. R., *not* Astoria, OR]

- Academic subjects should be spelled out.

Psychology and economics are proving to be my most difficult subjects this term. [*not* Psych. and econ.]

Chemistry laboratory sections are scheduled in the afternoons. [*not* Chem. lab sections]

- Divisions of written works should be spelled out.

One of the most famous chapters in *Moby-Dick* is Chapter 32, "Cetology." [*not* chs., *not* Ch. 32]

Those twelve or so pages begin on page 116. [*not* p. 116]

- Company names should be spelled out exactly as used by the company itself. Use *Co.*, *Inc.*, *Ltd.*, and the ampersand only when used by the company itself.

Arrowood Book Company is a small regional publisher of literary titles. [*not* Arrowood Bk. Co.]

NUMBERS

Spelling out or using figures for numbers (53h, 53i, 53j)

Suppose that you are writing about the time of day, weight loss plans, or the cost of various products, services, or programs. Should you spell out the numbers you use, or should you use numerals?

The conventions vary from discipline to discipline. For instance, most scientific or technical journals stipulate that numbers be identified with numerals rather than spelled out in letters. Journalists follow their own set of conventions. College essay writing typically follows the conventions presented here:

- Spell out numbers that can be expressed in one or two words.

  None of the fifty-eight people on board were injured yesterday when a commercial jet made an unscheduled landing outside Pittsburgh.

- Use numerals when an amount cannot be expressed in one or two words.

  With an average paid attendance of 44,258, the football program will have no trouble meeting its budget this year.

- Spell out any number that begins a sentence.

  Fifty-eight people escaped injury yesterday when a commercial jet made an unscheduled landing outside Pittsburgh.

  If a particularly large or cumbersome number begins a sentence, consider recasting the sentence so that the number appears later.

  Four thousand two hundred and sixteen people passed through the turnstiles at the Philomath Rodeo last July.

  The Philomath Rodeo attracted a crowd of 4,216 last July.

- When several numbers appear in one sentence, be consistent: either use numerals in every case, or spell out every number. Take your lead from the rules governing the first number of the sentence.

  This week we served 157 patrons, which is 30 more than last week. [*The first number appears as a numeral, since it cannot be written in one or two words; the second number follows suit.*]

- Use numerals for street addresses, exact amounts of money, days and dates, exact times of day, statistics and scores, measurements, decimals, fractions, percentages, pages and divisions of written works, and identification numbers.

1515 Main Street	7 5/8	9.7
$34.95	pages 44–50	50%, 50 percent
3:35 PM	302 Fifth Street, S.E.*	chapter 60
Patriots won, 21–14	October 16, 1948	account number 0461
5,280 feet	a median score of 66	

- Spell out hours followed by *o'clock*, as in *nine o'clock*. Note that this expression is used with whole numbers only (not, for example, *7:30 o'clock*).

---

*Note that both numerals and spelled-out numbers are necessary here in order to avoid confusion.

EXERCISE 38.1 USING ABBREVIATIONS FOR PERSONAL AND PROFESSIONAL TITLES

NAME _____ **DATE** _____

A. Proofread the following sentences for errors in the use of abbreviations. If a sentence is correct as written, write C after it. If a sentence needs revision, make your correction above the line.

general

EXAMPLES   The World War II invasion of Normandy was led by a gen. who never went into poltics: Omar Bradley.

Mr. Greg Pfarr's paintings have been selected to appear in many juried art shows across the nation. *C*

1. The emergency room Dr. probably saved Rev. Daniels's life.

2. As a young man, Mister Gates dropped out of Harvard before he had earned his BA.

3. Sir Thomas More, now recognized as a St., was an English statesman.

4. The speaker of the house recognized the jr. congressional rep. from Indiana.

5. My chemistry prof. prefers that we call her "Ms. Babatunde."

6. Years ago, a high school diploma marked excellent academic achievement; today, many people return to school for an MA or a PhD after finishing college.

7. One of Gary Cooper's finest roles was the real-life World War II hero Sgt. York.

B. Proofread the following passage for errors in the use of abbreviations. Mark any corrections above the line.

A prof. of law at Puget State University, Jermaine Jones is campaigning to be elected state Sen. from his district. Mister Jones's father is a well-known medical Dr. in the community, and his mother teaches in the Phd program of Puget State's Communications Dept. A former Cpl. in the Marine Corps, he feels he has special qualifications that would make him an excellent rep. of his constituency.

EXERCISE 38.2   USING ABBREVIATIONS WITH YEARS AND DATES/
USING SYMBOLS

NAME _____   **DATE** _____

**If a sentence contains unacceptable abbreviations or symbols, underline these abbrevia-
tions or symbols, and write out the full versions on the lines provided. If an abbreviation is
incorrect, correct it on the lines provided. If a sentence as written is correct and acceptable
in formal prose, write *C* on the line after the sentence.**

EXAMPLE   The individual with the winning # will receive an annual income in excess of $60,000
± a contract to appear in lottery advertising. <u>number, plus</u> _____

1. Spenser & Carole plan to arrive at the box office early in the a.m. in order to be first in line
   for tickets. _____

   _____

2. My father's first job paid only a $ or so an hour, but I was paid $5.75 an hour for my first
   summer job. _____

   _____

3. The class begins at 7:30 a.m., but I don't like to wake up before noon. _____

   _____

4. The home-run record set by Roger Maris in 1961 has been marked with an * in the record
   books because of the unusual length of the playing season. _____

   _____

5. At how many m.p.h. is a hurricane considered a Category 4? _____

   _____

6. The weather report claimed that it was 104°F this afternoon, but the information meant
   little to Claudio, who was accustomed to the C scale. _____

   _____

7. The Pantheon in Rome was completed in 27 BCE, and it still attracts admiring visitors.

_____

8. Someone found a hundred $ bill in the parking lot. _____

_____

9. The # one problem facing the school is a lack of diversity among the faculty. _____

_____

10. The p.m. trains run once an hour except between 5:00 and 8:00 p.m., when they run every

twenty minutes. _____

_____

EXERCISE 38.3   USING ACRONYMS AND INITIAL ABBREVIATIONS

Identify ten of the following abbreviations or acronyms. List the abbreviation or acronym, spell it out, and use it in a sentence. If any are not familiar, look them up in a dictionary. (Many college dictionaries include a special section listing abbreviations and their meanings.) Use your own paper, and follow the format of the example.

EXAMPLE   Abbreviation/Acronym: DWI
Long form: driving while intoxicated
Sample sentence: Jack was cited for his third DWI offense.

ORGANIZATIONS

HBO	WNBA	NATO	USDA	UAW	PBS
NAACP	CIA	FEMA	AA	WHO	

SCIENTIFIC/TECHNICAL

DOS	ENT	RNA	RBC
HDL	EKG	REM	ROM

TERMS

ASAP	CPR	MIA	DVD
SALT	DMZ	AWOL	CD

EXERCISE 38.4 CHECKING FOR APPROPRIATE USE OF ABBREVIATIONS

NAME _____ **DATE** _____

Check for inappropriate uses of abbreviations in the following paragraphs. Cross out inappropriate abbreviations, and write your correction in the space above.

On Aug. 16, 1996, Helena became anorexic. At the time, she was five ft. eight in. tall. She weighed 150 lbs., which was not especially heavy for someone of her ht. and build. But her brothers teased her about her wt. in front of out-of-town relatives, and she felt humiliated. "I'll show *them*," she thought, and from that moment on she tried to lose weight by every possible means. She paid attention to advertisements from any co. that made diet colas or sugar-free foods. She learned to count the no. of calories in everything she ate. At first, no one really noticed; when they began to pay attn., Helena discovered that she liked being in the spotlight. Her psych. teacher urged her to get counseling, and her phys. ed. classmates whispered about her, but Helena did not want to change. She filled pp. of diaries with details about the things she had avoided eating even as she read cookbooks in her spare time, but she did not feel that either her obsession with food or her desire not to eat was peculiar.

One day, however — it was Mon., Nov. 17, 1998 — something happened to make Helena change her mind. As her history class discussed a ch. in their textbook on W.W. II, she was riveted by photographs of people liberated from a Ger. concentration camp. "Hey, they look like Helena," snickered a classmate, and Helena realized w. horror that it was true. She went home from school that day and wept. Then she did the hardest thing she had ever done: she asked her parents to help her find a Dr. who could make her better. Helena is still struggling with her med. condition, but she is finally on the rd. to recovery.

EXERCISE 38.5 WRITING NUMBERS

NAME _____ **DATE** _____

Read the passage below for any errors in the presentation of numbers. Underline any errors you find, and make your corrections in the space above each line.

The Seattle Art Museum, located at one hundred University Street, is 1 of the city's premier institutions. Its current building, which opened in nineteen hundred ninety-one, was designed by the architect Robert Venturi. At its entrance is a forty-two-foot mechanical sculpture by Jonathan Borofsky called *Hammering Man*, which resembles exactly that. A grand staircase rises from the 1st-floor lobby to the second-level gallery, which plays host to special event exhibits. One popular recent show there was an exhibit of the works of Louis Comfort Tiffany, which opened on October twenty-third of last year and closed on January twenty-first. The 3rd and 4th levels display works from the permanent collection.

The museum originally opened in nineteen hundred thirty-three in a building that now houses the Seattle Asian Art Museum. The permanent collection includes more than 5,000 works, ranging from paintings by European masters to stunning Native American artifacts. The museum also hosts 2 to 4 traveling exhibitions each year. It has accommodated as many as three thousand seven hundred fifty visitors on a single day. The museum is open Tuesdays through Sundays from ten-thirty a.m. until five-thirty p.m., with special late-night hours on Thursdays. Admission is eight dollars and fifty cents for adults and free for children under 12.

Italics

39

Italic type—type that slants like *this*—is used by word-processing programs and by printers in a variety of conventional ways. If you use computer equipment to write and print your work, you can probably produce actual italics. Otherwise, underlining is the standard substitute. If you cannot produce italics, you should mentally translate every mention of *italicizing* to mean "underlining."

ITALICS IN EVERYDAY USE

Look around, and you'll see italics used in many ways: on signs, in pamphlets, on the sides of trucks. On a recent visit to Chicago, a student looking for good, cheap food found this listing in a visitor's guide:

> *Gold Coast Dogs* (418 North State). Chicago is serious about hot dogs. A good Chicago hot dog is an all-beef critter with natural casing, in a steamed bun and topped with your choice of the following (aka *everything*): yellow mustard, relish, raw chopped onion, tomato wedges, a dill pickle sliced lengthwise, maybe jalapeño peppers if you're perverse, and celery salt. A good Chicago hot dog *never* touches catsup, brown mustard, cooked onions, cheese, or sauerkraut.

For what purposes are the italics used in this listing? Look around you for some examples of italics in use, and write down two or three interesting examples.

Italics for titles (54a)

Writers identify titles either with italics or with quotation marks. In general, italics are reserved for the titles of long or complete works, and quotation marks identify titles of shorter works or sections of works. Thus in a manuscript, a book title is italicized, but a chapter title is placed in quotation marks. The title of a book of poems is italicized, but the title of a particular poem is placed in quotation marks. The name of a television series is italicized, but the name of a particular episode is identified by quotation marks. (For a review of the use of quotation marks, see Chapter 35.)

- Italicize book, magazine, journal, pamphlet, and newspaper titles.

BOOKS	*Native Son, The Awakening, Ulysses* [Note that sacred books (the Bible or the Koran, for example) are not italicized, nor are the divisions within them. In general, writers do not italicize the titles of public documents such as the Constitution, the Kyoto Protocol, or Magna Carta.]
MAGAZINES, JOURNALS, PAMPHLETS, AND NEWSPAPERS	*Newsweek, Journal of the American Medical Association, North American Review,* the *American Scholar, Common Sense,* the *New York Times,* the *Chicago Sun-Times* [Note that *the* is not italicized or capitalized before the name of a magazine even if it is part of the official name. Similarly, the word *magazine* is not italicized or capitalized following the name. Only when the name of a city is part of the official name of a newspaper is the city name italicized (thus *New York Times,* New York *Daily News*).]

- Italicize the titles of plays, long poems, long musical works, choreographed works, paintings, and sculptures.

PLAYS	*A Midsummer Night's Dream, Rent*
LONG POEMS	*Paradise Lost, Paterson*
LONG MUSICAL WORKS	*The Joshua Tree, The Wall, La Bohème, Messiah* [Note that classical works identified by form, number, and key are not italicized (for example, Sonata in F Minor).]
CHOREOGRAPHED WORKS	Twyla Tharp's *Movin' Out,* Agnes de Mille's *Rodeo*
PAINTINGS	*Starry Night, The Peaceable Kingdom*
SCULPTURES	*The Sphere,* the *Pietà*

- Italicize the titles of television series, other television programs, and radio programs.

TELEVISION SERIES AND PROGRAMS	*American Idol, CSI*
RADIO PROGRAMS	*The Howard Stern Show, A Prairie Home Companion*

Italics for words, letters, and numbers referred to as terms (54b)

Use italics whenever you want readers to see that you refer to a particular word, letter, or number not for its meaning but for itself.

How many *m*'s are there in *accommodate*?

In the inscriptions on some old buildings, the *u*'s look like *v*'s.

The binary system contains only *0*'s and *1*'s.

Also use italics to indicate a word you are about to discuss or define.

The word *prognosticate* has Latin origins.

Italics for non-English words and phrases (54c)

Sometimes writers decide to use non-English words in their English prose. Some words or phrases, such as *Gesundheit* (German) and *gracias* (Spanish), are commonly understood by many English speakers and writers, even though these expressions are not part of English itself. When you use words such as these, italicize them (except as noted in the discussion that concludes this section).

> James Bond has a license to kill, but ethically he should only use it in circumstances where he could legally plead *se defendendo*, or self defense.
>
> In the Gorbachev era, the key word in Soviet-American relations was *glasnost*.
>
> That puppy has more energy and *joie de vivre* than it can handle.

However, notice this example: *He considered making the spaghetti from scratch but decided to buy it from Cosello's instead.* In this example, the word *spaghetti* is not given special treatment. Some originally foreign words are now considered part of the English language and do not need to be italicized. When in doubt about whether to italicize a particular word, consult a good dictionary.

Italics for names of vehicles (54d)

Italicize the names of specific ships, trains, aircraft, and spacecraft. Capitalize but do not italicize the names of specific production models.

SHIPS	the *Golden Hinde*, the USS *Missouri*, the trawler *Alice III*
TRAINS	the *Golden Zephyr*, the *City of New Orleans*
AIRCRAFT AND SPACECRAFT	*Columbia*, *Echo I*, the *Graf Zeppelin*
SPECIFIC PRODUCTION MODELS	Learjet, Volkswagen Rabbit, Stealth bomber

The initials *SS*, *USS*, *HMS*, and the like before a specific name are capitalized but not italicized. Do not italicize the word *the* before the name of a vehicle. Finally, neither italicize nor capitalize generic terms identifying classes or types of vehicles.

the space shuttle *Atlantis*

the aircraft carrier *Eisenhower*

the steamship *Titanic*

Italics for special emphasis (54e)

Especially in informal writing and in dialogue, italics can be used sparingly to help readers actually hear the intonations of a person speaking. Note the differences in the following sentences:

The workers insisted they could not finish until at least Monday afternoon. [*no special emphasis*]

The *workers* insisted they could not finish until at least Monday afternoon. [*The workers insist one thing, but perhaps someone else is saying something else.*]

The workers insisted they could not finish until *at least* Monday afternoon. [*This version suggests that the job will take longer than the Monday afternoon deadline.*]

Here is another example; this time the emphasis is straightforward:

If we want to achieve our objectives, we *must* vote, and together we *will* win.

EXERCISE 39.1 ITALICIZING TITLES AND WORDS, LETTERS, OR NUMBERS REFERRED TO AS TERMS

NAME _____ **DATE** _____

Most (but not all) of the following sentences contain titles or other words that should be italicized. Underline these words. If a sentence is correct as written, write C beside it.

> **EXAMPLES** As a result of his extensive travel covering events such as the Olympics for television's <u>Wide World of Sports</u>, Jim McKay has seen the world.
>
> The word <u>separate</u> is one that many people misspell.

1. Without realizing it, my mother often watches reruns of Law and Order episodes she has already seen.

2. The name of the magazine Young Miss was changed to YM because the former was seen as lacking sophistication.

3. Alice Walker's novel The Color Purple has been adapted as a film and as a Broadway musical.

4. The orchestra began with a brilliant performance of Stravinsky's Firebird Suite and ended the program with Prokofiev's Symphony No. 6.

5. My friend often uses the word infer when he means refer.

6. Interested travelers can send away for the brochure A Guide to Visiting Civil Rights Monuments.

7. Many of Tennessee Williams's major plays have been made into films — including The Glass Menagerie, A Streetcar Named Desire, and Cat on a Hot Tin Roof — but my favorite has always been The Night of the Iguana, directed by John Huston.

8. The newsstand had been ransacked, and copies of the Wall Street Journal, the International Herald Tribune, and the Chronicle of Higher Education were scattered together uneasily with High Society, National Lampoon, and Teen People.

9. Native English speakers in French or German classes finally find out the difficulties non-native speakers encounter here in the United States.

10. One Web site grades episodes of The Sopranos according to a formula known as StR, which stands for the length of time from the opening credits to Tony's appearance in a bathrobe.

11. Last year we saw one of the four original, handwritten, fifteenth-century copies of Magna Carta on temporary display at the Huntington Library.

12. Overlooking the town, a large M is painted on the face of Mount Sentinel.

EXERCISE 39.2 ITALICIZING NON-ENGLISH WORDS OR PHRASES

Choose and circle ten items from the list below. On your own paper, write a sentence using each of the items you chose. If the word or phrase should be italicized as foreign, be sure it is underlined in your sentence. You may need to consult a good dictionary for this exercise. (College dictionaries may include foreign words in the general alphabetical list or in a special section on foreign words. Check your dictionary carefully to figure out where it covers such words.)

1. a priori
2. au contraire
3. bona fide
4. bon mot
5. bon vivant
6. c'est la vie

7. coup de grâce
8. coup d'état
9. ersatz
10. fait accompli
11. fresco
12. glasnost

13. habeas corpus
14. habitué
15. hasta la vista
16. jeune fille
17. joie de vivre
18. machismo

19. sans souci
20. sotto voce
21. trompe l'oeil
22. vis-à-vis

EXERCISE 39.3   ITALICIZING THE NAMES OF VEHICLES

NAME _____   DATE _____

Underline each name that should be italicized in the following sentences. If a sentence is correct as written, write *C* beside it.

> **EXAMPLE**   The battleship <u>Arizona</u> remains in Pearl Harbor as a memorial to those who died there on December 7, 1941.

1. The Queen Elizabeth II remains one of the world's most luxurious ocean liners.

2. Low-cost airlines like Southwest and JetBlue have provided stiff competition for many of the major carriers.

3. The Intrepid, a World War II aircraft carrier, has become a floating museum permanently anchored in New York City.

4. Fans of science fiction know that Captain Kirk and his crew traveled through space on board the starship Enterprise.

5. In 1937, the explosion of the Hindenburg effectively ended the use of airships for passenger service.

6. My grandparents rode on the Twentieth Century when they traveled by rail from New York to Chicago.

7. The first Mercury capsule, Freedom 7, carried astronaut Alan Shepard at speeds exceeding five thousand miles per hour.

8. The maiden voyage of the gigantic Spruce Goose, though brief, ushered in the modern age of air travel.

9. Norine likes cruising in her grandmother's Chevy Vega.

10. The Enola Gay will forever be remembered as the aircraft from which an atomic bomb was dropped on Hiroshima.

EXERCISE 39.4   ITALICIZING FOR EMPHASIS

NAME _____   **DATE** _____

A. Using your own paper, briefly analyze the emphasis created by the use of italics in the following sentences.

EXAMPLE   *I* heartily agree with you.
Italicizing *I* suggests that although the speaker agrees, someone else disagrees; italicizing *I* implies and highlights a contrast.

1. It seems that some of my co-workers will do *anything* to get ahead in the company.

2. We all expected that *you* would lock the front door.

3. Sometimes it seems as though spring will *never* arrive.

4. My daughter often complains that *all* the other kids are doing something I won't allow her to do.

5. Reading a book is easy. What is difficult is *writing* one.

B. Read the following passage, noting the use of italics for emphasis. Underline any other words that should be in italics. Circle any words that should not be italicized. Keep in mind the likely context for this kind of writing.

The Vikings were *dreaded warriors* who disrupted trade routes, seized valued treasures, and *terrorized* those they attacked. Because they were *excellent seafarers*, the Vikings often *attacked quickly*, arriving by ship from the sea or from a river. Then they left equally quickly, carrying the *spoils* of the day. Given their remarkable success, it is not surprising that some histories now hail this period as the *Viking Age.*

Hyphens

40

Writers use hyphens to form compound words (such as *after-school* in the phrase *my after-school activities*), to write out fractions (*one-half*) and two-digit numbers (*twenty-two*), to divide words at the end of a typed line, and to prevent misreading. This chapter discusses each of these uses.

HYPHENS IN EVERYDAY USE

Hyphens play a number of roles in our everyday lives. You might go to your part-time job, listen to hip-hop or old-fashioned love songs, and eat a Tex-Mex meal and wash it down with a medium-size Coca-Cola, all while wearing flip-flops and a T-shirt. Make a list of some of the hyphenated words or phrases you run across in a day.

Hyphens with compound words (55a)

English is full of **compound words** (such as *backpack*, *underline*, and *payday*) that frequent usage has joined together to make single words. Other compound words are spelled with hyphens, as in *left-handed*. And some are spelled as two separate words, as in *lame duck* and *mountain range*. When you use compound words, you may have to consult a dictionary to verify the spelling. If your compound word is a noun and your college dictionary does not list it, the compound word is probably two words and should be written as such.

Sometimes you may wish to construct and use compound words as modifiers. How to do so correctly is the subject of the discussion that follows.

Forming compound adjectives

Often, you will want to combine words into adjectives that are not listed in a dictionary.

The little boy had *carrot-colored* hair and matching freckles.

The people in this office are a *well-matched* group.

By linking these words with hyphens, you turn them into single adjectives that modify the nouns that follow them. The basic reason for using hyphens in cases like these is to make your meaning clear.

Here are some tips to help you hyphenate compounds correctly:

- Hyphenate a compound adjective appearing before a noun; do not hyphenate the compound adjective when it follows the noun. In the previous examples, the adjectives *carrot-colored* and *well-matched* precede the nouns *hair* and *group*, respectively. If the adjectives followed the nouns in those sentences, hyphens would not be used.

  The boy had freckles to match his hair, which was carrot colored.

  The people in this office are well matched.

- Never use a hyphen to join an adverb ending in *-ly* to another word.

  Her radically different approach produced excellent results.

  A crowd of morbidly curious onlookers gathered at the accident scene.

- When using comparatives or superlatives, creating compounds depends on what the adjectives are describing. Do not hyphenate if both modifiers describe the noun.

  The second course provides more extensive coverage.

- Do hyphenate if the first modifier describes the second modifier.

  This is the best-paid job in the city.

- Use suspended hyphens to shorten a series of compound modifiers sharing the same word (or words).

  This summer, the eight-, nine-, and ten-year-old campers were placed in a single group.

Using hyphens to create your own compounds for special effect

Suppose you wish to describe a picture that you are sending to family or friends. You are in the picture, and the look on your face is not exactly cheerful. You might write, *Don't worry about that down-on-my-luck expression.* You have strung four words together with hyphens. By so doing, you are telling your readers that the four-word combination has a single meaning. In theory, you could replace *down-on-my-luck* with a single adjective such as *dejected*, as in *Don't worry about that dejected expression.*

When speaking or writing informally, we often create spur-of-the-moment compounds. Though informal (and hence not always appropriate in formal writing situations), such compounds add flair and can make for more interesting prose.

We enjoyed another August-in-October day.

After four hurry-up-and-wait hours in the airport, I was ready to fly anywhere.

Again, note that the hyphens connect words that form a single modifier positioned in front of a noun.

Sometimes the same words use hyphens when functioning as a modifier but use no hyphens when functioning as separate modifiers and nouns.

The stained glass cast colorful shadows on the pews. [stained glass = *adjective + noun*]

Stained-glass artistry made the church distinctive and inspiring. [stained-glass = *single adjective*]

Officials estimate we need a month of rain to replenish the city's water supply. [water supply = *modifying noun + noun*]

The plumber says our water-supply pipe has corroded and needs replacing. [water-supply = *single adjective*]

Using hyphens with fractions and compound numbers

Writers conventionally use hyphens to spell out fractions. The fraction *3/4* would be spelled out as *three-fourths*. Here the hyphen acts (as it always does) to connect separate words in order to form one unit, one thing—in this case, one fractional number.

Compound numbers from *twenty-one* to *ninety-nine* are also spelled out with hyphens. Numbers higher than *ninety-nine* are not hyphenated, no matter how long they may be when written out, except for parts from *twenty-one* to *ninety-nine*. (Remember that numbers expressed in more than two words can also be written as numerals.) For example, to reproduce the number *300,354* in words, write *three hundred thousand three hundred fifty-four*. Note that the one hyphen occurs in the part of the number between *twenty-one* and *ninety-nine*.

Hyphens with prefixes and suffixes (55b)

Over the years, many **prefixes** (letters added to the front of a word) and **suffixes** (letters added to the end of a word) have been attached to some words so frequently that now no hyphen is used to connect them. *Unusual, disinterested, predestined*—these are all examples of words containing prefixes and no hyphens.

However, several prefixes and suffixes do commonly take hyphens. Prefixes attached to numerals or to capitalized words always take hyphens, as in *pre-1914* and *un-Christian*. When a prefix is attached to a compound word, use a hyphen, as in *pro-civil rights*. Other prefixes that commonly take hyphens include the following:

all- as in *all-inclusive*	*quasi-* as in *quasi-complete*
ex- as in *ex-softball player*	*self-* as in *self-employed*
half- as in *half-convinced*	*twenty-* as in *twenty-odd*

Suffixes that commonly take hyphens include the following:

-elect as in *treasurer-elect*　　　*-odd* as in *forty-odd years old*

Unfortunately, there are a number of exceptions to the general guideline. *Halfback* and *selfhood* are exceptions; over time, the hyphen has been dropped from these words. And some suffixes, such as *-like* and *-wise*, sometimes take hyphens and sometimes do not (for example, *warlike, elephant-like*). The only way to identify such exceptions is to consult a dictionary.

Hyphens to clarify meaning

Sometimes hyphens are crucial to meaning. Consider these sentences:

The couch needs to be recovered after the flood.

The couch needs to be re-covered after the flood.

The first sentence says that the couch is lost (perhaps washed away) and needs to be found. The second sentence says that the couch's upholstery needs repair. There also are significant differences between *procreation* and *pro-creation* and between *re-create* and *recreate*.

Hyphens are also commonly used to separate suffixes from their roots whenever the combination would result in three identical consonants in a row. Thus *skill+less* is spelled *skill-less*.

When adding a prefix results in the repetition of a vowel (*anti-imperialist*, for example), a hyphen is often used. However, this practice is violated too frequently to be considered a reliable guideline (consider *reenlist, cooperate*, and the like). When in doubt, consult your dictionary.

Combinations of single letters and roots are nearly always hyphenated, unless they form the names of musical notes or keys. Here are some examples: *T-shirt, I-beam, F sharp, B major.*

Hyphens can also create momentary confusion at the end of a line. Suppose that you are reading this sentence:

Darius sells men's clothing for Macy's, and Michael is a bus-
boy at the Ringside.

For at least a moment, the word *bus* appears to be part of that sentence; for just a moment, it sounds as though Michael is a transportation vehicle. Here is another example:

When I get up late and have early-morning appointments, I may carelessly skip breakfast.

Although such hyphenation follows the guidelines presented in the next section, in these cases it still leads to confusion. Whenever you hyphenate at the end of a line, make sure that you do not inadvertently send a confusing message.

Hyphens to divide words at the end of a line (55c)

One of the very last things writers do is produce a final copy. More and more frequently, this copy is printed from computer equipment. Most computer software eliminates the problem of end-of-line hyphenation through justification or word wrap (moving the whole word to the next line). But if you are typing on a typewriter, you may find that you do not have enough room to fit a word on a line. If you must break a word, follow these conventions:

1. Place the hyphen after the last letter on the line, not at the beginning of the next line.
2. Divide words only between syllables, and never divide a one-syllable word. Either squeeze a one-syllable word onto the end of the line, or shift it to the next line. If you are not sure about the syllabic breaks for a particular word, check your dictionary.
3. Whenever possible, begin the part of the divided word on the new line with a consonant (*medi-tate* rather than *med-itate*).
4. Divide words that contain doubled consonants between the doubled letters (as in *occur-ring*) *unless* the doubled consonants are part of the root word (not *calling* but *call-ing*).
5. Never divide the last word on a page (so you will never begin a new page with only part of a word).
6. Never leave a single letter at the end of a line or fewer than three letters at the beginning of a line.
7. Do not divide contractions, numerals, acronyms, or abbreviations.

    UNACCEPTABLE   Though the eclipse was scheduled to begin at 9:-
    38 AM, heavy cloud cover made observation impossible.

    Ellen called to let you know that she would-
    n't be able to meet with you until after 2:00 PM.

    The children collected donations for UNI-
    CEF during the last week of October.

8. Divide words that already contain hyphens only at a hyphen.

    UNACCEPTABLE   The plane seated twelve and was equipped with a jet-pro-
    pelled engine.

    ACCEPTABLE   The plane seated twelve and was equipped with a jet-
    propelled engine.

EXERCISE 40.1 HYPHENATING COMPOUND WORDS AND COMPOUND MODIFIERS

NAME _____ **DATE** _____

Many (but not all) of the sentences below use hyphens or compound words incorrectly. If a sentence needs revising, write your version on the lines. If hyphens and compounds are used correctly, write C on the line below the sentence.

> **EXAMPLES** Minh spent his afternoon entertaining the six-year-olds, seven-year-olds, and eight-year-olds.
> _Minh spent his afternoon entertaining the six-, seven-, and eight-year-olds._
>
> Stained-glass artistry made the church distinctive and inspiring.
> _C_

1. Many consider it ill mannered not to follow-up with a thank you note after a job interview.

   _____

   _____

2. Researchers conducted a door-to-door survey to determine the favored site for the new play-ground.

   _____

   _____

3. The apartment is fully-equipped with a stove, refrigerator, microwave, and stacked washer drier combination.

   _____

   _____

4. The before-and-after photographs reveal the extent of the painting's restoration.

   _____

   _____

5. My brother was out-of-work for almost a year before he found a full time job with an advertising agency.

   _____

   _____

6. The so called psychic reader asked me a lot of leading questions in the hope that I would give her enough hints to make a prediction.

_____

_____

7. She shook the last few nickels and pennies out of the coinpurse and held them out in her sticky hand.

_____

_____

8. Almost everything about U.S. elections is geared to the two party system.

_____

_____

9. Many argue that abortion is not just a two-sided or three-sided question.

_____

_____

10. After two days of pitching and yawing on a fishing boat, I feel weak-kneed, windburned, and weather beaten.

_____

_____

11. His strangely-perfect hair sat like a helmet on his head, so we were convinced that it was a toupee.

_____

_____

12. The sales clerk's in your face attitude would be more at home in a wrestling-ring than in the hardware department.

_____

_____

EXERCISE 40.2 HYPHENATING PREFIXES AND SUFFIXES, AND FRACTIONS AND COMPOUND NUMBERS

NAME _____ **DATE** _____

A. Each item below is either a number or a word starting with a prefix or ending with a suffix. Construct sentences that use the specified words correctly. Consult your dictionary as needed.

> **EXAMPLE**   thirty-six+odd
> After thirty-six-odd years, she trusted her own judgment. _____

1. 4/10 (write using words) _____

   _____

2. pro+tax reform_____

   _____

3. pre+existing _____

   _____

4. non+American _____

   _____

5. post+World War II _____

   _____

6. all+inclusive _____

   _____

7. anti+Washington _____

   _____

8. sub+marine _____

   _____

9. machine+like _____

_____

10. mid+stream _____

_____

11. anti+freeze _____

_____

12. in+decisive _____

_____

13. 405,222 (write using words) _____

_____

14. 4,000 (write using words) _____

_____

15. ex+convict _____

_____

B. Check the words in the following passage for the correct use of hyphens. Add any needed hyphens in the space above the word; cross out any extra hyphens.

Dining Out for Life is a program that brings to-gether volunteers, corporate sponsors, and restaurants for one special night each year to raise funds for organizations that pro-vide services for people with HIV and AIDS. Co created by ActionAIDS volunteers in Philadelphia in 1991, Dining Out for Life became a national event in 1993 when ActionAIDS offered licenses to service programs a-cross the nation. Since then, Dining Out for Life has grown throughout the country and is now produced in thirty three cities in the United States and Canada. More than twenty five hundred restaurants a year donate a portion of their pro-ceeds — up to as much as one third — on a designated night to the licensed agency in their city. In ex-change for their financial support, restaurants are listed in a city-wide marketing campaign to increase customer traffic. In addition, volunteers (so called "ambassadors") greet patrons at the participating restaurants, ex-plain the mission of the agency being benefited, and give patrons the opportunity to make donations of their own. Each year on the night of Dining Out for Life, more than twenty two million dollars is raised to support the missions of AIDS agencies.

EXERCISE 40.3   HYPHENATING TO CLARIFY MEANING

NAME _____ **DATE** _____

Use each of the specified words below correctly in a sentence. Consult your dictionary if necessary.

EXAMPLE   pro-creation <u>The pro-creation camp has definite opinions about how science ought</u> <u>to be taught.</u>

1. procreation _____

   _____

2. re-cover _____

   _____

3. recollect _____

   _____

4. re-collect _____

   _____

5. resort _____

   _____

6. re-sort _____

   _____

7. retread _____

   _____

8. re-tread _____

   _____

9. recoil _____

_____

10. re-coil_____

_____

11. protesting _____

_____

12. pro-testing_____

_____

13. cooperate_____

_____

14. co-operate _____

_____

NAME _____ **DATE** _____

Proofread the following paragraph for confusing or inaccurate hyphenation. Underline the errors you find, and correct each in the space above it. Consult a dictionary whenever necessary.

A well known first in exploration was the 1953 mountain climbing expedition that reached the top of Mount Everest. Edmund Hillary, a New-Zealander, usually receives credit for being the first person to scale the famous peak, but his team-mate, Tenzing Norgay, who reached the summit with Hillary, was doubt-less at least partially-responsible for the success of the expedition. Norgay was a Sherpa, one of the mountain dwelling people who live and work in high altitude Himalayan villages. Hillary hired him to guide the climbers up the 29,000 foot mountain. Perhaps because Norgay was a hired-helper instead of a planner of the climb, and perhaps because he was a non white member of a British expedition during the final days of British imperialism, his name was an after-thought in most accounts at the time. Although he was il-literate, Norgay was multi-lingual, speaking at-least seven languages, and he created several books by dictating them. He was only thirty nine when he climbed with Hillary, and he later earned financial rewards by opening a mountaineering school in India. Second and perhaps third generation Norgay climbers will carry on the tradition. Tenzing's son Jamling Norgay once explained that his father had dis-liked the idea of his children scaling Everest; he had wanted them to be well-educated and well-paid instead, so he sent each of them to American schools. However, Jamling, who had wanted to climb the mountain since he was eighteen-years-old, finally led an expedition up Everest and fulfilled his own life-long dream.

NAME _____ **DATE** _____

Many of the following sentences employ unacceptable hyphenation. Underline any improperly hyphenated word; make your correction in the space above the line. On the line below the sentence, explain briefly what is wrong with the use of the hyphen. If a sentence is acceptable as written, write C on the line below the sentence. (Note: Treat proper nouns like all other nouns.)

EXAMPLE   Ellen called to let you know that she <u>would-</u>   *wouldn't*
n't be able to meet with you until after 2:00 PM.
<u>Contractions should not be hyphenated.</u>

1. The plot hatched by the insurgents was the most fiendish and diabol-
ical that we had ever heard of.

   _____

2. When we visited the Senate, we were surprised to encounter a group of lobbyists waiting outside our representative's door.

   _____

3. Despite the fact that the measures taken by the conservationists were well-in-
tentioned, the results ended up being detrimental to the environment.

   _____

4. The honeymooners enjoyed watching the pedestrians they passed as they strol-
led through the streets of Paris.

   _____

5. After two days alone with a toddler, he had run out of both patience and ideas.

   _____

6. The space shuttle program has produced some huge successes for NA-
SA, but many people witnessed its most horrifying tragedies.

   _____

7. Baseball trivia buffs will recall the 1987 St. Louis versus Minnesota World Series as the first in which the home team won every game.

_____

8. We spent the afternoon driving the overheated car slowly through the mountain pass.

_____

9. We worked hard to learn English so that we could overcome the problems we had faced as recent immigrants.

_____

10. Trying to help, Maggie poured her own milk and spilled it all over the kitchen floor.

_____

PART 9

FOR MULTILINGUAL WRITERS

"The story of the American people . . . is told in the rich accents of Cherokee, Spanish, German, Dutch, Yiddish, French, Menomenie, Japanese, Norwegian, Arabic, Aleut, Polish, Navajo, Thai, Portuguese, Caribbean creoles, and scores of other tongues."
— HARVEY DANIELS

PREVIEW QUESTIONS

These questions are designed to help you decide what you need to study. Read each sentence, and underline the correct word or words from the choices provided within the sentence. (Answers to preview questions are at the back of the book.)

1. Mari, who enjoys listening to (the *or* no article) music, attended (a *or* no article) concert performed by (a *or* the *or* no article) Philadelphia Orchestra.

2. We can save (the *or* some) money on (the *or* no article) dinner if we use (the *or* some) coupon that I cut out of (a *or* the) student newspaper.

3. This chili needs (the *or* some) onions and peppers.

4. Dinner included (rice *or* rices) and (bean *or* beans).

5. The (three laughing *or* laughing three) children threw a ball for the (brown large *or* large brown) dog.

6. I waited for more than half an hour before the bus finally (arrive *or* arrived).

7. Since I have been going to the writing lab, I (got *or* have gotten) better grades on my papers than I (do *or* did) before.

8. Before the popularity of cell phones, people (cannot *or* could not) stay in touch as easily because pay telephones (are *or* were) their only way of making calls.

9. The pills are (in *or* on) a bottle (in *or* on) the second shelf (in *or* on) the medicine cabinet.

10. Ulrike arrived (at *or* to) the airport (on *or* at) 9:00 p.m., and her brother was waiting (at *or* on) the gate to (pick up her *or* pick her up).

11. The paper is due (in *or* on) Monday, but the exam will take place (in *or* on) the first Wednesday (in *or* on) December.

12. (Are *or* There are) several different ways to examine the problem.

13. Ajay was standing at the bus stop when the accident (was happening *or* happened).

14. She is exhausted because she (has been studying *or* been studying) for hours.

15. My six-year-old sister can (reads *or* read) very well.

16. I agreed (to open *or* opening) the store on Monday.

17. This large pot is the best for (to make *or* making) soup stock.

18. The house that (my uncle owns *or* my uncle owns it) needs a new roof.

19. If it rains for several days in a row, the roof (may leak *or* would have leaked).

20. If I finish my paper, I (watch *or* will watch) a video.

21. If you (would not have bought *or* had not bought) a car, you would not have been able to accept your new job.

22. If you (lived *or* would live) in New York, you (would probably have *or* probably would have) a hard time finding an affordable apartment.

Clauses and Sentences

41

In English, sentences are built from one or more **clauses**, groups of words containing both a subject and a predicate.

> He opened the door *that was painted red.* [*independent clause + dependent clause*]
>
> She just left for the airport *because the flight is late.* [*independent clause + dependent clause*]

A sentence itself can be an independent clause. An **independent clause** has a subject and a predicate; it is grammatically complete and expresses a thought, and it can stand alone as a sentence. A **dependent clause** cannot, in contrast, stand alone. Instead, a dependent clause must be connected to a clause that can stand independently (see Chapter 16). Because clauses are the basic building blocks of English sentences, they sometimes require special attention. Writers must make sure that all required sentence elements are explicitly stated in a sentence and are logically positioned and correctly connected with one another.

CLAUSES AND SENTENCES IN EVERYDAY USE

Signs and newspaper headlines often omit sentence elements that are otherwise required, as these examples illustrate.

NO HOT WATER TOMORROW
(*There will be no hot water tomorrow.*)

JUDGE REBUKED FOR STATEMENT TO JURY
(*A judge has been rebuked for making a statement to the jury.*)

Collect other examples like these, and see if you can formulate general rules about what elements can be omitted and what elements cannot (for instance, articles can but prepositions cannot).

Explicit subjects (57a)

In formal English, every sentence must have an explicit subject and an explicit predicate. The subject position in a sentence must be filled, even if it is filled only by a pronoun.

> The *temperature* is dropping.
>
> The *rain* continues to fall.
>
> *It* is cold and rainy tonight.
>
> *You* are not going to believe this.

Although you might write "Went to the mall" or "Running late" in a note to a friend or family member, neither expression would be acceptable in college writing. (See also Chapter 24 on sentence fragments.)

> *Letty and I* went to the mall.
>
> *We* are running late.

Explicit objects (57a)

Transitive verbs are verbs that generally require a direct object. Even if this object is clear from the context, it needs to be stated in the sentence. Although your dog may respond to "Give!" a written sentence needs to include more information. (See also Chapter 16 on types of verbs and sentence structure.)

> Give me the *ball*.
>
> Give her the *receipt* for her purchase.

Word order (57b)

Because word order shows how sentence elements are related in an English sentence, make sure that you leave subjects, verbs, and objects in their typical positions in the sentence. (See Chapter 16 for the typical patterns of sentences using transitive, intransitive, and linking verbs.)

> We ate spaghetti for dinner. [*subject + verb + direct object + prepositional phrase*]
>
> The spaghetti was delicious. [*subject + verb + subject complement*]
>
> Dinner gave us an opportunity to talk. [*subject + verb + indirect object + direct object*]

Noun clauses (57c)

When a sentence is built from several clauses, the clauses within the sentence can act in the same way as individual nouns. These **noun clauses** can act as subjects, subject complements, direct objects, and objects of prepositions. They are generally introduced by a **relative pronoun** (*who, whom, whose, which, that, what, whoever, whomever, whichever,* and *whatever*) or by *when, where, how, why,* or *whether.*

> *Whoever ate the cake* left crumbs all over the kitchen. [*noun clause acting as subject*]
>
> The auditorium was *where the concert was held.* [*noun clause acting as subject complement*]
>
> I asked *what was going on tonight.* [*noun clause acting as direct object*]
>
> I will look under *whatever magazines are stacked there.* [*noun clause acting as object of preposition*]

If a noun clause at the beginning of a sentence is long, a native speaker is likely to relocate the clause later in the sentence. In such a case, *it* or some other word needs to fill the subject position.

> *That the gym wall collapsed during the earthquake* made everyone on campus worry.
>
> *It* made everyone on campus worry *that the gym wall collapsed during the earthquake.*

Infinitives and gerunds (57d)

An **infinitive** is the base form of a verb preceded by *to* (*to play, to sleep, to read*). A **gerund** is the base form of a verb with *-ing* added (*playing, sleeping, reading*). Although these forms are easy to distinguish, it's not always easy to tell which one fits into a particular sentence. Usually when following a verb, an infinitive conveys an expectation, a hope, a wish, or an intention; on the other hand, a gerund following a verb is likely to convey a fact.

INFINITIVES

I expect *to receive* my check after work today.

The committee agreed *to present* its report on Friday.

Robert decided *to buy* a car.

His brother refused *to go* to the grocery.

GERUNDS

We appreciated *getting* a round of applause from the audience.

Margaret enjoys *playing* tennis.

The teacher kept *scheduling* appointments right after class.

Although many verbs are always followed by infinitives and others always by gerunds, some verbs can be followed by either of the two. In some cases — with verbs such as *continue, prefer, start,* or *like* — the choice of infinitive or gerund has little effect on the essential meaning of the sentence.

I like *to eat* tacos.

I like *eating* tacos.

In other cases — with *remember, try, forget,* or *stop,* for example — the choice of infinitive or gerund will completely change the meaning of the sentence.

I stopped *to practice* the piano. [*The verb* stop *with an infinitive means "in order to do something"* — here, in order to practice.]

I stopped *practicing* the piano. [*The verb* stop *with a gerund means that the activity* — in this case, practicing — ended or was discontinued.]

After a preposition, however, a gerund, not an infinitive, is always used regardless of the intention/fact distinction used with verbs.

These shoes are my favorites <u>for</u> *running.*

This sentence cannot use an infinitive placed directly after the preposition:

These shoes are my favorites <u>for</u> *to run.*

Adjective clauses (57e)

When a sentence is built from several clauses, a clause within the sentence can act in place of an adjective, modifying a noun or a pronoun. Such a clause should be placed close to the word it modifies and is often introduced by a **relative pronoun** such as *who, whom, whose, which,* or *that* or by *when* or *where.* (Sometimes the relative pronoun is understood and can be dropped, but do not drop a relative pronoun that is the subject of a verb.)

The <u>children</u> *who attend that school* wear uniforms.

| **INCORRECT** | The <u>store</u> *that Janet's mother owns* <u>it</u> is across the street. |
| **CORRECT** | The <u>store</u> *that Janet's mother owns* is across the street. |

INCORRECT	The <u>office</u> *that Mark works* is across the street.
INCORRECT	The <u>office</u> *Mark works* is across the street.
CORRECT	The <u>office</u> *that Mark works in* is across the street.
CORRECT	The <u>office</u> *in which Mark works* is across the street.
CORRECT	The <u>office</u> *where Mark works* is across the street.

Conditional sentences (57f)

Conditional sentences are sentences in which one situation depends on the occurrence of another situation (expressed in a clause introduced by a word such as *if, unless,* or *when*). Conditional sentences can indicate different degrees of confidence in the likelihood or truthfulness of the possibility expressed in the *if* clause.

- If the statement in the *if* clause is very likely to be true, then both verbs can be in the present tense or in another appropriate tense.

  If you *sneeze*, you *are* allergic to the cat.

  When it *snows*, driving *is* difficult.

  If you *have studied* all semester, you *have learned* what you need to know.

- If the *if* clause predicts the future and is likely to be true, the *if* clause uses the present tense. The independent clause, however, uses either the future tense or a modal that shows future time.

  If you *watch* the film again, you *will decide* what to say in your review.

  If we *eat* at China House tomorrow, we *may order* the won-ton soup.

- If the statement in the *if* clause is doubtful, the *if* clause uses *were to* with the base form of the verb or a past subjunctive. The independent clause uses *would* with the base form of the verb.

  If you *were to bake* bread every day, kneading the dough *would seem* easy.

  If he *played* tennis all year, he *would win* all his matches.

- If the statement in the *if* clause is not possible, the *if* clause uses the past subjunctive. The independent clause uses *would* plus the base form of the verb.

  If I *made* the rules, we *would have* ice cream twice a day.

  If you *were* tall, blond, and handsome, you *would have* no more friends than you already do.

- If the statement in the *if* clause is not possible and also is placed in the past, the *if* clause uses the past perfect. The independent clause uses *would* with the perfect form of the verb.

  If you *had lived* in ancient Rome, you *would have worn* a toga.

  If you *had invented* the traffic signal, you *would have collected* a fortune from your patent.

EXERCISE 41.1   EXPLICIT SUBJECTS AND OBJECTS

NAME _____ DATE _____

Revise each item so that it has an explicit subject and object as necessary. If an item does not contain an error, write C on the line below.

> **EXAMPLE**   Is a coffee bar in my apartment building.
>
> **REVISION**   There is a coffee bar in my apartment building. _____

1. Can be frustrating to drive during rush hour.

   _____

   _____

2. Are many different reasons to take a writing course.

   _____

   _____

3. Going to be late; see you around 6:30.

   _____

   _____

4. When I asked the man on the street corner for directions, he showed the way to the restaurant.

   _____

   _____

5. Some people avoid caffeine because gives them a headache.

   _____

   _____

6. There's no difference between us.

   _____

   _____

7. The poster publicizing the charity said "Give!" in big letters.

_____

_____

8. Mama gathered up the ravioli and put in the boiling water.

_____

_____

9. The neighbors watched the birds hunting for insects on the lawn.

_____

_____

10. Was even windier in Chicago than I'd expected.

_____

_____

EXERCISE 41.2 EDITING FOR WORD ORDER

NAME _____ **DATE** _____

Revise the following sentences as necessary. If a sentence does not contain an error, write C on the line below.

    EXAMPLE   On vacation she wants to go.

    REVISION   She wants to go on vacation. _____

1. An enjoyable activity ballroom dancing is.

   _____

   _____

2. Myself I consider lucky to be part of a large family.

   _____

   _____

3. To exercise regularly most doctors advise their patients.

   _____

   _____

4. Worried the hikers became when night began to fall.

   _____

   _____

5. Free checking the bank is offering to all new customers.

   _____

   _____

6. Uncle Miguel not was able to extend his visa.

   _____

   _____

7. A job she asked for.

_____

_____

8. I put all my pennies and nickels in a big jar.

_____

_____

9. Slow and steady wins the race.

_____

_____

10. Comes in first the runner from Kenya.

_____

_____

EXERCISE 41.3   USING NOUN CLAUSES, INFINITIVES, AND GERUNDS
APPROPRIATELY

NAME _____ **DATE** _____

Revise the following sentences as necessary so that each contains an appropriate noun clause, infinitive, or gerund in the proper position. If a sentence does not contain an error, write *C* on the line below.

EXAMPLE   It pleases me you like me.

REVISION   It pleases me that you like me. _____

1. That the Declaration of Independence was written in 1776 most people know.

   _____

   _____

2. It makes me angry some people in my class try to get good grades by cheating.

   _____

   _____

3. Twenty children in the class received an award for to read ten books in a month.

   _____

   _____

4. My friend considered to run for student body president but decided against to do so.

   _____

   _____

5. The staff expects completing the project by the end of the week.

   _____

   _____

6. I expect understanding more as I proceed with my studies.

_____

_____

7. Prem hoped meeting a girl that his family would like.

_____

_____

8. I need to get more sleep before finals.

_____

_____

9. Her mother stopped to drive on her ninetieth birthday.

_____

_____

10. Johann enjoyed to see as many new movies as he could afford.

_____

_____

EXERCISE 41.4   USING ADJECTIVE CLAUSES WELL

NAME _____ **DATE** _____

Revise the following sentences as necessary so that each contains an appropriate adjective clause positioned well. Make sure the sentence does not include unnecessary words or omit necessary relative pronouns. If a sentence does not contain an error, write C on the line below.

EXAMPLE   The doctor prescribed medicine for her headache that was no help.

REVISION   The doctor prescribed medicine that was no help for her headache.

1. A young person makes a more positive impression who has good manners.

   _____

   _____

2. Any employee of this company works thirty hours or more a week receives full benefits.

   _____

   _____

3. We're celebrating our anniversary with dinner at the restaurant that my husband and I went on our first date.

   _____

   _____

4. My brother who stayed in Ukraine now he wants to come to New Jersey.

   _____

   _____

5. The part of the trip frightened me most was being questioned by immigration authorities.

   _____

   _____

6. The apartment house that our family first lived it has now been torn down.

_____

_____

7. The results of the test, which we all prepared for, demonstrate the progress that we have made.

_____

_____

8. The sound of the kookaburra, which it is an Australian bird, is often heard in movies set in African or South American jungles.

_____

_____

9. The book that is the biggest is not necessarily the best.

_____

_____

10. The student practices the most gains the most.

_____

_____

EXERCISE 41.5   WRITING CONDITIONAL SENTENCES

NAME _____ **DATE** _____

Revise each of the following sentences as necessary so that both the *if* clause and the independent clause contain appropriate verb forms. If a sentence does not contain an error, write *C* on the line below.

EXAMPLE   If you had loved me, I would stay.

REVISION   If you had loved me, I would have stayed. _____

1. If people in the library are carrying on loud conversations, it would be difficult to study.

   _____

   _____

2. If I would have grown up in the United States, I could have learned English more easily.

   _____

   _____

3. If the weather had not been so bad, the flight had arrived on time.

   _____

   _____

4. If I were the only person in this class, I would get the highest grade.

   _____

   _____

5. If he did not wear a seat belt, he would not have survived.

   _____

   _____

6. If my landlord's rules were not so strict, I had been able to have a dog.

   _____

   _____

7. Even if he would have lived in ancient Egypt, he would probably not be a king there.

_____

_____

8. If everyone sits down, we could start taking the test on time.

_____

_____

9. If the course is challenging, he worked hard and earned an A.

_____

_____

10. If it stopped raining, we will go biking.

_____

_____

Nouns and Noun Phrases

42

Whether speakers and writers refer to *books, pens, rice, milk,* or *philosophy,* nouns are crucial components of English sentences. Because nouns are so important, their forms in English require particular attention. This chapter identifies some of the complexities of using count and noncount nouns, specific singular and plural forms, appropriate articles, and modifiers in English.

NOUNS AND NOUN PHRASES IN EVERYDAY USE

Sometimes English speakers use noncount nouns as if they were count nouns in the rapid verbal exchanges of everyday life—for example, in coffee shops ("Two coffees to go, please") or supermarkets ("That's two breads and a cottage cheese"). Listen for exchanges like these, and record some examples. Then try revising these exchanges to the more expansive style of written English. Two examples are supplied below.

> two coffees → two cups of coffee

> two breads and a cottage cheese → two loaves of bread and a container of cottage cheese

Count and noncount nouns (58a)

In English, distinguishing count and noncount nouns is important. These two types of noun may differ in their own forms (singular and plural), and they also may require different articles or other determiners. **Count nouns** identify individuals or things that can be counted. They usually have both singular and plural forms: *child/children, rabbit/rabbits, house/houses.* **Noncount nouns** identify masses or collections without individual or separable parts. Noncount nouns (also known as *mass nouns*) usually have only a singular form and include many abstract nouns (*sincerity, honor*), feelings (*anger, love*), foods (*flour, sugar*), beverages (*coffee, tea*), groups of items (*equipment, food*), substances in the various states of matter (*air, water*), and natural events (*lightning, snow*).

COUNT	tree/trees	chair/chairs	bean/beans	word/words	fact/facts
NONCOUNT	wood	furniture	rice	vocabulary	information

The meanings of count and noncount nouns are often closely related.

COUNT	NONCOUNT
chicken/chickens	chicken
(living animals)	(the animal as food)
wines, breads, fruits, cheeses	wine, bread, fruit, cheese
(varieties of the noncount noun)	(noncount nouns)
works, foods, loves	work, food, love
(instances of an abstract concept)	(abstract nouns)

Some nouns, depending on their meaning, can be either count or noncount.

The students handed in their *papers* on Wednesday. [*count*]

The printing company uses white *paper* for most jobs. [*noncount*]

Five *lambs* were born this spring. [*count*]

The leg of *lamb* was roasted with garlic and rosemary. [*noncount*]

If you do not know whether a noun is count, noncount, or both, this information is included in the *Oxford Advanced Learner's Dictionary* and the *Longman Dictionary of American English*.

Plural forms (58b)

Some languages do not use separate plural forms, but English requires the appropriate singular or plural form each time a count noun is used: *She bought a dozen rolls, six cookies, and a loaf of bread.* The correct form of a count noun needs to be used each time the noun appears, even if the sentence otherwise identifies the number of items (*a dozen rolls* or *six cookies*) or if the singular or plural form is obvious or has already been supplied.

In addition, although noncount nouns are not counted directly, their numbers can be expressed indirectly (*loaves* or *slices* of bread, not *breads; heads* of lettuce, not *lettuces*). In such cases, the count nouns may be singular or plural. The noncount nouns remain singular.

Determiners (58d)

A **noun phrase** consists of a noun (called the **head**) and all its modifiers.

His older brother works downtown.

In this example, the noun phrase *his older brother* consists of two modifiers (*his* and *older*) and the head (*brother*).

The words that identify or quantify the noun head are called **determiners**. A determiner must begin any noun phrase that has a singular count noun as its head.

my old <u>car</u>   *that* big, fat <u>cat</u>   *the* new <u>road</u>

COMMON DETERMINERS

a, an, the
this, that, these, those
whose, which, what
each, every, several, some, any, all, both, no, either, neither, many, much, (a) few,
    (a) little, enough
the numerals *one, two,* etc.
my, his, her, its, our, your, their
possessive nouns and noun phrases (*Jamie's, my sister's*)

Not every noun phrase has to begin with a determiner—only noun phrases with a singular count noun as the head. A determiner may or may not be used, depending on the meaning, if the head is a plural count noun or a noncount noun.

Letters arrive daily from around the world. [*plural count noun with no determiner*]

She mailed *the five letters* that she had written. [*plural count noun with determiner*]

Whether a determiner is necessary (with a singular count noun) or depends on the context (with a plural count noun or a noncount noun), certain determiners are used with certain kinds of nouns.

- *A, an, every,* and *each* are used with singular count nouns.

  a dog, *an* elephant, *every* day, *each* book

- *This* and *that* are used with singular count nouns or noncount nouns.

  She opened *this* window.

  He ate *that* leftover chicken.

- *These, those, (a) few, many, both,* and *several* are used with plural count nouns.

  these CDs, *those* boxes

  a few students, *many* classes, *both* feet, *several* books

- *(A) little* and *much* are used with noncount nouns.

  She ate *a little* soup but not *much* pudding.

- *Some* and *enough* are used with noncount nouns or plural count nouns.

  some pizza, *some* hamburgers

  enough travel, *enough* trips

Articles (58e)

The articles *a*, *an*, and *the* are frequently used in English. Multilingual speakers often find them difficult to use correctly because they carry small nuances of meaning.

Using *the*

If the identity of a noun is known or is about to be made known to readers, use the **definite article** *the* with the noun. The identification of such a noun may come from information provided to the reader somewhere else in the text, from the context of the conversation or written material, or from general knowledge. The identification of the noun may also come from information in the noun phrase itself (*the* gray cat <u>in the corner</u>), from a superlative adjective that specifically identifies the noun (*the* <u>most playful</u> of the kittens), from an ordinal number (*the* <u>second</u> room on the left), or from use of the word *same* (*the* <u>same</u> restaurant where we had eaten last week).

Here are some more examples:

Although *the two residence halls* share a dining facility, *the campus* also has *a cafeteria near the classroom buildings*. Because of its location, *the cafeteria* is especially busy at noon.

In this passage, the writer assumes that the reader already knows which campus is under discussion and also knows that it has residence halls and classroom buildings. When the writer mentions *the cafeteria* in the last sentence, the phrase refers back to information in the preceding sentence — *a cafeteria near the classroom buildings*.

The *president* will return to Washington immediately.

From general knowledge and the context (the mention of Washington), a reader knows which president the writer means — the president of the United States.

Please close *the window* before *the apartment* gets any colder.

Because this sentence is directly addressed to someone, the speaker assumes that this person knows which window — the open one — and which apartment.

Using *a* or *an*

If the identity of a singular count noun is not known to readers, use an **indefinite article:** *a* (before a consonant sound) or *an* (before a vowel sound). In deciding whether to use *a* or *an*, listen to the sound of the noun rather than checking its spelling: *a child, a house, an excited child,* and *an hour.*

Use of the indefinite article tells readers that they lack the information needed to identify the thing intended. Whether or not the writer has a specific identification in mind, *a* or *an* shows that the reader does not.

Here is an example:

> I want to get *a goldfish* for our apartment.

The goldfish in this sentence is hypothetical, not an actual or specific goldfish. It is indefinite to both the writer and the reader (*a goldfish*).

> I saw *a goldfish* yesterday at the pet store, and I decided to buy it. *The goldfish* has flecks of gold and orange and a big tail.

The goldfish mentioned in the first sentence is an actual fish known to the writer, who saw it at the pet store, but not yet known to the reader (*a goldfish*). When the second sentence refers again to the fish, the goldfish is then known both to the writer and to the reader (*the goldfish*).

The indefinite article is used to refer to an indefinite thing, not to an indefinite quantity. It can be used with a singular count noun but not with a noncount noun or a plural count noun. Instead, use *some* to indicate an indefinite quantity.

> This soup needs *some* salt.

> I saw *some* geese flying south today.

Using the zero article

The term **zero article** describes the use of a plural count noun or a noncount noun without an article (no *a, an,* or *the*) or any other determiner. (The noun may, however, be described by other adjectives.)

> The bakery serves *coffee, tea,* or *cocoa* with delicious *cookies,* chocolate *brownies,* or rich *pastries.*

Although generalizations can use articles with singular count nouns, they often use the zero article to make the most general statement. Notice the progression in the following sentences from a generalization (*first love*) to a hypothetical instance (*a first love*) to a representative instance (*the first love*).

> *First love* is rarely true love.

A first love may be a romantic introduction to dating relationships.

The first love may be intense and romantic, but the second love is more likely to incorporate reality as well.

The third sentence uses a formal style, common in academic papers. *The* would not be used in this way to generalize in conversation or informal writing.

Modifiers (58f)

Positioning modifiers correctly is an important part of using English smoothly. Modifiers in a noun phrase can precede or follow the noun head. Some modifiers that precede a noun have a **required position** and must always be placed in a certain position; others have a **preferred position**, generally but not always following a commonly accepted sequence. Modifiers that follow a noun are most likely to be phrases (the house *across the street*) or clauses (the house *that Sam rents*).

Guidelines for required modifier positions

BEGINNING THE NOUN PHRASE

- Place determiners at the beginning of the phrase.

  My new apartment is right here.

- Place *all* or *both* before any other determiners.

  I carried *all* my clothes up the stairs.

- Place numerals after any other determiners.

  These *three* pictures are my favorites.

AFTER DETERMINERS AND BEFORE NOUN MODIFIERS

- Place adjectives between the determiners and any noun modifiers. (See the later discussion of preferred positions.)

IMMEDIATELY BEFORE THE NOUN HEAD

- Place nouns that are modifiers immediately before the head.

  The large *living room* window has a view of the lake.

Guidelines for preferred modifier positions after determiners and before noun modifiers

- Place subjective adjectives (indicating the writer's attitude) early in the sequence.

  Those three *hideous* school photographs make my children look devilish.

- Place objective adjectives (adding descriptive detail) after subjective ones.

  My mother's lovely *glazed* ceramic vase is in the hallway.

- Describe size early.

  Her *gigantic* drooling bulldog scared me.

- Place objective adjectives for which there is no preferred sequence in the middle, separated by commas.

  Those gorgeous, *glittering* diamond bracelets adorned every actress at the ceremony.

- Describe color late.

  The soft, fluffy *pink* pillows were tossed on the couch.

- Place a proper noun derivative after color and before noun modifiers.

  The deep blue *Mexican* floor tiles have lively accent colors.

- Describe materials after color and before noun modifiers.

  Those heavy, old-fashioned green *velvet* bedroom curtains make the room very dark.

EXERCISE 42.1   IDENTIFYING COUNT AND NONCOUNT NOUNS

NAME _____ **DATE** _____

Underline the common nouns in the following short paragraph. Then identify each common noun as either a count or a noncount noun. The first noun is marked for you.

              noncount

In the <u>history</u> of the English-speaking theater, there is perhaps no playwright more influential than William Shakespeare (1564–1616). Many of his plays were written to be performed in London's Globe Theater, where he was a member of the resident company. The theater itself was a small, two-level enclosed structure, open at its top to allow daylight to enter. Two pillars supported a roof over the stage to protect the players and their costumes from rain. During Shakespeare's time, productions of his plays included no scenery and only a few props. Members of the audience viewing a play had to imagine its various settings. Today, a new Globe Theater carries on these traditions with great success.

EXERCISE 42.2   USING APPROPRIATE DETERMINERS; STATING PLURAL FORMS EXPLICITLY

NAME _____ **DATE** _____

Each of the following sentences contains an error with a noun phrase. Rewrite each sentence correctly on the lines provided.

EXAMPLE   They made a important linguistic breakthrough.

REVISION   They made an important linguistic breakthrough. _____

1. At the end of the eighteenth century, the two country of England and France were at war.

   _____

   _____

2. As part of his overall strategy to dominate British Empire, France's ruler, Napoleon, invaded Egypt.

   _____

   _____

3. In Egypt, a group of French army engineers traveled to a town of Rosetta, not far from the city of Alexandria, to establish a fort.

   _____

   _____

4. There, while preparing for construction of the fort, some soldiers discovered the unusual stone half-buried in the mud.

   _____

   _____

5. This stone, later called the Rosetta Stone, would become an unique find for historians.

   _____

   _____

6. The stone was covered with writing in three different language.

_____

_____

7. The Rosetta Stone was key that unlocked the secrets of the ancient Egyptian language.

_____

_____

8. Solving this puzzle has helped scholars around a world learn more about the great civilization of ancient Egypt.

_____

_____

9. Who knows how much other historical secrets remain to be discovered?

_____

_____

10. Every information that researchers learn about the past tells us something about human life both then and now.

_____

_____

EXERCISE 42.3   USING ARTICLES APPROPRIATELY

NAME _____ **DATE** _____

Insert articles as necessary into the following passage. If no article is needed, leave the space blank.

EXAMPLE   I saw ____a____ child climbing a tree.

I spent many hours in Northwood Park making sketches for my art class. _____

first assignment was to make _____ sketch of _____ specific location. I chose

_____ park because it included both scenic views and lively activity. There is _____

playground on _____ east side of _____ park where groups of _____ children

come to play every day. On _____ Tuesdays after my class, I made _____ drawings

of some of _____ children. Sometimes _____ small girl or boy stopped to see what

I was doing, and I asked them to pretend that I simply wasn't there. _____ playground

has _____ swings and _____ slides and _____ teeter-totter, but _____ most

popular activity for most children was chasing other children. _____ sketches I made

in _____ Northwood Park earned me _____ encouraging note from my teacher,

who suggested that I should think about _____ art degree or _____ career in

design. In my drawings of the children, I tried to capture their exuberance and _____

freedom.

EXERCISE 42.4 POSITIONING MODIFIERS

NAME _____ **DATE** _____

Modifiers for each noun are listed alphabetically in parentheses after the noun. Indicate the order in which the adjectives should precede the noun. If two modifiers could be placed in either order, separate them with commas.

> **EXAMPLE** <u>popular New Orleans jazz</u> album (jazz/New Orleans/popular)

1. _____ class (algebra/first-period/my)

2. _____ building (one-story/that/ugly)

3. _____ road (gravel/narrow)

4. _____ program (computer/new/user-friendly)

5. _____ cooking (home/inexpensive/tasty)

6. _____ injury (elbow/minor)

7. _____ question (surprising/trick)

8. _____ cats (Siamese/two/well-groomed)

9. _____ cloth (batik/orange/unusual)

10. _____ assignment (dull/reading/this)

Verbs and Verb Phrases

43

Along with nouns, verbs are crucial sentence components in English. Unlike some other languages, English requires that every sentence have a verb. If a sentence does not have a verb that adds lively action to it, the sentence must include a form of the verb *be*.

The students *read* their books.

The children *skip* along the walk.

The rain *falls*, and the thunder *booms*.

The boy *is* very tall for his age.

VERBS AND VERB PHRASES IN EVERYDAY USE

Everyday interaction, especially in making requests, calls for a delicate balance between the need to get things done and the need to show consideration for other people's feelings. Modals—auxiliary verbs that show possibility, necessity, and obligation—are an important device for softening the bluntness of a message. You can direct someone to do something (*Close the window*), but it's more considerate to say *Could you close the window?* Note also the difference between saying *Let's go* and *Shall we go?* The first is more of an order, while the second is an invitation.

Notice the kinds of requests people make, both those containing modals and those formed in other ways. For example, if someone says *The phone is ringing*, is the actual meaning "Please answer the phone"? Record some of your observations. Identify any patterns you notice, too—for instance, in the ways instructors make requests of students, customers make requests of sales personnel, or men and women make requests of people of their own or the other gender.

Forming verb phrases (59a)

Verb phrases include the **main verb** (the base form of a verb or a past or present participle) and one or more **auxiliary verbs** (also called *helping verbs*), which are added to show the intended tense and form of the verb. The most common auxiliaries are forms of *be, have, do, will,* and *shall.* (See also Chapter 17.) In English, the words in a verb phrase must follow a particular order.

> The children *play* soccer.

> The children *are playing* soccer.

> The children *have been playing* soccer.

> The children *may have been playing* soccer.

Notice that you cannot rearrange *The children have been playing soccer* as *The children been playing soccer have.* A new order is possible only if you change the original statement to a question: *Have the children been playing soccer?*

Auxiliary and main verbs

Up to four auxiliary verbs may precede a main verb, but the use of four is quite unusual. The auxiliary verbs must be placed in this order in a verb phrase:

1. modal (such as *can, could, may, might, shall, should, will, would, must,* and *ought to*)
2. perfect (*have*, which must be followed by a past participle)
3. progressive (indicated by a form of *be* and followed by a present participle)
4. passive (indicated by a form of *be* and followed by a past participle)

If *be* or *have* is the first auxiliary verb in a verb phrase, it needs to indicate present tense or past tense. Its form should also agree with the subject. (In contrast, a modal auxiliary does not change form.)

> I *was weeding* the garden when you *were sleeping* this morning. [*The auxiliary verbs* was *and* were *indicate past tense and agree with their respective subjects.*]

> She *has* already *eaten*. [*The auxiliary verb* has *indicates present tense and agrees with* she.]

Modal + base form

Modal auxiliary verbs include *can, could, may, might, shall, should, will, would, must,* and *ought to.* These verbs do not change form (always *can,* not *cans*) and are followed by the base form of the verb (not, in English, by an infinitive form). Only one modal at a time can be used in a sentence.

> The dog *can growl*. [can + *base form*]

> The cook *should* have been working.

Perfect *have* + past participle

The perfect tenses include a form of *have* (*have*, *has*, or *had*) followed by the past participle of the verb (the participle that does not end in *-ing*).

> The students *have gone* to class all day. [have + *past participle* gone]
>
> The baby *has been* crying all day. [has + *past participle* been]

Progressive *be* + present participle

Progressive verbs include a form of the auxiliary *be* (*am*, *is*, *are*, *was*, *were*, or *been*) followed by the present participle of the verb (ending in *-ing*). If the word *be* is itself used as an auxiliary, it must follow a modal such as *can*, *could*, *may*, *might*, *shall*, *should*, *will*, *would*, *must*, or *ought to*. (If *be* indicates the passive voice, it is followed by the past participle, not the present participle ending in *-ing*.)

> We *are eating* sandwiches for lunch today. [*form of* be + *present participle* eating]
>
> We *could be camping* by tomorrow night. [*modal* could + be *itself* + *present participle* camping]

Passive *be* + past participle

Passive verbs include a form of the auxiliary *be* (*am*, *is*, *are*, *was*, *were*, or *been*) followed by the past participle of the verb (never ending in *-ing*). If the word *be* is itself used as an auxiliary, it must follow a modal such as *can*, *could*, *may*, *might*, *shall*, *should*, *will*, *would*, *must*, or *ought to*.

> The dog *chases* the cat. [*active voice*]
>
> The cat *was chased* by the dog. [*passive voice*]

Modals (59b)

The modal auxiliary verbs include *can*, *could*, *may*, *might*, *shall*, *should*, *will*, *would*, *must*, and a few other words, such as *ought to*. Used for making requests, giving instructions, revealing doubts, expressing possibility or probability, and predicting, modals express a writer's assessment of available options.

> The final exam *might* be very difficult.
>
> You *could* begin studying now.
>
> *Would* you like to borrow these books?

Using modals to refer to the past

The modal auxiliary verbs generally indicate the present tense or the future tense. Adding a perfect auxiliary verb to a modal allows you to indicate past tense. (However, *had to* needs to be substituted for *must* to indicate past tense.)

If you want to get to work on time, you *should* catch the next bus. [*present/future*]

If you wanted to get to work on time, you *should have* caught the next bus. [*past*]

You *must* finish repairing the roof before it rains. [*future*]

You *had to* finish repairing the roof before it rained. [*past*]

Using modals to make requests or to give instructions

Modals are used in both statements and questions that make polite requests and supply instructions or directions.

Can you walk the dog?

Would you please pass the spaghetti?

Could you fix the salad for dinner?

Although these requests are arranged in an increasingly polite order, all three of them allow for the possibility that the request cannot be fulfilled. As a result, they are less assertive and more polite than they would be using *will*: <u>*Will you walk the dog?*</u>

The choice of modal controls the degree of assertiveness expressed, as the following instructions illustrate. Notice how they move from more demanding to less demanding.

You *will* report to work tonight. [*requires that instructions be followed*]

You *must* report to work tonight. [*acknowledges no option besides following instructions*]

You *should* report to work tonight. [*strongly urges following instructions*]

You *may* report to work tonight. [*somewhat formally allows but does not require following instructions*]

You *can* report to work tonight. [*less formally allows but does not require following instructions*]

Using modals to indicate doubt and certainty

Modals can also express the degree to which a statement is likely to be accurate or true. Notice how the following sentences move from most assertive or definite to most tentative.

The total seems too high; you *must* have made a mistake in the bill.

The total seems too high; you *may* have made a mistake in the bill.

The total seems too high; you *might* have made a mistake in the bill.

Present and past tenses (59c)

A complete sentence in English has to include a verb or a verb phrase (main verb + auxiliary verbs), each indicating a **tense**—the time at which the action of the verb takes place. The main verb in a sentence cannot be a **verbal**—an infinitive (*to walk*), a gerund (*walking*), or a participle (present *walking* or past *walked*) without the auxiliaries needed to form a verb phrase.

> After the earthquake, many homes *collapsed*. [*past tense*]
>
> My parents *call* every week; they *called* last night. [*present tense; past tense*]
>
> My uncle rarely *calls*. [*present tense*]

When you use the third-person singular in the present tense, be sure to add the *-s* ending (he *calls*). When you use the past tense, be sure to use the *-ed* form (they *called*) or the appropriate irregular form for the past tense (they *ran*).

Perfect and progressive verb phrases (59d)

Some sentences require a perfect or progressive tense rather than a simple present or simple past tense. These complex verb phrases are formed by using perfect and progressive auxiliaries with present-tense verbs, past-tense verbs, or modals.

Distinguishing the simple present and the present perfect

The simple present conveys current action or a current situation.

> His dog *barks* every night.
>
> She *lives* in apartment B.

If a sentence describes ongoing activity beginning in the past but continuing in the present, the verb tense needs to include both the past and the present, using the present perfect or the present perfect progressive.

> His dog *has barked* every night during the past week.
>
> She *has been living* in apartment B for two years.

Distinguishing the simple past and the present perfect

The simple past conveys actions that happened at a definite time in the past.

> He *bought* his books on Wednesday.
>
> Last summer, she *ate* lunch at the deli every day.

If a sentence describes ongoing action beginning at an indefinite time in the past, the verb tense used should be the present perfect or the present perfect progressive.

Ever since he started working in the bookstore, he *has bought* his books early.

Since last summer, she *has been eating* lunch at the deli every day.

Distinguishing the simple present and the present progressive

The simple present conveys actions that happen during a period of time, possibly including the present but not necessarily happening at the moment.

She *enjoys* skating.

She *watches* the skaters at the rink downtown every Sunday.

The present progressive conveys an action continuing at the present moment.

She *is watching* the skaters at the rink this morning because she *enjoys* skating.

Distinguishing the simple past and the past progressive

The simple past conveys actions that happened at a definite time in the past, even if those actions continued for a period of time.

She *attended* summer school during June and July.

He *bought* his new car last month.

Even when this type of past action endures over a period of time, English speakers are unlikely to use the past progressive tense unless the ongoing past action occurred at the same time as another past action.

She *was attending* summer school when she *received* the scholarship offer.

He *was buying* his new car when his old car *was stolen*.

Participial adjectives (59e)

Certain verbs form adjectives that describe emotions created by circumstances. For such verbs, the present participle (*disappointing*) and the past participle (*disappointed*) express very different meanings. The past participle is used to describe the person who feels the emotion involved; that person feels *bored, depressed, excited, frightened,* or *satisfied*. The present participle is used to describe the person or thing that creates the emotional response: that person or thing is *boring, depressing, exciting, frightening,* or *satisfying*.

The *fascinated* crowd watched the magic show.

The *fascinating* magic show attracted huge crowds.

Because words such as *interested* and *interesting* are used so often, be sure to use them correctly or use alternate phrasing that expresses what you intend.

I am *interested* in economics.

Economics *interests* me.

Economics is *interesting*.

Watch out for incorrect forms, as in *I am interesting in economics.*

EXERCISE 43.1   USING THE PRESENT, THE PRESENT PERFECT, AND THE PAST
FORMS OF VERBS

NAME _____ **DATE** _____

Rewrite the following passage by inserting the appropriate form of the verb in parentheses.
Remember to use *have* with main verbs to form the present perfect. The first answer is supplied as an example.

As I _____have grown_____ (grow) older, I _____ (start) to think more

seriously about my future career. When I _____ (be) a child, I

_____ (want) nothing more than to work in my family's small grocery store,

which I _____ (begin) to do when I was fifteen. I _____ (help)

out in the store for four years now, and I _____ (see) for myself how difficult

and often boring it _____ (be) to manage a store. Even though my family

_____ (appreciate) my help with the business, they always _____

(know) of my interest in pursuing an education, and today they _____ (sup-

port) me in my efforts at school. I _____ (know) I _____ (be) a

dutiful employee of my parents, but I still _____ (look) forward to a future of

my own different from their life.

EXERCISE 43.2   USING SPECIFIED FORMS OF VERBS

NAME _____ **DATE** _____

Using the subjects and verbs provided, write the specified sentences on the lines provided.

EXAMPLE   subject: Bernie   verb: touch
sentence using a present form: <u>Bernie touches the soft fur.</u>
sentence using the auxiliary verb *had*: <u>Bernie had touched a squid before.</u>

1. subject: we   verb: write
sentence using a present form:

_____

_____

sentence using an auxiliary verb + the past participle form:

_____

_____

2. subject: I   verb: attend
sentence using a past form:

_____

_____

sentence using an auxiliary verb + the present participle form:

_____

_____

3. subject: people   verb: believe
sentence using a present form:

_____

_____

sentence using an auxiliary verb + the past participle form:

_____

_____

4. subject: bells   verb: ring
    sentence using a present form:

_____

_____

    sentence using the auxiliary *had* + the past participle form:

_____

_____

5. subject: children   verb: play
    sentence using a past form:

_____

_____

    sentence using the auxiliary verb *were* + the present participle form:

_____

_____

6. subject: police   verb: look
    sentence using a present form:

_____

_____

    sentence using an auxiliary verb + past participle form:

_____

_____

7. subject: parents   verb: wait
    sentence using a past form:

_____

_____

    sentence using an auxiliary verb + present participle form:

_____

_____

8. subject: rain   verb: fall

sentence using a past form:

_____

_____

sentence using an auxiliary verb + a present participle form:

_____

_____

9. subject: car   verb: run

sentence using a present form:

_____

_____

sentence using an auxiliary verb + a past participle form:

_____

_____

10. subject: roof   verb: leak

sentence using a past form:

_____

_____

sentence using an auxiliary verb + a present participle form:

_____

_____

EXERCISE 43.3 IDENTIFYING TENSES AND FORMS OF VERBS

NAME _____ **DATE** _____

From the following list, identify the form of each verb or verb phrase used in each sentence.

    simple present   past perfect

    simple past   present progressive

    present perfect   past progressive

    EXAMPLE   Judge Cohen considered the two arguments. <u>simple past</u>

1. The doctor ran a complicated series of tests. _____

2. The city has hosted the spring festival for ten years now. _____

3. The owners of my building are planning a complete renovation. _____

4. Before her death, Mrs. Rodriguez had been ill for several years. _____

5. Blanche and Stella have always depended on the kindness of strangers. _____

6. Just as we took our seats, the movie began. _____

7. As guests were arriving, Cheryl was still getting dressed. _____

8. She is exercising to reduce stress. _____

9. During the opening act, the clown was frightening the small children. _____

10. Natalie wants to open a restaurant. _____

EXERCISE 43.4 USING VERBS APPROPRIATELY

NAME _____ **DATE** _____

Each of the following sentences contains an error with verbs. Correct each sentence on the lines provided.

> **EXAMPLE**   Quinine is used as a treatment for fever until the middle of the twentieth century.
>
> **REVISION**   Quinine was used as a treatment for fever until the middle of the twentieth century.

1. Quinine was know to the people of the Andes before the seventeenth century.

   _____

   _____

2. The bark of the cinchona tree, which grows in the Andean rain forest, has produced quinine.

   _____

   _____

3. Until the Spanish explorers arrived in the New World, Europeans have never heard of quinine.

   _____

   _____

4. They were extremely interesting in the fever-reducing properties of the cinchona tree.

   _____

   _____

5. Once the Spanish had discover quinine, they shipped it back to Europe.

   _____

   _____

6. Jesuit missionaries who traveling in the tropics in that century used quinine to treat fevers.

_____

_____

7. Soon, quinine was being called "Jesuit powder," and some people who were not Spanish or Catholic not trusted it because of its association with the Jesuits.

_____

_____

8. Eventually, the use of quinine became widespread, and modern historians believe that without the drug, the Europeans cannot have colonized tropical areas.

_____

_____

9. British colonials mixed the bitter quinine with gin and lime, and the gin and tonic is invented.

_____

_____

10. After World War II, synthetic drugs have worked better than quinine for treatment of malaria for a time, but when some strains of malaria became resistant, quinine made a comeback.

_____

_____

_____

Prepositions and Prepositional Phrases

Prepositions are words that indicate the relationship — location, direction, or time — of a noun or pronoun to another part of the sentence. They distinguish putting a chair *near* the fireplace from putting a chair *in* the fireplace, serving chicken *under* the rice from serving it *over* the rice, and wearing a skirt *above* the knees from wearing a skirt *below* them.

PREPOSITIONS AND PREPOSITIONAL PHRASES IN EVERYDAY USE

In many professions, you will find phrasal verbs — made up of a verb plus a preposition that functions as an adverbial particle — that are part of a specialized vocabulary. Examples include *log on* (computers), *blast off* (space exploration), and *kick off* (football or soccer). Make a list of some other phrasal verbs that are used in a field of special interest to you.

Using prepositions idiomatically (60a)

English prepositions are especially troublesome because they are used idiomatically. For example, a cup may be placed *on* the table, the dog may jump *on* the sofa, a ring may be worn *on* the finger, your friend may live *on* the second floor of an apartment *on* First Street, or you may invite someone for dinner *on* Saturday night. Here are some guidelines for using the prepositions *in*, *on*, and *at*.

- *In* expresses the idea of enclosure, and *on* expresses contact with a surface. Notice how the following sets of examples move from literal to figurative applications of these prepositions.

  The laundry is *in* the washer.

  My brother works hard *in* the heat or *in* the rain.

  Paula has fallen *in* love.

  The cereal is *on* the shelf.

  His hat is *on* his head, and his coat is *on* his back.

I found several books *on* American history, but I will also look for information *on* the Internet.

- *In* is used with locations in space (enclosing a place) or locations in time (enclosing an event).

  In 1989, my aunt arrived *in* Los Angeles *in* April.

  I take math *in* the morning.

- *On* must be used with days of the week, days of the month, and street names (though not with exact addresses), just as if a date is placed on a calendar or a location is placed on a map.

  My appointment is *on* Thursday.

  The final paper is due *on* May 11.

  Brad is moving to a small house *on* Maple Avenue.

- *At* specifies an exact location — in space or in time.

  I will meet you *at* the museum *at* noon.

  He lives *at* 4919 College Way.

  At home, I always watch the news *at* ten.

  Notice that *at* is used with *night*, even though *in* is used with other times of day.

  I take classes *in* the morning, work *in* the afternoon, and study *at* night.

Using two-word verbs idiomatically (60b)

Phrasal verbs are two-word verbs that may look like a verb plus a preposition, but in these cases the preposition acts as an adverbial particle.

> Sheila ran into Gwen. [*Ran into is a two-word verb; into is an adverbial particle here.*]

> I *dropped* the carrots *into* the stew. [*Into is a preposition; into the stew is a prepositional phrase.*]

Phrasal verbs have idiomatic meanings. In this case, *ran into* means *encountered* or *met*. English has hundreds of these expressions. Here are a few examples:

TWO-WORD VERB	DEFINITION
ask (a person) out	arrange a date
blow up	explode
call (an event) off	cancel
drop (a person or thing) off	leave at a certain place
put away	place something back where it belongs
shut off	turn off or stop a flow
wear out	reduce to shabbiness or inefficiency

There are several ways to distinguish between a preposition and a two-word verb. A preposition introduces a prepositional phrase, and other words can be added between a verb and a prepositional phrase. A phrasal verb, however, is a two-word unit. This unit generally cannot be separated by other words except for the direct object of the verb. (Some types of two-word verbs are exceptions, however.) Notice the word order in the following sentences:

I *made up* a bedtime story for my son.

I *made* a bedtime story *up* for my son.

A bedtime story is the direct object of *made up*. This direct object can follow the phrasal verb, or it can be placed between the two words of the verb. Should the direct object be a personal pronoun, however, the pronoun has to be placed between the two parts of the verb: *I made it up for my son.* Other words, however, cannot divide the two parts of a phrasal verb: *I made for my son up a bedtime story* does not make sense in English.

In contrast, a prepositional phrase can be separated from the verb and can be moved around within the sentence. Other words and phrases can also be added freely between a verb and a preposition.

For my son, I *made up* a bedtime story.

I *made up* a bedtime story with wild animals for my son.

I *made* a bedtime story *up* last night for my son.

Phrasal verbs are complicated because some types do not follow this pattern. Sometimes the second word acts like a preposition and may be separated by other phrases.

He *depends on* her to run the office.

He *depends* completely *on* her to run the office.

In some cases, the preposition cannot be separated from the verb, even by the object of the verb.

Sheila *ran into* Gwen. [*not* Sheila ran Gwen into]

Whenever you are uncertain about what an expression means or how it functions within a sentence, check it in the dictionary. The *Longman Dictionary of American English* includes detailed information about the various types of two-word verbs.

EXERCISE 44.1   USING PREPOSITIONS IDIOMATICALLY

NAME _____ **DATE** _____

Insert an appropriate preposition into each of the following sentences.

    EXAMPLE   We read the article _____ in _____ the newspaper yesterday.

1. Too many students _____ public schools today perform poorly.

2. Often students' low scores _____ standardized tests mean that they will be held back.

3. Some students may not be allowed to graduate _____ the end of their senior year.

4. One solution to the problem is to make sure that teachers know how to motivate the students _____ their classrooms.

5. Encouraging and involved parents can also have a positive effect _____ their children's attitudes toward school.

6. Every evening, students need to do the homework assigned _____ school.

7. Local businesses need to encourage students so that they are prepared _____ jobs or higher education.

8. Students need to come _____ school ready to learn.

9. They should get to school precisely _____ time.

10. Once _____ the school building, students should be ready to focus on their classes.

NAME _____ **DATE** _____

Identify each italicized expression as either a two-word verb or a verb + preposition.

EXAMPLE   *Look up* Jeremy the next time you're in town. _____two-word verb_____

1. Alois *gave up* her bus seat to an elderly woman with a cane. _____

2. Our instructor has asked us to *hand in* our papers by Friday. _____

3. *Look in* your dictionaries for the definitions of the words on this list. _____

4. James *lifted* his daughter *up* on his shoulders so she could see the parade. _____

5. Would you please *put* the garbage *out* on the sidewalk? _____

6. My sister once cried when she *stepped on* a beetle. _____

7. If the weather doesn't improve, we are going to have to *call off* the picnic. _____

8. On our tour through San Francisco, the guide *pointed out* the city's famous sights.
   _____

9. The laughing children *ran up* the hillside. _____

10. Marco *ran up* numerous bills during his months of unemployment. _____

Answers to Preview Questions

PART ONE   1. F   2. F   3. F   4. F   5. T   6. F   7. T   8. T   9. T   10. F
11. T   12. F   13. T   14. T   15. T   16. T

PART TWO   1. T   2. F   3. T   4. T   5. F   6. F   7. T   8. F   9. F   10. T

PART THREE   1. F   2. F   3. T   4. X   5. OK   6. X   7. <u>eludes</u> (should be *alludes*)
8. <u>scampered</u> (suggested correction: *thundered*)   9. <u>literally</u> (suggested correction:
nearly)   10. C   11a. Possible answers: porter, portable   11b. Possible answers:
biology, biography   12. –ly   13. *Coddle* comes perhaps from *caudle*, and it means "to
treat with extreme or excessive care or kindness."   14. Possible answers: *wedlock,
matrimony*   15. Depending on the quality of your dictionary, your answer probably
includes at least two of the following: an established law, the physical makeup of an
individual, the structure or composition of something, the mode in which a state or
society is organized, and the basic laws and principles of a nation or social group.
16. They're   17. separated, lose   18. heard, developed   19. used, whose, every day
20. professor, believe

PART FOUR   1. novel, surgeon, Henry Perowne, Saturday   2. mother, pride, daughter,
gold, Torino, Italy   3. would have wished, had seen   4. might speak   5. Everyone,
who, some, who, it   6. Whose, this   7. In, of, with, into   8. I   9. whom
10. Whom   11. She, him   12. me   13. am   14. doesn't   15. gone   16. lie
17. would   18. wants   19. its   20. a   21. their   22. have   23. is   24. bad
25. bigger   26. really   27. most helpful

PART FIVE   1a. I   1b. C   1c. I   1d. I   2a. I   2b. C   2c. I   2d. I   3a. C
3b. I   3c. I   3d. C   4a. I   4b. I   5a. C   5b. C   5c. I   6a. C   6b. I
6c. I   6d. C

PART SIX   1a. no   1b. yes   2a. <u>so</u>   2b. <u>but</u>   3. no   4a. <u>who listen to loud
music through ear jacks</u>   4b. <u>because it has antioxidant properties</u>   4c. <u>Although
some doctors endorse this new treatment for melanoma</u>   5a. compound
5b. simple   5c. complex   6a. wordiness   6b. C   6c. passive verbs, wordiness
6d. wordiness, weak verb   6e. weak verb

PART SEVEN   1. . . . banquet hall, the men . . .   2. . . . two hours, but she . . .
3. . . . china was totally . . .   4. . . . Bart, who spends . . .   5. . . . positions: short-order . . .
6. . . . a "bookhouse," I . . .   7. C   8. Yes, I . . . coffee; however, give . . .

9. . . . of shoes"?   10. . . . shouted "Stop!"   11. . . . judges' . . . defense's . . .
12. . . . just doesn't want . . .   13. . . . Samuel L. Jackson . . . Dr. Martin Luther King Jr.
14. . . . its . . .   15. . . . was theirs.   16. . . . "I did not know . . . evening," Peter said.
17. . . . was 'very taxing,'" Vincent reported.   18. . . . older brothers, and . . . her that
she shouldn't be going out with me.   19. C   20. . . . instant — and the ability. . .
21. . . . literature: good and bad.   22. C

PART EIGHT   1. Most . . . New York City . . . Empire State Building.   2. . . . says,
"Expect . . .   3. . . . sisters — she was born . . .   4. . . . Ph.D. . . . University of Texas.
5. Marie and Pierre Curie . . .   6. C   7. C   8. . . . 8:15 a.m., so . . .   9. . . . take a number.   10. . . . in California, . . . in Arizona.   11. Six people . . .   12. . . . ten thousand . . .
13. . . . *adieu* . . .   14. . . . the *New Yorker* . . .   15. . . . *Morning Edition* . . .   16. C
17. Halloween . . . Christmas . . . Thanksgiving and Hanukkah . . .   18. . . . poem
Beowulf . . .   19. . . . *The Corrections* . . .   20. . . . the best known.   21. . . . rarely performed . . .   22. Fully 85 percent . . . mayor-elect.   23. . . . mindful . . .   24. . . . better
coverage . . .   25. C   26. . . . one- and two-family homes.

PART NINE   1. no article, a, the   2. some, no article, the, the   3. some   4. rice,
beans   5. three laughing, large brown   6. arrived   7. have gotten, did   8. could
not, were   9. in, on, in   10. at, at, at, pick her up   11. on, on, in   12. There are
13. happened   14. has been studying   15. read   16. to open   17. making   18. my
uncle owns   19. may leak   20. will watch   21. had not bought   22. lived, would
probably have

Index

Note: A page number beginning with E *indicates a reference to an exercise.*